ONLY THE SWORD
OF
THE SPIRIT

> This book is
> presented for review
> by
> Kindred Productions
> Price:
>
> Please send copy of review
> to
> 169 Riverton Ave.
> Winnipeg, MB R2L 2E5
> Canada

Perspectives on Mennonite Life and Thought is a series jointly published between Kindred Productions, the Historical Commission of the General Conference of Mennonite Brethren Churches and the Center for Mennonite Brethren Studies of Winnipeg, Manitoba, Fresno, California, and Hillsboro, Kansas.*

1. Paul Toews, ed., *Pilgrims and Strangers: Essays in Mennonite Brethren History* (1977)

2. Abraham Friesen, ed., *P.M. Friesen and His History: Understanding Mennonite Brethren Beginnings* (1979)

3. David Ewert, ed., *Called to Teach* (1979)

4. Heinrich Wölk and Gerhard Wölk, *Die Mennoniten Bruedergemeinde in Russland, 1925 - 1980: Ein Beitrag zur Geschichte* (1981)

5. John B. Toews, *Perilous Journey: The Mennonite Brethren in Russia 1860 - 1910* (1988)

6. Aron A. Toews, *Mennonite Martyrs: People Who Suffered for Their Faith 1920 - 1940*, translated by John B Toews (1990)

7. Paul Toews, ed., *Mennonites and Baptists: A Continuing Conversation* (1993)

8. J. B. Toews, *A Pilgrimage of Faith: The Mennonite Brethren Church in Russia and North America 1860 - 1990* (1993)

9. Paul Toews, ed., *Bridging Troubled Waters: Mennonite Brethren at Mid-Century* (1955)

10. Peter Penner, *Russians, North Americans and Telugus: The Mennonite Brethren Mission in India 1885 - 1975* (1997)

11. Jacob A. Loewen, Wesley J. Prieb, *Only the Sword of the Spirit* (1997) The publication of this volume was assisted by a grant from the Loewen/Quiring Trust.

*Volumes 1-4 were published by the Center for Mennonite Brethren Studies (Fresno)

ONLY THE SWORD OF THE SPIRIT

by

Jacob A. Loewen & Wesley J. Prieb

Winnipeg, MB Canada  Hillsboro, KS USA

ONLY THE SWORD OF THE SPIRIT

Copyright© 1997 by the Centers for Mennonite Brethren Studies, Fresno CA, Winnipeg MB, and Hillsboro KS.

All rights reserved. With the exception of brief excerpts for reviews, no part of this book may be reproduced without written permission of the publisher.

All scripture quotations, unless otherwise indicated, are from the Revised Standard Version of the Bible, copyright by the Division of Christian Education of the National Council of the Churches of Christ in the USA. Used by permission. All rights reserved.

Canadian Cataloguing in Publication Data

Loewen, Jacob A. (Jacob Abram), 1922 —

Only the sword of the spirit

(Perspectives on mennonite life and thought; 11)

Includes bibliographical references and index.
ISBN: 0-921788-44-4

I. Mennonites – History. I. Prieb, Wesley J.
II. Title   III. Series

BX8115.L66   1997   289.7   C97-920067-9

Published simultaneously by Kindred Productions, Winnipeg MB R2L 2E5 and Kindred Productions, Hillsboro KS 67063

Cover design by Graphic Creations, Winnipeg MB

Book design by Graphic Creations, Winnipeg MB

Printed in Canada by The Christian Press, Winnipeg MB

International Standard Book Number: 0-921788-44-4

Dedication

Wesley J. Prieb would like to thank his mother, Katherine Jantzen Prieb, for reading the *Martyrs Mirror* to him as a child and for modeling an only-the-sword-of-the-Spirit lifestyle for him throughout her life.

Jacob A. Loewen would like to recognize both the late Reverend Johann Toews (affectionately known as "*Grossvater* Toews") and his spiritual mentor, the late Reverend John A. Harder, for laying a foundation for his understanding of Anabaptist values by their life and example.

Together they would like to thank Peter E. Schellenberg and Solomon L. Loewen, who as professors at Tabor College, introduced them to truth beyond the biblical. Together they also want to pay tribute to the Young Centre for Anabaptist Studies of Elizabethtown College for simultaneously appointing them research fellows, thus permitting them to work together for several months to develop an earlier version of this book.

In Remembrance

This book is also dedicated to the memory of co-author Wesley J. Prieb who passed away October, 1997, while the book was in press. Co-author Loewen, the Historical Commission, the Centers for Mennonite Brethren studies and Kindred Productions join to pay tribute to Wes for his confidence that this book could move many church people to recover an Anabaptist vision of the church. Wes, for this inspiring confidence we thank you!

Contents

Preface i
Introduction vii

PART ONE

Menno's Vision

1. "Only the Sword of the Spirit!" 3
2. The Significance of Menno Simons' Only-the-Sword-of-the-Spirit Stance in World History and in Scripture 19
    i. In World History 19
    ii. In Scripture 22
    iii. In Mennonite Experience 26
3. Menno's Feet of Clay 29

PART TWO

The Story Of The Northern Stream Of Mennonites: In Northern Europe, Southern Russia And America

4. The *Doopsgezinde* of the Netherlands 37
5. Mennonites in Northwest Germany 53
6. Mennonites in the Prussias 67
7. The Mennonite Commonwealth in South Russia 1789-1860 85
8. Awakening in Russia 99
9. Johann Cornies and His Vision 105
10. Pietist and Baptist Influences 113
11. The Outworking of Borrowed Pietist Values in the Mennonite Brethren Context 123
12. The Emergence of the *Selbstschutz* and the Mennonite Brethren Contribution to it 135
    Mennonites in North America 142

13. American Mennonites: Citizenship and Property 145
14. Social Class and Wealth 155
15. The Canon and The Congregation 163
16. Vulnerability to Outside Influences 179

PART THREE
The Twelve Anabaptist Values And Readers' Responses

17. When Mennonites Adjusted Their Worldview to become Two-kingdom Citizens 189
18. From Stewardship to Ownership and a Social-class-based Society 195
19. When Mennonites Developed a Church State and Decided to Defend it with the Sword 201
20. When Mennonites Shifted Their View of the Canon 207
21. When the Function of the Mennonite Congregation Changed 213
22. When Mennonites Achieved Physical Isolation as "God's Chosen People" in Their Own "Promised Land" and Then Lost Their Reason to be 223

PART FOUR
The Hope

23. Stories of Fidelity 231
24 The Hope for Ongoing Renewal 243

Postscript

Personal Reflections on the *Only-the-Sword-of-the-Spirit* Ideal, by Jacob A. Loewen 253
   How I Found My Roots *in Gewaltverzicht* 253
   How I Became Proud to be a Mennonite 261

Bibliography 265

Index 329

Preface

The origin of this book

In 1984, I (Jacob A. Loewen) began an urgent quest to rediscover my Anabaptist/Mennonite roots. This quest was a direct result of an anguished question my son asked me: "But Dad, why in Heaven's name did you not give me a foundation in Anabaptist/Mennonite peace principles? You gave me foundations for so many of life's crucial questions, but why not in this?" Then my son left the Mennonite Brethren church, because his pastor had just written him that since 54 percent of the local church's young men had chosen to go active in the last war, his home church no longer could take a firm position on nonresistance. Both Bill's question and his action jolted me severely. They forced me to face squarely an unease that had plagued my life ever since I had become a conscientious objector in 1940.

Then on June 4, 1993 I suffered a severe stroke. My right side—and I was fully right-handed—was now paralyzed. When I recovered as much as I could, the specialists told me that I probably had three more years in which I could expect to work (of course, always with my handicap). I then asked God, what part of his plan for my life was still undone. One of the three things I felt that God was still asking me to do was to give a final testimony to my church about Anabaptist/Mennonite peace principles. What follows is that testimony!

Since I was afraid that my professional writing style was not suited for the average members of our congregations, I asked my friend and colleague, Wesley J. Prieb, a retired English professor, to help me. I am deeply grateful that he has consented to join me in this testimony.

A scholarship peculiarity?

I also need to alert the readers to an idiosyncrasy in the scholarship about which those versed in history are bound to complain. The quoted translations from Menno Simons' own writings (Elkhart, 1876) and the references to Peter M. Friesen's Mennonite Brethren church history (Halbstadt, 1911) are largely from the German versions and in the author's own free translation, rather than in one of the officially-recognized English versions. The reason for this is that the study originally began as an entirely personal quest to rediscover my Anabaptist roots, following my son's indicting complaint cited earlier.

As I repeatedly waded through the Anabaptist sources, especially the writings of Menno Simons in German, I began to make my own free translation for my son who does not know German. Eventually an attachment developed to these personal ad hoc translation efforts. When this quest for my Anabaptist roots was later extended to develop this book, the original translation efforts were maintained as a nostalgic tribute to the years of intense immersion in the German texts.

Where Scripture is quoted in the text, it is from the Revised Standard Version (RSV) unless otherwise indicated.

Wesley J. Prieb's introductory remarks

My share in this book

My involvement in this publication included (1) making some contributions to basic research and writing, especially Chapter 23 and the conclusion, (2) helping to shape the broad outline and to order the materials, (3) tightening up the order and the way in which ideas are presented, and (4) adjusting the language level and the grammatical and semantic structures to facilitate easier reading and understanding of the text for the average reader.

It is my hope and prayer that this publication will help readers not only to understand the gospel but to live the gospel as they formulate strategies of peacemaking as members of the Body of Christ in this world.

Prieb's & Loewen's joint remarks

Evangelical diversity

While this study may at times seem to speak about evangelicalism as if it were a homogeneous movement, it recognizes full well that the movement actually is a very diverse and complex one (Hollinger 1990, 5, 281-283; Kraus 1979b, 39-61). One needs to look at it on several planes to see the full picture. On the plane of world acceptance we have the extreme right represented by organizations like the Christian Coalition, who are engaged economically, active politically and usually highly militaristic in orientation (Wink 1992, 28). On the extreme left on that same plane there is the Evangelical Left (Michaelson 1978, 16-19) represented by *Sojourners* which challenges the culture of the day calling for world-wide economic and social justice (Michaelson 1979, 63-82; Sider 1989b, 156-169; Driver 1978, 86-110; Gish 1970, 13-48). On the world-denying plane we have the world-condemning fundamentalist evangelicals who see modernism and heresy lurking behind every bush (Lindsell, 1976; Dollar 1973; H. S. Bender 1956, 2, 418-419). They reject the "world" in its ideology, especially in the way they view the religions of others. On the same plane we also have groups like certain Old Order and other Mennonites who reject the modern world pretty well in its entirety and fixate on a previous form of culture. In between these various ends there is a broad spectrum of groupings that this study chooses to refer to as "Mainstream Evangelicalism" (Bloesch 1973; J. L. Burkholder 1979, 23-38).

This study sees the entire spectrum of evangelicalism in sharp contrast to Anabaptism as characterized by a deep and noble common concern for the salvation of the human soul in the here and now and its preparation for a blessed hereafter. But by and large the movement, however, lacks the concern for the whole person and the wide range of discipleship issues that are at the very heart of Anabaptism. Bluntly stated, mainstream evangelicals tend to emphasize the purity of one's belief system, Anabaptism, on the other hand, emphasizes Bible-based Christ-like action and discipleship (Hollinger 1990, 5, 281). We think this difference can be succinctly illustrated with the following anecdote: A fundamentalist asked an Old Order Mennonite, "Are you really saved?" The Mennonite thought seriously for a while and then slowly answered: "I think you should really ask that question of my neighbors, they know best how I live!"

Recently a variety of new voices and new currents (e.g., Noll, 1994, especially chaps. 1 and 5-8) have appeared on the American evangelical scene. Some of these are challenging many of the more objectionable elements of certain strains of evangelicalism. However, like Luther and Zwingli during the Reformation, many current individual leading evangelicals have personally expressed deep sympathy for Anabaptist concerns, but most of these same leaders have resolutely said that because their financial support comes from people who do not trust Anabaptist values, they cannot publicly voice their endorsement for a truly Anabaptist position. This is certainly true of most mainstream evangelicalism; for example, at the Lausanne World Conference on Evangelism (1974) and the (1978) Bermuda Evangelism Conferences, the leadership of both conferences felt that their supporters would not permit them to publicly endorse Anabaptist concerns advocated by a few Mennonite representatives and many of the Third World delegates who were participating.

Furthermore, it is probably correct to say that many Mennonites, who consider themselves committed evangelicals today, should really define themselves as Anabaptists who happen to share an array of concerns with some evangelicals. This problem is especially acute for the Mennonite Brethren, who since their very inception in 1860, have emphasized many pietist evangelical concerns, often at the expense of their true Anabaptist roots. For this reason this study calls both individuals and entire Mennonite congregations to recognize and to return to their Anabaptist biblical roots.

Our position on evangelism

We are aware that we may be misunderstood at times when we make critical observations about contemporary and popular forms of evangelicalism. Do we as authors of this study believe in evangelism? Yes, we certainly do! We are committed to it! The early Anabaptist/Mennonites were intensely evangelistic. They boldly proclaimed their faith to the world and were willing to die for their convictions and for their right to share the Good News about Jesus. The scaffold and the stake often became their pulpit as they shared the Good News about the salvation Jesus had wrought for all. The blood of the martyrs was the seed of a rapidly growing church. But the purpose of this early Anabaptist/Mennonite witness was not statistical church growth. It was to help people enter the narrow gate and to walk the narrow road of discipleship (Hertzler 1971, 19-27). This the Anabaptists saw as the prerequisite to becoming citizens as Christ's Kingdom of Peace.

The Anabaptist/Mennonite concern was not to build bigger and better houses of worship, or to establish increasingly larger congregations. They were pilgrims on this earth and citizens-in-training who were in transit to their heavenly homeland. Caves, barns, or even shade trees and boats served as houses of worship where they studied the Word and encouraged each other to grow in the faith.

There are examples of biblical evangelism today! Much of contemporary popular evangelism, however, has been compromised by high-tech entertainment values, Hollywood-style glamour, pie-in-the-sky escapism, phony health/wealth promises, cheap grace without discipleship, "sanctified" materialism, patriotic nationalism and even pious militarism.

"Famous" evangelists and preachers are often living in the fast lane. They are misappropriating contributions given for God's work among the poor and needy. Their lives do not reflect the power of the gospel they are preaching. They are deceived by their own "positive-thinking, feel-good" gospel. Many genuine Anabaptist/Mennonite church people are concerned about this. Thus when we use the word evangelicalism in this book, it is the above kind of evangelicalism we are referring to. Concerned people (and the present writers with them) would like to see a lot more honest, biblical evangelism done in the power of God's Spirit and in the full light of God's Word. This was the brand of evangelism our Anabaptist/Mennonite forebears practiced during the Reformation. This is the evangelism which our Mennonite Brethren pioneers launched in 1860. Such evangelism demands the following:

> Accept God's Word as authoritative!
> Be born again! Be radically converted!
> Follow Christ's call to discipleship diligently!
> Function as a member of Christ's "Kingdom of Peace!"
> Conform to Christ's example in Word and deed.
> Live a simple life of sharing and stewardship.
> Remember genuine deeds of discipleship are the best proof of faith!

This is evangelism in the power of the sword of the Spirit! This evangelism we support wholeheartedly!

The Anabaptist vision: monogenetic or polygenetic?

One of the most persistent criticisms of H. S. Bender's (1944, 67-88; 1957, 29-56; 1980a, 13-32; Gross 1986, 352-363) Anabaptist Vision statement has been that it does not give enough recognition to the multiplicity of original views held by the various early Anabaptist leaders and the various branches of the movement that developed (Deppermann, Packull & Stayer 1975, 83-121; Stayer 1988, 109-116). Even though this present study limits itself, as much as possible, to the northern stream of the Anabaptist movement, it recognizes that even within that stream, Menno Simons' voice and views are not the only ones.

Almost from the very inception of the movement in Northern Holland, Melchior Hoffman, the catalyst who started the revival movement, introduced a chiliastic theme (Neff 1913, 1, 342-347) that produced some tragic effects at Münster, Oldeklooster and elsewhere. Again, Obbe Phillips, one of the very earliest leaders, who baptized Menno himself, held views that differed appreciably from those expressed by Menno Simons, who is generally considered the father of peaceful Anabaptism in Holland (H. Penner 1955, 48; Brock 1991a, 21). In fact, almost every one of the early elders appointed within the northern stream held some divergent views.

The northern stream may not have had its *Schwertler* (sword carriers) and *Stäbler* (staff carriers) distinction that dogged the southern wing (H. S. Bender 1956a, 11; 1959, 4; 488-489; 4, 607; Teufel & Hein 1967, 4, 140; Verduin 1964, 63-94), but it had its own share of divergent emphases on a wide variety of issues, including very different positions on the use of force, even the sword. Looking back today, however, one sees a growing consensus that Menno's views and writings do set the overall tone for the northern stream, especially the sharp distinction Menno drew between himself and the militants at Münster (Haas 1980, 72-84).

In fact, even limiting oneself to Menno's views alone, one has to recognize the development and the shifts and these not only in emphasis, but in actual substance that took place in Menno's life. A prominent example is discussed in chapter 3, regarding Menno's ambivalence and shifts of position on the Christian's responsibility toward government and the magistracy.

Introduction

When you open your door and invite Jesus to enter your house (Rev. 3:20) he expects you to open all the doors, not just the front door. If you accept him as Lord of your house, he wants to occupy every room. In fact, he wants to become a permanent resident and live with you and have an active part in your everyday life. Radical conversion is not simply a single visit in the front room. It is a lifelong process of walking with Jesus Christ who wants to become the Lord of the entire household.

When Menno Simons, an ordinary sixteenth-century Catholic priest in the Netherlands, was converted, he sought to practice and teach total obedience (Bornhäuser 1973; Hillerbrand 1962a; 387-399; Horst 1986b, 194-203). For him it was not enough to expose only the front room through courteous hospitality. Conversion meant accepting Jesus as the permanent Lord of the entire house. It meant entering the kingdom of peace and becoming a citizen of heaven, accepting forgiveness and cleansing through the mercy of God. It meant becoming a forgiving agent, living a life of sacrificial servanthood, and walking the narrow road of Christian discipleship. It meant living by the ethical and moral standards of the Sermon on the Mount.

This book is about inviting Jesus into every facet of your personal inner life, but it also appeals to the entire church to do the same. It demonstrates that fidelity, not perfection, is possible as a goal of Christian living. It recognizes that many of those who followed after Menno invited Jesus into only one or two rooms and kept him out of many other rooms, and shows how partial surrender tends to pollute the entire house. Yet it also shows that there is always hope about opening more rooms. Housecleaning always remains an option. It is the authors' hope and prayer that this book may inspire individual readers and whole congregations to discover the joy of total obedience to Jesus and to live in residence with him as the Lord of the entire house. This lifestyle, following Menno Simons, is called "living by the sword of the Spirit."

Part One defines the vision of Menno Simon, and asks what it was that dramatically transformed the life of this respected, rather ordinary young Catholic priest in a comfortable parish in the northwestern corner of Europe. What had he discovered in Scripture that made him willing to risk his personal reputation, a secure church future and his very life to become Northern Europe's most wanted religious fugitive (H.G. Mannhardt 1919, 24; Williams 1962, 393)? Was he just a firebrand revolutionary, another wild-eyed visionary like the Anabaptists of Münster, with his head in apocalyptic clouds? The answer is a definite no! Menno had both feet on the ground when he made the fateful decision to obey whatever truth he discovered in the Bible (Zijpp 1957, 74-79). He had no illusions about the consequences. He knew that he and others who followed this vision would have a huge price to pay.

Here, in a free translation and paraphrase (Simons 1876), is Menno's discovery in a nutshell.

> The Scripture teaches us that there are two opposing princes and two opposing kingdoms. One is the Prince of Peace, the other the prince of discord. Each prince has his own kingdom and each kingdom shares the nature of its prince (A:242).

> The Prince of Peace is Jesus Christ, his kingdom is the kingdom of peace, which is his church. His messengers are messengers of peace and his word is the word of peace, his body is the body of peace, his children are the seed of peace, his reward and inheritance, is the reward of peace (Heb. 7, Is. 9, Lk. 1, Is. 52, Rom. 10, Jn. 14, Col.3, Zech. 8). In short, under this king and in his kingdom everything one sees, hears, does and permits is peace (B:441).

> The born-again have a spiritual king over them who rules them with the unbroken scepter of his mouth, namely his Holy Spirit and his Word. . . His name is Jesus Christ.(A:242).

> (God's children) are children of peace, their hearts overflow with peace, their mouth, speaks, of peace and they walk the way of peace. They are full of peace in attitude and behavior. They seek, wish for and know nothing but peace. They are ready to abandon land, life, everything for the value of peace (B:442-443).

> All those who are moved by the Spirit of Christ know no other sword, but the Lord's Word, their weapons are earnest and powerful prayer, a strong pure faith, a living hope, an unblemished life so that the gospel of the kingdom, the message of peace be spread (A:95).

> We confess and teach no other sword, no violence in Christ's kingdom and the church, other than the sharp sword of the Spirit, the Word of God (A:120).

> No Christian is permitted to fight with the sword . . . The Christian fights only with the Word of God which is a sharp two-edged sword (A:621).

> For this reason we do not fight with carnal, but only with spiritual weapons with patience and the Word of God and in putting our trust in Christ, against all flesh, against the world and the devil, nor shall there ever be found among us any other weapons (B:470).

> Those who have been born again . . . lead a repentant and new life . . . They are children of peace who have beaten their swords into plowshares and their spears into sickles and they know war no more . . . Their (only) sword is the sword of the Spirit (A:240-242).

In the view of Menno Simons' living "only by the sword of the Spirit" involved much more than the doctrine of nonresistance—the abstinence of killing in war. He saw it as a total life of abstinence from the use of force or coercion, which he called an "only-the-sword-of-the-Spirit" lifestyle (Horst 1992, 163-180). If Martin Luther (Luther 1883-1932; 1955; Röbler 1937, 2, 703-708) reformed propositional truth about salvation (Bainton 1950; 1952), it was Menno who reformed the saved person's total lifestyle. He called the believer to accept Jesus not only as Savior but also as Lord and companion on the road of discipleship.

Part Two tells the story of Menno's followers in the northern stream of the Mennonite movement in Europe. The story begins in the Netherlands and then proceeds through North Germany, the Prussias and South Russia to North America over four-and-a-half centuries. This narrative reveals how gradual shifts in belief, values and practices compromised Menno's vision. It also shows cycles of collective renewal and housecleaning.

Part Three identifies twelve specific areas in which the northern stream of Anabaptists/Mennonites has gradually strayed from the scriptural vision Menno Simons proclaimed. These shifts, which usually slipped in unnoticed but then often worked in tandem, fall into two categories: those that relate to the believers' citizenship and lifestyle, and those that relate to the Scripture and the nature and function of the believing community. In each of the two categories the first shift seems foundational or direction-setting, and those that follow often seem to be a result or an outworking of the first.

In the first category are the following shifts:

(1) The believers' citizenship: from citizenship in only Christ's kingdom of peace to also becoming citizens of the kingdoms of this world.

(2) Separation from the world: the shift from radical separation characterized by an "only-the-sword-of-the-Spirit" lifestyle to only the refusal to wield the sword of war.

(3) Property: from stewardship of God's earth to private ownership.

(4) The covenant community: from a community of equals to a class structure largely based on differences in wealth.

(5) Governance in the believing community: from governance by the Spirit of God mediated through the *Lehramt* (the ministers and teachers of the church), to the development of a Mennonite secular state.

(6) The exercise of power: from "Only the sword of the Spirit" to a just war with the sword of iron.

In the second category appear the following shifts:

(7) The Scripture and its exegesis: from a focused canon, which placed primary emphasis on Christ's teachings in the New Testament, to a flat canon, which gave all portions of Scripture equal weight.

(8) The exegetical community: from the congregation as an exegetical community to a church controlled by professional exegetes.

(9) Decision-making: from community consensus to democratic majority voting.

(10) Church governance: from congregational control to ministerial or denominational control.

(11) The privileged community: from a persecuted suffering church to God's privileged chosen people in their own promised land.

(12) Identity: from a people with a clear vision of what it means to be disciples of Jesus to a loss of identity and vulnerability to outside movements and ideologies.

These twelve shifts serve as a yardstick to examine the experience of the northern stream of Mennonites, which originated in the Netherlands and later spread across Northern Europe into South Russia. This same yardstick is then applied to the Mennonite experience in North America where cycles of compromise and renewal have often coincided with those in Europe.

Statement of hope

Part Four stresses the importance of hope that must precede renewal. Hope must be based on realistic possibilities. We will offer examples of fidelity from the lives of real people and underscore the biblical encouragement for hope and faith. We also will provide practical examples of living by the sword of the Spirit. Our statement of hope is informed by the writings of John H. Yoder (1984, 4-5, also see, 1972), who suggested that the Radical Reformation should never be considered a one-time, once-and-for-all-times event. Entropy afflicts radically reformed individuals and radically reformed groups, just like it afflicts everything else. Just as God does not have grandchildren, so the Radical Reformation cannot have grandchildren. Each successive generation must individually and collectively be reformed anew. Especially when there are major changes in circumstances or in the cultural milieu, new radical decisions about spiritual renewal will have to be made repeatedly.

We believe that Mennonites today can repeat the experience of Acts 15. There, the believers under the guidance of God's Spirit decided what of their past (Jewish, in our case Mennonite) church tradition could be jettisoned, revised or changed for churches developing in other cultural settings.

We believe that even at the end of the twentieth century a congregation that is obedient to Jesus Christ can still find consensus on how to incarnate the ideals and values of the Radical Reformation. It can even today conclude with Acts 15 that it pleased God's Spirit and us to incarnate an only-the-sword-of-the-Spirit lifestyle.

An underlying thesis of this book is that by emphasizing nonresistance during war as a single agenda and test of fidelity, Mennonites have often closed other doors. It is as if we want Jesus to enter our peace room during wartime, but not when it concerns everyday issues of peace and peacemaking. And what about all the other rooms, our financial room or stewardship room? Unless all the rooms are occupied by the Lord of the House, even the peace room will eventually be closed. Jesus knocks at all our doors (Rev. 3:20-22).

The glasses we used: this study's perspective illustrated by analogies

The shifting of the twelve values in Mennonite history is not linear, but rather circular. At any one time the shifts may move in opposite directions in different parts of the world, or renewal movements can reverse the direction of the shifting in a given area. The angle of vision employed is illustrated in two analogies.

The prism analogy

When Newton, the scientist, first passed sunlight through a prism its rays of light were separated into their constituent wavelengths. These wavelengths showed up as a visible spectrum of colors which shaded into one another. Newton selected seven peaks or centers of color which he labeled violet, indigo, blue, green, yellow, orange and red. Between these labeled peaks, however, his eye discerned an almost infinite array of shades of color each blending into its neighbor without perceptible borders.

This analogy can help interpret the history of the northern stream of Mennonites. If the violet end of the spectrum represents fidelity and the red end represents compromise, the rest of the colors all shade into each other, including the red and violet. In the same way the events of recorded history shade into each other, making it difficult to establish precisely where either fidelity or infidelity begin or end.

The twelve core values inherent in Menno Simons' vision, when traced through history, can be seen to slide across four developmental peaks: fidelity, growth, compromise and new beginnings. These four peaks as well as the twelve core values can be shifted either left or right, often producing slightly different emphases or foci. The wide range of opinions expressed in the responses of the readers presented in the analytical section indicate how difficult it is to establish precise distinctions as to what constitutes fidelity or compromise.

The prism analogy also illustrates (1) the complexity of the value shifts involved, (2) the regional variations due to differences in political, economic or cultural circumstances, and (3) the dangers of glibly linking cause and effect.

The bounded versus centered set analogy

A second analogy comes from the fields of mathematics and semantics. It involves the distinction between bounded and centered sets (P. G. Hiebert 1978, 24-29; 1979, 217-227; 1983, 421-427).

A bounded set has fixed parameters or boundaries. Thus things or events are either inside or outside of the boundaries of a given set. For example, even numbers make up a bounded set and odd numbers another one. There is no question into which set a given number belongs since every number is either even or odd. Similarly, all triangles, regardless of their infinite variety of shapes or sizes, are united by a single common boundary: all are three-sided.

In a centered set, however, the relationship between items of a set is not established on the basis of their common boundaries. In fact, boundaries are largely irrelevant since the items belonging to the same centered set are so defined on the basis of their relatedness to a common center, irrespective of their distance from or proximity to that center. For example, the New Testament view of the church is that of a centered set. The center is Jesus Christ, and all believers in Christ, Jews or Gentiles, educated or uneducated, male or female, barbarian or civilized, circumcised or uncircumcised, slave or master, young or old, past or present are part of the church, if they maintain a relationship with Jesus Christ. God's new family, the church as a centered set, cuts across all traditional boundaries and divisions. As a bounded set each ethnic group and eventually each sub-group has to form its own church.

Applied to the interpretation of Mennonite history, bounded set thinking usually assumes that persecution and fidelity are consistently locked into a cause and effect relationship. In centered set thinking fidelity is linked to the believers' obedience to Jesus Christ, the center of the Christian faith. This permits the acknowledgment of fidelity wherever and whenever it occurs. For example, the Mennonite Brethren Church suddenly became a functional exegetical community at a time when the Russian Mennonite compromise in the harmful church-and-state linkage was at its height.

Another advantage of analyzing the Mennonite church's story in terms of a centered set is that it permits this study to deal with the "spirit" and not only with the external appearance of events. For example, if the church and membership in the kingdom of God are treated as a bounded set, then all people would be classified as either in or out of the church. Thus a person who affirms a church's doctrines and follows its prescribed patterns of conduct must be classified as being within that bounded set. In fact, however, that person's heart may be far from God or Christ, as Jesus so pointedly said of the very religious Pharisees of his day (Mt. 15:8). Thus someone could appear to be within the recognized parameters of a church while already having turned away from Christ.

On the other hand if "new life in Christ" is viewed as a centered set, where a person's relationship with Christ is truly the center, then our faith can be seen as a rope that links us to Christ, our anchor beyond the veil (Heb. 6:19). Being anchored in Christ does not confine believers to exist within certain specified boundaries or walls, but rather it frees them to go wherever the Spirit leads, as in Peter's going to the house of Cornelius, the Gentile (Acts 10). This type of cross-cultural contact was forbidden even for a converted Jew, but it was exactly what God was calling for in his new design, the church as a centered set.

The centered-set approach is even more helpful when it comes to judging others. For example, the Mennonite Brethren Church in 1860, working in terms of its own newly established bounded church set, condemned the mother church as corrupt, apostate and outside the will of God. It could not recognize that the mother church still had many believers who, like the people in Elijah's time, had not yet bowed their knees to Baal. In fact, it took 126 years for the Mennonite Brethren Church to recognize its "bounded set blindness" and to apologize for its error in judgment, as the Canadian Conference of MB Churches did in 1986 (Canadian Conference 1986, 8-9).

Had the young Mennonite Brethren Church operated as a centered set, it would have recognized that its own new beginning or return to Menno Simons' ideal of a scriptural church was not complete by any means. For example, the new Mennonite Brethren colony in the Kuban carried on the existing church/state compromise by setting up a *Gebietsamt* (colony government) identical to the original Mennonite colonies. In other words, a centered set approach permits us to speak of *degrees* of fidelity and compromise, providing a much more realistic picture of any situation. For example, in 1860, it would have enabled the renewed Mennonite Brethren to acknowledge the remnants of renewed life that still existed there. They might have recognized that the mother church was still "able to strengthen" its own links to Christ (Rev. 3:2) by reviving features of Christian obedience which for the majority had fallen into disuse.

Finally, the centered set approach permits us to be optimistic and assert that any individual, local church or entire denomination that is still linked to Christ, the center, can at any time take new active steps to reincarnate the *only-the-sword-of-the-Spirit* lifestyle. It has been done in the past! It can be done again today at the end of the twentieth century! Herein lies the Mennonite church's hope!

PART ONE

MENNO'S VISION

This section details Menno Simons' vision (Chapter One). It also includes a statement on the world significance of this vision, and a check on its "fit" with Scripture (Chapter Two). It concludes with a critique of some of the vision's most crucial shortcomings (Chapter Three).

CHAPTER 1

"Only the Sword of the Spirit!"

The Anabaptist movement was still in its infancy when, in about 1528, Menno Simons became convinced by Luther's writings that the authority of the Scripture supersedes human authority. He thus became a serious student of the Bible and began to question seriously the teachings and practice of the Catholic Church, especially on the mass, infant baptism and the believer's lifestyle.

In 1531, while Menno was still a priest at Pingjum, the Netherlands, a strange thing happened in the neighboring city of Leeuwarden. A tailor named Sicke Freerks Snijder was executed because he had been baptized a second time (Vos, 1959, 4, 523). This talk of a second baptism was new to Menno. He was even more surprised when he learned that Freerks was a pious, God-fearing man who believed that baptism should be administered only to adults upon a voluntary confession of personal faith.

Menno was deeply moved. Why would a person be willing to die for the sake of a second baptism? Why would the church kill a person for convictions based on a different understanding of the Bible? With great diligence he searched the Bible and found no basis for the position of the church. The innocent death of this martyr led to Menno breaking with the Catholic Church and, five years later, joining the Anabaptists. Menno described his conversion as follows:

> My heart trembled in my body. I prayed God with sighs and tears that he would give me, a troubled sinner, the gift of his grace and create a clean heart in me, that through the merits of the crimson blood of Christ he would graciously forgive my unclean walk and ease, seeking life, and bestow upon me wisdom, candor, and courage, that I might preach his exalted and adorable name and Holy Word unadulterated and make manifest his truth to his praise (Bender & Horsch 1936, 12).

Menno's conversion was deep and radical. He was overcome with a sense of divine mission. He felt himself called to rebuke an apostate church and to become a leader in the fledgling northern Anabaptist movement.

Menno over against the other Reformers

Menno Simons (Horst 1986a) probably was the least educated of the major reformers. Luther, Zwingli and Calvin all had a much better

3

educational foundation. Can his vision thus be trusted? Is it really important? And what would make his ideas and his ideal worthy of reconsideration at the end of the twentieth century?

What makes Menno exemplary is that when he became aware of the spiritual problems facing the people of his day, he went to Scripture for answers. He trusted God's Word to provide the necessary insight and guidance. He was totally committed to obeying the truths he found there, even if that meant suffering and death. The synthesis and practical expression of these truths represent the working of God's Spirit in the hearts and minds of this courageous reformer and his fellow-believers (Mast 1962, 35-41). These sixteenth-century discoveries in the Scriptures still speak potently to the problems of today, if people of integrity and commitment will once more incarnate them into a meaningful and comprehensive lifestyle (Brown 1853; Brunk 1992).

Like Luther, Zwingli and Calvin, Menno Simons realized that the Catholic Church of his day was perverting the gospel message about salvation by faith with its sale of penances and indulgences. Important as this insight was, he realized that this blatant corruption was not the root cause of the church's lack of spiritual power. The Catholic hierarchy, as Menno saw it, had sold its birthright when it became the state church under Constantine in 313. In this compromise the church had vitiated its fundamental peaceful character and its peacemaking mission.

Other Mennonite writers have summarized Menno's concerns in this regard. John Howard Yoder (1984, 107, 120, 135-136) says that in the church remodeled by Constantine, membership had become obligatory and universal rather than voluntary. The rejection of force and violence by the early church had given way to the doctrine of the just war, and the very word "church" had changed its meaning from "the assembly of believers" to designate the "governing hierarchy." To this list Wilbert R. Shenk (1991, 104) adds that the church now had become the "religious institution" of society, taking its place alongside all the other institutions as just another arm of the state. The Catholic hierarchy, as Menno saw it, had rejected Christ's example and teaching about being gentle, peace-loving servants of God who wielded *only the sword of the Spirit*. The Catholic hierarchy instead had appropriated the literal sword of worldly power to become the chief powerbroker of the medieval world. The church now controlled everyone and everything with the threat of hellfire in the beyond once the totalitarian government's sword of steel had ended their earthly existence here.

Menno Simons was not alone in recognizing that the Catholic Church was using the literal sword as a primary tool in its work. But he was unique in his determination to act on this insight (Luther 1962, 81-129). Zwingli and Calvin all began their work of reform by proclaiming the independence of believers from the existing political powers, the princes in Luther's case and the city council of Zurich in Zwingli's. All three began with a peace position. When it came to paying the price for following through on this insight, however, the mainline reformers chose the route of accommodation. They adjusted their message of reform to fit the requirements of the state authorities in order to live under the protection of the state's sword. Harold S. Bender (1956a, 7) evaluated the situation correctly when he said that even for the magisterial reformers, the sword of "war was not only an accepted instrument of national or political policy. It was also an instrument of the church. Men sought to serve God by using war as an instrument of religion, of the very kingdom of God itself."

This compromise with worldly powers demanded two crucial adjustments in the reformers' gospel. First, they had to identify the believers as citizens of two kingdoms—that of the spiritual kingdom of God and that of the political kingdom of the region's government, with the latter having preeminence in daily life. Second, they had to continue practicing infant baptism because the princes insisted that a uniform religious affiliation was essential for the political solidarity of the realm.

When the Anabaptists, in contrast, persisted in giving their allegiance only to God, the other reformers began to despise them as much, if not more, than the Catholic counter-reformers did (Bainton 1960, 1980). In fact, the other reformers spoke about the Anabaptist wing as "the degenerate child of the Reformation." Luther was so frustrated with them that he said the hangman was more useful in eliminating them than the theologian (Seebaas 1982, 8); or as in the case of Münster when he said, ". . . smite, slay and destroy the mad dog peasants" (Bender 1956a, 7).

Five sword-power abuses afflicting both the Catholics and the Mainline Reformers

What specifically did the Anabaptist reformers see in Scripture that did not permit them to make common cause with the mainline reformers? What was so important that they were willing to risk life and limb? They had discovered that the kingdom of God, as described in the New Testament, rejected five blatant power abuses commonly endorsed both by the Catholic Church and by the other Reformation churches who had joined hands with state governments. They were: (1) the misuse of the sword in defense of truth; (2) the misuse of the sword as an evangelistic tool; (3) the misuse of the sword to enforce morality, i.e., to exercise church discipline; (4) the misuse of the sword for the protection of one's material benefits; and (5) the misuse of the sword in war.

In defense of the truth

In response to the question of whether it was legitimate to use coercion and the sword in the defense of truth, Menno (1876) said:

> In the early church believers did no one any harm on account of a person's difference of belief. They exhorted the erring and the heretical with all fidelity (A:299).

> The Antichrist wants to defend and assert his cause with the sword, but Jesus Christ uses no sword or weapon (A:121).

The contrast between Menno Simons and mainline reformers is clear when we look at the use of the sword in the defense of truth. Ever since Constantine made Christianity the religion of the state, the church expected the state to use its sword-power to defend the truth the church professed. The mainline of the Reformation also advocated this practice. Luther, Zwingli, Calvin and the counter-reformers all accepted the use of the sword in the defense of truth not only as legitimate, but as obligatory. Thus the church, recognized by a given state, could expect the state to crush by force any dissident group to safeguard official truth.

The Anabaptists rejected this position, and held that sword-power could never legitimately be used to defend truth. God's truth never needed human defense, certainly not by the sword. As Conrad Grebel had warned Thomas Müntzer at the time of the Peasant Revolution: never use the sword to protect the gospel (H. S. Bender 1959, 4, 786; W. Mannhardt 1863, 8).

Anabaptists have been accused of violating this principle at Münster, where the sword was used in an attempt to usher in the millennial kingdom of God, but Menno and the Northern Mennonite mainstream have consistently rejected any association with or support for this aberrant event(Horsch 1911, 80-87; Keller 1980).

As an evangelistic tool

Menno was unequivocal in his belief that the decision to become a follower of Jesus was completely voluntary and personal. There was no room for coercion in evangelism. He wrote (1876):

> We have willingly chosen the way of peace and the gentle yoke of the Gospel (A:154).
>
> God's commands are to be followed on the basis of free personal choice (A:173).
>
> The truly born again and spiritually minded constantly conform to the dictates of God's Word and commands . . . They are not driven by the law, for that driver's whip has been broken; rather of their own free will, with a submissive spirit of love, they are ready for all good works and obedience (A:226).
>
> Christ uses only the sword of his Word to [convince people] (A:110).
>
> Faith is a gift of God and may not be forced upon people by any worldly power or sword (A:280).
>
> Enlarge, help, promote the kingdom of God in complete love and seriousness, without force, blood or sword, but through gracious consent and permission (A:318).

The Lutheran reformers, and certainly Catholic counter-reformers, saw the sword as a legitimate tool for evangelism. When princes of either persuasion captured towns or areas to enlarge their realms they made the inhabitants of the newly conquered area an offer they could not refuse—accept the true faith or die. The Anabaptists, however, rejected this use of the sword, not only because they believed it was wrong to kill others, especially unbelievers, but because they firmly believed the decision to become a disciple of Jesus Christ was to be purely voluntary (Horst 1986b, 194-203). Coerced conversion was unbiblical and incongruent with the very nature of the peaceful kingdom of God.

There is no question that the Anabaptist stance that faith should not be imposed from without but be arrived at by personal conviction is a central pillar of God's design. God wants to draw all people to him, but he wants them to make the choice personally. God has only children, no grandchildren. All who want to be his children must choose to do so voluntarily. Thus each person in every generation must personally make a commitment to follow and obey Christ. Menno disavowed anyone claiming to be a disciple of Jesus by virtue of having Christian parents or Christian ancestors:

> If Jews claim to be children of believing Abraham, they were not saved by their ancestry [but by their faith and obedience] (1886, A:11).

To exercise church discipline

Once the reformers and counter-reformers were in control of a given area, they used their respective prince's sword-power to enforce their views on the form of baptism, church discipline, church offerings, and other areas. Even the persecution of the Anabaptists/Mennonites needs to be seen in this light. Persecution was not merely malicious intolerance. Both Catholics and Protestants exercising it saw it as legitimate church discipline. Menno (1876) took a different position:

> The Antichrist rules by means of hypocrisy and lies, with force and the sword, but Christ rules with patience by means of his Word and his Spirit. He needs no other sword or weapon (A:110).

> In the early church believers did no one any harm on account of anyone's difference of belief. They exhorted the erring and heretical with all idelity (A:279).

> Gellius Faber says that the authorities are doing right when they do not let our evil practices continue, but stop us with all available force . . . but has Christ or the apostles ever appealed for the help of the authorities to rescue and protect the church of God (B:154).

To protect material benefits

On this issue, Menno (1876) wrote:

> The New Testament says that all true believers shall suffer patiently rather than fight back with swords and firearms (A:175).

> You should be ready to be robbed of all your goods for your brother's sake, remember what Jesus gave up (B:372).

[True Christians] seek only peace and are ready to leave land, property, life and all for the sake of peace (B:442-443).

Menno did say that governments existed to protect property, but then noted that anyone who called on the government to protect personal property was not acting like a Christian (Stayer 1972, 172). Menno's attitude toward property and its protection with the sword is most clearly seen in his and his followers' readiness to sacrifice everything they possessed in order to remain true to what they believed to be right.

According to Menno's interpretation of Scripture, all genuine disciples of Jesus Christ have been spiritually regenerated, and thus they have received both a new spiritual nature and a new heavenly citizenship. As citizens of this spiritual kingdom, followers of Jesus are completely separated from the love of, or the attachment to this world and all things in it (1876; also see E. Graber 1944):

Our way of behaving is not . . . focused on perishable money or property (A:19).

We declare ourselves ready before God and men to give our possessions, gold, house, farm, and everything we have, little though it may be. To this we add our sour sweat and our labors to succor the truly poor and suffering as the Spirit of the Lord, his Word, and true brotherly love teach us (A:21).

Menno defined property broadly. He used the term not only to designate real estate, chattels and personal possessions, but also all economic privileges and every kind of material benefit. All were to be considered as given in trust by the Lord to honest stewards.

Since early Mennonites were rejected and harassed by both the reformers and the counter-reformers, persecution, relocation and economic insecurity were their daily lot. They had little opportunity to accumulate land or wealth. Thus the conviction that the sword was not to be used to defend material privileges or property can be abstracted as much from their readiness to endure persecution and their demonstrated willingness to sacrifice their possessions for the cause of their faith, as from their teaching on the subject.

The fidelity of the Anabaptist/Mennonite believers to the last premise, however, was not fully tested until they had the opportunity to gain economic privilege as merchants and shipowners in the Netherlands and as farmers, whalers and artisans in the Hamburg-Altona area a century later. Unfortunately, this is probably the area in which Mennonites have most readily compromised their non-use of the sword.

The other reformers and Catholic counter-reformers found the Anabaptist attitude toward property and economic privilege totally incomprehensible. For them the kingdom of this world was as real and legitimate as the kingdom of heaven, if not more so. They saw themselves as citizens of both kingdoms (Bauman 1964, 40-44; B. N. Gingerich 1985, 248-267; Hillerdal 1955, 22-26), with this world actually having preeminence in daily life. Because of this, governments were forever suspecting the Anabaptists of being dangerous revolutionaries and because the Anabaptists worked so hard to help the poor and the outcasts the other reformers frequently accused them of trying to be saved by works instead of faith (Ehrt 1932, 179; Neff, Hege, & Epp 1959, 4, 202; Simons 1956, 569).

To fight for the country

In Menno's view, every use of the sword (except the sword of legitimate government) violated the nature of God's kingdom and the behavior of its citizens. True disciples of Jesus, the prince of peace, were citizens of a spiritual kingdom—the kingdom of God in Jesus' teaching. Kingdom citizens, Menno believed, resolutely renounced the use of "worldly" sword-power to achieve any God-given ends, because such goals could be achieved only with the sword of the Spirit. He rejected the use of coercion in all areas of life—religious, social, civil and international. Among these, the concern about not using the literal sword, that is, the abstinence from killing in times of war, was probably one of the least emphasized concerns in his writings (Krahn 1982, 172; Simons 1956, 247, 423-424, 555).

Menno's swordless lifestyle

Menno's reasoning about the non-use of force, or the sword, as he refers to it, appeared in numerous places. Like other reformers, he spoke about two kingdoms (R. Friedmann 1980, 23-27; H. Isaak 1974, 44-60). But his two kingdoms were mutually exclusive: a true child of God could belong to only one of them, the kingdom of God (1876).

> The born-again have a spiritual king over them who rules them with the unbroken scepter of his mouth, namely his Holy Spirit and his Word. . . . His name is Jesus Christ. They are children of peace who have converted their swords into plowshares and their spears into sickles and know no more war (A:242).

Christ did not conquer his kingdom with the sword, but through suffering! How can some then think that they can create the kingdom of God with the sword? (B:628).

For Menno, therefore, all true followers of Christ must manifest a similar attitude toward the sword:

> We confess and teach no other sword, no violence in Christ's Kingdom and the church, other than the sharp sword of the Spirit, the Word of God (A:120).

> For this reason we don't fight with carnal, but only with spiritual weapons with patience and the Word of God and in putting our trust in Christ, against all flesh, against the world and the devil, nor shall there ever be found among us any other weapons (B:470).

> True Christians know nothing of revenge; they do not cry revenge! revenge! as the world does but sigh and pray Father, forgive them for they know not what they are doing (Luke 23:34, Acts 7:60). According to the instruction of the prophets they have made their swords into plowshares and sickles of their spears. They sit at Christ's feet as if he were their winestock and fig tree and know war no more (Is. 2:4, Mic. 4:3-4) (B:442).

> We know nothing about killing, much less do we authorize or teach it, for we believe that no one who kills another can participate in the kingdom of God (A:121).

This lifestyle permits no self-defense:

> Everyone should guard himself against all false teaching, such as the sword, self-defense, etc., all of which are nothing else but the gilded flower behind which the evil one hides (B:629).

Nor is the sword to be used to protect others:

> Christ did not want to be protected by Peter's sword, how could any Christian then seek to protect himself with the sword (B:624).

> Peter was instructed to put his sword in his sheath (Jn. 18:10). All Christians are commanded to love their enemies

and to do good to those who do harm them, to pray for those who abuse and persecute them (B:442).

All who revert to the use of the sword are no longer considered members of the fellowship of peace:

> Since Christ opposed his enemies only with the sword of his mouth . . . how can we, who are to be like him, fight with any other sword? (B:623).

> Many have forgotten on what basis they were baptized, namely on the cross (of suffering) and they now accept the use of the sword. They recommend, even praise (its use)...(B:612).

Menno did, however, like the Schleitheimer Confession (Jenny 1951), recognize the legitimate use of the sword of government:

> We leave the sword of the civil police to those who have been charged with it, let everyone beware that lest he transgress in regard to the sword, and as a result receive the sword's punishment (A:120).

> Look, my friends and fellow believers, through these and other Scriptures and evidence we are taught and warned not to take of the literal sword and not to teach or to approve its use (except the accepted sword of government, if and when it has to be used), but (to take) only the sharp, powerful, two-edged sword of the Spirit which proceeds from the Lord's mouth, i.e., the Word of God (B:470).

For the last several centuries Mennonites have lifted up nonresistance—the abstinence from using the sword in war—as *the* most distinctive characteristic of the Anabaptist/Mennonite movement. Abstinence from killing in war was not, however, the most fundamental of Menno Simons' concerns. If his thinking was not—dominated by the Old Testament commandment—"thou shalt not kill"—was he then motivated by the New Testament commandment to "love thine enemies"? (J. L. Burkholder 1959, 4, 1079-1083)

There are a few examples of loving one's enemies in the early Mennonite story (Simons 1956, 44-45, 555). One of the most popular is that of Dirk Willems, who was fleeing across the ice with the inquisitional police in hot pursuit. Willems got across safely, but a pursuing police deputy broke through the ice and was about to drown. Willems, seeing the plight of his pursuer, turned around and pulled the deputy to safety. The grateful deputy was now going to let his rescuer escape, but the authorities from the other side of the water began to threaten the deputy's own life if he permitted the escape. To save his own neck the deputy recaptured Willems. Willems subsequently paid for his deed of mercy by being burned at the stake (Braght 1938, 741-742).

However valid the biblical injunctions for avoiding the use of the sword may be, Menno Simons' position went well beyond them. For him the literal sword was merely one instrument of force and he opposed not only that one instrument but also the very use of force itself. Force had no place in God's kingdom of peace. This kingdom knew only the sword of the Spirit. Peter Brock (1981, 19) seems to have grasped this insight when he says that Menno's nonresistance can only be understood as a part of his broader worldview.

Although Menno's vision was first elucidated by exposing power abuses in both the Catholic and Reformed churches, his study of the Bible and interaction with the Anabaptist movement led him to a cluster of convictions and beliefs that can be described as living "only by the Sword of the Spirit." There are twelve distinctive elements in this cluster of convictions.

The twelve distinctives of the only-the-sword-of-the-Spirit lifestyle

1. Disciples of Jesus are citizens of the kingdom of peace

Menno, while differing in detail from the positions held by some of the Swiss Anabaptists, took Jesus' teaching on discipleship and peace very seriously. For him, followers of Jesus were no longer citizens "of this world"; they had been re-born as citizens of the kingdom of God that Jesus had come to establish. While alive, the followers of Jesus were, indeed, "in this world" but they were never "of" it. They were merely pilgrims journeying through it while they proclaimed their loyalty to the kingdom of God.

> Since we are poor despised strangers and pilgrims, rejected and looked down upon by all people, yea, we are considered and treated as refuse. (1876, B:428).

> But we are poor miserable pilgrims, according to our flesh, afflicted strangers, who, not because of any outrage or evil committed, but because our witness for Jesus and our own consciences have to flee from the tyrannical and bloody sword to save ourselves with our poor wives and our small children

and go to foreign countries in order to eke out our survival in sorrow and suffering (B:454).

Because the disciples of Jesus are citizens of Christ's kingdom of peace they renounce the use of the sword-power of this world in all its forms and contexts and depend exclusively on the sword of the Spirit, God's Word.

2. Citizens of the kingdom of peace must separate themselves from this world

> The Gospel writings teach us that the Church of Christ in her teaching, life and worship must be a people completely separated from this world (1876, B:53).

> Separation [from the power structure of this world] is a command of God (B:400).

Menno understood that total obedience to Jesus as Lord meant walking the narrow road of separation and radical nonconformity. It meant renouncing all use of sword-power and living by the sword of the Spirit. Menno knew that the world would punish nonconformity and that the call to discipleship was an invitation to take up the cross of self-sacrifice. He knew that the blood of the martyrs was the seed of the church.

3. The followers of Jesus should live together as a community of equals under Jesus as Lord and Master

The believing community Menno envisioned was to be one of equals. The Radical Reformation flatly rejected both the feudal pattern of nobles and serfs and a medieval church governed by a hierarchy of professional clergy. The Radical Reformation also rejected the distinction between the clergy and laity of the Reformed churches. Menno recognized only one Lord and Master in the fellowship of believers. Those who had responsibility in the congregation were called servants rather than leaders. Ideally authority did not rest in any office of leadership, but rested in the congregation, which called individual members to fill whatever functions the fellowship needed. The Anabaptist ideal firmly insisted that there was no distinction between clergy and laity, no difference between secular and sacred work, no distinction between social classes and no difference based on wealth.

4. Disciples are stewards, not owners of property

As strangers and pilgrims, the early Anabaptists did not place a high priority on legal ownership of property. They were admonished not to set their hearts on the things of this world. The Anabaptist rule was: "Live a simple life but always eat your own bread" (Brons 1891, 179). Menno believed that Christians should be productive and that the fruits of their labor should be freely shared with others. Their attitude toward material goods always should be that of stewards, rather than that of owners (Stayer 1991, 161; Verduin 1964, 231-232).

5. The believing community should be governed by the Spirit of God mediated by its servants—the ministers and teachers

It is better to be a prophetic and even persecuted minority walking on the narrow road of Christian discipleship than to become a Mennonite state responsible for civil government under the direction of their own leaders. Menno believed in the separation of church and state and did not envision a state ruled by Mennonites.

6. Disciples are to live by the sword of the Spirit in building the kingdom of peace

> Christ only used the sword of his Word (1876 A:110).

> Our [only] sword is God's Word (A:118).

> The kingdom of God can be maintained only by the sword of the Spirit and not by the sword of the flesh (B:154).

For Menno Simons, living by the sword of the Spirit included much more than abstinence from the sword of the flesh during war. It was to involve every facet of life and faith, even the defense of the gospel itself. True believers use only the sword of the Spirit (Stayer 1972, 310).

7. The Anabaptists read the Bible as a focused rather than as a flat canon

The Anabaptists believed that the New Testament superseded and in large measure replaced the Old Testament in which force and violence were permitted by God (Simons 1956, 422-423). On the basis of the New Covenant, force and domination of others were replaced by love and servanthood (Urry 1978, 49). Gordon Matties, professor of Old Testament at Concord College, expressed it well when he said that for Menno there was an even more pertinent canon within the New

Testament itself (personal conversation with author Loewen). This core canon was the Sermon on the Mount (Matt. 5-7), Jesus' instruction about the nature of the final judgment (Matt. 24-25) and the Epistle of James (H. Loewen 1985, 34; J. Reimer 1988, 25; J. A. Toews 1955, 12-21).

8. Menno Simons believed that the believing community should serve as an exegetical community in interpreting Scripture

Menno recognized that finite human beings, even when completely honest, will not necessarily arrive at the same interpretations of a given Scripture. The Anabaptists felt that believers should not automatically accept any preacher's message as "truth." They should personally search the Scripture and arrive at the personal conviction that the message given did, indeed, accord with God's revealed truth.

A second test was to submit personal interpretations to the scrutiny of the group of believers (W. Klassen 1968, 67-77). The Anabaptists considered the exegesis of Scripture to be the task of the entire congregation, which under the guidance of God's Spirit, the supreme interpreter, studied the Word and then formed a consensus as to a passage's meaning and application (Rues 1743, 10). Menno saw the congregation as the actual locus of all authority under Christ. (1876)

> We leave it to you and all the pious people to judge who are the true preachers of peace (A:385).

> Everyone must personally give careful attention to God's Word and abide by what it says (A:389).

> Readers, I warn you that you watch what [teachings] you believe and support (A:256).

> [To people who question us about our teaching] we answer in love that they shall search the entire Scripture diligently in order to ascertain whether the apostles and prophets willingly and undismayed gave themselves to their ministry, even when they knew that this meant death (B:461).

> I wish that every Christian would do what Christ taught when he told us to "search ye the Scriptures" (Jn. 5:39) in like manner as the Thessalonians daily searched the Scriptures (Acts 17:11) (B:645).

When you yourself search the Scriptures, they will instruct you (B:645).

About his own teaching as truth he says:

There is no reason to put me to the sword. If I [am erring and] do not recognize the truth, I am wishing with all my heart that others will correct me (A:299).

9. Menno Simons believed that the church can best make decisions on the basis of consensus under the guidance of the Holy Spirit

The early Anabaptists firmly believed that under the headship of Christ all members in the Body of Christ, the church, were equals. This truth was reinforced by several other Anabaptist emphases, such as the priesthood of all believers and the church as a fellowship of equals with differing but coordinated individual abilities so that the whole body could function efficiently.

Menno believed that the church should always hold its doctrinal positions open for review and revision. Furthermore, he held that the statement of faith of a given congregation should be arrived at on the basis of group consensus. Whenever there was a doctrinal or lifestyle disagreement, the whole fellowship, aiming to be of one accord, would simply seek the mind of God together until it could conclude: "It pleased the Spirit of God and us" (Acts 15:25-28; W. Klassen 1968, 67-77).

10. Menno Simons believed that the congregation should fully participate in church governance as part of the Body of Christ

The Radical Reformation placed church authority in the context of the congregation, which was the highest court of appeal in terms of theology and lifestyle. It was the seat of church authority. The chosen leaders were called *Diener*, ("servants of the church") a reminder of where actual authority resided.

11. Menno Simons believed that church members should practice sacrificial servanthood rather than seek privileged status as God's chosen people

The call to discipleship, Menno believed, was a call to suffer with Christ and a call to narrow-road living. "Whosoever would follow me, let him deny himself, take up his cross, and follow me." The call to missions was a call to bring the good news of the gospel to all people and all nations. There was no room for exclusiveness or special privileges.

12. Menno Simons believed that the people of God should be identified by their discipleship, not by doctrine and ideology

The fundamental identity test for the believer is to accept Jesus as Lord and to walk in his steps in living *only by the sword of the Spirit*.

The twelve vision statements, here briefly introduced, will be expanded and used as a yardstick to examine the fidelity of the northern stream of Mennonites in its pilgrimage.

The Significance of Menno Simons' Only-the-Sword-of-the-Spirit Stance in World History and in Scripture

I. In World History

Menno's teaching made the renunciation of coercive force in all of life the principal distinguishing feature separating the Anabaptists from the mainstream of the Reformation. Furthermore, he provided both the Anabaptists and their critics with some of the clearest statements on what a "swordless" lifestyle called for. Through the centuries serious students of Christ's teaching have repeatedly asked the question: Is nonresistance merely a "Mennonite idiosyncrasy" or is it really something of abiding significance? This study maintains that Menno's discovery of abstinence from force *is* vital to Christian faithfulness. Indeed, it sees the renouncing of the use of force as being of world consequence, for the following reasons:

The way of the sword and the "will to power"

In his book *Creative Mythology,* Joseph Campbell (1968, 386) traces the history of "the programmatic exercise of power" by one group of people over other groups. As he and other scholars of mythology have noted, many societies have built violence into the very fabric of their culture by means of supposedly supernaturally inspired creation myths based on violence and the premise that "might makes right." For example, the Babylonian creation myth in *Enuma Elish* builds violence and the right of might into the very nature of the gods and makes their violence the cornerstone of creation. This motif of violence reappears in the foundation myths of society after society (Freund 1965, 106; Shenk 1991, 106).

Campbell sees this early Babylonian *Enuma Elish* myth acted out repeatedly in human history. According to Campbell, when the people in the Near East between 7500 BC and 4000 BC learned to domesticate plants and animals, it became possible for them to settle in villages. Their increasing production of surplus made possible urbanization and the specialization of labor (Childe 1951), culminating about 3500-3000 BC in city-states such as Ur of the Chaldees, Abraham's original family home. As these city-states grew more powerful, they began to subjugate not only the countryside around them but also their neighboring city-states. They no longer made raids in the earlier tribal spirit of plunder or revenge, but rather now executed systematic campaigns of conquest and subjugation. Ever since, history has been a long grim story of one group of people forcing its will on other groups (Campbell 1968, 386).

In a recent book, Walter Wink addresses the same theme and speaks about world domination systems, which he characterizes as outer realities like objects, people, and institutions, and inner (spiritual) realities related to the very nature and structure of the created universe (1992, 3). In the Scripture, according to Wink, these world domination systems are called *stoicheia tou kosmou* (the elements of this world) and they are characterized by the three complex New Testament concepts: cosmos, aeon and flesh (Col. 2:8; 1992, 51-63).

Wink also begins with the Babylonian creation myth *Enuma Elish* and states that the national motto of the Chaldeans was: exterminate your enemies. "Violence was for the religion of ancient Mesopotamia what love was for Jesus" (1992, 13-14). It arose as a guiding political philosophy around 3000 BC with the appearance of the Sumerian and Babylonian city states and has been the prevailing doctrine ever since (1992, 39-40). It pervades the entire world of our day. It has even clothed itself in current day-to-day religion, not only in the creation myth. Thus it now takes the form of the myth of "redemptive violence" and becomes identified with world-wide religious nationalism—and in some cases even Christian nationalism (1992, 27-31).

Writing about the post-World War II era, the orientalist Hans Heinrich Schaeder (1960, 30-32) noted that the twentieth century has experienced the full effect of this world-historical process of groups of people imposing their will on other groups by force. At least twice, however, this practice of dominating others by force has been successfully challenged by a religious movement that renounced sword-power, and based its *modus operandi* on love of neighbor, mutual aid and self-sacrifice. The source of power in such movements was not traditional sword-power and violence, but the moral power of love and self-giving.

The first such movement was that of Buddha (563-483 BC), who rejected the Hindu caste hierarchy based on Brahminical rules of social order and warrior-based power and instead called for "a return to the roots" of love and the giving of oneself for others (McFarlane 1986, *1*,

97-98; Schumacher 1980, 138-145). The second, and possibly even more successful, challenge to "might-makes-right" sword-power, was made by Jesus, who challenged both the Roman military empire and the Jewish ecclesiastical power structures. He demanded a radical return to the "original intents of God" (Roloff 1971, 9-25; also cf. Trocmé 1973).

Wink says that it was Jesus who made the people aware of world domination systems and proclaimed "God's domination-free order of nonviolent love." So Jesus overturned some very rigidly held mores of his time. But not for long! Eventually this domination system proved too strong even for the Christian church that Christ founded and it too joined the very domination system it was designed to replace (1992, 45-50).

Secular sword-power seduces the only-the-sword-of-the-Spirit church

Schaeder (1960, 30-32) continues, and asserts that both of these religious movements—Buddhism and Christianity—were quickly seduced by the world's historical power process. They too "became infected with the will to power" and as a result they "betrayed" their core of moral power based on love and self-sacrifice and began to depend on the sword of steel. For Christianity this happened when Constantine made it the religion of the state in 313 AD (Harnack 1981). According to John Howard Yoder (1984, 135),

> the pre-Constantinian Christians had been pacifists, rejecting the violence of army and empire . . . because they considered it morally wrong; the post-Constantinian Christians considered imperial violence to be not only morally tolerable but a positive good and a Christian duty.

By the Middle Ages the Christian church had become a superpower that could use both the church's religious power and the sword-power of its subordinate "worldly" states to "conquer the world on God's behalf." In the words of Joseph Campbell, "the cathedral of God's love and the chalice of Christ's blood freely self-given for others, had been openly and brazenly turned into tools of force. The Pope now was both the king of kings on earth and the earthly representative of God himself" (1968, 390).

The Left wing of the Reformation returns to an *only-the-sword-of-the-Spirit* stance

During the Reformation the Anabaptists revived Christ's call to return to the original intents of God and renounce all physical, ecclesiastical and secular power (Hillerbrand 1958, 92-93). They envisioned an assembly of God's people based on true love and self-giving—a church operating exclusively on moral power, which Menno Simons and Scripture call "the sword of the Spirit." According to Menno (1876, A:165),

> It is the believer's greatest delight and joy to walk and to live according to God's will and Word in all powerlessness in the pure unfeigned love of God. Here even the volunteers who gladly serve others never lack love as they follow Christ's commandments.

In this century Mohandas K.(Mahatma) Gandhi (1970, 1-402; Shridharani, 1972), Martin Luther King Jr. (W. Miller 1968, 57-85; Washington 1986, 5-74), Mother Teresa (Chawla 1992) and Rigoberta Menchu (1983) have stepped forward to model a lifestyle that renounces force while still confronting the injustice of their world. Of the four, Gandhi has most clearly verbalized why the Christian church, including the Mennonite mainstream, is so ineffective today in standing up to the economic, social and political injustice of the contemporary world order (Prabhu 1959, 33):

> I rebel against orthodox Christianity, as I am convinced that it has distorted the message of Jesus . . . When it got the backing of the Roman Emperor, Christianity became an imperialistic faith as it has remained to this day.

One of Gandhi's biographers, James W. Douglas (1968), says Gandhi rejected organized Christianity because he wanted to remain true to Christ and his teaching.

II. In Scripture

The biblical basis for Menno Simons' rejection of the "will to power"

The Anabaptist rejection of the "will to power" was based on four New Testament premises: (1) the miracle of the incarnation; (2) the teaching of Jesus; (3) the lifestyle of Jesus; and (4) the nature of the new birth (Klaassen 1962b, 1-12).

1. The miracle of the incarnation

Early Mennonites reading the Gospels were overwhelmed by the truth that "the *Word*," which had been with God from eternity and which was everything that God was, had now chosen to become "flesh," that is to say, a human being, in order to live among humans and to teach them what it means to live as genuine children of God (John 1:1-14).

They were touched when they saw that this Jesus did not take on the likeness of angels, but came in the nature and flesh of frail humanity so that he could learn to feel with human beings who were tormented by fear, buffeted by temptation and denigrated by suffering (Heb. 2:14-18).

The Anabaptists were deeply moved that this Jesus, "the only begotten" Son of God, rather than claiming power as God's Son and as God's representative on earth, willingly laid aside all his divine prerogatives and "made himself nothing." As a person of flesh and blood, he humbly obeyed God's will, even when that included his shameful death on a Roman cross (Phil. 2:5-8).

These early Anabaptists reasoned that if Jesus Christ, the Son of Almighty God, found it necessary not only to reject earthly power but also to lay aside all the power prerogatives of divinity, then they, as disciples of Jesus, must follow his example and renounce all earthly power as well.

2. The teaching of Jesus

The Anabaptists used the Sermon on the Mount as their primary source, for there Jesus said:

> You have heard that it was said, 'You shall love your neighbor and hate your enemy.' But I say to you, Love your enemies and pray for those who persecute you (Matt. 5:43-44).

> You have heard that it was said, 'An eye for an eye and a tooth for a tooth.' But I say to you, Do not resist one who is evil. But if any one strikes you on the right cheek, turn to him the other also; and if any one would sue you and take your coat, let him have your cloak as well; and if any one forces you to go one mile, go with him two miles (Matt. 5:38-41).

They believed that obeying the teachings of Jesus was the definitive mark of a person's status as a child of God:

> Blessed are the peacemakers, for they shall be called sons [children] of God (Matt. 5:9).

3. Jesus' lifestyle on earth

The early Anabaptists saw Jesus explicitly and intentionally rejecting earthly sword-power and force during his temptation (Matt. 4:1-12). In his first temptation to turn stones into bread, Jesus consciously rejected economic power. He also rejected abusive power in his identification with the poor and the outcasts as seen in the parable of the rich man and the poor beggar Lazarus and in his warnings to the rich:

> And Jesus said to his disciples, "Truly I say to you, it will be hard for a rich man to enter the kingdom of heaven" (Matt. 19:23).

> Jesus said to him, "If you would be perfect, go sell what you possess and give to the poor, and you will have treasure in heaven; and come, follow me" (Matt:19:21).

Even more important was Jesus' rejection of economic power in his own lifestyle:

> And a scribe came up and said to him, "Teacher, I will follow you wherever you go." And Jesus said to him, "Foxes have holes, and birds of the air have nests; but the Son of man has nowhere to lay his head" (Matt:8:19-20).

In the temptation on the mountain to control the kingdoms of this world Jesus rejected political power and the desire to dominate others (Kraybill 1978, 41-42). The disciples heard him say:

> You know that the rulers of the Gentiles lord it over them, and their great men exercise authority over them. It shall not be so among you; but whoever would be great among you must be your servant, and whoever would be first among you must be your slave (Matt. 20:25b-27; also compare Mark 10:42-44; Luke 22:24-27).

Finally, in the temptation to jump off the pinnacle of the temple, Jesus rejected abusive religious power. At the end of his life he even rejected an appeal to divine power when he refused to call on the twelve legions of angels God had ordained to protect him. He permitted himself to be arrested as a common criminal and instructed Peter to stop trying to defend him with the sword of iron:

And behold, one of those who were with Jesus stretched out his hand and drew his sword, and struck the slave of the high priest, and cut off his ear. Then Jesus said to him, "Put your sword back into its place; for all who take the sword will perish by the sword. Do you think that I cannot appeal to my Father, and he will at once send me more than twelve legions of angels?" (Matt. 26:51-53; also compare Luke 22:49-51; John 18:10-12)

Early Anabaptists firmly believed in the validity of Jesus' reason for rejecting the sword, when he said:

My kingship is not of this world; if my kingship were of this world, my servants would fight, that I might not be handed over to the Jews; but my kingship is not from the world (John 18:36).

They resolutely decided to follow Jesus' example and to abstain from the use of the sword and force in all its forms.

The only power Jesus laid claim to was spiritual power (Luke 4:18-19; Acts 10:38), because the kingdom he had come to establish was to be peopled by citizens who required no force to keep them in line and no "economic blessing" to keep them faithful. Citizens of Christ's kingdom of peace were such by personal choice and, like him, they relied exclusively on love and self-sacrifice to provide the moral authority they needed.

In washing the disciples' feet, Jesus demonstrated how his ideals of powerlessness, humility and servanthood could be expressed in the culture of that day:

[Jesus] rose from supper, laid aside his garments and girded himself with a towel. Then he poured water into a basin, and began to wash the disciples' feet, and to wipe them with the towel with which he was girded. . . . When he had washed their feet, and taken his garments, and resumed his place, he said to them, "Do you know what I have done to you? You call me Teacher and Lord; and you are right, for so I am. If I then, your Lord and Teacher, have washed your feet, you also ought to wash one another's feet. For I have given you an example, that you also should do as I have done to you. Truly, truly, I say to you, a servant is not greater than his master; nor is he who is sent greater than he who sent him. If you know these things, blessed are you if you do them" (John 13:4-17).

4. The nature of the new birth and the resulting life of discipleship

Those who have truly entered the "narrow gate" by being born again and have committed themselves to the narrow road of discipleship have become citizens of God's spiritual kingdom (Brock 1991a, 33). As a result, they renounce all the attractions of power in this world, whether religious, political or economic. True disciples of Jesus might be "in this world," but they are definitely no longer "of this world" (John 13:17; see also Hauerwas & Willimon 1989, 11-12). Here are Menno Simons' own words:

> The Scriptures everywhere present Christ as humble, gentle, merciful, just, holy, wise, spiritual, patient and longsuffering, peaceful, loving, obedient . . . This is how the Spirit sees God or Christ and this is the example he constantly holds before our eyes for we are to be like that and live like that. Achieving this is the goal of all God's born-again children. (1876, A:323-324).

III. In Mennonite Experience

A name for the "renunciation of force" in Menno Simons' teaching

In spite of Menno's voluminous writings on the sword, neither he nor his immediate followers ever developed a satisfactory label for the teaching. The most widely used label in German has been *Wehrlosigkeit*, usually translated as "nonresistance" (Hershberger 1950, 156-162; J. A. Toews n.d.; 1955). This label seems to be drawn from Jesus' command in the Sermon on the Mount, "Do not resist one who is evil" (Matt. 5:39; Bender 1956a, 5-18; Crous 1957, *3*, 907). Another source in the Sermon on the Mount is "Blessed are the peacemakers" (Matt. 5:9; Hershberger 1958; Mosemann 1926, 898; J. E. Toews 1986b, 45-56). Subsequent scholars have rejected the traditional term *Wehrlosigkeit* and proposed *Gewaltlosigkeit*, "the abstinence from the use of force" (Bauman 1968, 38; 1971, 128-140). Clarence Bauman's term is doubtless superior as a label for Menno's teaching, but it has not achieved the acceptance it deserves. Likewise the term *Gewaltverzicht*, "the renunciation of force," proposed by Heinold A. Fast (1971, 29; Strauss 1971), has received inadequate attention, even though it is probably the best so far proposed.

However, when we try to express this concept in English, there seems to be no easy equivalent even to the word *Gewaltlosigkeit*. Several groups of Mennonites borrowed Thieleman J. van Braght's expression "defenseless." Thus the Conference of United Mennonite Brethren in North America, formed in 1889, changed its name to Defenseless Mennonite Brethren in Christ in North America. This lasted until 1937, when the name was changed to Evangelical Mennonite Brethren (H. F. Epp 1956, 2, 262). Similarly the Egli Amish, founded in 1864, changed their name to Defenseless Mennonite Church of North America. It carried this name until 1948 when it was changed to Evangelical Mennonite Church (Rupp 1956, 2, 264-266).

In the world at large today "pacifism" is the most common label for opposition to war, but Mennonites have often shied away from that term (Hershberger 1928, 111-118; 1959, 4, 104-105; 1969; Smucker 1946; J. A. Toews 1955). John Horsch (1920) called "pacificism" a dangerous movement because it originated "outside of Christ" (Horsch 1926, 663-666; 1927, 650-652). Gandhi seems to have sensed some of the difficulties entailed in the word pacifism, because he said that in order for something to qualify as *satyagraha* (Gandhi's label for the "renouncing of force") (Groff 1990, 5, 323), the person must actually have the capacity to use force but voluntarily choose to forego its use (Erickson 1969, 198-199). Heinold A. Fast's term *Gewaltverzicht* is closest to Gandhi's thought and probably also expresses Jesus' view best.

Mennonite obedience to *Gewaltverzicht*

The absence of a good label, however, is not the most serious difficulty to plague this teaching through time. Mennonites quickly manifested a tendency to see it as a wartime issue, with little or no relevance for times of peace. For Menno Simons nothing could have been further from the truth. He wanted abstinence from the use of force to be a lifestyle, both for himself and for his followers. But as history shows, the refusal to bear arms in times of war has remained the bottom line for most of Menno's followers.

Initially the abstinence from using force eliminated the Anabaptists from participating in government. Their lack of interest in and support for the state was usually not appreciated by the powers of the day. As a consequence, a long history of persecution followed. This persecution in and of itself removed them even further from the centers of political and economic power. Except for a few aberrations like Münster, which were roundly rejected by the Anabaptist mainstream, the latter considered themselves completely outside of the sphere of political power and at least very marginal to economic power.

The radical vision of the Anabaptists in respect to the "will to power" and to following Jesus' example of renouncing force has often been compromised. Ironically it was their strong commitment to purity of belief and action that frequently led to all kinds of unexpected power abuses. Subsequent chapters will examine some of these contradictions.

Menno's Feet of Clay

In spite of Menno Simons' expressed vision of what a life of discipleship and *Gewaltverzicht*, or peace, was to involve, both his own practice and the practice of his early followers contained blind spots, which helped undercut Menno's noble ideals and kept them from becoming a comprehensive way of life for his followers. This was especially true once the persecution ended. Three notable trouble spots apparent already in Menno's day were his resort to the "sword of the tongue" to defend God's truth as he saw it, the punitive use of the ban within early Mennonite congregations, and his ambivalence toward government and magistracy.

The sword of the tongue

James, in his epistle, warned believers about the human "tongue" problem when he said, "If anyone thinks he is religious, and does not bridle his tongue but deceives his heart, this man's religion is vain" (James 1:26). Later he changed metaphors and referred to the tongue as a destructive fire (3:6), as deadly venom (3:8) and as an ambiguous source of both blessings and curses (3:10).

Menno's caustic tongue occupies an inordinate amount of space in his writings. He often seemed to impugn the very motives of those who differed with him, and sees them as stubbornly refusing to accept self-evident truth (H.J. Goertz 1986, 160-176). Some examples of Menno Simons' sharp tongue include the following (1876):

> Look, the God of this world has so blinded these obstreperous and wicked spirits (Gellius and his ilk) who deliberately fight against God's Word, and who block the truth with injustice, so that they end up warped and unable to repent (B:9).

> Dear Readers, here now you have the answers I am forced to give to that unsalted, blasphemous book that Gellius published in 1552 against God's pure truth and against His poor scattered church and by means of which he has so wretchedly falsified the pure, wholesome teaching of Christ (B:155).

> If Micron and Hermes feared God, as their sheep's clothing would seem to indicate, they would not have acted so

stupidly, as they have done in their writing. I suspect that the very one who moved Pharaoh to pursue Israel . . . who urged Antiochus to quickly reduce Jerusalem to a sepulcher . . . has motivated Micron and Hermes to write what they have written, so that their hidden hypocrisy, their massive, manifold and serious lies, their fame-seeking party spirit (I call it the way I see it before God), their pride, ingratitude, their undeserved slander, their falsification, their intentional misrepresentation of God's holy Word, their fractured interpretations, their sophist philosophy, their tragic seduction of poor miserable souls, their awful anti-Christ-inspired false teaching, their grievous blasphemies against both God the Father and his blessed son, their palpable darkness and their proud fleshly hearts (B:507).

Menno reserved his sharpest invective for those who dared criticize or question his interpretation of Scripture. According to Menno, his interpretation was God's interpretation (1876):

It will be hard for Johannes á Lasco to reduce to blasphemy our teaching (on the ban), which is not really ours, but that of the Lord Christ himself, because it flows straight out of the very Holy Writ (B:206; see also Simons 1956, 229, 452, 788).

Why was Menno Simons so willing to use the sword of the tongue? Doubtless he was deeply concerned about the accuracy of the interpretation of Scripture and the purity of church doctrine. Furthermore, both he and his followers were convinced they had discovered "the truth, the whole truth and nothing but the truth" (1956, 233, 235, 285). Thus Menno could categorically claim to have "the one and only manner of baptism which Jesus Christ has instituted and the apostles taught and practiced. Truth will remain forever unconquered" (1956, 287).

Menno's sharp tongue was not unique. Other reformers, even the counter-reformers, were equally convinced that they had the whole truth. They too felt fully justified in violently condemning those who differed from them, or even in exterminating them as heretics. John Calvin, for example, said of Menno that "nothing can be more conceited than this donkey, nor more impudent than this dog" (Simons 1956, 405).

Such vicious polemical writing seems to be a mark of the times. Luther described the generally revered church father, Origen, as nothing but Lucifer, "the great star that fell from heaven," whose name was "Wormwood" (Simons 1956, 279). Menno Simons and his coworkers, according to Luther, were *Winckelprediger*, (quacks, phonies, or completely unauthorized charlatan preachers) (Köhler 1957, 3, 418; Simons 1956, 400). Elsewhere he called them *Schwaermer* (fanatics) (Fischer 1954, 30), *Aufwiegler* (stirrers-up of trouble) (Bauman 1964, 37-44), and revolutionary heretics and blasphemers (Seebaas 1982). Zwingli, meanwhile, said the Anabaptists "bathe in gall" and daily produced more mischief and evil "than Africa can produce strange animals" (Clasen 1972, 11).

Clearly, Menno did not have a monopoly on the caustic tongue, but his harsh use of the sword of the tongue in defense of his teaching violated his own belief that God's truth needs no human defense. It also contradicted his instructions to his followers:

> Every one of you should exercise extreme care where, when and what he speaks, so that he not transgress against God or his neighbor (Simons 1876, B:635).

The effects of Menno's failure in this regard have manifested themselves again and again in the course of Mennonite history, as we shall see in later chapters.

Menno's argumentative defense of the truth continued and became even more virulent as he grew older. His final writings include lengthy polemical arguments refuting and condemning the ideas of Gellius Faber, Johann á Lasco, Micron, David Jories and others. If schism-based fanatic fidelity to minor differences of belief or practice has been called "the Mennonite affliction" (Hamm 1987, 38), its germ obviously was already present in Menno Simons himself.

Menno's vacillations on the ban and shunning in his concern for the "pure church"

Menno's second trouble spot had to do with the practice of the ban and shunning. In face-to-face societies, like the closed groupings in which the Anabaptists lived in Menno's time and for some centuries thereafter, everyone knew everything about everyone else. In such circumstances, social disapproval of ideas or behavior expressed in social withdrawal (quite apart from actual ostracism) could exert enormous pressure on deviant persons to bring their thinking or behavior into line. In fact, based on Matthew 18, the Anabaptists stressed that extensive private exhortation and serious group admonition always had to precede the application of the third degree of discipline, the ban and shunning (Wenger 1955).

Likewise, during the time the Anabaptists were "on the run" because of persecution, an individual's survival and safety depended on the complete loyalty of the rest of the group. The redemptive ban thus served as a means of pressure on the deviants to repent and conform in order to insure their physical safety.

Regarding the redemptive rather than the punitive intent of the ban, Menno wrote to some Frisian hardliners:

> The ban was instituted as a means to produce repentance. How can anyone speak a ban in a situation in which repentance is already visible, namely a contrite and broken heart; who would dare in such an instance to still insist on the ban? Oh my brethren, do not begin to put into practice such a (punitive) approach, for that would produce sin and not the reformation of the person (1876, A:387).

On another occasion Menno pleaded that the ban be applied only "with prayers, tears, a compassionate spirit, and out of great love" so that the erring one would quickly be "loved back" into the fold (Wenger 1955, *1*, 200).

But what Jesus (Mt. 18:15-18) and Paul (Rom. 16:17, 1 Cor. 5:1-11) had proposed as redemptive discipline readily became a punitive weapon "to keep the church clean" (Postma 1959, 63) or even to forcibly eliminate anyone who might challenge an autocratic leader's views. History is replete with examples of Mennonite leaders who used the ban to establish or maintain their authority (Krahn 1956, 121). P. M. Friesen (1978, 31) wrote that in Russia, "Under the guise of 'cleansing' the church, they threw their brother out of the church because his beard was either too long or too short, because of a button or hook." In the case of the 1860 Mennonite Brethren renewal movement, the ban was used as a weapon by the mother church to destroy the means of livelihood of communally paid persons like teachers and to ruin businessmen (Isaac 1908, 43).

Toward the end of Menno's life, several of the younger, more authoritarian individuals like Leenaert Bouwens and Dirk Philips were advocating the punitive use of the ban (van der Smissen 1895b). In fact, Bouwens had to be sidelined from leadership in 1561 because of his "domineering ambition" (Vos 1957). Eventually, the issue of gentle versus harsh use of the ban would become one of the reasons for the Frisian/Flemish split in the Mennonite church in the Netherlands (Brüsewitz 1956).

Throughout Mennonite history the sharp tongue and the punitive ban have often short-circuited the high ideals of the sword of the spirit lifestyle. From the very beginning Menno advocated the resolute use of the ban and avoidance to keep the church of Christ pure (F. C. Peters 1955, 26). Later, however, when the Anabaptist elder group in Holland grew in number and some of the other elders began to be rather harsh in their application of the ban and avoidance, especially also between husband and wife, when one member of the couple was placed under a ban (Neff 1955, 1, 221; Williams 1962, 495), Menno began to have second thoughts and in some cases actually opposed certain harsh applications of the ban. In fact, he advocated that the ban should be applied only to "worldly discourse" outside of the home and that it was not applicable within the members of a family (Neff 1913, *1*, 117).

Then in 1557, after lengthy and difficult negotiations, during which Leenart Bouwens even threatened Menno himself with the ban, Menno reluctantly agreed to adopt a harder line on the ban under pressure from his co-elders, Dirk Philips (Zijpp 1957, 79-80; 1958, *3*, 368-369) and Leenart Bouwens (Zijpp 1957, *3*, 827). This agreement soon led to serious tension between the three elders, because Menno soon reneged on his agreement and again began to intervene actively on behalf of a number of individuals whom he thought the other two elders were treating unduly harshly (Horsch 1939, 210-211; Zijpp 1957, 3, 827).

The differences between the other elders and Menno and the latter's own changes of position on this score permitted considerable confusion to develop in the various congregations. Toward the end of his life when Menno was already on his sick bed and could not even attend the conference discussions concerning the ban, the two factions actually started to mutually excommunicate each other in 1567 (Zijpp 1957, *3*, 828). The confusion over these shifts of position on the ban led to a series of church splits. The first, between the Waterlanders and the Flemish-Frisians occurred in 1556 (Neff 1955, 1, 221) with the latter taking the harder line and the Waterlanders emphasizing that only the Word in the congregation and not some domineering elder was the source of authority in the church (Zijpp 1957, *3*, 828-829). In 1586 and 1589 the Old Flemish and Old Frisian split from the Young Frisian and Soft Flemish with the latter again taking the Waterlander position (Neff 1955, 1, 222). Often the latter split is spoken of as the split between the Flemish and the Frisians (Neff & Zijpp 1956, *2*, 337-340; *2*, 413-414).

On the issue of who can apply the ban, however, Menno consistently insisted that only the congregation itself had that authority—no elder on his own had scriptural authority to do that, as some of the other elders were advocating or actually practicing (F. C. Peters 1955, 28-29; Zijpp 1957, 3, 827). But at least three times Menno himself strayed even from this position when, either alone or together with other elders, he banned other erring elders. For example, he and Dirk Philips banned Adam Pastor in 1547 (H. S. Bender 1956, 2, 278; Zijpp 1957, 3, 827), and he alone banned Frans Cuiper (1549) and Gillis van Aken (1552) on other occasions (H. S. Bender 1956, 2, 278). Quarrels about how strictly to apply the ban caused deep divisions among Mennonites for at least the next 150 years (Neff 1955, 1, 221).

Menno's shifting position on government and magistracy

A third problem area in Menno's vision was his ambivalence on the issue of government and the magistracy. He probably shifted his position in this area at least twice. Early on in his ministry he supported the sword of government and a believer's participation in the magistracy (Brock 1991b, 98, Horsch 1939, 210-212; Keeney 1968, 129). In fact, recently, H. Isaak (1992a, especially Appendix IV) has written an entire dissertation on Menno's early support of government and magistracy (also see 1992b, 57-82). He asserts that Menno saw at least three functions for such a Christian government. They are: (1) To implement peace and justice; (2) to promote the pure gospel; and (3) to protect the good and to punish the evil.

But after Müntzer's peasant uprising (Bender 1980b, 145-157; Berg 1990; Goertz & Klaassen 1982; Stayer & Packull 1980, 41-45) and the Münster (H. G. Mannhardt 1919, 7; Seebass 1982, 14-15) and Ooldeklooster (Neff & Zijpp 1959, 4, 52-53) debacles, where certain Anabaptists took to the sword (discussed more fully in chapter 4), Menno, fully supported by Obbe Philips (Zijpp 1957, 3, 826), changed his position and advocated that believers should abstain completely from both (Brock 1981, 22). This view persisted through most of Menno's active life.

Then, late in life, Menno found a safe haven within the lands and the jurisdiction of Count Bartolomäus von Ahlefeldt in central Schleswig-Holstein (Dollinger 1930, 128-132). As soon as he grew accustomed to von Ahlefeldt's benevolent rule, he once more began to feel that with governments like the latter's, believers could and should cooperate (Brons 1891, 86; Keeney 1968, 129).

Sutter (1982, 23) actually says that while Menno's views on government kept on changing in his lifetime, his "only-the-sword-of-the-Spirit" lifestyle and his overall pacifist position remained unwavering.

PART TWO

THE STORY OF NORTHERN STREAM MENNONITES

The historical part of this study is itself divided into three geographical sections: Northern Europe, Southern Russia and North America. Several chapters are dedicated to each. Each section will examine the fidelity of that part of the northern stream's behavior against the yardstick of Menno's only-the-sword-of-the-Spirit lifestyle; but each with a slightly different emphasis.

The Northern Europe section contains a chapter each on the Mennonites in the Netherlands, Northern Germany (southern German Mennonites [Marbeck 1929] are best treated together with Swiss Mennonites with whom they share a large part of their history) and in the Prussias. These chapters pursue the Anabaptist story in each area in more or less historical order. All three point out fidelity, growth and slippage, but they contain only a minimum of analysis.

The southern Russian story (six chapters) differs appreciably. First of all, it begins with the entire Mennonite group—Flemish, Frisian, German or whatever—that moved from Prussia to Russia in successive waves of migration. Eventually however, it zeros in on the authors' home church, the Mennonite Brethren, who separated from the mother

Mennonite church in southern Russia in 1860 as a result of a major renewal movement.

Second, in the Russian story as a whole, chronological history gives way to a more topical and analytical treatment of the developments there. The reason for this is that in the authors' view the developments in South Russia show the most compact and comprehensive picture of slippage and renewal in the northern stream's living out of Menno's vision.

The North American story (four chapters), while continuing the focus on the Mennonite Brethren, must, of necessity, also keep an eye not only on the various other branches of the northern stream that came to America, but also on the broader American Mennonite scene, because all the different strands of Mennonites originating in Europe can no longer be separated neatly and cleanly in the North American milieu.

Furthermore, this section also pays much more attention to the twelve values presented in the introduction and shows how they were violated during the Russian sojourn.

The *Doopsgezinde* of the Netherlands

Paradoxically, the Anabaptist/Mennonite movement in Holland probably owes its life and much of its early rapid growth to persecution. Menno Simons' own conversion was the result of the testimony of the early Dutch Anabaptist martyr Sicke Freerks Snijder, who was beheaded on March 20, 1531 in Leeuwarden. Menno was still a Catholic priest at the time, but was already afflicted with serious doubts about his church. When he heard the story of this martyr from the neighboring town he was forced to confront his doubts and ask: "Why would anyone be willing to be baptized a second time if that meant suffering such a terrible, premature death?" Sicke Freerks was a convert of Jan Volkerts Trypmaker (Zijpp 1957, 3, 826), a printer turned preacher, who himself was one of the first three converts baptized by Melchior Hoffman during the latter's first preaching visit to northern Holland and East Friesland in 1530.

The movement's subsequent phenomenal growth was an outstanding example of "the blood of the martyrs being the seed of the church." It was one of the periods of greatest fidelity to Menno Simons' vision of a church operating only by the sword of the Spirit (Braght 1938).

Several authorities have chosen 1614—somewhat arbitrarily—as the end of the persecution (Verheyden 1961; Swartzentruber 1954, 5ff). In fact, in southern Holland the persecution ended shortly after 1580, and in parts of northern Holland it happened about a decade or so later (Koolman 1955, 1, 102). But in East Friesland and North Germany it probably did not abate until 1614 (Krahn 1956, 2, 120).

Most historians agree that Melchior's 1530 visit to northern Holland marked the beginning of the Anabaptist movement in that country. Even though his visit was short, he and his helpers rebaptized some three hundred converts in Emden alone (H. Penner 1955, 51-52). In 1530-1531 Hoffman and his disciples also preached to and rebaptized many converts in other parts of Holland, especially in The Hague-Amsterdam area and the so-called Waterlander region of southern Holland.

The Catholic Holy Office of the Inquisition moved swiftly to destroy this new crop of "heretics." This bid for the destruction of heresy was based on Yahweh's Old Testament exhortation to his chosen people to eradicate the idolatrous Baal worship in their midst (Deut. 12:7-

11; see H. Quiring 1957, *3*, 41-42). There already existed a 1529 ordinance announcing that:

> All Anabaptists and every rebaptized person, male or female, who is of accountable age, shall be separated from life to death with fire, the sword or whatever. All these revolutionary uproar-makers shall be brought to justice (Loserth 1936, 27).

At first, local sympathy for these "upright believers" tended to sabotage the intentions of the Inquisition. But that ended abruptly when Jan Matthys and Jan van Leyden became carried away with the chiliastic dimension of Melchior Hoffman's message (Wenger 1955, *1*, 200-202). They and their followers seized the city of Münster by force of arms in 1535 to establish what they called "the kingdom of God on earth." Another group of Anabaptists of the same cast marched against the authorities in Amsterdam with swords drawn. As a result the inquisitional fury of the Holy Office knew no bounds. In 1535 it issued a new hard-hitting edict:

> Whoever will rebaptize people or any rebaptized person who refuses to renounce his rebaptism, or anyone sheltering rebaptized people shall be killed—men by beheading, women by drowning (H. Penner 1955, 52).

Soon burning at the stake was added to the methods of execution, because "it added so much more drama." In short order some 1500-2000 Anabaptists became martyrs (Braght 1938). An overwhelming majority of them came from southern Holland, but a substantial number also came from other parts of that country (Mellinck 1986).

It was at this point that Menno Simons' emerging leadership became so crucial to the Anabaptist movement. Menno, while not denying Hoffman's eschatological hope (W. Klassen 1986, 15-31), rejected force, especially the force of arms, as a valid means for establishing God's kingdom of peace. Instead he emphasized obeying Jesus' teaching and following Jesus' example in humble service and renouncing every use of the sword, except the sword of the Spirit. It was Menno who gathered all the *Vreedzamen* (the peaceful ones). It was his peaceful stance that saved the Dutch Anabaptist movement from annihilation (H. Fast 1976, 10-13). Under his gentle leadership the supposed "uproar makers" became known as "the quiet of the land" (H.-J. Goertz 1988a, 41; Keeney 1970, 15-19).

While the Inquisition during its first years was destroying so many of Menno Simons' co-disciples of Jesus, he himself was trying to encourage all new converts, saying:

> Remember those who have gone before! Look at how they ended! Follow their faith! They have loved God above everything else and seriously sought their soul's salvation. They separated themselves from the world and gave themselves wholly to God. They left all earthly things behind and did not count their lives as worthy, but have suffered for Christ willingly and freely (Dühren 1939, 26-27).

The testimonies of these martyrs are truly inspirational. The *Mennonitisches Lexikon* estimates that some eighteen thousand people were martyred in Holland (B.C. Roosen 1886, 4-6; Smissen 1913, *1*, 17). This high figure may include casualties of the war between the forces of the Inquisition and those of the independence movement.

Developments in southern Holland

Some believers hide their faith

Not all converts were willing to pay the ultimate price for their faith. Many so-called secret believers concealed their faith to avoid persecution. In a letter Menno chided one such group for permitting their infants to be baptized and for attending mass at Easter. Such compromises, he wrote, were unscriptural and could not be justified as expressions of Christian liberty, for Christ wanted open and obedient disciples (Horst 1982, 203-204).

The poorer and most vulnerable of the new Anabaptists resorted to the so-called "rabbits' defense"—they fled. Some headed for the northern parts of Holland where Catholicism had never taken firm root. Others clandestinely boarded ships bound for Baltic ports. Many with entrepreneurial skills headed for the Hanseatic cities along the Baltic coast with whom Dutch merchants—some of them Anabaptists—were doing a thriving business. An estimated 100,000 people were forced to flee during this period (Brons 1891, 106). Some southern Dutch Anabaptist churches were wiped out completely by the persecution (B. C. Roosen 1886, 5).

Eventually the Reformed wing of the Reformation also began to take hold in Holland. The new Reformed believers often were as eager as the Catholics to root out the Anabaptist "heretics." But in a few cases religion and politics joined forces to create unusual alliances, for example the *Doopsgezinden* and William of Orange.

The *Doopsgezinde* and William of Orange

At first Prince William of Orange, the regional governor appointed by the Holy Roman Empire (then headquartered in Spain), eagerly joined the persecution of Anabaptists. But his attitude changed dramatically when he was converted to the Reformed faith in 1568 (Neff & Zijpp 1959, 4, 956-957) and volunteered to lead like-minded Hollanders in a struggle for independence against the Spanish Crown and the Holy Roman Empire. His early ragtag soldiers, however, were no match for the seasoned Spanish troops headed by the Duke of Alba (Smissen 1913, 1, 17). As a result William and his supporters were quickly forced to flee to the Dutch countryside. Here he gathered a wide assortment of independence-minded people, especially converts of the Reformation, to continue the struggle for independence. In order to eliminate William as quickly as possible, King Philip of Spain put a price of 25,000 gold crowns on his head (Brons 1891, 127). Now, as one of the hunted himself, William forged a new relationship with those he had once persecuted.

Some wealthy Anabaptists paid a visit to Prince William shortly after he had been forced to withdraw from the city under pressure of the superior forces of the Duke of Alba. They presented him with a sizeable sum of 750,000 gulden (Schlabach 1988, 178; Zijpp 1957, 3, 829-830). "This gift," they told him, "has no strings attached to it. You may use the money as you see fit." They asked only that the prince remember them once he achieved victory in his struggle against the Holy Roman Empire.

William did remember his new benefactors, granting the Mennonites citizenship in 1578 as soon as the southern part of Holland achieved its independence (Reiswitz & Wadzeck 1821, 39). The Mennonites, along with all the other independence-minded groups, met with Prince William to form the Union of Utrecht in 1579. All parties pledged to be tolerant toward all other religious persuasions as part of their united struggle for independence (P. M. Friesen 1978, 24; Zijpp 1959, 4, 124-125). By participating in these negotiations the Mennonites were clearly signaling that they were patriots (Zijpp 1959, 4, 124-125) and that they intended to function as citizens of an independent Netherlands, which they hoped would emerge from the struggle.

The Union of Utrecht also marked the beginning of the end of the persecution for Anabaptists in the southern area, at least in those areas under Prince William's control. This agreement made the Netherlands unique in Europe. It established a state with no single official religion (Baasch 1927, 7; Brons 1891, 171).

The Mennonites had successfully communicated to Prince William that the right to refuse to bear arms was very close to their hearts. However, they had also convinced him that they weren't mere "duty-shirkers." They were willing to serve, but they wanted to serve unarmed. They also were willing to pay *Schirmgeld* (protection money), or even to pay for the military exemption privilege itself. Their willingness to pay for military exemption had already been demonstrated in their earlier gift to the prince, and their service readiness was demonstrated when they volunteered to dig trenches, build embankments and fight fires during enemy attacks.

Early Alternative Service

For reasons of his own, Prince William responded in kind toward the Anabaptists. This gave rise to his famous distinction in all future military call-ups: "All men are to present themselves with arms, all Anabaptist men with shovels and baskets" (W. Mannhardt 1863, 31)! When some local town governments nonetheless tried to force Mennonites to take up arms, even though they were offering to pay for substitutes (W. Mannhardt 1863, 30-32), William repeatedly intervened to uphold their right to serve unarmed. He probably was the first head of government to invent alternative service for conscientious objectors to war (Brock 1981, 28).

The Mennonites continued to refresh William of Orange's memory of their friendship by making additional gifts in 1665 and 1672, and by floating major loans for the country's treasury during the years 1666 and 1673 (Brons 1891, 145; W. Mannhardt 1863, 34-35).

Early Dutch entrepreneurship

The loans the Mennonites provided (Zijpp 1957, *3*, 824-830) not only helped the country but also gave the donors a front-of-the-queue position in the economic boom that followed independence, both in Holland itself and in its newly established overseas colonies. Thus the *Doopsgezinde*, as Dutch Anabaptists now called themselves, were active in founding and operating both the Dutch East Indies Company in 1601 (Cramer 1902-3, *12*, 611; Hege 1956, *2*, 122; 1958, *3*, 321-322) and the Dutch West Indies Company which was developed in 1621 (Baasch 18927, 373-374).

The arming of East Indies Company ships to repel pirates operating in the eastern seas produced one of the first internal tests of fidelity to abstinence from arms-bearing for *Doopsgezinde* churches (W. Mannhardt 1863, 34). In the face of these new developments the church at first passed a resolution saying that no church member was to own or work on an armed vessel. Violators were to be banned from the fellowship.

The revengeless *Doopsgezinde*

This total ban (Neff 1955, 219) soon was replaced, however, by the so-called "little ban," that is to say, exclusion from the communion table while a church member was on board an armed ship (Hershberger 1969, 86-87; W. Mannhardt 1863, 34, 51; Zijpp 1957, 3, 828). The "big ban" (complete excommunication) seemingly was applied only rarely, if ever, in the Waterlander area. Brock (1991b, 105), on the other hand, maintains that the ban was strictly enforced at first, but he cites no supporting evidence.

This armed-ship issue eventually led to the first split (1619-1631) among the *Doopsgezinde*. The Waterlanders stood for the "revengeless" position and the Flemish believers upheld the "defenseless" position (W. Mannhardt 1863, 33-34; Rues 1743, 26). As a result Waterlanders came to be popularly known as the "coarse" Mennonites, i.e., only "revengeless," but willing to engage in defense, while the Flemish-Frisian groups considered themselves the "fine," i.e., completely "defenseless" Mennonites.

There was a second major difference between the "coarse" and the "fine" Mennonites. As early as 1581 the "coarse" Waterlanders permitted their members to function as full-fledged participants in government. Surprisingly, the Dutch government permitted the *Doopsgezinde* to make a solemn promise of loyalty instead of demanding that they swear an oath for citizenship and for holding government office (H. Penner 1955, 56). Before long *Doopsgezinde* church members were part and parcel of the national sword-bearing government with a Mennonite deacon serving as mayor of Amsterdam. During WWI the minister of the navy was an active *Doopsgezinde* church member (Cattepoel 1958, 3, 243; Hershberger 1969, 87). In 1807 the church even began to draw salaries for their ministers from the state government, just like the Reformed and the Catholics were doing (Erb 1939, 75-82).

The emergence of class distinctions

Robert Friedmann (1940, 95) has already drawn attention to the fact that the converts in Southern Holland were largely urban and wealthy. He thinks they should really have become Pietists, because the latter's more internal, highly personalized religion would have suited them better. The converts in the north, on the other hand, were more rural and came from the poorer peasant, artisan or working classes. In the south, Mennonite wealth and commercial interests helped nudge them into joining the Utrecht agreement of 1579 which dealt with confessional, political and commercial concerns. This drew them into ever-increasing commercial activity (Baasch 1927, 7).

The loans the Mennonites made to the government not only established them as an essential cog in the economy, but also helped them become leaders in the resulting commercial enterprises. As their wealth grew, some of them lost their taste for simplicity and became addicted to increasing luxury. As someone put it, "their clothes were costlier, but their inner adornment was lost; love cooled and quarrels increased" (W. Mannhardt 1863, 65; Swartzentruber 1954, 5-26). Education also increased rapidly. Soon Mennonite sons and daughters were the scientists, artists, poets and professionals of urban Holland (Brons 1891, 140-148; F. Epp 1974, 37; Hershberger 1969, 87; Sprunger 1993). Their outreach in evangelism ceased (Krahn 1935, 167). Their motto now was: "We'll leave you alone, so please leave us alone" (Brons 1891, 160).

The paid minister issue

The wealthy educated *Doopsgezinde* began to feel less comfortable with lay preaching and congregational exegesis. They now wanted educated ministers who would speak with authority (Keeney 1968, 56). But since they still had no seminary of their own, such ministers had to be trained in Collegiant, Remonstrant, Socinian and even Roman Catholic seminaries (Brons 1891, 148). The result was an increasing love for individual independence. Before long individualism replaced community, unbounded tolerance replaced discipleship, luxury replaced simplicity, and so-called cultured living replaced their original lifestyle of *Gelassenheit* (a peaceful life of trust in the Lord) (C. Redekop 1985b, 95-107; Swartzentruber 1954, 22ff). Collective church discipline, especially the ban, soon became unthinkable (Brons 1891, 148).

The church begins to fragment

Up to this time the *Doopsgezinde* had been meeting in small groups in private homes, but now they began to erect church buildings. When the *Dompelaars*, who also practiced adult baptism but baptized by immersion, began to push their idea of an invisible church without any binding confession of faith, many *Doopsgezinde* were drawn into the movement. As a result splits like the *Lammists*, who placed the symbol of a lamb on their church gable, versus the *Sonnists*, who placed a sun emblem on their church gable, multiplied (Brons 1891, 139-140, 150-151; Zijpp 1937, 2, 606; 1957, 3, 829).

Even though many *Doopsgezinde* were already wealthy, educated members of the elite, some were still not satisfied. Seeking more status, they switched allegiance and joined the larger and more prestigious Reformed Church. It is estimated that during the eighteenth century four-fifths of all Mennonites in southern Holland left their church and joined other groups, principally the Reformed. After 1750 intermarriage became a common occasion for changing churches (Brons 1891, 156-157).

In 1735 the Lammists finally realized that ministers trained in the seminaries of other denominations were causing severe problems for their church and so they opened the first *Doopsgezinde* seminary (Brons 1891, 154). These paid educated ministers, especially those who became bishops/elders, quickly began to reach for authority; thus Vos (1914, 195) says, "The elders soon had the say-so in everything and ordinary church members in nothing." Bornhaeuser (1970, 30-32), following Vos, says that between 1537 and 1565 the voice of elders was decisive in everything.

Developments in Northern Holland
Persecution in the north

Meanwhile in Northern Holland, where the Holy Roman Empire remained at least in minimal control, the Inquisition continued unabated. Believers were imprisoned, interrogated, tortured and put to death. The Inquisition even put a one hundred gulden (some say five hundred gulden) reward on Menno Simons' own head hoping to lure some disgruntled Anabaptist into turning him in (Bender & Horsch 1936, 26-27; Brons 1891, 106-113; Williams 1962, 345).

There was one very incongruous example of early Anabaptist violence in 1534 when three Anabaptist "apostles" ran through the streets of Leeuwarden brandishing swords, and proclaiming that the day of judgment had arrived and the time had come for everyone to repent. But on the whole it was Menno Simons' apolitical, peaceful, baptism-minded position that saved the movement from self-destruction and helped the movement survive and spread (Dyck, Keeney & Beachy 1992, 3, 25; Cramer 1971, 7, 586-594). Even the Catholic Cardinal Hosius seems to agree with Menno's positive influence when he says: "Menno Simons speaks and teaches with simplicity and an upright heart, just as he has learned it from the Scriptures" (Dühren 1939, 25).

The desire to read the Word

What possibly was even more decisive for the success of the movement was the intense desire of the largely illiterate country people to learn to read and to study the Word of God personally. Then once having developed a personal conviction about the truth of Scriptures, they sought to follow it, even to the point of death. A Catholic monk, stymied in his own work, once railed,

> You Anabaptists are a fast people. You do everything you can to get access to the Scriptures yourselves. Before you were baptized, you couldn't distinguish "a" from "b," but now, as soon as you are baptized, you can read and write and interpret the Scriptures (Brons 1891, 139).

Another stymied Catholic complained: "Every farmhouse is a school in which the New and Old Testaments are being read" (H.-J. Goertz 1988a, 55).

Anna von Oldenburg

As the persecution continued, many of the Mennonites near coastal towns found it expedient to escape by sea. Others looked to some of the relatively independent nobles who controlled large tracts of undeveloped land in the north and east and who were willing to give shelter to religious dissidents. Among those who received them on their lands was Countess Anna of Oldenburg, East Friesland, the wife of Count Enno, who after the latter's death, became the regent of the duchy from 1540-1562 (Neff 1955, *1*, 124; H. Penner 1955, 61).

For a time Anna ignored all threats from Charles V, the Holy Roman Emperor, about sheltering heretics. But in 1554 when she received word of her own impending excommunication from the emperor's sister, then regent of the Netherlands, she became frightened and issued sharp decrees against the Anabaptists, here called "Mennists" for the first time. But Anna's decrees were carried out only half-heartedly, and in some cases not at all. Some Anabaptists heeded her expulsion orders, however, and fled to other principalities farther north and east. Some went to Schleswig and Holstein where they found refuge on lands under the jurisdiction of the tolerant nobleman, Bartolomäus von Ahlefeldt. Wherever these Mennonite refugee groups went, they drained swamps, developed lands and established local economies, bringing prosperity to their shelter-givers as well as themselves (Neff 1955, *1*, 124; Smissen, Hege & Krahn 1955, 27).

How the Anabaptists survived the inquisition

In order to understand how the Mennonite refugees in the north were able to function so self-sufficiently during the five or more decades during which they were repeatedly uprooted by persecution, a closer look is required of the socioeconomic and political developments in the region at the time.

Politically the control of the Holy Roman Empire over northwestern Europe was slipping. In fact, the Frisians had never fully bowed to the Pope and the mass. Furthermore, individual princes and other local authorities were frantically seeking political and economic independence (Brons 1891, 71).

The earlier system of serfs controlled by landed nobles had already largely disintegrated. Nobles now controlled only 10 percent of the land while peasants owned from 42-85 percent of the land in different areas of northwestern Europe. But times still were not easy. The average wage earner still needed 70 percent of daily earnings for food alone (Blum 1957, 807; Jansma 1986, 98; Vries 1974, 25, 35, 50).

In the cities, commercialization and industrialization were demanding ever-increasing numbers of workers (Baasch 1927, 4-5). In order to induce peasants to leave the land and to come to the cities to work in the factories and other commercial enterprises, the governmental authorities collaborated with the mercantile classes to artificially depress the price of the peasants' agricultural products. The result was that many were forced to leave the land (Baasch 1927, 4-5).

Other entrepreneurs who were unable or unwilling to compete with the heavily capitalized urban ventures, moved their commercial efforts to more rural areas. This allowed many peasants to remain on their land and supplement their subsistence farming with outside employment. Some of these entrepreneurs merely brought in raw materials and product ideas, encouraging cottage industries to make the goods, which the entrepreneurs then marketed. The peasants thus began to cultivate previously unknown skills such as weaving, dyeing, woodworking, leatherworking, metalworking and pottery-making (Jansma 1986, 97; Vries 1974, 57,120).

Trade and specialization

Meanwhile, foreign trade with the Eastern Baltic region was beginning to bring in vast quantities of cheaper grain (Holland produced only ten percent of its need at that time) (Baasch 1927, 35) and cheap raw materials from Eastern Europe (Baasch 1927, 1-2; Malowist 1958, 27; Vries 1974, 171), where serfdom was now flourishing and where wages and prices were low (Blum 1957, 807-809). This permitted local

Dutch farmers to specialize in products like butter, cheese and processed meats for which there was great urban demand (Baasch 1927, 28).

These specialized farmers now became increasingly dependent on outside labor to provide transportation, marketing, fuel supplies, fertilizer, hay, etc. The result was that many new crafts, skills and special services developed to fill this need (Vries 1974, 120). Thus at mid-sixteenth century, in the area from which Mennonites originated in Northern Holland, Vries suggests the following occupational profile (adapted from Vries 1974, 226-227):

Farmers	36.80%
Fishermen	1.20%
Industrial workers	14.02%
Trade and transport	10.50%
Laborers	15.09%
Social services	4.40%
Miscellaneous	7.00%

These widespread economic and social changes also made the people of the region much more open to new religious ideas (R. Friedmann 1940, 95). The years 1520-1530 have been characterized as years of deep dissatisfaction with the Catholic Church, especially with the growing magical interpretation of the mass (Jansma 1986, 90). Additionally, at least one scholar—Helmut Isaak (1986, 76-77)—claims that the general economic depression (1527-1530) in Northern Europe greatly influenced the rapid spread of Anabaptism. Thus when Menno's version of the Reformation gospel reached these people, many responded with alacrity.

Menno's converts were thus drawn from a wide spectrum of occupations and it was because of their diverse occupational makeup that Mennonite groups fleeing persecution were able to set up relatively self-sufficient communities wherever they were given shelter. This diversity of skills made them very attractive to nobles who were desperate to find people willing and able to develop their land holdings and the local economies.

Even though the persecuted Mennonites were able to function as relatively self-sufficient economic units, their short periods of residence in any one place precluded accumulating much wealth. If Peter J. Klassen's (1964, 46-49) judgment is correct, they never were able to acquire much more than they required to meet the needs of their own group, to take care of a few other fleeing Mennonites in transit and to give minimal help to fellow-believers who were getting established in some new refuge.

Working for the right to exist

The result of vicious and widespread persecution and frequent relocation was that early Mennonites in Northern Holland came to see work, not as a way of acquiring property or accumulating material benefits and wealth, but as a means of earning their basic right to exist. When these Mennonite refugees tamed wild lands on the estates of nobles, turned inhospitable swamps into valuable productive land or established industries like weaving and pottery-making, the material benefits mostly accrued to the noble landowners who were giving them shelter and protection (Abel 1978, 35-36; Baasch 1927, 27; Brons 1891, 109; P. Friesen 1978, 46). Kaiser Fredrick Wilhelm I, for example, expelled the East Prussian Mennonites from the Memelland Delta as soon as they had converted the previously unusable delta into productive land (Schreiber 1955, 23). Through it all, the Mennonites themselves gained only their basic right to survive and to practice their faith. For their part, they seemed satisfied as long as they had simple shelter from the elements, meager sustenance, minimal clothes for their bodies and the privilege to practice their faith. Given these basics, they asked for no more (F. Epp 1974, 30; Simons 1956, 285). In 1821 the nobleman, royal councillor and friend of the Mennonites, G. Reiswitz (Neff 1959, 4, 282-283) wrote about their virtues as follows:

> One must consider these people, because of their hard work and saving nature, as the honey bees of the republic. One does not fear them, because they are totally different from those of the events of Münster. One can learn many good things from them, such as humility, contentment, moderation and especially their active love on behalf of those in need.

Mennonites in government financing

Over time, North Holland Mennonites also became wealthy and heavily involved in government financing, as had their counterparts in the south. When the city of Groningen was attacked by German forces, the Mennonites provided a 150,000 gulden loan to the government for its defense effort. In 1785 the West Frisian government asked for and got a 200,000 gulden loan from the Mennonites in exchange for permitting them to perform marriages in their churches. During the war with Britain, West Friesland Mennonites advanced 500,000 florin to the government, and in the war with France they provided a 400,000 florin loan (Brons 1891, 144-145, 160).

Later Dutch Developments

Meanwhile the *Doopsgezinde* church in northern Holland as a whole continued to hold to nonresistance as an official doctrine. The 1639 "armed ship" resolution was reaffirmed as late as 1716. A North Holland Mennonite sailor on a Dutch warship was banned as late as 1793. Eventually, however, even the "fine" Mennonites also shifted to the so-called "little ban," which merely excluded people from the communion table while they were on board armed ships. Thus by 1785-87 a sizeable number of Mennonites were already serving in the armed forces, some even as officers. This situation prompted a sharp rebuke from the Altona-Hamburg Mennonites in 1787 (W. Mannhardt 1863, 34, 51-52).

Military exemption

When Napoleon, who tolerated no objections to arms-bearing, annexed Holland to his empire in 1810, the *Doopsgezinde* quietly acquiesced and dropped nonresistance as an article of faith. Those who could not accept this shift in doctrine emigrated to North America. Van der Zijpp (1930, 25-26) maintained that the conscientious objector stance was dead in Holland after 1800. For a short period it still was possible for individual conscientious objectors to pay 300-400 florin of liberation money to escape bearing arms (W. Mannhardt 1863, 54). Soon, however, the cost of such liberation payments rose to 2000 florin per person. At first the church as a whole helped those individuals who desired to avoid military service by helping to pay for their exemption (W. Mannhardt 1863, 54-55). Eventually, however, this support dwindled and poor conscientious objectors had no alternative but to serve in the military. From 1822 on, Mennonites everywhere in Holland joined the national and political mainstream. They were more or less indistinguishable from other Dutch citizens (K. Bartel 1981, 33). By World War II there was a record of only one Dutch Mennonite seeking conscientious objector status (Crous 1957, 3, 907).

A major complaint voiced by theologians and church leaders of this time was that Menno's writings on nonresistance were not sufficiently systematic nor complete. As Mannhardt saw it, early Mennonites were so busy dissociating themselves from Münster that they failed to develop an appropriate systematic theology for their stance. Probably the real answer lies in the fact that later generations made nonresistance, a minor part of Menno's teaching, to be the core of his vision (W. Mannhardt 1863, 28, 35).

Isaak Molenaar, a late example of fidelity

At the beginning of the nineteenth century, when *Doopsgezinde* as a whole had largely abandoned nonresistance, there is a fascinating example of individual fidelity to it—the minister, Isaak Molenaar (1776-1834). After serving in several parishes in Holland, Molenaar was called to the ministry in Krefeld (Cattepoel 1939, 5-28; Lau 1896-1897; Risler 1951, 26-26) just across the border in Germany, where he served until his death. In Krefeld Molenaar continued to call the Mennonite church community back to its only-the-sword-of-the-Spirit roots. His appeal, however, was not based so much on the earlier Mennonite call for complete separation from this evil world, as it was a call to return to Menno's only-the-sword-of-the-Spirit lifestyle. Molenaar's teaching called for a lifestyle here on earth that would visibly demonstrate what the coming Kingdom of God would be like (Froese 1990-1991, 113; Neff 1957, *3*, 724-725; Rembert & Crous 1955, *1*, 737-738).

Like his Dutch audiences before, however, the Krefeld Mennonites largely rejected Molenaar's passionate appeal to return to Menno. But the *Doopsgezinde* historian, C. B. Hylkema, reverently calls Molenaar the father of the Dutch and Krefeld revivals from 1830-1850 (1911, 63-69; also see Neff 1957, *3*, 724-725).

Sharing material benefits

The Mennonites did not fail to share their material benefits during this period. The Groningen Mennonites eagerly joined William of Orange's drive to help beleaguered Anabaptists in the Palatinate who had been sentenced to death there. Between Amsterdam and Groningen some 500,000 gulden were raised and at least 140 lives were saved (Brons 1891, 145).

In 1672 a Mennonite merchant-shipowner thought his entire fleet had been lost at sea. When all ships arrived safely and with ample wares, he made a thank offering of thirty thousand gulden in cash, fifteen thousand coats, fifteen thousand pairs of shoes, twelve thousand pairs of socks and one thousand shirts, plus much bedding and food, all to be given to the poor. In 1717, when a violent storm damaged dykes and caused extensive flooding in West Friesland, the Groningen Mennonites again shared what they had with the victims, regardless of their religious affiliation (Brons 1891, 145, 170).

Although the Mennonites of the Netherlands retained elements of Menno Simons' vision, especially in the areas of charity and social reform, their amazing upward mobility appears to have diverted them from the narrow road of Christian discipleship and nonconformity to a pattern of cultural accommodation based on economic and political privilege. The only-the-sword-of-the-Spirit lifestyle, advocated by Menno Simons, suffered its first compromise in the land that gave him birth. It was not, as we shall see, the last.

Mennonites In Northwest Germany

The story of the Mennonites in northeastern Holland and northwestern Germany divides into at least three area segments. There are the developments in East Friesland, including both rural communities—such as lands belonging to Countess Anna—and in urban communities like Emden, Norden and Leer, with Emden emerging as the crucial hub. The second region was Schleswig-Holstein, with urban centers like Wismar, Lübeck and Friedrichstadt, and rural village areas like Fresenburg (Goverts 1925, 41-560 and Wüstenfeld. The urban centers of Hamburg and Altona, which later became one metropolis, are the third region. The interests of the Mennonites in the metropolitan area and the city of Emden ultimately became decisive for all Mennonites in the region.

Mennonites in East Friesland

Historians generally suggest that the Anabaptist movement in northwestern Germany had its inception with Melchior Hoffman's preaching and his baptism of three hundred people in Emden (Neff 1913, *1*, 565-573), East Friesland (then Dutch, now German territory) in 1530. Menno Simons worked in Emden during 1543-1544. When persecution erupted in the region, a sizeable number of converts found refuge with Countess Anna of East Friesland, who offered them a safe haven on some of her uninhabited and underdeveloped lands (H. Penner 1955, 61-62).

Before long several more Anabaptist church groups were established in surrounding areas, where local authorities granted them worship privileges, for example Leer (south of Emden) and Norden (well north of Emden). These privileges were reaffirmed during a number of consecutive leadership changes in the various jurisdictions (H. Penner 1955, 62).

Some chronicles state that the Anabaptists first appeared in this area in 1528. The East Friesland nobleman and historian, Eggerink Beningha (1723, 652; see also Neff 1913, *1*, 163; 1955, *1*, 274), however, neither identified the people he called Anabaptists, nor did he indicate from where they came or how they developed. His assertion may be based on a letter Count Enno, Anna's husband, wrote to Philip of Hesse, noting that already in 1530 there had been several unbaptized children (Cornelius 1852, 20) in the area for a number of years. Some

53

sources suggest that they were children of refugees who fled there in 1526 from Münster (C. Krahn 1956, 2, 119).

A similar claim was made by J. P. Mueller (1887, 11), who felt there was good evidence that Anabaptists from Switzerland arrived in the area as early as 1528, since persecution had broken out in their homeland the year before. It is also possible that these early arrivals, perhaps Waldensians (Schlabach 1983, 230-231 quoting Peter Burkholder 1837, 11-27), merely prepared the "soil" for Melchior Hoffman's phenomenal success in 1530.

Unlike in many other regions, where Anabaptists often represented a revolt not only against Catholicism but also against the magisterial reformation, the Anabaptists in East Friesland actually preceded the Calvinists and Lutherans. However, once either the Reformed or Lutherans came into the region, persecution of Anabaptists always followed (Williams 1962, 343).

Female martyrs

Jennifer H. Umble (1987, 1-3, 76-77), in her study of the *Martyrs' Mirror*, discovered that a sizeable number of women martyrs came from this region. Among them were Lijksen Dirks, who was drowned in a sack and Kalleken Strings, an otherwise quiet woman who sang hymns and exalted the Scriptures to all onlookers as she was being led to her martyrdom. Annekin Jans could be considered the first female Anabaptist theologian, since she urged women to stand up for their faith to show that women were no less worthy than men to bear Christ's cross.

While some Mennonites were finding shelter on the unused lands of certain friendly nobles, the group as a whole still faced numerous hostile edicts that prohibited harboring them, lending them money and leasing them land. If they were permitted to settle down anywhere, they usually had to wrest that land from the sea by building dykes or draining unproductive coastal swamps (A. Fast 1947, 3; Krahn 1956, 2, 119-122).

Payments to buy toleration

In spite of their contributions to land development, the edicts of the inquisition still took their toll. Even though the Holy Roman emperor's control of East Friesland never was firm, his threats against local authorities caused many of the latter to yield to the demands of the representatives of the Inquisition. Many rebaptized believers lost their lives and others, like Menno himself, had to be on the run constantly. The *Martyrs' Mirror* tells moving stories of many East Friesland Anabaptists who laid down their lives for their faith. However, the number of martyrs was not as great as in the South where von Alba, the Holy Roman emperor's representative, and his forces were more in control. Even where favorable local authorities gave the Anabaptists some protection, it was not without cost. They had to make substantial financial payments to those who gave them shelter. However, it probably was the most successful Anabaptist movement on German soil (Hege 1913, *1*, 426).

Regional government protection

These favorable authorities, wanting to avoid the revolutionary overtones of the Anabaptist name, began to give the religious refugees less offensive labels. For example, in 1612 Count Enno III reaffirmed the "Mennists" religious liberty on his lands, but exacted twenty thousand thaler for a ten-year extension of these privileges. His successor renewed the privileges for a six thaler annual tax per family. Others called them "Ukowallist," "Obbists" and "Dirkists" after the name of other Anabaptist leaders. In 1658 their privilege was again renewed in exchange for a six thousand thaler loan. In 1660 the new ruler of the duchy again extended their privileges but, in exchange he asked them to forgive the loan made by his predecessor. In 1690 when Mennonites asked for another renewal of their privileges, they were given thirty days to pay 350 thaler to the ducal treasury or face expulsion. The issue was finally settled with a six thaler tax per person for the wealthy, four thaler for the less wealthy, and the very poor exempted altogether. It was under Enno III that the first known substitute oath for Mennonites came into use. It said, "I hereby declare with good conscience with 'yes' or 'no' that this is the fullest truth" (Hege 1958, *3*, 269-270; Mueller 1887, 85, 111, 120).

In spite of all promises of tolerance by the authorities of the area, Mennonites had to continue paying large sums annually as fines for their "intolerable" religion. In 1821-22 the Mennonites of Norden, weary of these heavy financial burdens, petitioned the local government to accept them as full participants in civic matters. They pointed out that even though Mennonites represented only four percent of the population they contributed 12 percent of the city's revenue (Mueller 1887, 227-231; Shepansky 1980, 55).

Mennonites in the textile industry

Both urban and rural Mennonites seem to have been deeply involved in textile weaving. Burial records from 1700-1740 list a total of sixteen professions. Of a total of 122 deceased Mennonites, 42 were listed as weavers and an additional 21 as professionals in trades related to weaving, like dyeing. Abraham Fast (1947, 5-6) called it the "Mennonite" industry.

In Emden itself all the major merchants were Mennonite. They controlled the oil presses, grain sales, liquor distilling, whaling (Brinner 1913) and marine shipping (Baasch 1827, 163-165). By 1905 the distilling tax on Mennonite distillers on two million liters of liquor amounted to 684,049 marks. It was said in Emden that only rich people could afford to belong to the Mennonite church. In 1891-92 the average Catholic, Reformed or Lutheran church members in that city spent 8.40 marks per child per year on education, while the average Mennonite spent 73.70 marks per child (A. Fast 1947, 6-8).

Care of the poor

Mennonites still were a model in their care for the poor. Their church always maintained a sizeable treasury to help the unfortunate among them. This also included giving loans to help the jobless to get established in some trade. Many non-Mennonite poor also received Mennonite assistance. In addition, urban Mennonites maintained hospitals, parks and bathing places as well as homes for rural Mennonite girls working in the cities (A. Fast 1947, 6, 17).

The struggle over the punitive ban

Church discipline became a critical issue when Leenaert Bouwens was installed as elder in Emden. Bouwens, a very active person, reportedly baptized ten thousand people during his ministry. As church elder he became increasingly authoritarian and punitive. If a male member of the church was excommunicated, his wife was expected to shun him completely. If she hesitated, Bouwens threatened to ban her, too (Vos 1957, *3*, 305). It was on one of these occasions that Menno reacted vigorously and wrote appeals to stop such use of force in the church. Menno, in this instance and more generally, sought to be more redemptive when using the ban (Brons 1891, 79-80; A. Fast 1936, 8; Williams 1962, 495).

In the course of time the churches in the area were afflicted with numerous divisions. First, there was the Flemish/Frisian split over the issue of the ban and other concerns about how to live the simple life. In the Emden area all churches were considered Flemish. Later a group of German-speaking Mennonites appeared in the area. Anna Brons (1891, 73-74, 252-253; Smissen 1913, *1*, 271-273), wife of Isaak Brons, said that the differences between the groups, however, never involved fundamental doctrines and usually dealt merely with local and national concerns.

Mennonites sacrifice their witness for the right to worship

After 1614, when the persecution substantially subsided (Hege & Zijpp 1957, *3*, 452; Oyer 1990, 696), Mennonite missionary outreach in the area began to weaken. On several occasions, in their struggle to worship freely and avoid bearing arms, they promised to practice their religion quietly and to abstain from all proselytizing. On one occasion Mennonites were accused of having proselytized when a Mennonite married a Lutheran woman and she joined her husband's church. A lengthy court case resulted (Krahn 1935, 167; Mueller 1887, 40, 179-188).

Mennonite officeholders

As long as Mennonites were not considered full citizens, there was little pressure for them to hold government office. In due time, however, as their wealth increased, Mennonites began to accept public positions and served as magistrates, councillors and even as mayors. In 1822 the King of Hanover ordered that qualified East Frisian Mennonites should accept government posts. If they refused, all their privileges were to be annulled. Eventually these appointments even included military offices. Isaak Brons, for example, directed a society in Emden for the promotion of the German navy. Isaak Brons also served in the parliament in Frankfurt and in the first national parliament of the German Empire (Smissen 1955, *1*, 436). Another unnamed elder from the Emden church at one time was a city senator and a member of the Danish council during the time of Danish control (K. Bartel 1891, 41-42; H. S. Bender 1939, 89-91; A. Fast 1947, 17).

In 1744 the East Frisian area came under Prussian control. This eventually led to the loss of Mennonite military exemption under the Hanoverian regime in 1848 (K. Bartel 1981, 47; Mueller 1887, 175).

Mennonites in Schleswig-Holstein

In August 1555, while the six Lutheran Hansa cities were still reaffirming their original edict against Reformed and Mennonite immigrants within their jurisdictions, a number of Mennonites were already finding refuge on the lands of the tolerant nobleman Count Bartolomäus von Ahlefeldt in central Holstein. He had learned to know the Anabaptists during his military service in Holland and had decided to give them protection on his property. One of the villages the Mennonites established there was Wüstenfeld. Menno Simons found shelter in this village when he fled from the Cologne area in 1554. Many of his writings were printed there. It was here also that Menno Simons died in 1561 (Keeney 1968, 129).

Coastal cities

Wismar in Schleswig was not included in the Hansa city edict, so some Mennonites found shelter there. Menno lived in this community during 1547 and organized a small church. It was from Wismar that he wrote his letter to the believers in Prussia in 1549. In 1555 a Lutheran preacher in Wismar reportedly worked up such a rage against Menno and his followers during a sermon that he suffered a stroke and died in his pulpit (Brons 1891, 77, 83-84).

In 1554 Menno, again living in Wismar, together with Elders Dirk Philips, Leenaert Bouwens, Gillis van Aken, Herman van Tielt, Hans Busschaert and Hoyte Rienex, conducted a secret elders meeting and issued a nine-article declaration called the Wismar Resolutions (Zijpp 1959, 4, 966). Of these resolutions, five dealt with the ban. The sixth called for elder approval for marriages. Article seven seems to have dealt with the believer's right to invoke the aid of secular courts, and article eight dealt with arms bearing. It did not seem to demand absolute nonresistance. Article nine stated that only a person ordained by a congregation or an elder could teach and admonish. Historian John Horsch complained that all the existing texts of this declaration were so corrupted that articles seven and eight were next to unintelligible (Bender & Horsch 1936, 43). This meeting appears to be a complete departure from congregational consensus, reflecting instead hierarchical church government. Another explanation could be that the elders met secretly because persecution made larger congregational meetings dangerous (Bornhaeuser 1970, 33).

Lübeck, another Schleswig town, also sheltered a Mennonite congregation. Menno met David Joris there in 1546. Most of the church people had to vacate the town, however, following the 1555 eviction edict (B. C. Roosen 1886, 14). A small church of seven families remained there. Jacob Denner came here from Altona after the church split in the latter city and preached in Lübeck for awhile. In 1770 new preacher B. C. Roosen caused serious tension when he insisted on audible prayer instead of the traditional silent prayer. It was also in the Lübeck church where younger members of the congregation were asked to preach on designated Sundays. Some of these younger members served the church remarkably well (B. C. Roosen 1887, 32-33, 49-50).

Two more innovations developed in Lübeck. In 1786 the church began holding services in High German on Wednesdays, but continued to use Dutch on Sundays. In 1789 it permitted believers from other churches to share in open communion (B. C. Roosen 1887, 32, 55).

Eiderstedt and Friedrichstadt, two more Schleswig cities, permitted Mennonites to enter their domains as early as 1623 with complete commercial and religious liberties, including exemption from the oath of allegiance (H. Fast 1965, 18-31) and miliary service (Neff 1956, 2, 401; Bethke 1965). In both of these cities separate German, Flemish and Frisian Mennonite congregations eventually developed. Mennonites there prospered and soon began to supply the mayors and councillors of both cities (W. Mannhardt 1863, 59-60; Neff 1937, 2, 4-5; H. Penner 1955, 69; Sutter 1982, 102).

Rural Schleswig-Holstein

Central Schleswig-Holstein was under the jurisdiction of the Count Bartolomäus von Ahlefeldt. When even some of the coastal cities felt that they had to move against the Anabaptists, the latter found refuge in the rural villages in the area. Thus when Menno himself had to leave Wismar due to a new edict in August of 1555, he found refuge in the domains of von Ahlefeldt. Here in Wüstenfeld-Fresenburg (Brons 1891, 86; Krahn 1959, 4, 461) he was able to write, to establish a printing press—actually built by von Ahlefeldt (Krahn 1956, 2, 394-395) and to preach freely. In fact, it became Menno's permanent home for the later years of his life. It was here that he lived as a cripple and finally died in 1561 (Krahn 1957, 3, 577, 582). A monument commemorating Menno's life and work was established here in 1902 (Krahn 1956, 2, 394-395).

The Mennonites on the whole prospered in rural Schleswig-Holstein. Mennonite refugee families established businesses in several of the villages there. The van der Smissen family, which eventually moved to Altona in 1677 and became famous there, had its roots and developed its early prosperity in this area (Krahn 1959, 4, 549; Muente 1932a, 1932b; Rauert & Kuempers-Greve 1992).

Hamburg-Altona Mennonites

Following the Münster affair, in which an aberrant group of Anabaptists who opted to become militant to achieve God's purposes in 1535, the North German Hanseatic cities—Hamburg, Luebeck, Bremen, Rostock, Stralsund, Lüneberg, and others—agreed to refuse entry to so-called "revolutionary" Anabaptists within their city walls. This edict was reaffirmed in 1555 and remained in effect at least until 1650. It supposedly was read from all Lutheran pulpits every three months. In 1572 Lutheran pastors in Hansa cities again complained about the heretics in their area but were unable to do much about it because the Amsterdam commercial houses, to which these North Sea ports were beholden, and William of Orange himself, were pressuring all the Hanseatic city councils, including Hamburg, to permit entry for Anabaptists (Baasch 1915, 215-216; B. C. Roosen 1886, 6-7,11).

In spite of the official rejectionist stance toward all Anabaptists (H. Fast 1962, 1982), records show Dutch Mennonite entrepreneurs and merchants present in Hamburg as early as 1575. In order for the city to be able to trade with Amsterdam, Anabaptists thus had to be tolerated in the city's trading area. From about 1600 onward the Hamburg city council extended many liberties and privileges to them. However, they were to remain quiet and not proselytize. In this way Mennonite merchants, who belonged to a forbidden faith and who refused to bear arms, came to be tolerated, if somewhat secretively (Dollinger & Smissen 1956; Buesch 1797). Some Mennonites, still feeling exclusion, became Lutherans to improve their status in the city (Dollinger 1937, 2, 239-244; Dollinger & Smissen 1956, 2, 639-643; H. Penner 1955, 67; B. C. Roosen 1886, 7).

By 1605 some 130 Mennonite families had established residence contracts and/or citizenship in Hamburg (Dollinger 1937, 2, 239; Schowalter 1938, 33-48). Coordt Roosen, one of the earliest of these entrepreneurs, manufactured gunpowder (Driedger 1993, 11). Since Mennonites did not swear the oath of citizenship, those who were not citizens had to pay numerous other taxes and promise to desist from "all tumult and disturbances," including proselytizing (B. C. Roosen 1886, 8). In 1672 King Leopold of Hanover launched a lawsuit against the Hamburg city council for harboring hundreds of heretics within its jurisdiction. The city council sidestepped the issue by saying they sheltered no violent revolutionaries. The "heretics" they had accepted were peaceful people who benefitted everyone in the city (Dollinger 1937, 2, 239-244; Driedger 1993, 11).

Early Mennonites in Altona

Geographically, Hamburg-Altona formed a single entity. Politically, however, the two had a long history of separate administrations. Hamburg since the thirteenth century had been an independent city belonging to the Hanseatic League. By 1600 it already was a city of forty thousand inhabitants, while Altona was a little hamlet ruled by the Count of Schauenberg (Wichmann 1896).

In 1576, a Brabant Mennonite named Francis Noé and his family fled from Holland and established friendship with Count Ernst von Schauenberg of Altona. The latter consigned a plot of land to Noé in exchange for one thaler per year protection money (Bolton 1790a, 270; 1970b; Neff 1957, 3, 328). He then made Noé his official court supplier (Piper 1893, 92; B. C. Roosen 1854b, 9).

In 1601 Count Ernst was given permission from the Hanover government to open a free trade zone in Altona (Ehrenberg 1893). To operate it successfully he invited Mennonite entrepreneurs to establish their business enterprises there. He wanted them to develop a viable competition to the older, larger and more established trade zone of the city of Hamburg. Some of the Mennonites who accepted the count's offer came from Fresenburg in Holstein. The church they organized in Altona followed the Flemish tradition (H. Penner 1955, 67; B. C. Roosen 1886, 26-27).

In contrast to Hamburg, Count Ernst openly and explicitly promised the Mennonites military exemption in addition to the general liberties of religion, commerce, profession and citizenship usually associated with a free trade zone. These privileges were reaffirmed in 1622 and 1635. When the Schauenberg bloodline died out in 1640, the king of Denmark began to administer the city of Altona. In 1641 King Kristian IV reaffirmed all the Mennonite privileges enjoyed under the previous von Schauenberg administration (Bolton 1790a, 283; W. Mannhardt 1863, 57; B. C. Roosen 1886, 11, 18; Schowalter 1937, 103-116).

Merger of the Altona-Hamburg congregations

At first the Mennonites in Hamburg and Altona functioned as two separate congregations, though they exchanged services from time to time. In about 1682 they merged to form a single congregation to be known as Hamburg-Altona (Dollinger & Smissen 1956, 2, 642-643; Schowalter 1939, 59-70; Shepansky 1980, 54-73).

After 1700 the merged churches suffered numerous internal struggles. This prompted a sizeable number of Hamburg-Altona Mennonite families, who did not want to be involved in these quarrels, to emigrate to Pennsylvania (B. C. Roosen 1886, 63).

During the years 1700-1740 the church continued to affirm that the congregation was the exegetical authority. The first two preachers of the joint church still were "love preachers," or laymen who donated their time. But in 1717 it was decided to hire a salaried professional clergyman at an annual salary of six hundred marks. By 1726 the salary had been raised to one thousand marks. The next year another minister was appointed. By 1774 the church had four salaried ministers (Dollinger & Smissen 1956, 2, 641; B. C. Roosen 1886, 8-11, 65-66; 1887, 8-11).

By 1729 tension arose between the paid ministers and the congregation regarding ultimate authority. The congregation ruled that only persons banned by the entire congregation would not be allowed to vote on church issues. Those banned only by the ministers still retained their congregational voting rights (B. C. Roosen 1887, 17).

Roosen, a popular Mennonite minister

Some ministers were enormously popular, however. One of these was Gerrit Roosen (Piper 1893). On one occasion he was expelled from the city for baptizing a maid who worked for his minister's family. (B. C. Roosen 1854b, 10). But the subsequent popular outcry caused the expulsion to be revoked. A descendant, B. C. Roosen, later became an honored citizen, credited with almost single-handedly achieving tolerance for "heretical" Mennonites. He was such a personable individual and successful entrepreneur that local commerce felt they could not do without him. Because of people like B. C. Roosen, Mennonites soon dominated the whaling off Greenland and were major players in all types of marine commerce (Oesau 1937, 1955; G. Roosen 1712; B. C. Roosen 1851, 78-108; 1905; Shepansky 1980, 55, 60).

Mennonites were growing in influence and image. In 1636 a Lutheran pastor complained that the Mennonite church was so big and that "everyone" was attending there. With popularity, however, some slippage in Mennonite fidelity became apparent. It was decided to no longer excommunicate those who married outside of the church, provided that they promised to continue attending some "evangelical" church (B. C. Roosen 1886, 31,17).

Various fidelity issues

In 1712 a Hamburg church member and shipowner mounted cannons on one of his vessels. This provoked a stormy church confrontation. The church resolved to ban him if he did not immediately remove the guns (Dollinger & Smissen 1956, 2, 641; B. C. Roosen 1886, 66-67). But the armed ship issue did not go away easily. The church had to deal with it repeatedly (Brinner 1913, 163; M. Driedger 1993, 64).

At this time most of the Mennonites still were not citizens but only resident aliens who were considered very beneficial to the local economy. In time, however, this changed, for in 1642 some wealthy Mennonites were asked to accept public office. As a result, members of the Mennonite church now began serving as city councillors and magistrates. According to Ernst Crous there were twenty major Mennonite businesses in the city in 1783 (Crous 1938, 22-32; Dollinger & Smissen 1956; Sutter 1979, 299-305). Friedrichstadt ran a close second (Lichdi 1977, 18-19; Sutter 1979, 299-305; 1980, 42-53; 1982, 102, 127, 214).

Problems in the church

During the last half of the seventeenth century the church fell into a sad state of affairs. Church records show repeated bannings because of drunkenness, fighting and immorality (M. Driedger 1993, 44). B. C. Roosen wondered aloud whether the quarrels and church splits of the previous decades did not have a bearing on the current difficulties (B. C. Roosen 1886, 55-56).

Morally the condition of the church seems to have been much better later in the eighteenth century. By 1756 only seven known cases of immorality had occurred. Four had happened in 1723 alone. Of these, two involved enlisted men. Church growth, however, was exclusively by birth. There is no record of new conversions and baptisms from the outside. In an effort to slow the drain of members to other churches, the earlier ban on mixed marriage was now discontinued (Dollinger & Smissen 1956, 2, 639-643; B. C. Roosen 1887, 17; Shepansky 1980, 63).

Sweden attacks

In 1686 King Kristian V of Denmark, while administering Altona, organized the Mennonites as a fire brigade. During the war with Sweden in 1700 the Mennonites again served in that capacity. When the Swedes won, the Altona Mennonite Church was forced to pay a Swedish tax of seven hundred thaler. In 1713 the Swedes threatened to burn the city unless they received another payment of 120,000 Prussian thaler. When the city could not meet this payment, the Swedes made good their threat and set it on fire. Of some 1,546 buildings in the city only a few survived (B. C. Roosen 1854b, 12-13).

In that fire one Altona Mennonite merchant lost two of his three breweries. Workers at the third brewery saved it by lavishing beer on the Swedish soldiers until they were docile enough to be led away (B. C. Roosen 1886, 71-72).

Following the fire, Heinrich van der Smissen, the biggest Mennonite merchant in Altona, purchased much of the burned out property and rebuilt scores of low-cost houses as residences for tradespeople and factory workers. He almost single-handedly helped return the city to prosperity (B. C. Roosen 1886, 71-75).

Even though van der Smissen, in daily life, was the wealthy and powerful owner of the largest Altona commercial enterprise, everyone who knew him testified that he remained a devout humble Mennonite. He owned a fleet of ships, extensive harbor facilities, large shipbuilding docks, numerous factories, breweries and major real estate developments. Yet he lived humbly and generously shared with others (H. Penner 1955, 68).

Following the devastating fires of 1711-1713 set by the Swedish army, the congregation decided to replace its burned building with a new and larger church. When the structure was about to be dedicated it was discovered that wealthy members had installed separate family pews. This occasioned an anguished congregational meeting about introducing social status differences into the church. The assembly arranged to have the offending pews judiciously removed before the dedication took place (B. C. Roosen 1887, 7-8).

Later developments in Germany

About this time, the issue of national loyalty appeared as a Mennonite church issue. In 1749 the emperor declared a national day of thanksgiving for his military victory. After some heart-searching the Mennonite church did offer a short prayer for the emperor as part of a worship service. On the occasion of the death of King Kristian in 1746, the church paid lip service by draping the pulpit and ministers' chairs in black (B. C. Roosen 1887, 20). Eventually, however, German nationalism engulfed all the Mennonites (J. Friesen 1989, 61-72) and in 1934 under Hitler all German Mennonites formally renounced nonresistance (Brock 1991a, 136).

Into the eighteenth century, congregational life was governed by rather standard practices. The church elected persons to church positions. Ministers customarily sat while delivering their sermons. All men would kneel for prayer, while the women stood up. Prayer was silent and would continue until the minister got up from his knees (Rues 1743, 46-47, 60).

Baptismal candidates were asked three questions: (1) Is your heart free from sin and do you intend to follow God in a holy life? (2) Do you believe in the church of God and Jesus Christ? (this was taken from the Apostles Creed, but they left out the part about hell) (3) Do you promise to heed the teaching of the church and try and follow it faithfully? (Rues 1743, 51-52)

Charity continued to be an important part of church life. The church raised offerings to help Anabaptist refugees from the persecution in Switzerland. A special offering was also taken when harvests in West Prussia failed and churches there needed help. Hamburg-Altona joined the Dutch churches to raise money to purchase the liberty of some Algerian slaves. During the Polish/Russian war and the subsequent flooding in the Vistula Delta in 1736, funds were raised for war victims. When Königsberg suffered a devastating fire in 1765 funds were collected for relief. At home the church instituted regular offerings for the widows of preachers, and for young people engaged in theological studies. In 1762 it collected money for the city council to help the city's poor (B. C. Roosen 1887, 29-31, 57-58).

The military and nonresistance

When the Prussian government finally moved to eliminate all exemptions from military service in 1893, most nonresistant Mennonites on German-controlled soil had emigrated. Some of the wealthy established families who had not left Germany were able to retain their military exemption privileges because of their economic power and political connections. An order-in-council in 1868 gave these families the alternative of rendering alternative service or paying a three percent tax. That same order-in-council, however, forbade any additional Mennonite families to share this privilege. In fact, it forbade the establishment of any additional Mennonite communities. All German Mennonites outside of the listed families were obligated to render military service (H. S. Bender 1956, 2, 496; 1957, 3, 689; Mannhardt 1863, 58).

The twentieth century

During the twentieth century peace concerns began to dim (Correll 1913, 1, 706-713; Crous 1957, 237-248; Hein 1933, 104-113; Neff 1924, 76-87) and all German Mennonites opted to become part of the national mainstream. Following the lead of the famous Mennonite parliamentarian, Herman von Beckerath (1801-1870; Niepoth 1955, 1, 259), Mennonites no longer claimed that they deserved nor did they ask for any privileges (Neff 1955, *1*, 259). They no longer felt that the original Anabaptist distinctives had any relevance for them.

When National Socialism began to develop after World War I, Mennonites embraced its philosophy wholeheartedly (H.-J. Goertz 1977, 259-289). They identified fully with Hitler's national aspirations and even sent him a telegram of support (H.-J. Goertz 1988a, 1). There were no Mennonite conscientious objectors in Germany by this time.

New twentieth-century fidelity

But after World War II many Mennonites who had served in the military and had witnessed some of the atrocities perpetrated by the Nazis against minorities like Jews, Gypsies and Slavs, began to rethink their behavior and the peaceful ideals of Anabaptism that they had forsaken. This resulted in some dramatic testimonies of repentance and changes of heart among Mennonites (S. Bartel 1994, 28-57, 144-153; Haury 1988, 50-55; Schellenberg 1988, 50-52). Many German Mennonites have now recaptured at least a part of their original Anabaptist vision of an only-the sword-of-the-Spirit lifestyle (Casalis 1971).

CHAPTER 6

Mennonites in the Prussias

The story of East and Polish Prussia began with the Crusades. In 1199, an order of German knights, eventually called the Teutonic Knights, was organized in Riga for crusade purposes, but the Pope commissioned the knights to also capture "the pagan territory of Prussia for Christ and the church." The order thus established Germanic villages throughout the southeastern Baltic region. At its height the order governed 93 "Germanic" towns and had 1,400 dues-paying villages under its control (Schumacher 1957, 28).

After the demise of the order in 1546, three centers of power survived: East Prussia (Königsberg and east to the Memel region); Royal or Polish Prussia, called West Prussia after Frederick Wilhelm I's annexation of the region (extending from the Elbing west to Danzig including most of the Vistula Delta); and Prussia proper, usually referred to as Brandenburg-Prussia, with its center around the cities of Brandenburg, Potsdam and Berlin.

The three Prussias were eventually all brought under the dominion of Brandenburg-Prussian Hohenzollern (Göbel 1956, 2, 788). East Prussia was annexed in 1656 and Polish Prussia in 1772, the latter as part of the first partition of Poland. This area was then renamed West Prussia (H. Penner 1959, 4, 923-926). Finally, in 1862 all the Germanic states, including former Dutch East Friesland, were united under William I and from then on the whole was called the Empire of Germany and its ruler the *Kaiser*.

Early Anabaptist refugees in Prussia

As soon as the Inquisition (H. Quiring 1937, 422-423) edict against the Anabaptists in Holland had begun to take effect, thousands of new converts, whose lives were in danger, began to seek safety and refuge elsewhere. Many sought a safe haven along the southern Baltic coastline. Since Dutch merchants, including Mennonites, had ships going to the far reaches of the Baltic coast, many Anabaptists used this as their avenue of escape. Some sources speak of non-conformists being in the eastern Prussian region as early as 1530. But whether they were actual Anabaptists has not been documented.

The earliest known arrivals

The Polish Prussian coastal cities of Königsberg, Elbing and Danzig and the East Prussian towns of Riga and Memel were part of the great

Hanseatic trading league for which Amsterdam served as financial and commercial hub. As early as the fifteenth century Dutch traders were operating a bank in Danzig. Dutch traders had trading partners or actual Dutch representatives in all the coastal cities, and Dutch ships, many of them built in the Baltic, constantly plied these ports and Amsterdam. Thus when the first wave of inquisitional fury hit the converts of Melchior Hoffman in Holland in 1530, many of them fled on ships bound for these Baltic ports (H. Penner 1987, 19).

After the peasant revolt, Münster and the major edict against Dutch Anabaptists by the Holy Office in 1535, the traffic of Anabaptists into this easterly region became a veritable flood. All of them had to come surreptitiously because the name "Anabaptist" still carried the taint of "violent revolutionaries," and the name "Mennist" still was not well enough established (Abr. Friesen 1975, 228; 1992, 131ff; H. Penner 1955, 42-43).

In 1535, some two hundred Anabaptists (sixty families) were expelled from Moravia because of their faith. These people somehow managed to find a new home in the Thorn-Graudenz area of Royal Prussia. This group probably represents the first official Mennonite settlement in Prussia. Some Swiss Mennonites, also refugees from persecution, joined this group in 1570 (H. Penner 1959, 4, 920-926; 1987, 21).

Another early Anabaptist/Mennonite settlement, with refugees from Holland, was established in Oberland, East Prussia on 4,250 acres in 1539. When it was later discovered that these settlers did not conform to the official Lutheran dogma on baptism and communion, they were ordered expelled. Those settlers who actually left this settlement found new homes either in Elbing, the Vistula Delta or in Danzig (Händiges-Elbing 1938, 27; Keyser 1940, 3; H. Penner 1959, 4, 922).

Also in 1539 some Dutch Anabaptists tried to negotiate a refuge for themselves in the Brandenburg-Prussian area, but the effort failed and so these refugees instead found shelter in the Danzig Werder located in the Polish Prussian area (H. Penner 1955, 70-71).

Land acquisition patterns in Prussia

When the Anabaptist refugees first arrived, two kinds of settlements were possible in the region. The first involved making long-term land leases called *emphyteusis*. Such lease contracts, usually valid for twenty to forty years, regulated many features beyond mere land rental and annual taxes. Village-size areas were often leased as a unit and its settlers were thus committed by contract to form their own internal government. Dues were collected by the internal group authority, usually a mayor, and paid in a lump sum to the lessor. This practice was originally begun by the Teutonic Knights. Often these lease contracts specified things like the right to practice a specific religion, to operate schools, to set up dyking and drainage commissions. At the beginning most of the Mennonite settlements in the delta area were all established on the basis of *emphyteutic* leases. After 1757 it became possible to purchase even *emphyteutic* property outright (Ludwig 1961, 87ff; Nottarp 1929, 18-26; Schreiber 1955, 20; Schumacher 1958, 63; H. Wiebe 1952, 91ff).

The second kind of settlements were called *coelmer* villages, which were remnants of the Teutonic Knights' era. They were freehold towns whose lands could be purchased outright. The *coelmer* villages, settled by imported Germans, were located on high areas of the delta and originally had been horse pastures. Eventually the Mennonites were able to buy up many of these villages. This often began with a group of Mennonites extending financial credit to the current village owners and then assuming ownership as one by one the latter fell delinquent in their payments (Nottarp 1929, 17; H. Penner 1955, 72).

"Hollanderies"

All these large scale self-governing villages—whether *emphyteutic* or *coelmer*—were called *Hollandereien* (Quirin 1952, 55), because so many of the settlers were of Dutch origin. Since these German and Dutch settlers had settled in large homogeneous concentrations, they were able to retain their language and culture without coming under any strong Polish linguistic or cultural influence (Schumacher 1958, 186). Eventually all these *Hollanderein* came under the control of their own village mayors (Ludwig 1961, 46; Randt 1912, 22), had their own fire insurance and fire brigades (H. Penner 1963, 19) and their own dyking authorities (Kahlstorf 1935, 35-38).

Mennonites in Hanseatic cities

Danzig

Like all Hanseatic cities, Danzig was afraid of permitting "revolutionary" Anabaptists to take up residence within its city walls. The early Mennonite refugees were thus forced to settle in the unwalled villages, or "forecities," just outside of the Danzig city walls. In 1603 all the forecity residents, including the Mennonites, were allowed to register as property owners in these villages. Some Mennonites managed to find entry into Danzig itself. The earliest were Dutch business representatives and as such were tolerated as resident aliens, since Danzig depended so heavily on the goodwill of the large Amsterdam trading houses. Thus, long before Mennonites were legally permitted to own property in the city of Danzig, some already owned property in the name of the Dutch trading partner or under some local partners' name. The first land registered as actually being owned by a Mennonite citizen seems to have been in 1653. The first Mennonite church in the city was built on that property in 1660 (H. G. Mannhardt 1919, 49-54; H. Penner 1987, 53-54; Reiswitz & Wadzeck 1821, 24-25).

Menno Simons reportedly visited Danzig in 1549. He probably visited only the forecities outside of the Danzig city wall, because until 1772 the Danzig city council decreed that only Lutherans and Reformed church members could reside and practice within the city walls. Menno may have made several visits to the area. He wrote at least one epistle to Mennonites in Prussia (Händiges-Elbing 1938, 28; H. G. Mannhardt 1919, 41; also see Fellmann 1938, 25-44).

During the 1656 war with Sweden all Danzig forecities were burned to the ground, partly as Swedish plunder and partly as a Danzig city defense strategy. At that time several dozen more Mennonite families from the forecities were given residence permits to live inside the city walls, but they continued as resident aliens without full citizenship (Brons 1891, 260-261; H. G. Mannhardt 1919, 55; W. Mannhardt 1863, 107).

Ten years later there was a long and difficult debate in the Danzig city council about whether Mennonites, who belonged to a non-recognized religion, could be recognized as registered shipowners. Since Mennonites were by then economically powerful and Danzig authorities wanted to remain on good terms with them and their Dutch supporters in Holland, the registry was approved even though it did not accord with city statutes (H. G. Mannhardt 1919, 50).

About the middle of the eighteenth century, the craft guilds in Danzig demanded that Mennonites be restricted to certain trades, and some temporary restrictions were imposed. In those trades that were certified as legitimate for Mennonites, however, they gained the right to own land and to acquire citizenship. On the whole, Danzig opposition to Mennonites always seems to have been based more on economic jealousy than on religious grounds (Brons 1891, 252; W. Mannhardt 1863, 107-108).

By the beginning of the eighteenth century, the earlier revolutionary overtones of the Anabaptist name had all but disappeared. In 1749 Mennonites resident in the city were finally given the right to Danzig citizenship "because of their enormous contribution to the local economy." This led to two new developments. First, the Catholic bishop was able to get the Mennonite military exemption confirmed by the Polish King Sigismund III for all Mennonites in the delta around Danzig, not only for those on the bishop's property. Second, when the next Polish king gave an eviction order in 1770 for all Mennonites in the Danzig city area, the city council had the courage to ignore the order since their expulsion would seriously undercut the city's prosperity (H. G. Mannhardt 1919, 76-80; W. Mannhardt 1863, 105; H. Penner 1987, 96-97).

In time several Danzig Mennonites, such as Adam Wiebe and Peter Miller, became famous as architects. Many famous buildings in the area, like the courthouse and the archbishops' residence, were built by Mennonite architects. Others excelled in engineering, and one even established a reputation as an inventor (H. Penner 1987, 81, 204-208).

Elbing

The city of Elbing seems to have been more accepting of the Anabaptists from the very beginning. Dutch immigrants are reported to have arrived there as early as 1519-1521. The struggle between the Teutonic Order and the Polish crown had seriously devastated the area and new settlers were badly needed to revive the local economy. The name Anabaptist appears in the records there for the first time in 1530 in connection with names like Dirks and Jans, who were inscribed in the registry of citizens. A second wave of Mennonites arrived in 1545. The church founded by these refugees is considered to be the oldest Mennonite church in the delta (Händiges-Elbing 1938, 27).

Polish authorities were not happy with Elbing's tolerance of Anabaptists, but whatever expulsion orders—the first was in 1520—were issued by the central government, the city usually found it financially unwise to carry them out. By 1585 Mennonites like Jost van Kampen and Hans van Keulen were prominent local citizens. The former had purchased a piece of property and built the first Mennonite house of worship on it in 1590. As early as 1610 and 1635 all Mennonites were permitted to become citizens of Elbing as long as they would agree to assume full citizen responsibility, which could include serving as councillors and magistrates. However, they were exempted both from the oath of loyalty and from military service upon the payment of *Schirmgeld* (protection money) (Brons 1891, 255; Crichton 1786, 31-32; Händiges-Elbing 1938, 35; Keyser 1940, 3; H. G. Mannhardt 1919, 49; W. Mannhardt 1863, 71-72; H. Penner 1987, 56; Reiswitz & Wadzeck 1821, 25-26).

The first expulsion order against the Mennonites in the city was given in 1550. A second in 1571. These expulsion orders by the central government were based on some local complaints that these foreign refugees were depriving local citizens of their livelihood. However, the orders fell on the deaf ears of the city fathers, who considered the Mennonites essential to the economic health of the city. In 1612 Sigismund III once more ordered the Mennonites expelled, but again the city council refused. In fact, the council had a secret agreement with its most prominent citizens that they would protect all the Mennonites within the city's jurisdiction (Brons 1891, 255-258; Crichton 1786, 17-19; Reiswitz & Wadzeck 1821, 26).

During the pestilence that wiped out a large part of Elbing's population the Mennonites contributed 12,000 florin for the burial of the city's dead. The list of the victims includes fifty-two Mennonite names (H. G. Mannhardt 1919, 87; Neff 1937, 2, 5).

During the war with Napoleon in 1815, a young Elbing Mennonite volunteered for the Polish army and was then excommunicated by his church. A year later he asked the Elbing city authorities to help him be reinstated as a Mennonite church member. The city council president sent a strong message to the presiding church elder, ordering him to reinstate the young man at once. However, during the subsequent court proceedings, the judge declared the elder free of wrongdoing. In fact, he assured him that he had acted properly in disciplining the young man, since the latter had, indeed, violated a fundamental statute of the Mennonite faith (W. Mannhardt 1863, 46-47; Reiswitz & Wadzeck 1821, 236ff; 1824, 233ff).

An examination of the local high school records in 1784 reveals some fifty-five students identified in the records either as Anabaptists or as Mennonites. By 1923 Elbing Mennonites were among the city's more illustrious citizens. The first paid seminary-educated minister in Elbing reportedly was hired that year (A. Goertz 1966, 225; Kauenhoven 1961, 16; Neff 1937, 40).

Königsberg

The East Prussian city of Königsberg was another early refuge for Mennonites, but it never was an easy place for them (H. Quiring 1937, 2, 538; Quiring & Zijpp 1957, 3, 221-222). There were constant threats by local authorities against them. In 1554 all the professors at the university in Königsberg were asked to swear that they would not tolerate any Anabaptists in their institution, either as instructors or as students. However, Mennonite merchants doing business with Holland seemingly were operating out of Königsberg already in the year 1536. There exists an official record of 1579 with a petition to Count Georg Friedrich of the city to permit Mennonites to reside legally in Königsberg and other East Prussian localities. The ducal response was negative; only adherents of the Augsburg Confession would be tolerated. This edict was repeated in 1585, 1586, 1661, 1679 and 1689, but all the while Mennonites acquired property and practiced their trades in the city. Reiswitz's explanation of the apparent contradiction is that expulsion orders given by the crown were never really enforced locally. While permanent residence remained forbidden, Mennonite merchants were always given indefinitely renewable short-term residence permits. Later when a judge, Pribinder by name, investigated the situation for the crown and reported what a great benefit Mennonites were, the king approved a letter of privilege for them (Hartknoch 1686, 498, 947; W. Mannhardt 1863, 111; H. Penner 1987, 222; H. Quiring 1937, 2, 538; Reiswitz & Wadzeck 1821, 31; Verduin 1964, 19).

When Brandenburg-Prussia annexed East Prussia in 1698, the territory continued to be governed under Polish law. This meant that the existing Polish military exemption for Mennonites there remained in effect (W. Mannhardt 1863, 100).

In 1710 the Dutch government again appealed to the authorities in East Prussia to be hospitable to Mennonite refugees there. Since the pestilence of the early 1700s had annihilated so much of East Prussia's population, all the new Mennonite immigrants to the Königsberg area now were promised freedom of religion and occupation, as well as exemption from military service. As a result in 1716 the Mennonites Jan Pieters Spronck, Heinrich von Hofen, Jakob Schroeder and Isaak Kroeker were given citizenship because they were famous distillers and they had paid 6,190 thaler in taxes on their products over the previous five years (W. Mannhardt 1863, 117-118; H. Penner 1958, 3, 324; Quiring & Zijpp 1957, 3, 221).

In 1718 the Mennonites there were still meeting in the home of a cloth merchant who had royal permission for a textile factory. In 1720 a Danzig city Mennonite minister received permission from the Königsberg City Council to celebrate a public communion service for Mennonite believers. The first Mennonite meeting house was finally purchased in 1752 and the first actual church built in 1768. Many Lutherans began to attend there, but those who wanted to actually join had to go to Holland to do so, because local proselytism was strictly forbidden. In June 1724, following another expulsion order, some six hundred families left the city, but forty families remained. Of these, a Mennonite named Dyck was granted full citizenship even though he would not swear an oath of allegiance (Crichton 1786, 35; H. Penner 1987, 97; Reiswitz & Wadzeck 1829, 196-199).

At about this same time some over-zealous Prussian recruiters forced some Königsberg Mennonite youths into the military, torturing the young men and violating some women, but a Mennonite church appeal to the Prussian king brought the release of the young men taken (Verduin 1964, 166).

There were numerous expulsion orders—1585, 1586, 1661, 1679, and 1684 (W. Mannhardt 1863, 110-111)—but none of them ever were carried out because "Mennonites were producing such a large percentage of the city's revenue." In 1724 the king again took a strong stand and ordered a "final and total" expulsion of all Mennonites from Königsberg. When the Mennonites began departing, however, the ministers of war and commerce protested loudly that their expulsion would mean a tremendous loss of revenue both for the city and the realm. The king thus made an about-face and invited the Mennonites back, provided they would also open a textile mill to supply his armed forces with material for uniforms. A royal decree in 1740 made citizenship available to all Mennonites (W. Mannhardt 1863, 118-119; H. Penner 1987, 223; H. Quiring 1937, 2, 538; Verduin 1964, 60).

The Königsberg Mennonite church operated two homes for the poor, each of which had space for six families. In 1766 the relatives of a deceased person in one of the poor homes sued the church for all assets the person had owned when he entered, even though the latter had lived in the home without charge for many years. The court decided unanimously in the church's favor (H. Penner 1987, 223-224).

Mennonites in the delta areas

The Vistula Delta

The Vistula Delta (Ratzlaff 1971) was historically divided into four major sections: (a) the Danzig Werder, which stretched west of the Vistula River, (b) the Great Werder, which was located between the Weichsel and Nogat Rivers, (c) the Small Werder, which was east of the Nogat River and (d) the Marienburger Werder, which was on the Vistula upriver from the Nogat River junction. The latter, however, was often treated as a part of the Great Werder. Up to 1550 the area, except for a few high spots, had remained largely uninhabited (H. Penner 1940, 65).

The first of the Werders, the Danzig Werder, was settled at the request of the Bishop of Kujavien (*Kujavy*), who had title to large tracts of flooded delta land there. This invitation was first extended in 1547-

1550. There was a degree of malice in the Catholic bishop's invitation. He saw it as a way to get back at the Lutherans who controlled Danzig city (H. Penner 1987, 52-53).

The bishop invited these refugees onto his properties to establish Mennonite towns, including Seidlitz, Altdorf and Schottland. Historian Cornelius J. Dyck and others suggest there is good evidence that Dirk Philips spent some time preaching in Schottland (Dyck, Keeney & Beachy 1992, 31; H. G. Mannhardt 1919, 41-42).

Draining the Vistula Delta

These lands all needed to be drained. The total area involved some one hundred square miles, some of it three to seven feet under sea level. Only the high spots had previously been occupied by the Teutonic Knights as horse pastures (H. G. Mannhardt 1919, 41-42).

Already in the thirteenth and fourteenth centuries under the Teutonic Knights several dykes had been built along the Vistula and Nogat rivers. When the Teutonic Order collapsed in 1456, the Danzig Werder came under Danzig city control. Most of the rest of the Werder area came under direct Polish crown control (A. Driedger 1957, 3, 481-482). The new administrators, however, took no initiative to maintain the existing dykes. When local citizens also failed to assume that responsibility, authorities considered importing Dutch settlers to drain the region, even though the Dutch Anabaptists still were being treated like Jews, who had to pay up to eight times the rent charged previous renters (A. Driedger 1957, 3, 481; H. Penner 1987, 54-55; Schumacher 1957, 25).

Anna Brons found some Anabaptist families living in Marienburg, the old headquarters of the Teutonic Knights, as early as 1526. In 1547 a Dutch banker named Loysen acquired a large tract of delta land in the Great Werder as payment for services rendered to the Polish crown. He now proceeded to import Anabaptist settlers to drain the land. Another parcel of low-lying delta land in the Danzig Werder was acquired in the same year by Bommel and Florissen, two wealthy Anabaptists, already resident in Prussia. They, too, had acquired the land as reward for service to the Polish crown 1539-1554. Bommel became a citizen of Danzig in 1550 (Brons 1891, 242; H. Penner 1940, 67; 1959, 4, 922).

The first major Mennonite drainage work in the Werder area began in 1547. Over the years the whole delta area was brought under flood control and eventually became fertile farmland. It took about one hundred years of hard work before all three Werder areas were drained and equipped with windmills, sluice gates, dykes and countless drainage canals, including a sixty-mile seawall. The price had been high. It has been estimated that 80 percent of the original settlers died of marsh fevers. Even though several major floods devastated the region, the settlers were always able to recover quickly. Some anti-Mennonite elements periodically tried to pin the blame for such natural disasters on the Mennonites' "strange" religion. At the beginning most of the land could be held only under *emphyteutic* lease contracts, but in 1850 that law changed, permitting Mennonites to make outright purchases of all former *emphyteutic* land in the delta (Crichton 1786, 31; A. Driedger 1957, 3, 481; H. G. Mannhardt 1919, 71; H. Penner 1955, 71; 1959, 4, 923).

The military exemption issue

When Mennonites first arrived in the Werder area, they were considered foreigners and as such they were not expected to defend the country but had to pay *Schutzgeld* to hire mercenaries for the defense of the region. Surprisingly, their earliest lease agreements with the Bishop of Kujavien in the Danzig Werder exempted them from all military obligations, including *Schutzgeld* payments. But after Mennonites had resided in the area for decades, pressures mounted for them to participate in the defense of the region.

As long as Mennonites were considered only strangers or resident aliens, their exemption from military service posed no severe problem. Furthermore, since Mennonites willingly paid for substitutes, this issue was readily solved. Throughout the eighteenth century, however, Mennonites were still paying double or triple taxes (H. G. Mannhardt 1919, 63, 84-88; H. Penner 1987, 100).

Paying for substitutes instead of serving in the military was practiced widely in Europe at this time, so the Prussian situation was not unique. In 1749 the payments by Mennonites in Danzig to Polish King August amounted to 5000 florin annually. In 1757, due to economic difficulties, this sum was reduced to 2000 florin and in 1759 to 1500 florin (W. Mannhardt 1863, 108-109).

The first showdown over military service in the Danzig Werder came in 1613. This conflict was resolved by Mennonites making a group financial payment in lieu of their exemption. One result of this first major payment was that the Mennonites now became vulnerable to random extortion by corrupt government officials working in conjunction with the unscrupulous landowners. One royal chamberlain, Haxberg, tried to extort fifty thousand thaler from the Mennonites in

1585 (W. Mannhardt 1863, 105; H. Penner 1955, 76; 1959, 4, 923; Schön 1886, 44).

Stephen Funk: an example of fidelity

When Carl VII of Sweden besieged the Polish city of Thorn in 1703, a teacher from the Culm Mennonite church, Stephen Funk, brought a load of foodstuff, which the Swedes had purchased, into their camp. While there, Funk listened to a sermon by the Lutheran army chaplain. The king noticed that the Mennonite wrote down each Scripture passage the chaplain cited. The king then asked that he be brought before him. He asked why he had been recording all the Scripture references. Funk replied that he wanted to check their interpretation when he returned home. The king then ordered him to prepare a sermon about peace and war, to be preached before him fourteen days hence.

Two weeks later Funk returned and delivered the sermon as ordered. Afterward the king questioned him privately. Did a Christian ever have a right to go to war, he asked? Funk said that Christians did not have such a right. Then the king asked if a Christian king had any right to engage in war. This time the Mennonite hesitated, but finally said, "A king might possibly have a right to mount a defense, if his kingdom were attacked, but under no conditions could he undertake to attack another kingdom" (as King Carl was doing just then against Poland). Attacking others, Funk said, was something that went against everything that Jesus taught and lived. The king then told Funk, "I hope you will always stand up for faith like that" (Brons 1891, 330-331; H. Penner 1955, 76).

State church dues

Another Mennonite tribulation involved state church dues. The Polish state was Catholic and imposed Catholic church dues on all residents, including the Lutherans and the Reformed (Hartwich 1722, 331). After Brandenburg-Prussia had annexed East and West Prussia, the Lutheran church gained ascendancy. Thus Mennonites frequently had to pay dues to both churches simultaneously. The argument was that since Mennonites did not pay their preachers, the other churches were thus at an unfair disadvantage (Nottarp 1929, 21, 42, 52).

In 1789 such church-dues payments became linked to original land ownership. Thus when a Mennonite purchased land from a Lutheran owner, he was now assessed Lutheran church dues, because the land was "Lutheran Church dues land." Fredrick Wilhelm II rejected such obligations based on previous ownership of the land, but linked payments instead to the Mennonites military exemption (Litten and Nottarp 1931, 3; Nottarp 1929, 29, 44-48).

Military exemption

In 1623 the Polish Catholic bishop of Kujavien arranged to have the privileges, which he had up to this time personally extended to the Mennonites, confirmed by King Sigismund III. These privileges were extended to include Danzig city residents in 1681. Over the years all the Mennonites in the Polish Werder area developed a united front and appealed directly to the Polish crown and received military exemption for all Mennonites in lieu of annual exemption payments. This blanket exemption was first given to them by King Wladislaus IV in 1642. The 1642 exemption, with some modifications, was reconfirmed by successive Polish kings six times during the following century. Though not overtly expressed in these royal guarantees, their military exemption was, nevertheless, based implicitly on the Mennonites' religious beliefs (W. Mannhardt 1863, 80-93, 105-106).

In 1764 some Mennonites residing in the village of Schwetz close to Culm were capriciously evicted by their landlord. This group then asked for and received privileges from Frederick the Great. They now resettled in Brandenburg-Prussia in the town of Neumarkt, where they established a liaison with the pietist Herrnhuter Brethren. Members of this group eventually emigrated to South Russia and settled in the village of Gnadenfeld, where they fostered renewed interest in Bible study, new birth and Christian fellowship, all of which contributed greatly to the mid-nineteenth century renewal movement in Russia (H. Penner 1955, 77).

The Memel Delta

By 1713 some Mennonites in the Vistula Delta were becoming landless. A group of them decided to migrate to the Memel Delta, which they were being asked to drain. When they arrived they discovered their land rents would be double that of all other settlers, but they still settled there. Ten years later these immigrants organized the first Mennonite church in the area. Records from the following year show that Mennonites had marketed 3,700 hundredweight of cheese, called Tilsit cheese (H. Penner 1955, 74; 1987, 217-218; Verduin 1964, 21).

Various difficulties

About that time rumors were being spread that many Lutherans were converting to the Mennonite faith. In fact, a large number of Mennonites were joining the Lutheran church. Nevertheless, the government gave Mennonite churches a strong warning not to permit Lutherans to become members of their church, if they wanted to retain their religious privileges. One report says that for a time they were forbidden to conduct even private services, but an appeal to the king brought a return of their worship privileges (Crichton 1786, 33; H. Penner 1987, 218-219).

When the plague in the early eighteenth century wiped out a large percentage of the East Prussian population, the Mennonites were invited to repopulate the Memel Delta area. In 1716 the Mennonite J. P. Sprunk received permission from Fredrick Wilhelm I to open a brandy distillery in Tilsit. But in 1724 the same military-minded Fredrick Wilhelm of Prussia ordered a group of Mennonites expelled because they refused to heed his order to take up arms (H. Penner 1959, 4, 924; Verduin 1964, 13).

During the 1730 flurry over Arianism and Unitarianism the enemies of the Mennonites succeeded in getting an approval for an official eviction order against them on grounds of heresy. However, during the three-month period set for their departure, further negotiations reestablished not only their permission to stay, but also all their religious privileges. The crown's new tolerance was contingent upon their establishing a textile industry in the region. At that time the number of Mennonite families in Memel had reached 105. As in the Vistula Delta, Mennonites in Memel area were permitted to install their own local self-government with Mennonite mayors in charge of their villages. The land was leased for thirty years under *emphyteutic* contracts (Crichton 1786, 33-34; H. Penner 1987, 207, 220-222; Schreiber 1955, 21).

Mennonites in Memel received permission to build the first church-schoolhouse in 1767, but the school was ordered to operate strictly on local finances and not to expect any governmental assistance (Reiswitz & Wadzeck 1829, 203).

During an 1806 royal visit to the area, Mennonites gave the king thirty thousand thaler as a gift. The king then commended them for their diligence and their excellent care for the poor. However, a few years later about six hundred Mennonite families were evicted from the area because the king had declared the region "Lutheran territory" (Reiswitz & Wadzeck 1821, v; Verduin 1964, 7, 73).

Later developments

By the time Frederick the Great annexed Polish Prussia and renamed it West Prussia in 1772 (Baer 1909), the Mennonites there had switched from Dutch to German as their language of worship (J. A. Duerksen 1990, 107-109). Eventually they began to identify even with German nationalism (J. Friesen 1980, 61-72).

After the annexation, Fredrick the Great organized a census which showed that some 13,500 Mennonites owned or leased 150,000 morgan (morgan=.5 hectare) of land. That same year the Mennonites feted the Kaiser with a massive banquet and then asked him to reaffirm their earlier Polish military exemption. Since Frederick believed in freedom of conscience and "needed money as badly as men," he promptly agreed to exempt them from actual military service on the condition that they finance his military academy at Culm with an annual payment of five thousand thaler. By 1774 not only were Mennonites as a group forbidden to purchase more land, they were obligated to pay an annual group tax of five thousand thaler to support Frederick's military academy in lieu of military exemption for Mennonite sons (F. Epp 1974, 48; H. G. Mannhardt 1919, 124; H. Penner 1955, 79-80).

Military recruitment under the Hohenzollern was cantonally based. Because of this, the extensive Mennonite ownership of land caused great hardships for all other groups in the region. Thus the next emperor, Fredrick Wilhelm II, while reaffirming their religious liberty, imposed serious limitations on the Mennonites' further acquisition of land in 1789. This restriction later was modified, so that Mennonites could purchase uninhabited and previously uncultivated wasteland (H. Penner 1955, 80; Schreiber 1955, 30).

The first Mennonites to volunteer for military service early in the nineteenth century were summarily excommunicated. But from 1806-1815, when the Werder area came under the control of Napoleon (who tolerated no military exemption), Mennonite loyalty to nonresistance became very tattered (W. Ewert 1937, 284-290). It was also during French rule that *emphyteutic* lands first became available for purchase, an opportunity Mennonites accepted eagerly (Schreiber 1955, 23; Schumacher 1958, 236-240).

End of military exemption

When Prussia terminated the Mennonite military exemption in lands it controlled in 1867, the decree permitted conscientious objectors to render non-arms-bearing service under military command. The end of military exemption, however, also ended all land purchase restrictions so that the Mennonites who remained could readily increase their holdings and prosper. Once again the price of becoming full citizens meant abandoning the cherished principle of nonresistance (Erb 1939, 75-82; H. Penner 1955, 83-84).

Many Prussian Mennonites refused to compromise and emigrated to Russia or North America. The major trek to Russia, however, came when the Prussian government shortly thereafter again restricted land purchases for Mennonites. This prompted thousands of Mennonites to accept Russian Empress Catherine the Great's offer of eternally guaranteed exemption from the military, if they abstained from proselytizing.

Those Mennonites who remained in Prussia decided, in 1870, to make the conscientious-objector position optional for church members because "it is difficult to determine with absolute certainty from Scripture whether or not it is wrong to render military service to the state." They now unanimously accepted the Lutheran "two kingdom view," arguing that the Bible commanded "to give Caesar what belongs to Caesar and to God what belongs to God" (H. G. Mannhardt 1919, 175-177).

Many Mennonites subsequently joined the Protestant mainstream and began to serve in the army and in government, e.g., Johann J. van Kampen became the city official of Allstadt. In WWI 138 Mennonites volunteered for the army and an additional 350 were drafted. Of these, twenty-nine were commissioned officers, sixty-five served as non-commissioned officers and four were military doctors (H. G. Mannhardt 1919, 11; H. Penner 1955, 171, 175-176).

An elderly Prussian pacifist

When Mennonite fidelity to the peace stance in Prussia had already been abandoned by the majority, there occurred a rather touching example of loyalty to it in practice.

A group of ruffians decided to have some fun with a well-known Mennonite practitioner of peace. At dawn the young fellows showed up at the old man's house and without a word began to remove the thatch from the elderly couple's house. The elderly couple awoke. The lady of the house was greatly alarmed, but her husband quietly said, *"Mame, wie habe Jast"* (Mother, we have visitors). "Quickly prepare food for our guests!"

So while the rascals were removing thatch, the old couple prepared a lavish breakfast. When it was ready, the old Mennonite called the young men to breakfast and said the following table prayer: "Lord, we thank you for our visitors. We know that all our comings and goings are in your hands and you plan all things for our good. We may not always realize the benefit at once, but we humbly accept all that you give us. Bless our guests in their undertaking. Thank you for the food and all the good with which you bless us! Amen!"

Then the old couple cheerfully fed the work crew. The young fellows were so taken aback by the kindness and the warmth of the old couple, that after breakfast they repaired not only the damage they had done, but also the rest of the roof that needed attention (W. Mannhardt 1863, 44).

Citizenship gained, but ethical standards diminished

As Mennonites prospered and became more accepted as citizens, many of their early values paled and fell into disuse (W. Mannhardt 1863, 102-103). Their zeal for new converts had disappeared. They were concerned primarily with retaining their in-group privileges. They even gave up their right to evangelize (Maercher 1888, 2(1/3), 369). Church member behavior, which earlier had been beyond reproof, now often violated not only church standards but also legal ones as well. H. Penner (1987, 171-172) lists growing problems with cheating on excise taxes, careless indebtedness, drunkenness, dancing and carousing, beating servants, and even murder (Brons 1891, 160; Reiswitz & Wadzeck 1821, 11).

Changes in the ministry in Mennonite churches

Even in church leadership conditions had changed drastically. Some leaders, like Pastor Mannhardt, encouraged discipleship, mutual admonishment, mutual aid, moral life and democratic church practices, including consulting with other churches in the region on difficult ethical and moral questions (Brons 1891, 332). But not nearly all preachers and elders were as committed and conscientious. Many exercised arbitrary powers. The elected *Vermahner* (exhorters) of the church now grabbed the reins of authority and became congregational rulers. They made decisions, promulgated decrees and signed documents without consulting their fellow church members (Brons 1891, 332; Hein 1959, 4, 424).

Early on in the church the distinction between the office of elder and minister had been one of function rather than rank. This changed over time. The elders and ministers no longer called themselves servants; only the deacons still bore that label. Eventually some elders insisted on being called "governing elder." Most elders were chosen from among the well-to-do because only they could afford to spend so much time for the church without pay. The first theologically trained and paid minister was appointed in 1826 (Krahn 1956, 124; H. Penner 1987, 170).

Polish Mennonite charity

On charity and sharing the Mennonites' record seems to have been somewhat better. The poor, the old and the unemployable were supported by a special treasury administered by the deacons. Those who suffered loss through theft, flood or fire could count on help from the congregation. Often other Protestants and even Catholics were helped in this way. Each church had a number of deacons, and churches of the Flemish wing also had deaconesses. The churches maintained homes for the homeless, orphans and widows, and hospitals for the sick, but the latter were now operated largely on levies rather than voluntary contributions as had been the case earlier. In fact, the church now organized its own church police to supervise member morality and to collect all church dues and levies (Reiswitz & Wadzeck 1821, 46-47). In 1622 the first large-scale mutual fire insurance organization was set up by Mennonites in the Danzig and Great Werder areas (H. Penner 1959, 4, 920-926; 1987, 169; Reiswitz & Wadzeck 1821, 42-43).

When Menno's works became an embarrassment to the church leaders

When the *Kleine Gemeinde*, a conservative reform movement within the Russian Mennonite Church, emerged in Russia in 1812 they wanted to return to Menno Simons' teachings. Since they could not obtain his writings in Russia, they appealed to Danzig Mennonites for copies. A wealthy Danzig Mennonite, Peter von Riesen, heard of the *Kleine Gemeinde's* request and took it upon himself to print a new edition of Menno's works at his own expense during the 1830s. After the first section of the complete writings had come off the press, von Riesen took copies to the local school teachers to get their approval and backing. Through them the local bishop became aware of the reprinting effort and at once rallied his fellow elder/bishops to condemn the project and to order all the books already printed to be destroyed. At an elder/bishops' meeting in Marienburg it was decided that the material was "too dangerous" to release. The bishops reasoned officially, "If we let any Mennonite have this book, the information contained in it will eventually fall into non-Mennonite hands and that will turn everyone against us and put all our privileges in jeopardy." The bishops apparently were in the process of jettisoning nonresistance as an essential church doctrine, and they feared that the public availability of Menno Simons' writings might complicate matters. Von Riesen thus had to write to Russia to say he would be unable to fulfill his promise to provide the requested copies because the elders had burned what he had already printed (H.-J. Goertz 1988b, 2; Reimer & Gaeddert 1956, 3-15; Peter Toews 1911).

What a tragic irony—their own spiritual father's writings were now considered too dangerous in the hands of the church people, just as the Catholic Church had seen Scripture in the hands of the people as a threat before the Reformation.

The Mennonite Commonwealth In South Russia 1789-1860

Following the latest round of the Russo-Turkish war in 1877-1878, Russian empress Catherine the Great looked to western Europe for settlers to colonize the steppes of New Russia. One of her German-speaking emissaries, Baron von Trappe, contacted the Mennonites in Prussia, especially the poor and landless, and offered such an invitation to them. The Mennonites in the Danzig-Vistula Delta area sent two delegates—Jakob Höppner, Flemish (D. E. 1937, 2, 346), and Johann Bartsch, Frisian, (Neff 1955, 1, 240)—as scouts to Southern Russia to inspect the land and to negotiate for certain privileges, especially freedom of religion and the right to refuse to bear arms (D. H. Epp 1956, 2, 811; P. M. Friesen 1911, 72; D. Rempel 1933, 11-12; Urry 1989b, 52). This immigration resulted in the establishment of two adjacent colonies, Chortitza and Molotschna (J. Quiring 1928, 1-49), which were more or less autonomous under the guidance of a government-established Guardians Committee (Ehrt 1929, 76-79; 1932; Krahn 1959, 4, 1068-1069). Eventually this lead to the development of a Mennonite Commonwealth in southern Russia (D. Rempel 1973, 259-308; 1974, 5-54).

The Mennonite commonwealth in Russia

In Prussia the Mennonites had already secured a partial right to internal self-government. At first this local government consisted only of the *Lehramt*, the ministers and teachers of the church. However, the growing responsibility of such leadership to collect land rent and taxes, to organize fire-fighting and to be responsible for dyke construction and maintenance led to a budding civil government even in Poland. When the Mennonites arrived in South Russia, they immediately added to their traditional *Lehramt* a full-fledged *Gebietsamt*, a colony-wide civil authority (Urry 1989b, 71).

From the very beginning in Russia the *Gebietsamt* seemed to have greater legitimacy than the *Lehramt*. When the emigrants left Danzig, they had no elders or ministers with them. The group was made up of landless people who required no exit permission, as the landholding *Lehramt* members did. While wintering in Dubrovna, the group elected a new *Lehramt* but since they felt that ordination by an elder was necessary, they did not fully trust its legitimacy. While they asked for and received confirmation for those they elected by letter, the doubt about the legitimacy of the *Lehramt* lingered until several elders from Danzig came in person and carried out the ordinations in Russia (Krahn 1955, *1*, 568).

The *Gebietsamt*, on the other hand, was duly elected by all the colonists and confirmed by the Russian government's Settlement Guardians Committee, giving it double legitimacy. This *Gebietsamt* eventually developed into a comprehensive local civil government. How did this development come about, given Menno Simons' contrary teaching on such matters? These Mennonites evidently no longer affirmed with their forebears that both the sword of war and the sword of political power were beyond the scope of kingdom citizens (Wenger 1945, 250).

Thus, on their arrival in South Russia, this northern Mennonite stream began to operate under two separate authority structures. On one hand, there was the church with its *Lehramt*, headed by an elder. On the other hand, there was the village government with an executive committee composed of an unpaid mayor (*Schulze*), two assistants and a paid clerk, assisted by one unarmed and unpaid "police" deputy per ten households. All the villages of a colony were linked together under the overall leadership of a central authority (*Gebietsamt*), which consisted of a paid mayor-in-chief (*Oberschulze*) and his office staff. Severe tensions soon arose in this dual power structure. The *Lehramt* felt that scripturally and historically it was the maximal authority under God, but in Russia the law of the land considered the *Gebietsamt* as maximal. This made clashes between the two inevitable (D. Rempel 1933, 53-59).

Mennonites on the run had been able to function as relatively self-sufficient economic units even during the era of persecution. In South Russia the self-governing colony structure and the national government's mandate for Mennonites to become models in agriculture, trades and industry—to become a sort of a "development engine" that would stimulate the economy of the entire region—provided them with almost unlimited economic opportunities. When they embarked on this road, probably none of them were fully aware of what a Pandora's box of power possibilities, including abuses, they were opening. In fact, most of them were completely unaware of how much of "this world's political power" their self-governing colony structure was putting into their own hands.

Once the colonies were able to produce agricultural surpluses and their trades and their industries turned out a wide range of manufactured goods for market, their economic influence and power began to extend far beyond their boundaries. As their economic influence grew, so did their political power. Without any hidden or sinister intentions on their part, they soon wielded political power in regional governments. In fact, eventually they even made their presence felt in the national government, when Mennonites became deputies in the *Duma*, the Russian parliament.

As they now exercised these various powers, the Mennonites of South Russia fell into power abuses of diverse kinds, violating pretty well every premise of Menno's vision. These compromises, however, were challenged and interrupted by spiritual renewal movements that attempted to call Mennonite believers back to their roots. There are clusters of compromise and potential power abuses that must be examined:

(a) The *Gebietsamt* as the de facto state exercising governmental sword-power in the Mennonite community;
(b) Mennonite relations with their nomadic tribal neighbors;
(c) Mennonites as employers of other Mennonites and of non-Mennonites;
(d) Mennonite landholders and their power monopoly in the existing colony structure;
(e) The development of the Mennonite estate system; and
(f) The growth of Mennonite industry.

The *Gebietsamt* exercising civil governmental power

The Mennonite *privilegium* in Russia authorized the colonists to govern their own civic and community affairs. This meant that colony authorities could issue local ordinances and have their own police deputies enforce them. At first the number of such ordinances was minimal, but as the commonwealth developed, they and the concomitant deputy control increased sharply (D. H. Epp 1946, 74-75; D. Rempel 1933, 11).

The *Gebietsamt* levied taxes, issued travel documents, preserved law and order, issued orders for communal labor and hired herdsmen for the communal livestock herding. In short, it performed all the necessary functions of civil government, undercutting Menno's basic premise that believers, as citizens of the spiritual kingdom of God, were only pilgrims in transit through this world. Furthermore, in the exercise of this civil government and magistracy, they were expressly violating article six of the Schleitheim Confession of faith. It is ironic that the very Russian law that guaranteed their minority privileges also led to the creation of a Mennonite state and to the eventual complete merger of the Mennonite church and state (John B. Toews 1977, 88; 1982, 33).

Mennonites and their nomadic neighbors

The Russian sojourn began with several decades of relatively peaceful development. There were a few minor property problems like horse and lumber thefts when Mennonites first arrived on the steppes of New Russia in 1789. Even though the Turks and their sometime "bandit" Cossack allies had been defeated and driven out by the Russians during the Russo-Turkish war in 1768, and the Zaporozhe Cossacks had been forcibly removed in 1774 just prior to the Mennonite arrival, numerous other nomadic tribes still roamed the steppes (Hildebrand 1888, 68,75; D. Rempel 1933, 15; Urry 1989b, 134; also see C. Redekop 1982, 71-90).

The arrival of unarmed Mennonites brought these semi-nomadic and somewhat predatory peoples a bonanza of potentially easy booty. Fortunately, there seem to be no recorded incidents of Mennonites killing such looting tribespeople. The new settlers did, however, appeal repeatedly to Russian authorities for protection against them. The authorities responded promptly with heavy-handed frontier-style justice, indiscriminately punishing and killing suspects whenever an injustice was reported (Hildebrand 1888, 68). The Mennonite complaints became the occasion for repeated violent governmental retribution against such tribal offenders. These appeals for protection already show a major departure from Menno's ideal that no Christian should call upon the secular "sword" for the protection of personal property (D. H. Epp 1946, 131-134; G. Epp 1989a, 133-134; Urry 1989b, 93).

Mennonites as employers

During the early years in Russia most Mennonites could depend on their large families to provide all necessary labor. Eventually the more prosperous needed additional labor. At first this was provided by landless relatives or friends, who were given access to a generous plot of land on the landholder's property. Here they could build a house, plant a garden and perhaps grow some grain. Such live-in workers were called *Anwohner* (adjunct residents). In exchange for such privileges the able-bodied members of these families worked for the landholder, who usually paid them in kind. On the whole it was a satisfactory arrangement for both parties. They all prospered.

The more prosperous also needed outside help to run their households. At first this was provided by Mennonite servants and maids. It was in connection with maids that another cultural problem appeared. Historian Adolph Ehrt (1932, 66-68) called attention to the fundamental problem when he noted that all Mennonite women were without voice or vote in church and colony affairs and had the status of minors, who were "not capable of independence." This dependent status made maids especially vulnerable to both physical and sexual abuse. Minister Jacob D. Epp's diary mentions maids who were mistreated and even abused sexually. When they sought redress their complaints were ignored because they had no status. This problem became acute when young Russian women began to replace Mennonites as maids (H. Dyck 1991, 394).

As the population in the colonies increased, there soon was no more space for *Anwohner*. As a result, "slum" sections developed on the edge of the larger Mennonite villages. These people were called *Einwohner* (renters), *Kleinhaeusler* (little-house people), or *Armenreihe* (the poor row). They did not even have a garden plot or a cow to put on communal pasture. Some relied on charity, either individual or communal. Thus, by the mid-nineteenth century, more than two-thirds of the Mennonites in Russia were landless (H. Dyck 1989, 187; Krahn 1935, 171; Urry 1989b, 60).

From the beginning the *Anwohner*, just like full landholders, had been obligated by colony law to provide an annual quota of grain to be stored for emergency famine relief. But as their access to land dwindled, this annual quota became an increasingly difficult burden for them to bear. *Kleinhaeusler* and *Einwohner* were seldom able to contribute to this fund. In fact, they often subsisted on the previous years' gathered emergency food (Klaus 1887, 266-270).

There is no question that in the case of Mennonite labor, Mennonite landholders not only unjustly used their power, but also worked actively to achieve a stratified society in which the landed exercised political and economic violence on their own landless brothers and sisters in the faith. This was something their official confession of faith could never condone, because it called for a community in which all members had equal status and shared equally in the returns from everyone's labors (A. Braun 1937, 2, 612-613; J. J. Toews 1951, 206; Urry 1985, 18).

Mennonite employers also hired Russian laborers, whom they treated as serfs, if not slaves, much as did the Russian landowners around them. They made little effort to improve their wages, nor did most of them create better working conditions, although Mennonite agriculturalist Johann Cornies did introduce a labor statute that at least prevented some of the more serious abuses (D. Neufeld 1922, 23-26; J. C. Toews 1954, July 14, 5, Aug.4, 1-3; Urry 1978, 144; 1985, 24; Urry 1989c, 107).

Unlike Russian landowners, however, Mennonites usually toiled in the fields together with their outside laborers, often working as hard or harder than their employees. The discrepancy between Mennonite employers and their non-Mennonite employees was marked, first, in the overall social distance that separated the two. Servants did not share the master's table. On returning from their common work, they were strictly segregated: most Mennonites went to a comfortable house, the Russians went to the workers' barracks or a sod hovel. Where the distance was most marked, however, was in the unequal return that each received from their common labor (F. Epp 1962, 24; Urry 1985, 24; 1989a, 106-107).

Mennonite governmental sword-power was also exercised on these outsiders who worked in the colonies. Colony authorities frequently had to discipline non-Mennonites for offenses like drunkenness, disorderly conduct and theft, all of which Russian law punished by flogging. As a result, Mennonite deputies found themselves flogging increasing numbers of non-Mennonite offenders.

Mennonite "justice" followed the local frontier style. Guilt or innocence was decided on the spot. Communication with the nomadic tribes in the area was not always easy. If there was difficulty identifying a specific culprit, all suspects were flogged to teach a lesson to both the guilty and the innocent.

Probably the harshest injustice felt by outside labor was in cases of real or imagined theft. Any suspicion of theft by a servant resulted in severe lashing by the employer or by colony deputies. For example, a Mennonite one day discovered a Russian stealing grain from his bin. Since it was late Saturday afternoon, the Mennonite nailed up the grain bin with the Russian in it. On Monday morning he notified the mayor's office and the deputies came, extracted the thief and flogged him (Calvin W. Redekop to Jacob A. Loewen, 5 Jan. 1990).

Mennonite landholders and their power monopoly

An even more revealing Mennonite use of sword-power to defend material advantage occurred in connection with the struggle between landholders and the growing number of landless in the Mennonite colonies themselves (Loewen & Prieb 1996, 17-30). When the Mennonites settled in South Russia, their government charter spelled out certain legal procedures that helped produce a crisis in the mid-nineteenth century. Especially problematic was the restriction of voting in colony affairs to landholders (D. Rempel 1933, 71).

Contributing factors

When the Mennonite colonies were established, all church members were landholders. At this stage choosing the civic village or colony leadership was equivalent to a church election; the entire church family participated. These elected officials were empowered by Russian law, not only by colony mandate, to make ordinances, resolve civic disputes, assess fines and mete out physical punishment. But they were basically responsible to the entire church community. At first, all church members had relatively equal say in running the affairs of the colony. But as the landless population grew, a new problem surfaced. The landless might be church members in good standing, but they were ineligible to vote or run for office. That privilege was reserved for landholders. As a result, by mid-nineteenth century two-thirds of all Mennonites had become disenfranchised because they were landless (Aus den Kolonien 1863, 974-975; Die gegenseitigen Verhaeltnisse... 1864, 25-27; Krahn 1935, 171).

The second troublesome Russian rule was that the property grant entrusted to a colonist was indivisible: only one son, usually the youngest, could inherit it. Older sons were expected to find professions or establish themselves elsewhere. The sixty-five dessiatine land grant per family was to remain forever undivided (D. Rempel 1933, 12).

There were a number of subsidiary contributing factors:

(1) Each of the two original colonies had a large unassigned area to be used for communal pasture, road allowances and future expansion. Any temporarily unused land could be rented out to individual colony members with the proceeds going into a common treasury. Since only landholders could vote, colony administrations were in the grip of those who controlled land grants. The latter could use their voting rights and the resulting economic power to their own advantage, and they fully exploited this advantage. Landholders now stopped establishing new villages because they themselves were renting large tracts of unassigned colony land at two kopecks per dessiatine (2.7 acres) per annum. They were also the only ones able to set the price and to decide to whom the land was to be rented. They would sublet the land to those sons who could not inherit the family property, or they sublet it to landless non-relatives for three or four rubles per dessiatine, thus making hundreds of percent profit. Eventually the public rental price of land rose to eight, twelve and even eighteen rubles per dessiatine per annum. This practice swelled the coffers of the rich and assured that the poor would remain poor (Aus den Kolonien 1863; Die Freiwirte in den Deutschen Kolonien Südrusslands 1863; Die gegenseitigen

Verhaeltnisse... 1864; F. Isaac 1908; Klaus 1887, 269; Krahn 1935, 171; D. Rempel 1933, 71).

(2) Following the end of the Russo-Turkish war, the Czar gave land grants in New Russia to certain nobles of his court. The tribal people on these lands now became serfs, providing cheap labor for the nobles as well as the Mennonites. But when all the serfs in Russia were set free in 1861, many emigrated to Turkey, leaving a vacuum in the supply of cheap labor. The landless Mennonites seemed like a good solution to the whole labor shortage problem (D. Rempel 1933, 71).

Then, too, the nomadic Nogais formerly had control over vast tracts of unfarmed land, much of which they had rented to Mennonites. With their sudden departure, the Russian government gave the land to Bulgarian immigrants, thereby squeezing out the Mennonite renters. These landless Mennonites were now completely at the mercy of their landed co-religionists. They had no land on which to raise food. They had no voting power to change their circumstances. They could not get travel documents to move elsewhere (Klaus 1887, 250; Rempel 1933, 71; J. C. Toews 1954, Sept.15, 4; Urry & Klippenstein 1989, 24).

Preserving a pool of cheap Mennonite labor

To preserve their pool of cheap Mennonite labor, the *Gebietsamt* and landowners compromised Menno's vision in the following ways:

(a) They introduced family-based, rather than their earlier land-based, taxation. During the Crimean war the Russian government demanded that the Mennonites provide wagons for military transport. Colony authorities, in turn, ordered each family to supply a wagon. The landless Mennonites often had to borrow money to buy a wagon and horses and then operate the wagons themselves. This aggravated the existing social and economic disparities (Urry and Klippenstein 1989, 12, 18).

(b) They increased the tax burden on the landless. This included cutting down the amount of land *Anwohner* were permitted to cultivate, restricting from eight to two the number of animals *Anwohner* could put on communal pastures, raising pasturage fees and imposing new school, pasture and herd levies (Aus den Kolonien... 1863, 974-975; Die gegenseitigen Verhaeltnisse... 1864, 370; P. Klassen 1964, 106-113).

(c) They introduced stringent mobility restriction. The village *Schulze* could control the movement of the landless from one Mennonite village to another, but even more, the *Oberschulze* could deny them a passport to leave the colonies altogether. People gaining permission to move elsewhere could be repatriated if they got into trouble during the first five years. Worst of all, this Russian law was used as a pretext to demand taxes up to five years in advance from departing Mennonites (D. Rempel 1933, 70-71; Urry and Klippenstein 1989, 24).

(d) They applied religious and civil ordinances selectively. When the merchant Isaak Matthies (Isaac 1908, 43) became a Mennonite Brethren, the parent church placed him under a church ban and ordered him shunned. This action excused its members, who owed him thirty thousand rubles, from paying their debt. Meanwhile, colony authorities proceeded against the merchant in conjunction with his creditors, whom he owed fifteen thousand rubles. He was ruined financially. His business and his home were sold at debtors' auction (P. M. Friesen 1978, 348).

(e) They formed collusions between church and colony authorities. A blatant example was the action of the landholding consistory bishops, excluding the Ohrloff Elder Johann Harder. They piously claimed to be unable to help landless church members seek justice because their church work confined them to dealing only with "the heavenly Canaan" (F. Isaac 1908, 54-56), while the *Oberschulze*, with whom the bishops were conniving, labeled the petitioning landless as rabble rousers and revolutionaries and initiated two falsehood-laden denunciations against them with the Russian authorities. The bishops also introduced church rules that made it a religious offense to oppose the authority of the *Gebietsamt* and authorized the police deputies to use physical discipline against all church members who offended colony authorities. There also is some evidence that they gave landholders two votes in church affairs (H. Dyck 1991, 230; Ehrt 1932, 50; D. Epp 1984, 74-75).

(f) They exiled Abraham Thiessen, an early advocate for the landless, to Siberia (P. M. Friesen 1911, 498; Krahn 1969, 73-76; John B. Toews 1977, 89).

(g) They displaced Mennonite craftsmen with Jewish workers who were willing to work for lower wages (H. Dyck 1989, 192; Urry 1989a, 111).

Mennonite estates

A little spoken about, but equally significant property development in regard to economic power, was the establishment of Mennonite estates outside of the boundaries of the Mennonite colonies. This only became possible after 1817, for until then Mennonites were forbidden to buy land beyond their original settlement grants. At their height, around 1914, there were some five hundred Mennonite estates in Russia, controlling an estimated million acres of land. The largest estate, that of Wilhelm Martens, was reputed to have had in the vicinity of 300,000 acres. These large estate owners represented only 3 percent of the Mennonite population, but they controlled 30 percent of all the land in Mennonite hands. They alone employed 22 percent of the Mennonite population, though Al Reimer (1989, 2-6) asserts that the major part of their labor force was Russian or Ukrainian (Krahn 1935, 170; J. C. Toews 1954, Sept.15, 4; Urry 1988, 15).

Even though the stories of servant mistreatment are not many, the estates represented a blatant power abuse. As Mennonite estate-owners became wealthy, they increasingly aligned themselves with their Russian noble counterparts. Before long they had become a conspicuous cog in the oppressive system of "noble" landowners. The unhappiness of their "serfs," together with urban worker dissatisfaction, eventually produced both the 1905 and 1917 revolutions.

Active Mennonite participation in this system can be seen not only in the way they conformed to Russian patterns of treating and paying labor, but also in the way they participated in government. Local political officeholders up to this time had been drawn exclusively from the ranks of the nobles, who were estate owners. Since Mennonites now also owned estates, they, too, began to function as nobles, even though they were still officially classified as peasants. At one time five of the seven positions on the regional government council in Melitopol were filled by Mennonite estate owners and at one time two Mennonites even served in the Tsarist Duma, the Russian parliament. In this way Mennonites became part of a vast system of power abuse that helped spawn the 1917 revolution which eventually almost destroyed Mennonite existence in Russia. Since Mennonite estate owners were considered ethnic foreigners, their estates were singled out as targets for reprisal (L. Friesen 1989; A. Reimer 1989, 9; D. Rempel 1933, 91; J. C. Toews 1954, July 21, 3; Aug.11, 4-5; Urry 1985, 19, 25).

Industrial development

Traditionally, Mennonites have considered themselves as "people of the land." Cornelius Krahn (1935, 169) cites a Mennonite villager in Russia who said, "God is our father, the soil is our mother, nature is our teacher." In a similar vein, Adolf Ehrt (1932, 17-18) cites Jacob Kroeker, who at a Mennonite anniversary celebration said land may also have been a cause of Mennonite downfall because "[We] love the sickle more than the pursuit of peace and the ownership of the earth more than our spiritual inheritance."

In southern Russia, however, the Mennonites' unprecedented economic growth opened new industrial possibilities, particularly in farm-related fields like grain milling and the manufacture of implements and livery vehicles. Grain milling began early with individual or village windmills that ground the village-grown grain into flour or feed (Haxthausen 1972). Windmills were in large part a carryover from the Mennonites' earlier delta drainage experience in Prussia. By 1908 there were more than a hundred such windmills in Chortitza and Molotschna, as well as another seventy-three motor-powered mills. By 1914 two-fifths of all flour and feed mills in Russia were located in the south, largely on Mennonite lands. The four largest Mennonite mills had an annual production turnover of over six million rubles, of which the Niebuhr mill in Alexandrovsk alone produced 50 percent (Ehrt 1932, 92; Urry 1985, 12; 1989a, 102, 113).

The first two Mennonite farm-machine innovations were the multiple share plow called the *Bugger* and the *Drillbugger*, an implement which combined plowing and sowing into a single operation (John B. Toews 1982, 6).

Three factors were especially crucial to the rapid expansion of the manufacture of agricultural machines:

(1) The increasing affluence of Mennonites who were able to rent land beyond their colony allotment. This increased acreage made larger and more efficient farm implements highly desirable, if not necessary.

(2) After 1817 Mennonites were allowed to buy as much land as they could afford and were no longer restricted to the original sixty-five dessiatine allotment in the colonies. This led to the development of estates where more, larger and more efficient machines were needed to cultivate vast expanses of land.

(3) Johann Cornies' efforts through the agricultural society improved both the quality and quantity of Mennonite agricultural production (W. Quiring 1939, 160-168). By the time he died in 1848, the production of farm implements by Mennonite manufacturers was in full swing. Mennonite factories and craftsmen produced all kinds of farm wagons and luxury horse-drawn carriages (D. H. Epp 1985, 289-371). In fact, Mennonite-produced vehicles were among the most renowned in Russia. For the farmers there were machines for tilling, harrowing, seeding, cutting, raking, threshing and cleaning the harvested grain. In addition there were all kinds of grinding and cutting machines to produce flour and animal feed (Niebuhr 1955, 15-30; D. Rempel 1933, 279; Urry 1985, 16).

By 1911, 6.2 percent of all farm machinery in Russia was of Mennonite manufacture. By 1914, eight Mennonite manufacturers were producing 10 percent of the gross Russian output in farm machinery. Mennonite-made machines operated everywhere in Russia, from the eastern Ukraine to the far reaches of Siberia. Indeed, Mennonite manufacturers were competing with American implement giants like McCormick and International Harvester (Carstensen 1984); the latter in fact opened a factory near Moscow in 1912 (Ehrt 1932, 92; John B. Toews 1982, 6; Urry 1985, 2, 1989a, 119).

The impact of wealth on Mennonite society

The rapid increase of wealth, especially among Mennonite estate owners and industrialists, had a dramatic effect on Mennonite community solidarity. No longer comfortable in Mennonite villages, the rich escaped their community's pressures and control by moving to private estates or to nearby Russian cities (G. Epp 1989b, 239-260). In so doing they did not withdraw from Mennonite life entirely, continuing to invest large sums in better schools and hospitals. The wealthiest two percent contributed roughly 30 percent of the operating costs of alternative service programs. James Urry adds, however, that there are clear indications that the rich also cheated in the property values they reported to the colonies for such tax purposes (Ehrt 1932, 88; Urry 1985, 21; 1989a, 116).

The rich formed a separate in-group whose members socialized with each other and whose children intermarried to create vast family fortunes. Adolf Ehrt (1932, 93-96) argued that this produced two Mennonite economies, the capitalist economy of the estate owners and industrialists and the peasant economy of most Mennonite villagers. Two more economies could also be identified: the landless laborers who were exploited by both groups and who survived at more or less subsistence level, and the "poor row" who were dependent on private or public dole (Urry 1985, 17).

The rich were generally condescending toward other Mennonite colonists, but to the landless poor they manifested definite disdain. They considered the poor irresponsible and lazy, unwilling to put forth the effort necessary to improve their lot (Urry 1985, 19).

Estate owners and industrialists felt superior to Russian peasants and serfs and observed strict class distinctions. As their wealth increased the master-servant distinction became more marked. Servants who displeased their estate-owning masters could expect instant and rough retribution (Urry 1985, 24).

Officially, all Mennonites, including estate owners, were still classified as peasants even though some of them functioned as nobility. How much solidarity Russian peasants felt with Mennonite peasants, even when the latter were still poor, has not been documented. But there is no question that when peasant and worker unrest began at the beginning of the twentieth century, the peasants reacted not only against the Mennonite wealthy but also considered the poorer Mennonites traitors to the peasant class. Especially during the 1905 revolution, nobles made a conscious effort to deflect the revolutionaries' anger away from themselves toward the Mennonite "foreigners" (J. C. Toews 1954, Aug.11, 4-5). These two factors help explain why the Mennonites reaped so much suffering (Urry 1985, 26-28).

When the elite removed themselves physically from village observation and control they also largely withdrew themselves from the authority of church and colony leadership. This not only weakened overall Mennonite community solidarity, it also greatly increased the insecurity of Mennonite leadership in both church and colony. To combat the erosion of authority, church and colony leaders now sought greater control. The church, which formerly had the upper hand, now found itself reduced to junior partner status. Eventually both church and colony leadership worked together to protect their interests (John B. Toews 1982, 9-11).

Mennonites and citizenship

Even though Mennonites in Russia always saw themselves as non-Russians, they functioned as citizens from the day of their arrival in 1789. Although they did not at first participate in Russian society and government as such, in their colonies they functioned as full-fledged citizens of their own commonwealth, which itself was but an extension of the national Russian state.

The renunciation of the sword of war had become the Mennonites' chief distinguishing characteristic. This, too, was guaranteed by their original immigration *privilegium*. When that privilege was threatened in 1870, many left for the new world. There have been questions about whether this exodus was really motivated by fidelity to nonresistance (G. Wiebe 1900; 1981). Nonetheless, this mass exodus convinced the Russian government that it had to reach some form of accommodation with the Mennonites. Those who remained now initiated a Mennonite-financed alternative service program. The money for the program was raised by a fifty kopek tax per one thousand rubles of Mennonite property (Ehrt 1932, 66; H. Janzen 1949/1981, 108; Neff 1913, *1*, 11;

Suderman 1943, 35; John B. Toews 1974, 8-13; 1986, 9-14; Urry 1991, 11-16).

The first Mennonite alternative service program in Russia was established in 1880 with some four hundred young men serving. The annual cost to Mennonites was about seventy thousand rubles. By 1913 this program had grown to one thousand men costing about 350,000 rubles annually (Hershberger 1955, *1*, 692-699). Eventually, two alternative service possibilities were developed: forestry (A. Braun 1913, *1*, 663-664) service and service in the military medical corps (H. Rempel 1980, 2-12). During World War I Mennonites not only provided the twelve thousand young men to serve in both these capacities—about 6,000 in each (Hershberger 1955, *1*, 693), they actually bore the burden of paying for both alternative service efforts. In 1917 the cost reached a staggering $1.5 million (H. Rempel 1980, 2-12; Hershberger 1955, 692).

In a relatively short period of time the Mennonites of Russia underwent a breathtakingly sudden shift from a people in pilgrimage, seeking religious freedom and basic human rights, to a stratified class society with economic, political and religious power vested in a privileged minority that controlled both church and state (R. Kreider 1951, 17-33). At the same time this amazing shift was creating increased pressures for a major round of reform.

CHAPTER 8

Awakening In Russia

The previous chapter detailed a variety of developments in the economic and social domain of the Mennonite colonists' life in Russia. The story involves an uncomfortable account of wide-spread slippage in regard to Menno's ideals on the abstinence from the use of force in daily life. But that is not the end of the sad story. Similar kinds of slippages were also occurring in the realm of the Mennonite's religious life and church affairs. This disheartening state of affairs, however, was soon to be interrupted by several renewals and new beginnings.

Tensions between the *Lehramt* and the *Gebietsamt*

At first the new commonwealth power structure in South Russia exhibited minimal strain. As we have said, the insecurity of the only-ordained-by-letter *Lehramt* created some concerns. However, the Russian authorities, having negotiated the basic agreements with the scouts, Johann Bartsch (Neff 1913, *1*, 128-129) and Jacob Höppner (Urry 1989b, 68-69), continued to treat the two men as the Mennonite leaders, disregarding both the *Lehramt* and the *Gebietsamt*. This irritated both of these authority structures. For the *Lehramt* its uncertain start was to have long-range implications. It started an ongoing cycle of concern about its legitimacy and the extent of its authority. The insecurity led to the unjust accusation of Höppner by the church and colony leadership, his imprisonment and sentence of exile to Siberia. Fortunately the sentence was never carried out. He was eventually vindicated by the tsar. However, since Höppner leaned toward the authority of the *Gebietsamt*, this episode helped to increase the *Lehramt's* insecurity (D. H. Epp 1956, *2*, 811; P. M. Friesen 1978, 91ff.).

The development of a *Volkskirche*

For average colonists in their isolated villages, however, the colony situation fostered what could be considered a normal religious and reasonably comfortable civic life. At this stage both the church and the civil government were communally operated largely on a consensus basis. Every head of household was a landholder, a church member and a voting member of the colony. Before long, however, civic power problems such as those previously described resurfaced in the churches. Several related factors were involved:

(1) The churches ceased to function as live exegetical communities and now depended on a diet of "canned" sermons handed down

from previous generations, which often were poorly read (P. M. Friesen 1978, 94, 113).

(2) With the passage of time, the lives of many of the colonists no longer exhibited a radical faith in God. The tavern, rather than the church, was becoming the preferred gathering place (H. Dyck 1991, 23, 92, 360; P. M. Friesen 1978, 118, 494; Kreider 1951, 27).

(3) The *Lehramt*, frustrated by the lack of church response to its teaching and admonition, began a quest for more authoritarian control. This drastic shift in ministerial attitudes can be seen in the fact that only deacons were still being labeled "servants" (D. H. Epp 1984, 71; John B. Toews 1982, 9).

(4) Most expressions of Christian charity had by now become fully institutionalized in the form of colony dues and levies (H. Dyck 1991, 99, 191; P. M. Friesen 1978, 615-617, 876).

(5) Morality in the homes and community was slipping. Sexual promiscuity, wife and child abuse, and sexual abuse was on the rise (Loewen & Prieb 1996, 30-39).

What had once been a Radical Reformation church which demanded that professed faith be demonstrated in life and deeds, had become a comfortable in-group of traditional religionists. The Mennonites' earlier radical obedience, marked by adult baptism on the confession of personal faith, had shriveled to a mere continuance as non-war-making members of an ethno-religious community. What had begun as a voluntary believers' church was now for all practical purposes functioning as a *Volkskirche* (state church). The real reasons for joining the church had been reduced to being able to marry and inherit property, privileges still restricted to members (L. Driedger 1988, 14; A. Fast 1936, 12; Francis 1948, 101-107; W. Sawatsky 1988, 6; J. A. Toews 1975a, 21; John B. Toews 1982, 10).

Already while en route to their Russian colony allotments in 1787 there had been a feeble effort at spiritual renewal, an attempt to heal the two-century-old split between the Flemish and the Frisians. This effort took place while members of the two factions were "overwintering" together in the Russian village of Dubrovna. Worshiping together on the way to their new homeland, they had decided that the two church groups should forget their differences and merge into a single church. From now on the members of the two groups would be permitted to intermarry, something that had previously been forbidden. This healing effort was never fully implemented in the Chortitza Colony (Krahn 1955, *1*, 569-573), and was not even attempted among all the subsequent waves of settlers who came to Russia. In the larger and more dominant Molotschna Colony, the second major colony to be founded, the earlier bickering continued unchecked (Hildebrand 1888, 21ff; Francis 1951, 173).

Moral decadence

The moral decadence in the colonies was another reason some believers called for renewal. Jacob Epp, a Mennonite minister in the Chortitza Colony, reported in his diary that the Mennonites of the early 1800s knew what faith demanded of them. There was no need for an extensive written law, since the demands of public and private morality were implicitly understood. There still was an awareness that the Sermon on the Mount must be applied to daily life and that the life of Christ was a model worthy of imitation (John B. Toews 1988, 4).

That was the traditional ideal. But what was the reality? In his diary Epp (1838, 56) lamented, "When will this dissolute, wild life in the community end?" He records rowdies being excommunicated from the church for drunkenness and disorderly conduct; excessive drinking by the Osterwick mayor; growing instances of promiscuity and adultery; rumors of a schoolteacher having an affair; seduction by a woman of an older bachelor with the object of forcing him to marry her; a Mennonite girl bearing a son to a Russian lad; a Mennonite girl bearing a son to a Russian and having the baby baptized in the Orthodox Church; a newborn child born out of wedlock abandoned in a ditch by its young mother, possibly the first murder since migration; a father impregnating his stepdaughter; cases of sexual assault; cases of sodomy and even animal buggery.

The elders' quest for power

According to the Anabaptist/Mennonite ideal, when a church member's behavior departed from accepted church norms, the proper corrective approach involved several levels of churchly and ministerial admonition. If that failed, the ban and shunning were to be applied by the entire congregation. Banning by the individual elder or even by the *Ältestenkonvent* (the convent of elders), had traditionally not been condoned (F. C. Peters 1955, 28-29). However, now in the commonwealth structure, deviant behavior often involved both a religious and a civic dimension. Thus its punishment might relate not only to the church and its leadership, but also the wider village and colony government. This overlap led to conflict between the prerogatives of the *Lehramt*, led by the bishop, and those of the *Gebietsamt*, led by the *Oberschulze*. The first actual clashes came in 1789-1799. While the elders couched their concerns about these incidents in church language, there was no doubt that they involved a naked struggle for power (D. Rempel 1974, 54).

This tension between the two authority systems came to a head in 1806 in connection with a case about which history gives only the scantiest details. Novelist Al Reimer provides a fictionalized account of the circumstances surrounding this clash, while others provide a few additional details. A Mennonite youth was caught behind a haystack fornicating with a Russian peasant girl. The *Oberschulze's* deputies apprehended the two in the act and gave them a severe lashing, according to Russian law. When the bishop learned of this disciplinary event, he was furious. A sexual transgression by a church member was the domain of the church. He considered the mayor's action an infringement on the bishop's authority and demanded a public apology. The mayor countered by stating that this public interracial infraction was a disturbance of the public order for which he, the mayor, was responsible. The bishop, however, continued to insist on a public apology from the mayor-in-chief. When that was not forthcoming, Bishop Jakob Enns used what he considered his bishop's prerogative and arbitrarily excommunicated Klaas Wiens, the offending colony official, for insubordination to his elder/bishop and for using church-forbidden violence as punishment (A. Reimer 1985b, 76-77; Urry 1978, 206-207; 1989b, 74, 76-79).

Only four years later, in 1810, the same bishop began to feel that congregational discipline alone was no longer an effective deterrent to aberrant behavior. As a result Elder Jakob Enns, who had earlier excommunicated the *Oberschulze* for using physical punishment, now appealed to the *Gebietsamt* to bolster the church's authority by meting out corporal and financial punishments to those whom the church disciplined. Consequently church discipline could now be accompanied by village or colony discipline. The latter could include fines, other economic sanctions, imprisonment and lashing. In fact, Enns not only wanted to deliver church miscreants to "secular" colony justice, he even asked colony authorities to exile members of his own *Lehrdienst* who opposed his approach to church discipline (John B. Toews 1988, 12). Obviously church discipline had lost its redemptive intent and had become a punitive instrument of power. Ehrt (1932, 50, 56) saw the landowner-preacher-mayor system as the crucial factor that robbed Mennonite community life of much of its moral integrity. The church had forgotten that Menno Simons had said that the sword was not to be used for church discipline.

The *Kleine Gemeinde* renewal

When colony punishment was added to church discipline in 1810, not all church people were in agreement. Some felt the church was now following the Lutheran and Catholic path of power abuse. Instead of relying on the "sword of the Spirit," their community now depended on the "sword of the flesh." These people saw the new approach to discipline as disloyalty to Menno Simons' basic ideals. They labeled this abuse "spiritual decay," because they saw it as participation in magistracy (Klippenstein 1984, 23), which was expressly forbidden by the Schleitheim Confession. They were equally concerned about the moral and spiritual decay described earlier (Balzer 1948, 75-93; Wenger 1945, 251).

Robert Kreider (1951, 27) cites minister Heinrich Balzer, who said: "There is no moral superiority anymore between us and our pagan nomadic neighbors, the Nogai. We are involved in pride, ostentation, vanity, greed for more, lust for wealth, avarice, drunkenness, luxury, viciousness, masquerade, obscene songs, gambling and the smoking of tobacco—just like they are."

These "conscientious objectors" to Mennonite moral laxity called on the faithful to return to the teaching and lifestyle of Menno Simons himself. They urged people to live in such a way that it would be unnecessary to use the Russian flogging whip as a part of church discipline. Ministers Klaas Reimer (Al Reimer 1985a, 108-117) and Cornelius Janzen of Petershagen decried the use of the whip, fines and incarceration as a part of church and colony discipline. They called on the faithful to band together and shun the decadent parent church (C. Plett 1985, 6; Urry 1989b, 79).

The group which rallied around minister Klaas Reimer in 1812 was small, and so it received the derogatory name of *Kleine Gemeinde* (little church). Except for widespread ridicule, some threats of banishment, and incidents of minor harassment, like not exempting *Kleine Gemeinde* ministers from communal work parties organized by the *Gebietsamt*, the new church was not systematically persecuted by the mother church (H. Görz 1951, 57; Urry 1989b, 80).

At first this new group not only withdrew from the church's involvement in corporal discipline, it also refused to participate in village and colony government per se. It insisted that the *Lehramt* was all the authority the church and community needed. Before any major reaction against the dissidents could set in, however, the group found a protector in Johann Cornies of the all-powerful Agricultural Union, and he secured legal recognition for the group from the Russian authorities. After this, the grateful *Kleine Gemeinde* people and their leaders became wholehearted supporters of Cornies, and, in a sense, became full-fledged participants in an even more pervasive system of evil sword-power abuse that the Cornies' regime produced (F. Isaac 1908, 92; H. Görz 1951, 37; Urry 1989b, 89).

During the Crimean War, the *Kleine Gemeinde* was probably the only consistent voice protesting Mennonite participation. Later they repented publicly about the degree to which they had permitted themselves to be drawn into this war effort. Here, obviously, was a group calling for a return to a swordless society. Unfortunately, it remained a minuscule minority in the Mennonite community as a whole (Urry & Klippenstein 1989, 21-26).

Their concern to return to the vision of Menno Simons prompted them to search for a copy of his writings. Seemingly no copy was available to them in Russia. In fact, the leading Elder, Jacob Warkentin, of the mother church is reported to have said that he himself had never read Menno Simons' writings, nor did he ever intend to do so in the future. Thus the renewal leaders appealed to Danzig Mennonites for copies of Menno Simons' writings (Reimer & Gaeddert 1956, 3-4).

CHAPTER 9

Johann Cornies and His Vision

Cornies' vision

Johann Cornies (1789-1848) took seriously the Mennonite *privilegium* in Russia and decided to do his part to help Mennonites become the model farmers and the "development engine" they had promised the tsar they would be (D. H. Epp 1995). In this effort Cornies was fully supported by Senator Kontenius, chairman of the Settlement Guardians Committee in Odessa, which represented the immediate Russian government authority to which the Mennonite colonies related (F. Isaac 1908, 25-26; Urry 1978, 183).

Cornies started a model farm on his own private estate at Juschanlee near Ohrloff sometime around 1813. Five hundred dessiatines of this land had been a gift from the tsar. Some four years later Cornies' personal effort to improve agriculture and animal husbandry became the focal point of an agricultural society that eventually embraced all the Mennonite colonies in southern Russia (Krahn 1955, 14-20). By 1830, the year Senator Kontenius died, the Russian government had already elevated this society to the status of a "free academy," and not only named Johann Cornies as its permanent head, but also made him a lifetime councillor to the Russian government. Backed by the full authority of the Russian crown, Cornies thus became the de facto "Mennonite tsar" in southern Russia, who could single-handedly issue decrees and force both the Mennonite church leadership and colony authorities into compliance (Ehrt 1932, 39; F. Epp 1974, 166; P. M. Friesen 1978, 193; Görz 1951, 34; W. Quiring 1948, 30-34).

Cornies as a person

An interesting vignette from Cornies' early life provides insight into the man. One day when he was riding across his newly-acquired Juschanlee estate, he discovered an Armenian who was surreptitiously pasturing his herd of sheep on Cornies' land. Cornies was riding unarmed, while the intruder was well armed and aggressive. Nonetheless, Cornies confronted the man and demanded rent for the use of his land. The Armenian was furious, but Cornies quietly stood his ground until the intruder finally paid up. Cornies then told the man he wanted to get better acquainted with him and so he spent the rest of the day and also the night with him. By the time he left next day the two men had become friends (D. H. Epp 1946, 18-19).

Another glimpse of Cornies has been recorded by Horst Penner (1955, 130). Cornies is reported to have said: "I trust no one. I pay no attention to insults. I depend on God as my Savior. There are opportunities here (in the colonies) for all. But I want no one cold, no one lukewarm! In God's name work!"

The attitude of others toward Cornies has likewise not been lukewarm. People either have glorified him as a tough saint or condemned him as a cruel dictator. Many of the more pious Mennonites felt Cornies' use of power was out of line. Preacher David Epp (1838, 56) said in his diary that the "behavior of Johann Cornies is more despotic than Christian."

Cornies and the church elders

Under the umbrella of extensive Russian government backing, Agricultural Society administrator Cornies became increasingly autocratic. He antagonized the indigent and the irresponsible farmers whose farming privileges he unilaterally terminated and whom he then put to work together with the indigent under deputy supervision. He also infuriated the church leadership, especially Elder Warkentin, who represented more than two-thirds of all church members in the Molotschna Colony at the time. When Warkentin fomented opposition against Cornies and the Odessa settlement authorities who backed him, Cornies was able to have the elder declared unworthy of his office and forced the other elders to relieve him of his duties in 1842 (Ehrt 1932, 39; Just 1948, 100). Subsequent to relieving Warkentin of his duties the district was divided and three separate elders were installed in Warkentin's former jurisdiction. Elder H. Wiens, one of those installed, continued and even increased the spirit of opposition to Cornies' autocracy. Wiens was then not only declared unworthy of his church office, but was summarily banished from the Ukraine in 1846 (F. Isaac 1908, 116; Klippenstein 1984, 22).

The Wiens episode clearly indicates that the elders operated on the premise that the "Mennonite state," in the form of the *Gebietsamt*, was subject to the authority of the church and its elder. But the Russian administrator of the Settlement Guardians Committee, E. von Hahn, whose ear Cornies had, viewed the church as subservient to the state (F. Isaac 1908, 114-121). Von Hahn intervened once more when one of the newly elected elders baptized a Lutheran youth without obtaining government permission. This was illegal because Russian law forbade proselytizing other Christian groups. Hahn ordered the other elders to defrock newly-installed Elder Peter Schmidt (F. Isaac 1908, 113-121; Urry 1978, 379).

The *Kirchenkonvent*

Such repeated interference severely threatened the beleaguered Mennonite elders. Hoping to achieve at least some additional strength in unity, the elders, in 1851, organized a *Kirchenkonvent* (council of elders) and declared all Mennonite churches in the colonies subject to their jurisdiction (F. Isaac 1908, 122-123; H. Görz 1951, 61; cf. Hege 1955, *1*, 19).

This new body went against both the ideal and the traditional consensual practice of the Mennonite church. In the past the churches had related only to their own elder. Outside elders could be called into another district only as advisors. Furthermore, the individual elders had always acted only under guidance from their respective congregations and ministerial colleagues. Now for the first time in Mennonite history they had declared themselves to be an independent, superior legislative and executive body, with the power to speak and act for the church in binding fashion without consulting their congregations, ministers and teachers (D. H. Epp 1984, 71; F. Isaac 1908, 122-123; A. Unruh 1954, 39). In fact, the elders now referred to the entire church membership as *untergeordnet* (subordinated) (F. Isaac 1908, 122).

Cornies, the administrator

At first, the village and colony authorities welcomed and cooperated fully with Cornies' reform and development efforts (H. Wiens 1935, 347-350, 367-371), but eventually even their patience with his increasingly autocratic style grew thin. He was constantly imposing new ordinances ranging from levies to build schools, to demanding that chimneys be rebuilt with brick and mortar. In 1844 Cornies suddenly ordered the colonies to plant two-and-a-half million trees. Within a few years this quota grew to six million trees annually (H. Görz 1951, 45-50; *Die Mennoniten-Gemeinden in Russland* 1921, 23).

When Cornies died in 1848, the humiliated elders as well as the diminished *Gebietsamt* were determined to refurbish their tarnished authority. The mayoral candidate representing this common cause between the Mennonite elders and the colony authorities was David Friesen. His election initiated an era in which a strong and often ruthless *Oberschulze* could count on the elders to rubberstamp his actions. The elders, in turn, could count on the *Oberschulze*'s office to bring all its political clout to bear on issues where the church authorities wanted colony power support. Here was a clear case of church and state linkage, often employed in blatant sword-power abuses (F. Isaac 1908, 178-180; H. Loewen 1991, 156).

Despite his excesses, Cornies was not a villain. He was a man with a great vision for the Mennonite people. He had gained the ear of the Russian authorities to a degree that permitted him to impose his design upon the Mennonite church and "state" almost at will. But he was not on a quest for unbridled power. In fact, Cornies refused nobility offered to him by the tsar because "I want to remain a simple Mennonite" (Ehrt 1932, v-vi; Krahn 1935, 171). On the whole the Cornies era was one of unprecedented educational, social and economic development which raised the overall standard of Mennonite life within colonies to a degree seldom deemed possible (H. L. Dyck 1984a, 9-28; 1984b, 29-41).

Side effects of growth and prosperity

This growth and prosperity brought with it significant liabilities. As economic and health conditions improved, the population was able to grow rapidly and the number of landless families in the colonies increased to near crisis proportions. Cornies grasped the seriousness of the problem and tried to introduce new industry and trades to provide an adequate living also for the swelling numbers of landless. But it turned out there was neither enough capital nor enough entrepreneurs to achieve this goal. Thus at the time of Cornies' death over half of the families in the Mennonite colonies were not only landless, many were destitute (H. Görz 1951, 111; Krahn 1935, 165-177; Kuhn 1942, 14).

Furthermore, the prosperity of the landholders, coupled with the rapid population expansion, destroyed the original egalitarian society and produced a three-tiered one. On top was the landholding and governing minority. In the middle was the landless majority who could not vote in civic affairs. At the bottom were the non-Mennonite workers and servants employed by the landed minority. These workers, despite Cornies' efforts to introduce fair labor practices, often were no better off than the serfs under Russian nobility (F. Epp 1962, 24; R. Kreider 1951, 25; J. J. Toews 1951, 206).

Collusion between *Lehramt* and *Gebietsamt*

No relief was in sight for the landless. Colony regulations allowed only the landed to vote in village affairs. The ministers of the church, especially the elders, were part of the landholders. They themselves had been chosen because they were financially independent landholders. The elders saw their authority as assured by cooperating with the landed who controlled the economy and who provided a strong *Oberschulze* in David Friesen. *Oberschulze* Friesen, in turn, went out of his way to support the elders' agenda (H. Görz 951, 72; Thiessen 1887, 1-4; Urry 1989b, 199).

This new church hierarchy/colony leadership cooperation led to questionable practices. For one thing, the elders "created a new church sin," namely, disobedience to the colony *Gebietsamt*. In Chortitza the landholders introduced a resolution that no landless person could rent unused church-controlled lands. It did not pass. Landholders, however, seemingly were awarded two votes each in church ministerial selections (H. Dyck 1991, 204; D. H. Epp 1984, 74-75; Klaus 1887, 270).

There was a substantial breakdown of Christian mutuality in both church and community. When the landless appealed for redress to their fellow church members, the village and colony leaders, they were frequently denounced as rabble rousers and revolutionaries (F. Isaac 1908, 64ff). The fact was that the landed controlled even the vast areas of unassigned colony land, which they rented from the colony for a pittance and then sublet to others at inflated rates (F. Isaac 1908, 31; R. Kreider 1951, 27). When confronted by protesting landless people, *Oberschulze* Friesen is alleged to have shouted, "I will not give you landless even half a dessiatine of land" (F. Isaac 1908, 31; Urry 1978, 709).

The *Odessaer Zeitung* (2 April 1865, 151) provides a revealing vignette about the landholders' attitude toward the landless. The mayor-in-chief wanted to make a public announcement. In order to have sufficient citizen witnesses he sent a young landholder out to call together all the people who might be in the vicinity of the *Oberschulze*'s office. However, the young landholder returned shortly to report that there were no *Menschen* (people) out there, just a few *Kleinhaeusler* (landless persons).

The Mennonite power structure, and the Russian government

Wittingly or unwittingly Johann Cornies became instrumental in moving the Mennonite colonies further into the Russian governmental power orbit (John B. Toews 1988, 19). He did this in at least six ways:

(1) He helped tip the balance of power between elders and colony administrators in favor of the latter. The elders were thus forced to become dependent on a powerful *Oberschulze* who, for all practical purposes, was the local representative of the Russian state. Calvin

Redekop (1985b, 99-103; possibly after Tulles 1963) says this shift moved Russian Mennonites out of the "meetinghouse" milieu and firmly into an individualistic and capitalistic "counting house" mentality. Thus when the Mennonite Brethren revival and schism began, the elders could call on the *Oberschulze* and the Odessa Settlement Guardians Committee to help destroy the dissident movement without even considering the group's complaints or trying to talk to them as church protocol required (F. Isaac 1908, 176-180; Urry 1989b, 149).

(2) He also taught the elders that outside Russian governmental power sources could be used to do one's "dirty work," such as when he used the Odessa Guardians Committee to order elders deposed. Soon the elders would turn the tables and enlist a willing *Oberschulze* and the Odessa authorities themselves in an attempt to destroy the Mennonite Brethren upstarts on their behalf (F. Isaac 1908, 187).

(3) He was instrumental in "secularizing" education in the Mennonite colonies. Up to this point, teachers had been part of the ministry and thus servants of the church, subordinate to the ministers and certainly to the elder. After the Russian government gave Cornies full control of education in the Mennonite colonies in 1843, schools were effectively removed from church control and no teacher could be appointed without Cornies'—and therefore the Russian state's—approval (F. Epp 1962, 211; F. Isaac 1908, 276). On realizing what was happening, one elder is reported to have cried out, "Now everything has been taken out of our hands" (Görz 1951, 95).

(4) Cornies occasioned the discovery that an individual elder could appeal to Russian authorities and then use the latter's authority to help the elder get his way. One example was Elder Warkentin's early successes when he appealed to the Odessa authorities during the Halbstadt church building quarrel (F. Isaac 1908, 106ff). Another example was when Elders Fast and Harder sent Johann Cornies (Junior) and Philip Wiebe to the Odessa authorities to seek relief in the same church quarrel. This avenue was used several times in harassing the emerging Mennonite Brethren Church (F. Isaac 1908, 102-107, 145-149).

(5) During the Crimean War Cornies' Agricultural Union became the driving force that pushed the Mennonite colonies into large-scale participation in the Russian war effort (Urry & Klippenstein 1989, 14).

(6) He brought Russian government authority, in the form of the Odessa Guardians Committee, into the day-to-day affairs of the Mennonite colonies (Ehrt 1932, 39).

Sword-power abuses prior to the 1860 revival

In summary, the following sword-power abuses were widely present at the time of or immediately preceding the 1860 revival:

(1) The wealthy "landholding" Mennonites who controlled the colonies shamelessly exploited their landless brothers and sisters in the faith.

(2) Only the landed were given voting power in the colony structure, thus two-thirds of all the colonists remained disenfranchised and totally impotent to do anything about their situation.

(3) "Landholders" and the landholder-controlled *Gebietsamt* conspired to produce a vast pool of cheap landless Mennonite labor, totally at their mercy.

(4) The church *Lehramt*, working hand-in-glove with the *Gebietsamt*, claimed to be powerless to help landless church members in their struggle for justice, while at the same time giving landholders two votes on church issues (H. Dyck 1991, 204).

(5) Mennonite colony authorities were fully involved in magistracy and freely employed every form of punishment from Russian flogging to banishment from the colonies, often at the request of the elders as part of church discipline (Loewen & Prieb 1996, 17-44).

(6) The elders organized themselves into a *Kirchenkonvent*, which now declared all churches as subordinate, thus creating a hierarchical power structure hitherto unknown in the Mennonite church (D. H. Epp 1984, 17; P. M. Friesen 1978, 169, 171, 258; F. Isaac 1908, 106, 142ff).

(7) One elder, in cooperation with the colony leadership, could harass another elder and his congregation in an obvious struggle for power—for example, Elder Warkentin's role in the Ohrloff barley quarrel and his subsequent requests for the excommunication of Deacon Wall or his quest for the control of the new Halbstadt church building (F. Isaac 1908, 123-173).

(8) Mennonite peace principles were ignored and violence was perpetrated both privately and collectively (John B. Toews 1988, 7, 12).

(9) The elders were willing to forego the traditionally required spiritual exhortation and simply turned dissidents (like the emerging Mennonite Brethren) over to civic authorities for immediate physical punishment or imprisonment (F. Isaac 1908, 178-180; Klaus 1887, 266; R. Kreider 1951, 27; John B. Toews 1988, 20). This clearly violated three of Menno Simons' premises, namely the use of sword-power to force them to recant their conversion, to defend the truth and to impose one view of morality on otherwise-minded believers. Franz Isaac

assessed the situation correctly when he wrote: "Mennonites, who themselves are a barely tolerated minority, are completely unable to tolerate their own minorities" (1908, 345).

Pietist and Baptist Influences

Unlike the 1812 *Kleine Gemeinde* renewal, which was basically home-grown, the mid-nineteenth century renewal currents were heavily influenced by several streams of Pietism imported from abroad. Pietism is defined by *The Mennonite Encyclopedia* as a quest for personal piety based not on creed or doctrine, but on a "heartfelt" personal emotional experience. It originated in Germany at the end of the seventeenth century. Many early Anabaptist centers eventually became centers of Pietism (Ritschl 1880-1886).

Three streams of Pietism impacted the Mennonite colonies in South Russia. The Moravian variety focused on personal conversion, outreach in evangelism and missions, social justice, and serving the poor and needy. The Würtemberg stream added a strong eschatological interest, including dispensationalism. Finally, the Blankenburg stream developed a strong interest in Christian unity. Eventually this stream became nationalistic, emphasizing German language and culture and finally, German militarism. All of these Pietistic streams and some baptistic influences penetrated into both the Moltoschna and Chortitza colonies during the nineteenth century (J. A. Toews 1957, 1-3).

Molotschna Colony

Tobias Voth

One of the earliest renewal influences in Molotschna was the work of Tobias Voth (1791-1855), who came from Prussia to teach in the Rudnerweide congregation. Voth was a sincere and deeply pious Mennonite, but he was also an innovator who had been deeply influenced by the German Pietist, Johann Heinrich Jung-Stilling. Voth emphasized the need for an inner spiritual experience of Jesus Christ as personal Savior. In his educational and religious efforts Voth enjoyed the backing of Elder Franz Görz, who soon encouraged him to move to Ohrloff in order to broaden his religious and educational efforts (P. M. Friesen 1978, 97; Hamm 1987, 47).

In Ohrloff Voth established a literary society and introduced prayer meetings for missions. Historian P. M. Friesen (1978, 97) credits Voth with originating the practice of warm Christian fellowship that became the trademark of the Mennonite Brethren branch of the renewal movement. In Voth's case the outside influence had been filtered through

Mennonite glasses and shaped to Mennonite needs (John B. Toews 1988, 13-14).

John Melville

Less dramatic, but even more fundamental, was the influence of John Melville (1802-1886), the representative of the British and Foreign Bible Society in Russia (Urry 1980, 305-322). Melville was born in Scotland and had Presbyterian affiliation, but in Russia he functioned as an evangelist who fellowshiped with the *Stundo* Baptists. These Baptists were part of the larger *Stundist* movement (Krahn 1959, 4, 649-650), a nineteenth-century Pietist movement characterized by private devotional meetings. Under Melville's inspiration several Bible Society auxiliaries were organized in the Mennonite colonies under the local sponsorship of the Elders Peter Wedel of Alexanderwohl and Bernard Fast of Ohrloff. These auxiliaries raised funds for Bible distribution elsewhere, distributed Bibles locally, and encouraged group Bible study within the Mennonite colonies. One of Melville's Bible study groups had been established in Einlage, Chortitza. These Bible study groups helped to create the biblical awareness needed to initiate and to sustain the 1860 renewal movement. This made possible the eventual recovery of the practice of the church as an exegetical community in the Mennonite Brethren context (John B. Toews 1988, 14).

Developments at Gnadenfeld

Another important development was the arrival in Gnadenfeld in 1835 of a group of Mennonite Pietist settlers from Germany. These people represented a happy amalgam of the Schwetz Mennonite group from Poland who had moved to Neumark and who there had worshiped with the Herrnhuter (Moravian) Brethren. This group was well-educated and religiously very active. They had achieved a blend of the positive aspects of both Pietism and Anabaptism without sacrificing the central concerns of their Anabaptist/Mennonite heritage. This group stressed the need for personal salvation and a subsequent life of discipleship with concerns for evangelism and service to the needy.

Their late arrival in Russia made this group less conscious of the fact that Mennonites in Russia had agreed to refrain from missionary and evangelistic activity among Russians in exchange for the guarantee of their privileges. As a result, these new settlers reached out to their Russian neighbors (A. Braun 1938, 14-15; R. Kreider 1951, 23).

The Gnadenfeld church soon became known for its mission support groups, meaningful Bible studies, warm Christian fellowship and concern for social justice. It was here that people began to address their fellow worshipers as "brothers and sisters," which later became a key element in the new Mennonite Brethren name (P. M. Friesen 1978, 99).

Especially important in this group was the Lange family, originally of the Moravian Brethren. Wilhelm Lange was an ordained Mennonite minister and leader, and a number of his relatives and descendants followed in his footsteps. Even though his nephew, Friedrich Lange, was later removed from leadership under questionable circumstances, the Gnadenfeld enlightenment under Lange's leadership continued to spread its influence through the teachers and preachers the community produced (Urry 1989b, 160-174).

Jacob P. Bekker (1973, 25-26), one of the signers of the Mennonite Brethren document of secession, asserted that the tract and temperance societies established in Gnadenfeld became the models which the Mennonite Brethren Church later copied. Historian P. M. Friesen (1978, 99) described Gnadenfeld as the "womb" which produced the Mennonite Brethren Church. Gnadenfeld could be considered the center of Pietist renewal, just as Ohrloff was the fountain of intellectual renaissance under Johann Cornies and teacher Tobias Voth (J. A. Toews 1975a, 27).

Schism at Gnadenfeld

The religious and educational activities in Gnadenfeld enjoyed the approval of Ohrloff Elder August Lenzmann over an extended period of time. Suddenly and unexpectedly, however, Elder Bernard Fast intervened in the affairs of the Gnadenfeld church and deposed several members of the Lange family from leadership, seemingly even in the absence of proven guilt. As a result, the local congregation's leadership structure was so severely weakened that it lost control of the renewal movement that was just emerging. In the absence of strong overall leadership, differences of opinion within the movement soon led to its splintering (A. Braun 1938, 7-18; P. M. Friesen 1978, 103).

The first of these splits occurred in 1858-1859, when David Hausknecht and Heinrich Franz were being considered for the leadership of the Gnadenfeld school program. Hausknecht was more pious, while Franz was more academic. Johann Claassen and Jacob Reimer (later Mennonite Brethren leaders) backed Hausknecht, while others, including Elder Lenzmann, supported Franz. Among the Franz supporters were the Schmidt brothers, Nicholas and Johann, who had links with Christoph Hoffmann's (Neff 1937, 2, 325-326) Friends of Jerusalem, sometimes also called the Temple Church (Krahn 1959, 4, 693-694). This group advocated a theology more open than most Mennonites were used to or considered acceptable. This outside contact soon led to the second schism in 1861-62 in which Elder Lenzmann and teacher Franz called for a more closed Mennonite approach, thus separating from the Schmidt brothers and the more open approach of the Temple Church.

The Schmidt brothers and most of their followers now organized a local Temple Church in Gnadenfeld. Their aim was to be an alternative Mennonite church, but when the elders and *Oberschulze* conspired to imprison one of their leaders, Johannes Lange, the group decided to secede from the Mennonite Church in April of 1863 (F. Isaac 1908, 238; Krahn 1970, 171-172).

A multiplicity of renewal movements

Besides the Mennonite Brethren (Bekker 1973, 25; Krahn 1978, 4-11), who are an important concern of this study, the Gnadenfeld religious atmosphere over time produced a variety of other renewal movements. We have already referred to the Friends of Jerusalem, or Temple Church (Doerksen 1982, 169-178). Many of them actually left Gnadenfeld after they developed difficulties with the local authorities there and moved to Palestine in 1870. Members like Friedrich Lange of Mennonite origin played significant roles in the movement both in Russia and in Palestine (Krahn 1959, 4, 693-694; H. Sawatzky 1990, 7-103).

Another movement was *Die Brotbrecher* (the bread breakers), also called the Peters Church or the *Apostolische Brüdergemeinde* (the Apostolic Brethren Church). This group stressed the new birth and used only whole loaves of bread for their communion, during which individual participants each broke off a piece before partaking of it. This group never really developed a substantial following (A. J. Dueck 1989, 160 Krahn 1955, *1*, 141-142).

A later (1870) offspring was a chiliastic movement called The "Philadelphia" Church of the Revelation. Its founder was Claas Epp. Another elder of the group was A. Peters. When Russia began to curtail Mennonite privileges in 1870 and many Mennonites left for America, this group had a revelation that their salvation lay in the east. So they set out for central Asia in 1880 and settled among Muslim Mongolians at Ak Mechet and Aulie Ata. Here leader Epp grew ever more fanatical and finally claimed to be a fourth member of the trinity. This group developed serious difficulties with bandits who stole their cattle and even killed some of the group's members. The situation deteriorated until the group disintegrated in about 1891 (Bartsch 1907 [reprinted 1948, 1957]; 1956, *2*, 234; Bartsch & Krahn 1955, *1*, 29; Belk 1976).

The Gnadenfeld renewal also provided an impulse toward ecumenism in the *Allianz Gemeinde* (Alliance church). While never strong, this movement attracted such famous Mennonite Brethren as historian Peter M. Friesen. Most of the group migrated to North America, where they eventually joined the Mennonite Brethren (Neff 1913, *35*; P. M. Friesen 1978, 669, 918-925).

Pastor Wüst

Probably the single most influential individual in launching the 1860 renewal movement was Eduard Wüst (1818-1859). Wüst was a Pietist Lutheran pastor shepherding a German "free church" near Berdjansk, not far from the Mennonite colonies. P. M. Friesen (1978, 211-212) suggested that Wüst was to the Mennonite Brethren what Menno Simons had been to the Dutch/German Mennonite movement. Wüst was a powerful preacher and while many people came to hear him out of curiosity, they invariably left his meetings concerned about their soul's salvation. John A. Toews (1975a, 31) likened him to Moses, who was permitted to lead the people only to the boundary of the promised land, and who had to let "Joshua" actually lead the people into it.

As Wüst's popularity as a preacher grew, he became more enthused about "free grace" and Christian "liberty and joy." Thus while he continued to emphasize personal salvation, he gravitated toward a position of greater personal liberty (P. M. Friesen 1978, 511).

A Mariopol teacher, Kappes by name (first name unknown), took Wüst's freedom, ideas and practice even further, producing unhappy results. When Wüst finally recognized this and began to counteract Kappes' excesses, the latter launched a violent personal attack against Wüst, who had just fallen ill. Wüst's wife, writing about her husband's last days, says that when her husband realized he had overemphasized free grace and joy, he hoped and prayed for a chance to rectify his mistake, but his sudden premature death prevented him from doing so (P. M. Friesen 1978, 225-226).

Chortitza Colony

German Pietist influence

Meanwhile, in the Chortitza Colony, a totally separate renewal movement was taking shape. It began in Kronsweide and Einlage. In the village of Kronsweide in 1853 a young man named Johann Loewen began reading sermons written by the German Pietist preacher Ludwig Hofacker. Deeply moved, the young man began to search the Scripture and as a result discovered how he could make peace with God. This new convert spoke about his new faith experience so zealously and convincingly that soon others joined him to study the Bible and pray. Before long the group had grown to fifty converts (P. M. Friesen 1978, 281).

The German Baptist connection

In the village of Einlage, likewise, several persons experienced personal salvation on the basis of their study of the Bible after being inspired by Pietist/Baptist literature that had come into their hands. These new converts now established letter contact with the Hamburg Baptists and especially with their leader, Johann G. Oncken, who was the author of some of the literature that had sparked their spiritual interest (John B. Toews 1993, 81-96).

This correspondence was initiated during 1858-1860. Abraham Unger invited Oncken to visit them and help organize them into a church. It had not dawned on the group that such action might make them Baptists. Before Oncken could come, however, Gerhard Wieler, a young teacher who had become a Mennonite Brethren and was subsequently dismissed from his teaching post and exiled from Molotschna Colony, arrived back in his home village of Einlage. He informed the new believers there about the new Mennonite Brethren Church in Molotschna. He also warned the Einlage group that becoming Baptists would jeopardize their Mennonite status and its privileges. The invitation to Oncken was thus canceled (H. Epp 1907, 20ff; Urry 1989b, 182-183).

However, when Oncken visited Baptist congregations in South Russia somewhat later, he also contacted the Einlage group. Here he ordained the newly selected Abraham Unger as elder, Aron Lepp as minister, and Cornelius Unger and Benjamin Nickel as deacons, even though the latter was a church office largely unknown to the German Baptists. These ordinations caused the other colonists to assume that the group had become Baptists, even though the group affirmed their loyalty to the recognized Mennonite confession of faith. The mother church called them *Die Ausgetretenen* (those who have abandoned the church) (D. H. Epp 1984, 64; see also P. M. Friesen 1978, 461-467).

The Baptist connection introduced some thorny issues. The first had to do with tobacco. Oncken himself was a smoker. Eventually the

Einlage church excommunicated about a dozen influential members because of their use of tobacco (J. J. Toews 1959, 4, 60).

The second, more serious, issue dealt with military service, which the Baptists believed a Christian was obligated to render to the state. Disagreements on both issues led to the organization of two church nuclei, one Mennonite-oriented and the other Baptist-oriented. But the two groups continued in joint worship (P. M. Friesen 1978, 464).

The Baptist connections created not only ethical and doctrinal problems for the Mennonite Brethren, but also greatly colored the other Mennonites' perception of the new movement. Some Mennonites noted bitterly, "They accept fighting Baptists as good Christians, but treat us fellow Mennonites as spiritually dead," or "They accept smoking Baptists as church members, but we Mennonites have to be reconverted and rebaptized." (See Ehrt 1932, 58; D. H. Epp 1889/1948; *"Was sind die Mitglieder der Mennoniten Brüdergemeinde?..."* (1896, 23); "Baptisten oder nicht?" (1901, 23).

In 1866 two Baptist pastors, August Liebig and Karl Benzien, visited the Einlage congregation, which up to this time had followed largely Mennonite, including pacifist, ideals. This seems to have rankled Benzien, who was not a pacifist. He is reported to have said he would have to take it upon himself "to pull out the corroded Mennonite sword" (P. M. Friesen 1978, 465).

When Oncken visited Einlage a second time in 1869, he consecrated additional church workers on the basis of Baptist church polity. But by this time the group had established enough links with the Molotschna Brethren that when the first Mennonite Brethren general conference was convened in 1872 the Chortitza group decided to integrate fully with the now legally recognized Mennonite Brethren. A few of the Einlage believers found this unacceptable and transferred their membership to the Baptist Alliance Church across the river (P. M. Friesen 1978, 467).

New pacifist input was provided when the Quakers visited the Mennonite colonies during the Crimean War in 1854-1856 (Yarrow 1978). They tried to encourage Mennonites to resist economic and transport participation in the war effort in which Mennonites were, in fact, heavily engaged. This visit seems to have left no lasting impression (O. Gingerich 1951, 283-294; Scott 1964, 101-111; Urry & Klippenstein 1989, 21).

Summary of Pietist and Baptist influences

This assortment of Pietist and Baptist contacts brought the South Russian Mennonites face to face with a series of themes, ideas and values (Adrian 1965; H. Epp 1908). Some they embraced, while others they merely tolerated or ignored. These outside influences pulled the renewal currents in several directions simultaneously (Klassen & Neufeld 1985; P. J. Klassen 1993, 73-80). Some encouraged the recovery of Menno Simons' vision, while others undermined it. Cornelius J. Dyck (1977, 55-77) categorically states that the Mennonite Brethren affirmed their Mennonite roots from the very beginning with statements like, "in all articles of faith we are in accord with Menno Simons," or "we are living fruits of our founder Menno Simons." Dyck cites Frank C. Peters in saying that the MB revival was a return to the Anabaptist vision, rather than a deviation from it. Our perusal of the evidence does not permit us to be so confident.

Twelve borrowed Pietist themes

There are at least twelve distinct themes or ideas contained within the Pietist and Baptist influences on the Mennonite Brethren:

1. The serious study of Scripture

The two-pronged Pietist approach to Scripture in personal and group Bible study reinforced both of the traditional Anabaptist/ Mennonite approaches to the Scripture, which, in South Russia, had been allowed to lapse. This helped in the recovery of the exegetical community.

2. A personal conversion experience

This Pietist emphasis closely paralleled the Anabaptist/Mennonite call for a conscious personal decision to follow Jesus. However, the Baptist/Pietist conversion intensified the emotions involved and decreased the emphasis on discipleship.

3. Heartfelt spirituality

Mennonite baptism and church membership had become largely perfunctory catechism-based decisions, usually occasioned by a desire to marry or be able to inherit land. The Pietist conversion, in contrast, called for a deeply-felt spiritual encounter with God. The fellowship of believers further stimulated an ongoing spirituality. Pietism proved to be a big temptation to Anabaptists/Mennonites to switch from discipleship and community to make their religion primarily inward, personal and individualistic.

4. Warm fellowship in an atmosphere of freedom and celebration

Pietism provided a welcome alternative to Mennonite worship services that had become highly ritualized, austere and lifeless. The old sermons that were read contained few inspiring insights, made few appeals to the emotions and stimulated little warm fellowship.

5. A theology of grace

The Pietist slogan "saved by grace" had a beautiful ring to it. However it usually lacked the Anabaptist/Mennonite emphasis on discipleship and community. Furthermore, it suggested that since grace was experienced personally, the subsequent Christian life was also personal. This discouraged mutual exhortation and discipline, a salient feature of Anabaptist/Mennonite fellowship.

6. An emphasis on the return of Jesus Christ

This had already been a powerful element in Melchior Hoffman's first gospel preaching in 1530, and had sustained believers during persecution. It became a problem, however, when it was joined by dispensationalism, especially under Blankenburg influence.

7. Concern for evangelism and missions

Early Anabaptists/Mennonites, with their emphasis on the priesthood of all believers, had eagerly shared the good news with others. For many years now they had sacrificed this ministry to protect their military exemptions. Pietist and Baptist stress on evangelism brought relief from accumulated guilt over their failure to share the gospel with their Russian neighbors.

8. An emphasis on Christian unity

During the persecution and in their later colony living Anabaptists/Mennonites often felt isolated. They now saw opportunities to establish relationships beyond the narrow confines of their own communities.

9. German language and culture

Having switched from Dutch to German during their Prussian sojourn, Mennonites now felt at home in the German milieu (J. A. Duerksen 1967, 107-109). Since they disdained the Slavic and Islamic tribal cultures around them, they developed an uncritical and unhealthy attachment to things Germanic.

10. Militarism

This militaristic orientation of the Blankenburg Pietists was alien to the Mennonites. Since they were grateful for all the other spiritual values the pietists and Baptists brought, however, they tolerated it and tried to ignore its militarism, albeit unsuccessfully.

11. The conference approach to studying biblical and spiritual concerns

The Blankenburg Conference was composed of people who had covenanted to work together to accomplish certain goals. This became the model for the Mennonite Brethren General Conference in 1872—hence the name: *Bundeskonferenz.*

12. A leadership called by God

Anabaptists/Mennonites had traditionally recognized both the call of God and the call of the congregation. However, in practice they depended almost exclusively on the latter. Pietists, on the other hand, operated largely on the former.

The Outworking of Borrowed Pietist Values in the Mennonite Brethren Context

The Pietist and Baptist influences (H. Löwen 1989, 13-44) that the Mennonite Brethren renewal movement experienced produced both positive and negative consequences. Because these influences made themselves felt at different times, they are treated here as closely as possible to the actual sequence of their appearance in Mennonite Brethren experience.

Bible study and the exegetical community

The first positive influence that came to the Russian Mennonite colonies, even before the actual emergence of the Mennonite Brethren Church, was the revival of the exegetical community. As individuals alone and families studied God's Word together they realized the slippages that undermined their earlier vision of a live, committed discipleship community. The communally discerned insights discovered during their study of Scripture provided the basis for this renewal effort. The trigger event for the actual secession was the parent church's unwillingness to permit a separate celebration of the Lord's Supper for those who had experienced the new birth and who as a result had dedicated themselves to more Christlike behavior in word and deed. Individual Mennonite Brethren communities continued as active exegetical communities until after World War II.

The "pure church" emphasis

Next, there were the concerns associated with the "the pure church," which at the beginning had already afflicted Menno Simons. This emphasis prompted the early Mennonite Brethren to make many unwise, wholesale and not always accurate condemnations of the parent church (John B. Toews 1984, 87, 90).

The first component of a pure church was that it be made up of only "born-again" persons. In the early days of closed community living, it also included a strict monitoring of members' daily life and behavior. When violations occurred, admonition followed; and if that failed, banning and shunning were employed either to bring the straying person back or to rid the church of that which was unclean.

Today the use of church discipline, especially the ban or excommunication is rare. Unless the individual commits a flagrant sexual transgression or something equivalent, he or she will merely be released from church membership. Modern urban and professional living provides little opportunity to monitor daily "narrow-road" behavior. Besides, the "sins" of the current generation have become so much harder to identify. How does a church treat unfair labor practices (J. Redekop 1972a), ethical violations in business (C. Redekop 1985b, 95-107; Sider 1989b, 156-169), abuse of the environment (Daly 1980; White 1967, 1203-1207), racial prejudice (Sider 1979), conspicuous consumption (Sider 1977; Sprunger 1993), intolerance (J. H. Redekop 1972b, No. 23), or investment in abusive multinational corporations (Sider 1977, 1979; Ward 1961)?

The result, it seems, is that the concept of the "pure church" is now being redefined as "pure doctrine." Thus, instead of the early Anabaptist/Mennonite tolerance for individual opinion with room for private interpretation, the Mennonite Brethren and some other Mennonite congregations are now increasingly ready to "detect" and expose allegedly heretical ideas.

The exuberant movement

An early negative result of these outside influences, which made itself felt soon after the emergence of the Mennonite Brethren Church, was the influence of Pastor Wüst's teaching on free grace and joy. It produced within the new movement a group which has been called *Die Fröhliche Richtung* (the exuberant movement). It represented an unhealthy extreme of the Pietist emphasis on warm heartfelt spiritual experience.(P. M. Friesen 1978, 511; H. Löwen 1985, 118-125).

Two kinds of exuberant behavior were manifested. The first was an emphasis on personal liberty. Its proponents called themselves *Die Starken* (strong ones). This manifested itself largely in freely kissing persons of the opposite sex, previously strictly taboo in Mennonite society. In some cases preachers kissed other men's wives and the more attractive of the unmarried women. This produced some unfortunate results and was soon eliminated from Mennonite Brethren practice (J. H. Lohrenz 1950, 34-35).

The other dimension involved shouts of praise, dancing and jumping for joy. The latter behavior occasioned the German nickname, *Hüpfer* (the jumpers). Historian P. M. Friesen (1978, 208ff) noted that this aspect reached its peak during Johann Claassen's (Neff 1913, *1*, 356-357) second visit to St. Petersburg from November 1860 to June 1962. A leader in this group, Wilhelm Bartel, was a close friend of Kappes, the man who took Wüst's teaching to the extreme. When Bartel reported some of his joyous experiences in a letter to Claassen in St. Petersburg, the latter cautioned him against the inherent dangers. Bartel and his followers eventually withdrew from the Mennonite Brethren movement (E. Klassen 1978, 150-151).

This exuberant movement reached as far as the Chortitza Colony into the village of Einlage. But when in the spring of 1862 some of these "liberated ones" or "strong ones" in Einlage lapsed into sin, strong opposition within the main movement developed. By June of 1865 both emphases had been all but eliminated from the Mennonite Brethren mainstream (E. Klassen 1978, 151-152).

"Spiritual despotism"

Another negative development seems to have developed out of the Pietist emphasis on the call of God to the individual. It, likewise, made its appearance soon after the Mennonite Brethren Church emerged. This development, which seems to be related to the exuberance emphases, has been called "spiritual despotism" (P. M. Friesen 1978, 268-270, 457; Hamm 1987, 49; H. Löwen 1985, 120-124; J. A. Toews 1975a, 61-62). It also manifested itself in both colonies, in two Mennonite Brethren congregations in the Molotschna and in the revival group in Einlage, Chortitza. In one or two cases its proponents overlapped with people who were also involved in the exuberant movement. Three frontrunners in this regard were Benjamin Bekker, Bernard Penner and Gerhard Wieler. These men, among the first to be ordained to the ministry in the new church, soon saw themselves as spiritually superior to others and began to call themselves "apostles" (Urry 1989b, 190). As apostles "called directly by God" they no longer felt any need to consult the congregation or their ministerial colleagues, but felt free to legislate on their own. It was ironic that no sooner had they escaped the arbitrary authoritarian rule of the elders in the parent Mennonite church, then they and others fell into a new kind of power abuse. They mercilessly condemned everyone who did not support their ideas, even to the point of excommunicating anyone who voiced disagreement. In several cases they even tried to "deliver to Satan" those who opposed them (P. M. Friesen 1978, 275).

During the winter of 1864-65, however, the moderate leaders, including Johann Claassen, were able to assert their authority and put an end to this abuse of power. Then, as part of the June 1865 reforms, a number of the arbitrary and unjust excommunications were revoked and the church reaffirmed its loyalty to congregational government.

A dramatic rise in evangelism and missions

Pietist and Baptist influences stimulated a surge of interest in outreach (J. H. Lohrenz 1950, 53-59), which Mennonites as a group had agreed to forfeit when they came to Russia (R. Kreider 1951, 23; Rempel 1933, 321). In 1867 Heinrich Dirks, the first Mennonite foreign missionary from Russia, went to Sumatra under Dutch Mennonite auspices (Pannabecker 1957, *3*, 713-714; J. J. Toews 1967, 148-151). Abraham and Maria Friesen were sent to the Baptist seminary in Hamburg to prepare for missionary service. They then went to India under the Baptist Missionary Union in 1889. The Friesens were joined by Abram J. and Katharina Hübert in 1898 and by Heinrich and Anna Unruh in 1899. A total of eighteen Mennonite Brethren missionaries from Russia were sent to this field under Baptist auspices. P. Penner (1991, 17-23; 1993, 133-146), historian of the Mennonite Brethren mission in India, characterized their work there as Baptist in everything but their Mennonite name.

Another effect of the renewal was an interest in the spiritual condition of the Russian people. Even though the Mennonites had promised they would not evangelize members of the Russian Orthodox Church as part of their immigration agreement, now that they had personally experienced new birth, the Mennonite Brethren felt compelled to share the Good News with all their neighbors. The result was the local evangelism of tribespeople around the colonies and the launching of several mission efforts among the Russians farther afield. Early missionaries in these efforts were Johann Wieler, Jacob Froese, Adolph Penner, Hermann Fast (H. H. Janzen 1959, *4*, 393; Kasdorf 1991; G. W. Peters 1984, 29-39; Rempel 1933, 321; J. J. Toews 1967, 145-148).

In Russia the emphasis on evangelism led to the selecting of itinerant evangelists and preachers called *Reiseprediger* (traveling preachers), who evangelized fellow Mennonites. Before long a few hardy souls overcame their fear of violating the non-proselytism clause of their *privilegium* and began to also share the Good News with their Russian and tribal neighbors. Among these, names like Johann Wieler (J. J. Toews 1959, *4*, 948) and Adolf Reimer stand out. Throughout its history evangelism and missions have remained major emphases of the Mennonite Brethren Church (H. S. Bender 1956, *2*, 270; P. G. Hiebert 1988, 75-82; A. E. Janzen 1966; H. H. Janzen 1959, *4*, 393; J. H. Lohrenz 1957, 598; J. A. Toews 1975a, 92-94).

The *Bundeskonferenz*

Probably one of the most positive developments and certainly one of the greatest attractions of the new church was the early development in 1872 of the General Conference of Mennonite Brethren Churches, first called the *Bundeskonferenz* (Covenant conference). *Bundeskonferenz* usually has been translated as "General Conference," but that translation seems to miss the original covenanting intent. This new structure permitted all believers to participate in shaping church policy instead of having it handed down from a consistory of bishops. It represented a truly wholesome move in the direction of the priesthood of all believers. It was so popular that the parent Mennonite church soon found it expedient to adopt it too (H. Ediger 1914). It was clearly modeled on the Blankenburg Allianz-Konferenz (A. Braun-Ibersheim 1938, 11; H. Löwen 1989, 31-35; J. A. Toews 1977, 173).

The Christian unity issue

The early Mennonite Brethren were very concerned about unity versus purity, particularly in connection with the communion observance. They considered all members of the existing Mennonite churches to be unredeemed, and refused to have communion with them. They did, however, permit Baptists and Pietists to share the Lord's Supper with them. In fact, Adolph Ehrt has asserted that the Mennonite Brethren became "de-Mennonitized" under these outside influences.

If the Mennonite Brethren had wanted to have broader fellowship, it would have seemed most appropriate for them to have joined hands with the budding alliance movement among the revived Mennonites in Russia. In fact, an actual Mennonite Alliance Church movement was not formally launched until 1905. This movement never became strong, but Mennonite Brethren historian P. M. Friesen gave his loyalty to it. Now more recently, except for membership in the National Association of Evangelicals in the U.S. and the Evangelical Fellowship of Canada, the Mennonite Brethren have continued to avoid ecumenical associations ("Baptisten oder nicht?," 1901, 23; Ehrt 1932, 59; John B. Toews 1982, 26).

A weakened peace position

The Baptists and Pietists who influenced the 1860 renewal movement came from traditions that saw military service as a Christian obligation. In fact, in the case of Pastor Karl Benzien (J. J. Toews 1955, *1*, 275), there seems to have been a conscious effort to counteract the Mennonite ideal of *Gewaltverzicht* (abstinence from the use of force).

In the case of the Temple Mennonite Church, the Pietist "sword" ideals were quickly carried to full fruition and this group's taking of the sword in its own self-defense during the 1917-18 revolution became its undoing in Russia (Krahn 1970, 173; H. Sawatzky 1955).

The eschatological hope

The assurance that Jesus Christ would soon return has always sustained suffering Christians, including the Mennonite Brethren, in a wide variety of difficult circumstances. It also has frequently served as the basis for calls to fidelity and more dedicated discipleship. Due to the Blankenburg Conference influence, however, this hope became hostage to the dispensationalism of Plymouth Brethren Bible teacher, John Nelson Darby. This seriously undercut the Anabaptist/Mennonite focused canon and Christ-centered exegesis of the Scripture because certain passages were now assigned to specific dispensations. The exegetical community became severely inhibited, for only dispensational experts could be trusted to know which passages belonged to which dispensations. For example, Cyrus Ingerson Scofield, a renowned North American dispensationalist and editor of the famous Scofield Reference Bible, assigned the Sermon on the Mount to a future kingdom (A. J. Klassen 1965; J. A. Toews 1975a, 378).

The dramatic dated conversion

Even though Mennonites now are calling Anabaptism a "conversionist movement" (Brunk 1990, 5, 205) and Mennonite Brethren are calling conversion a "doorway to discipleship" (Schmidt 1980), the tendency to insist upon a dramatic dated conversion has not been without negative effects. It is true that the negative effects of the dated conversion took even longer than most of the other Pietist influences before its effect could be assessed adequately. There is no question that the early Mennonite Brethren wholeheartedly agreed with Menno Simons (1876, A:327) when he wrote:

> All those who are regenerated through the eternal and saving Word of God, have been changed, born-again and resurrected, so that their hearts and minds now think in terms of what is God-pleasing, what is spiritual and not this-worldly. They are people who seek after that which is eternal, and not that which is temporal. As a result their hearts are where their heavenly treasure is and their walk is one that becomes citizens of heaven and members of God's household.

This was the very experience the new Mennonite Brethren sought (Keeney 1961, 29-32). It became the Mennonite Brethren trademark and most prized emphasis (R. Friedmann 1949, 70; R. Kreider 1951, 30; D. Wiens 1965, 1-28). As long as they lived in relatively closed colonies with extensive face-to-face pressure for a commensurate discipleship, Mennonite Brethren conversion remained close to the early [Menno Simons'] ideal. Once the Mennonite Brethren began to circulate in open societies in modern Europe or America, however, the flaws of the emphasis on an emotional Pietist experience soon became apparent. The Pietist conversion differed from the Anabaptist/Mennonite discipleship commitment in that it was a highly personal, subjective and dated experience, and did not include the same strong emphases on *Nachfolge* (discipleship) (J. L. Burkholder 1957, 135-151) and community (R. Friedmann 1957, 115). Positively stated, the Anabaptist/Mennonite discipleship experience was a deliberate decision to study God's Word in the context of equally committed fellow disciples, to obey this communally discerned truth, and to give and to receive corrective exhortation. Historian Robert Friedmann (1940, 156-157; 1944, 120) suggested that for Anabaptists/Mennonites discipleship is a lifestyle that translates Jesus' words into deeds and that follows Jesus' example; for Pietists, discipleship is verbally preaching the gospel. Some aspects of Friedmann's view have been challenged by Schlabach (1983, 222-229), but in the end he agrees with Friedmann that Pietist gospel hymns and other literature were some of the chief avenues for Pietism's entry into Anabaptism (1983, 222).

On the North American scene this lopsided emphasis on conversion, under the influence of revivalism and evangelicalism, absorbed elements of American individualism (Bellah, et al 1985, 1987) and "cheap grace." As a result conversion now often lacks many of the crucial Anabaptist/Mennonite components, especially discipleship, mutual exhortation and community.

For many conversion-oriented Mennonites today the once-and-for-all-time dated conversion experience means at least a "passing grade" for heaven. While it is hoped that converts will "grow in grace," their ultimate salvation does not really seem to depend on it. As long as they do not die with any major unresolved church-defined "sin," their final entry into glory is assured by the original new birth experience, because that changed them from being "children of Satan" to "children of God."

From the vantage point of history, however, conversion, whether in the original form described by Menno Simons (1876, A:321-331) or in the 1860 Mennonite Brethren ideal described by Delbert Wiens (1965, 1-22), should rather be likened to a declaration of bankruptcy coupled with the declared commitment to make a new beginning. The declaration of bankruptcy releases converts from their past accumulated guilt and spiritual debts and permits them to begin anew. To paraphrase the well-known biblical analogy, conversion marks the person's entrance through the narrow gate, but unless such an entry is followed by a lifetime of narrow-road living and spiritual growth, which Menno Simons called discipleship, the original dated conversion may well terminate in a spiritual miscarriage.

Natural children can, of course, be born out of wedlock, but normally one expects a child to be born into a loving, nurturing nuclear family (and in some societies even a caring extended family) in which the new-born child will be nurtured, enculturated and disciplined. The Anabaptist/Mennonite new-birth ideal likewise foresaw the spiritually newborn as "born" into a loving spiritual church family with nurturing and disciplining functions. In contrast the pietist (in North America, the evangelical) conversion is a purely personal experience that may, but usually does not, include a nurturing context. It certainly carries no expectation of a disciplining context.

Two modern consequences of the personal dated conversion

Two consequences of the emphasis on the pietist-type conversion can be readily observed today. The first is the increased value that the conversion emphasis places on soul-winning, often at the expense of spiritual growth. This tends to align the Mennonite Brethren Church with flashy revivalism and mainstream evangelicalism in America, and which, as a consequence, makes many Mennonite Brethren suspicious of the earlier quiet Anabaptist/Mennonite discipleship and service.

Emphasis on soul-winning

Currently in North America soul-winning has teamed up with two further emphases. One is the evangelical emphasis on numerical increase called "church growth;" the other is the modern western emphasis on professionalism. As a result, Mennonite Brethren churches are hiring more and more pastors both to promote church growth and to provide a team of professionals who will do "professional quality" church work on behalf of a largely spectator congregation. This substitutes the paying salaried professionals for the original Anabaptist ideal of a functioning priesthood of all believers.

Push toward individualism

A second consequence is the way in which the emphasis on individual and personal conversion diminishes converts' resistance to the overwhelming American cultural push toward individualism. This individualism stands in the way of the original Anabaptist/Mennonite emphasis on mutual responsibility (Peck 1987, 52-58; Bellah, et al. 1987). As former closed Mennonite communities gave way to urbanization, most of life became a purely private and personal matter, making brotherly or sisterly admonition between believers increasingly rare.

The above powerful Pietist emphases were never properly reshaped and integrated with the Mennonites' values of discipleship and peace. Had it not been for the military service exemption that the Mennonite *privilegium* afforded, and the fact that becoming non-Mennonites would have meant vacating the Mennonite colonies, there is reason to doubt that the 1860 renewal movement would have been as quick to identify itself as Mennonite (H. Braun 1910, 3-5; J. F. Harms 1896, 3-4; W. Hiebert 1966, 6-7).

Was the Mennonite Brethren renewal a return to Menno Simons?

When one looks at how successfully this renewal movement recaptured the New Testament ideals that Menno Simons and other Anabaptists called for (J. A. Toews 1957, 1-3) one is likely to be disappointed. In spite of one of their earliest names, *Vereinigte Christliche Mennoniten Brüdergemeinde* (United Christian Mennonite Brethren Church), their concern about Christian unity and return to their Anabaptist roots was rather selective. Probably the most successful return to Menno's vision was the revitalizing of the church as an exegetical community. Inspired by Melville, Wüst and the Gnadenfeld example, congregational study of Scripture became a standard characteristic of all Mennonite Brethren fellowships. In regard to the two related features of congregational consensus, decision making and church authority resting in the congregation, their return to Menno was less clear.

Another area in which the Mennonite Brethren returned to the original vision was an equally deep concern about the "pure church." The new Mennonite Brethren believers viewed the larger Mennonite church and colonies as similar to Reformation-era state churches, in which infant baptism made everyone a member. Mennonite adult baptism and church membership had largely become mere rituals for marriage and eligibility to inherit land. The 1860 individual conversion emphasis was a conscious reaction to this casual view of Mennonite church membership. To the Mennonite Brethren Church's credit, their closed community living also emphasized discipleship by insisting that converts' lifestyles reflect the conversion they confessed (Krahn 1968, 223).

The newly-converted Mennonite Brethren first expressed their greatest concern about the pure church in connection with the Lord's Supper. Indeed, it was their independent celebration of communion (after the elder failed to honor their request for a separate communion service) that sparked the first open rift and led to the showdown between the emerging Mennonite Brethren and the mother church.

The Mennonite Brethren emphasized a redemptive approach to discipline similar to that of Menno Simons. They practiced extensive private and group exhortation before deviant individuals were banned or excommunicated, but they did not openly dissociate themselves from the practice of permitting colony discipline to accompany church discipline.

There also was some renewed affirmation of the do-not-go-to-war emphasis, but in regard to Menno's larger concern about renouncing power in all relationships there was only highly selective renewal. They immediately sought Russian governmental protection against the persecution of the contemporary Mennonite church hierarchy and the local Mennonite "state." In so doing they demonstrated that they were not nearly as ready to suffer for their faith as their early ancestors had been. Again, when they got a government land grant and set up their own Mennonite Brethren colony in the Kuban (Toews, Friesen & Dyck 1989), they perpetuated the same commonwealth power structure that had evolved in the mother church.

In regard to the equality of the believers in the church, the Mennonite Brethren tried to bring church government back into the fellowship of believers. In fact they tried to broaden the believers' participation in church government with the institution of a General Conference. Likewise, they soon abolished the institution of eldership in 1909 in Russia and 1920 in North America. This did not, however, eliminate the "elder complex." Individual Mennonite Brethren churches often had powerful individuals, usually ministers, who were bishops in everything but name (I. Block 1990, 28-38; J. A. Toews 1975a, 305).

Since there is no specific mention of peace and discipleship in the Mennonite Brethren Document of Secession, historian Theron Schlabach questions the degree of Mennonite Brethren loyalty to the peace dimension of Menno Simons' vision. Following James Urry's evaluation, Schlabach (1988, 236-237) sees the Mennonite Brethren embarking on the road to individualism at the expense of community, another of the important early Mennonite emphases.

In P. M. Friesen's version of the secession document (1911, 91ff) there are five references to Menno or his works. They are:

1. We are in agreement with our dear Menno . . . on baptism on faith as a seal of faith.

2. Menno Simons' *Fundamentbuch* (part of Simons 1876A) Vol. 1, pp. 115-121.

3. As he proved in his *Fundamentbuch*, Vol. 1, p. 148.

4. Menno's conviction as recorded in Vol. III [sic], pp. 334-335.

5. Finally there is the statement that "in all other articles of faith we are also in accord with Menno Simons" (also see P.M. Friesen 1978, 230-232).

The Emergence of the *Selbstschutz* and the Mennonite Brethren Contribution to it

By far the most tragic departure from *Gewaltverzicht* among Mennonites in Russia was the organization of the self-defense army (*Selbstschutz*) during the Bolshevik Revolution. As John B. Toews (1972, 13) has commented, this episode revealed that not even the very "bottom line" of *Gewaltverzicht*, the abstinence from the use of the sword of war, had developed deep roots in the individual Mennonite's convictions.

Antecedents to the *Selbstschutz*

The *Selbstschutz* episode had several antecedents in Mennonite history in Russia. The first of these took place shortly after 1870, when a minister named Claas Epp began to preach the immediate second coming of Jesus Christ. Epp had a vision that he was to find and to prepare a refuge for the faithful to escape the Great Tribulation (Rev. 3:8-10, 12:14). He interpreted the Russian government's threat to curtail or eliminate the military exemption of the Mennonites as a prelude to the coming tribulation. When Mennonites began to emigrate to America after 1870, Epp disclosed that God had revealed to him that the real deliverance lay not in the West, but in the East. In 1880 he thus led a group called the Philadelphia Church of Revelations into Turkestan (J. Harder 1980, 69-73).

The group wandered for some time, and finally settled in Ak-Mechet with the permission of the Muslim Khan of Khiva. However, predatory tribespeople began to steal their horses and cattle. When one of Epp's followers was killed in a night attack by marauders, the young men demanded permission to acquire weapons. The group also hired some armed local tribespeople to help them with self-defense (C. H. Smith 1941, 454-462).

A second such effort occurred in the Mennonite colony on the Terek River in connection with the 1905 revolution. In 1901 several hundred Mennonite families established a daughter colony at the foot of the Caucasus Mountains along the shore of the Caspian Sea. The surrounding mountains were inhabited by predatory tribes who had been kept back by the Russian army but who were still far from pacified. When the authority of the central government in the region was shaken during the 1905 revolution, these mountain tribes stepped up their harassment of the Mennonite colonists.

From 1905-1908 the Tereker settlers sent innumerable petitions and delegations to the Russian government officials pleading for military protection, but the latter merely replied, "Who invited you here? You would have done well to acquaint yourselves with the region in advance. We cannot help you; help yourself!" (Martin 1991, 1). In desperation the Tereker Mennonites hired Cossack warriors as guards. However, the Cossacks did not like long hours of guard duty. They preferred to burn down villages suspected of harboring thieves. When local politics made further Cossack employment unfeasible, if not impossible, and a wealthy Mennonite, Herman Neufeld, was kidnaped and held for ransom, the Mennonites faced the choice of flight or fight. They chose the latter and began to arm themselves. After several battles and dozens of casualties, the settlers ultimately gave up and returned to Molotschna Colony just in time to experience the emergence of the *Selbstschutz* there.

There seems to have been a third antecedent, namely a secret *Selbstschutz* organized by young Mennonite men in Melitopol. This group got its weapons and training from the Austro-German occupation forces. These armed young men tracked down the attackers of wealthy Mennonite estates on behalf of the estate owners and brought the captured culprits to the German occupation forces for punishment (A. A. Reimer 1930, 36-47; John B. Toews 1972, 15).

The specific causes for the development of the *Selbstschutz*
The immediate political and military circumstances

The treaty of Brest-Litovsk of April 1918, the separate peace-treaty that Russia and Germany signed to terminate their hostilities in World War I, led to the occupation of southern Russia by German and Austro-Hungarian troops. Since the Russian Revolution had already broken out the previous year, the destructive anarchy of bandits and revolutionaries was already in progress. Some of the largest and wealthiest Mennonite estates had already been plundered and their owners had been forced to flee. With the arrival of the Austro-German troops, those whose properties had been seized by revolutionaries now saw an opportunity to regain control. Among them were Mennonites who had come from Germany and Poland after the military exemption there had already been lost and who therefore had served in the Prussian or the Polish military. Some of these people now armed themselves under Austro-German army tutelage, and together with other estate owners organized posses that attacked and sought to retake estates seized by rebels. Interrogating those they captured, they searched out the rebel leaders, whom the occupation army then executed summarily (C. P. Neufeld 1989, 10; Al Reimer 1989, 5, 17; John B. Toews 1972, 15; J. C. Toews 1954, 1 September, 3).

The presence of the occupation army in the colonies, often quartered in Mennonite homes, exposed Mennonite youth to weapons and military force for the first time. Many became deeply enamored with the military precision of the drilling army units. Some accounts speak of young Mennonite men volunteering to join in the training exercises (C. P. Neufeld 1989, 13; John B. Toews 1972, 15; 1967, 26).

The Mennonites actually were a minority among the foreign (even German-speaking) settlers in southern Russia. None of the other Germans—Baptists, Lutherans and Catholics—hesitated to use arms. They eagerly accepted the training and weapons offered by the occupation army. They urged the Mennonites to follow suit so that together they could form a common front against the marauders (B. Dick 1986, 137; C. P. Neufeld 1989, 15).

When the Austro-German army had to withdraw some seven months later, following the signing of the Treaty of Versailles in November of 1918, a serious power vacuum developed in the area surrounding the Mennonite colonies. The White Army (tsarist government forces) in the south and the Bolshevik Red Army coming from the north had been unable to defeat each other. This standoff provided an excellent opportunity for anarchist bandits like Nestor Makhno to loot and plunder the unguarded Mennonite colonies, which lay between the opposing armies (K. Klassen 1913, 2; John B. Toews 1967, 26).

One must not underestimate the impact of the anarchists on the Mennonite psyche (A. Friesen 1913, 2-3; N.F. 1912, 2). As each day brought new stories of bloodshed, looting, raping and killing, one Mennonite is reported to have said: "To rob my possessions is one thing—but they won't touch my wife or my daughter. Then I'll grab the axe I keep handy for that purpose" (B. Dick 1986, 135).

When the Austro-German army withdrew after November 1918, not nearly all the foreign officers and soldiers left. Many stayed behind with quantities of arms and ammunition. These military men were most eager to organize the settlers into a defense force and were able to provide not only training and weapons, but also the officer leadership which such a defense force needed (A. A. Reimer 1930, 42; John B. Toews 1972, 15-16).

The White Army, amassed just south of the Mennonite colonies, was likewise eager to arm the Mennonites in order to augment its strength. It, too, actively lobbied the Mennonites to take up the arms it was ready to provide (B. Dick 1986, 136).

The erosion of Mennonite loyalty to nonresistance

The erosion of Mennonite loyalty to Menno Simons' peace ideals in South Russia has been well documented by scholars Helmut-Harry Loewen and James Urry. As they describe it, the rapid development of the Mennonite colonies and their remarkable prosperity in the second half of the nineteenth century was tragically accompanied by a corresponding erosion of loyalty to Anabaptist/Mennonite ideals of simplicity and peace (J. Dyck 1989). That this erosion affected laity as well as the clergy was brought to light vividly through a young man's question published in the *Odessaer Zeitung* (Y. 1907, 2). He asked, "Why do Mennonites employ Cossacks?" The young man wanted to know if hiring armed Cossacks to protect Mennonite property was not a sign of lack of confidence in God. He then answered his own question by suggesting that one could hardly expect God to be concerned about protecting anyone's property (*Ein ins-Leben-* . . . 1907, 3).

This young man's question sparked several responses in subsequent issues of the newspaper. One respondent, most likely a minister, quoted many Bible verses suggesting that a Christian had a duty to protect family and property, especially if such property was necessary for the sustenance of life. This obviously no longer reflected Menno Simons' view of the Christian attitude toward property.

An estate owner's response (*Ein Gutsbesitzer* 1907, 2), meanwhile, showed how firmly Mennonites were committed to law and order and the extent to which they had aligned themselves with landowning Russian nobility. With the latter they denounced the unreliable (Russian) peasants and serfs as always demanding more than they deserved. While strongly favoring the defense of property and the upholding of law and order, the estate owner recognized inherent dangers in this stance. Once one begins protecting property with the sword, it is logical to use armed force to recover stolen goods and maybe even to take punitive action against the thieves. And once you engage in punitive action, you are well on the way to also making preemptive strikes against potential aggressors. This estate owner probably did not realize how prophetic his observations were. Loewen and Urry (1991, 34-53) suggest that once law and order collapsed at the end of World War I, in South Russia, the emergence of the *Selbstschutz* was almost inevitable, given the prevailing attitudes.

The immediate impact of returning alternative service men

In the forestry camps and on the medical, service trains-young Mennonite men had worn military-type uniforms and operated under a rigid discipline much like the army itself. Some strong leaders emerged among them. They quickly became a challenge to the parochial and sometimes lax leadership in the churches and villages. In a number of instances these returnees were able to wrest leadership from their elders. This resulted in a drastic lowering of the age of the overall colony leadership (*Die Mennoniten-Gemeinden in Russland* 1921, 54-55). These younger leaders were appalled at the growing anarchy and were determined to stem the tide. They thus not only influenced public opinion, but actually formed the core of the volunteers for restoring law and order. It seems ironic that their alternative service experience had prepared them to wage "war" (Ehrt 1932, 114).

The Mennonite Brethren biblical justification for the *Selbstschutz*

The Mennonite Brethren shared the reactions of the Mennonite colonists in general. However, they seem to have made their own specific contributions to the development of the *Selbstschutz*. The powerful Pietist and Baptist influences that helped spawn the Mennonite Brethren renewal movement introduced ideas and allegiances that downgraded Mennonite peace principles. Pietism largely replaced the earlier Anabaptist values of discipleship, tolerance and community with an emphasis on an emotion-charged individual conversion and on soul-winning (Ehrt 1932, 59).

Mennonite Brethren loyalties to the Pietists and Baptists often outweighed their loyalty to their fellow Mennonites. Anguished letters published in the *Odessaer Zeitung* ("*Was sind die Mitglieder der Mennoniten Brüdergemeinde?...,*" 1896, 23; "*Baptisten oder nicht?*," 1901, 23) testify to the growing psychological distance between the Mennonite mainstream and the new Mennonite Brethren Church. One correspondent after another asked, "How can the Mennonite Brethren accept smoking and fighting Baptists as their spiritual brothers and sisters and share communion with them, but treat us, their fellow Mennonites, like 'pagans who must be shunned'?" (H. Löwen 1989, 41-47; R. Kreider 1951, 30; see also F. C. Peters 1959, 176-178; 1969, 2-3; J. A. Toews 1972, 2-4)

The ongoing flow of outside literature and ideas from Pietist and militant German sources into Mennonite Brethren homes and churches promoted not only Pietist spirituality but also German language, nationalism and militarism. John B. Toews has shown that the pietist/ Baptist influence continued long after the Mennonite Brethren secession. The first Mennonite Brethren confession of faith in 1873 drew heavily from a Baptist document (John B. Toews 1988, 136-137; also see H. Löwen 1989, 38-40).

Mennonite Brethren leaders made significant contributions to a meeting in Lichtenau, Molotschna in 1918, called to decide whether or not to organize a *Selbstschutz*. The debate was heated, but B. J. Dick, a young man who attended the meeting, reported that the conference achieved nothing. On the third day it finally passed a tepid resolution not to condemn either those who joined or those who abstained from joining the self-defense effort. More crucial, however, was the discussion that continued even after the resolution had already been adopted (B. J. Dick 1986, 136-137).

During the meetings, ex-German army and White Russian army officers hovered on the fringes anxiously awaiting a positive decision. While the meeting was still in progress word came that the Lutheran villages across the river from Halbstadt had decided to organize themselves into a defense unit. According to B. J. Dick, it was then that the Mennonite Brethren Church's most educated leader, Benjamin H. Unruh, added "the straw which broke the camel's back," by asking whether the Mennonite nonresistance stance was merely "an old church tradition" rather than a fundamental biblical principle. Had not God himself helped Abraham rescue Lot? Didn't David kill Goliath? Didn't Samson kill thousands of Philistine enemies while protecting God's people? (B. J. Dick 1986, 137).

Unruh was not alone. Jacob Reimer and Jacob Friesen, both of whom had received theological training in Germany and who also reflected Blankenburg Conference ideals (which voiced the German Pietist slogan: "When it comes to war then we shoot!"), joined Unruh to support the idea of self-defense (John B. Toews 1977, 78-107). Other Mennonite Brethren voices, like those of Benjamin B. Janz (1956) and Jacob Janzen, pled fervently and even eloquently for strict adherence to *Gewaltverzicht* based on the New Testament, especially Jesus' teaching in the Sermon on the Mount. But their contrary voices failed to carry the day. The door had been opened a crack and the waiting army officers quickly stepped into the opening to call local meetings in Rückenau, Gnadenfeld, Halbstadt, Alexanderthal and other villages to organize Mennonite defense force units. Benjamin H. Unruh and his students at the *Kommerzschule*, the Mennonites' highest educational institution in Russia, now became leaders in the self-defense organization, with Unruh serving as the official chaplain and his students as junior officers (B. J. Dick 1986, 137-138; John B. Toews 1982, 83).

The *Selbstschutz* was now a reality. This marked the end of four hundred years of continued abstinence from armed violence for the northern stream of Mennonites. This new army of some two thousand men tried to defend some seventy Mennonite villages with fifty thousand inhabitants, representing millions of rubles in investment and property. Initially there were some remarkable successes, but before long, especially when the Red Army temporarily joined forces with Makhno's anarchists, the Mennonite effort was doomed. It led to massive retaliation by both the anarchists and the Reds (Ehrt 1932, 114; John B. Toews 1972, 5,17).

Most Mennonites later decried the self-defense effort as a tragic mistake. But did this unfortunate experience succeed in making Mennonites more convinced practitioners of *Gewaltlosigkeit*? Subsequent history shows that Mennonites have remained hopelessly divided on this issue.

MENNONITES IN NORTH AMERICA

To begin this third section on Menno's followers' history, a few observations specific to the North American situation are necessary. First, the study continues its focus on the northern stream of Mennonites. It acknowledges, however, that in the American melting pot, a series of factors begin to increasingly blur that focus. Next, the study of the American story also focuses much more closely on the twelve value pillars of Menno Simon's vision and the concomitant slippages introduced early in the book. Finally, the special focus on the Mennonite Brethren Church is sharpened still more in this section.

The migrations
Several northern-stream groups of Mennonites who came to America earlier seem to have blended completely either into the southern stream of Mennonites or with the American mainstream. Among these are some very early immigrants from Holland who settled in the New York area in 1643 where they are referred to as Mennists (Baasch 1927, 364; H. S. Bender 1957, *3*, 863), a group that left the Hamburg area in about 1700 during a time of local church difficulties, and settled in Pennsylvania (Dollinger & Smissen 1956, 2, 642; M. Driedger 1993, 45), and a group from Prussia who left during the military exemption struggles there (E. G. Kaufman 1956, 2, 469).

An example of blurring on the American scene can be found in connection with the 1874 immigration of the revived Mennonite Brethren, who rejected the merger overtures (F. Epp 1974, 238-241) of the North American Mennonite revival movement that had arisen among the southern stream of Mennonites at about the same time as the Mennonite Brethren emerged in Russia. As a result of this refusal in 1874, some non-revival Mennonite immigrants from Russia, especially those from the more progressive Molotschna Colony and some immigrants from Prussia, accepted the hand of welcome and fellowship of the renewed American Mennonites and merged with the North American revival stream in the General Conference Mennonite Church (E. G. Kaufman 1956, 467, 469). However, neither the Mennonite Brethren nor the General Conference Mennonite churches (L. Harder 1971) have ever equaled the Mennonite Church (as the largest group within the southern stream of Mennonites from the Palatinate, Switzerland and France is commonly called in America) either in size or in influence.

Other non-revival Mennonites from Chortitza Colony in the Ukraine came to Canada en masse in 1874 and settled in the East and West Reserves in southern Manitoba (Epp-Thiessen 1982, 40). They were later joined by many of the *Kleine Gemeinde* people from the Molotschna colony who also had not participated either in the 1860 Brethren revival nor in a similar revival in the Crimea in 1869 that led to the founding of the Krimmer Mennonite Brethren Church (H. S. Bender 1957, *3*, 242-243). These people settled either in Nebraska or in Manitoba (C. Krahn 1957, *3*, 460; D. F. Plett 1985, 1986).

The Krimmer Mennonite Brethren Church also came to America in 1874 and settled either in the Midwestern United States or in Saskatchewan (H. S. Bender 1957, *3*, 243; C. F. Plett 1985).

For a number of decades the Old Colony groups (Krahn 1959, *4*, 38-42), such as the Chortitza Colony people now residing in the two reserves in Manitoba were usually called, maintained their isolation and their not-part-of-this-world stance. When the use of the English language in colony-run schools became an issue in Canada in the early 1920s, several contingents emigrated to Mexico during 1922-1925 (Francis 1955, 109; Fretz 1955, *1*, 645; 1957, *3*, 663-665; H. Sawatsky 1990, *5*, 580-582), and to Paraguay during 1926-1928 (I. Dyck 1970; Fretz 1955, *1*, 645; M. Friesen 1977; W. Smith 1959, *4*, 118). The latter group was joined in 1930 by the bulk of the 1500 Mennonites who had been able to leave Russia in 1929 (A. E. Janzen 1959, 117-120; C. Krahn 1959, *4*, 78) and who now also went to the Chaco, Paraguay to found Fernheim Colony there (H. Duerksen 1990; P. P. Klassen 1988, 1990, 1991; W. Quiring 1936, 1938, 1953). From 1948 to 1952 that part of the *Kleine Gemeinde* which rejected the revival that was then affecting Manitoba Mennonites, moved to Mexico to join the earlier Old Colony immigrants there (H. L. Sawatsky 1990, *5*, 580; Schmiedehaus 1948, 1982).

American melting-pot influences

Several American melting-pot influences led to many common experiences for the various immigrant Mennonite groups. On the inter-Mennonite level there was their cooperation and common service in the relief efforts toward their starving brothers and sisters in Russia through Mennonite Central Committee (hereafter MCC), organized in the aftermath of the first World War (C. J. Dyck, et al 1980a, 1980b, 1980c). Later their common service in MCC projects in other parts of the world provided common bonds. Then there also was their common participation in Civilian Public Service during World War II. This juxtaposition of young men from all Mennonite church groups produced much cross-fertilization of ideas between them. Many lasting personal friendships were formed in these various types of common service. A considerable number of cross-church marriages also resulted. As a result the purity of the originally separate streams of Mennonites has become ever more compromised.

In regard to outside influences, over and above general American culture, there were a multiplicity of impinging religious currents that frequently produced very similar reactions in the otherwise separate Mennonite groups (B. S. Hostetler 1987). Among these influences were the Sunday school movement (H. S. Bender 1959, *4*, 657), the Bible school movement (H. S. Bender 1955, *1*, 332-333), dispensationalism (D. Ewert 1990, *5*, 240-241), millennialism (H. H. Janzen 1955, *1*, 559-560), fundamentalism (H. S. Bender 1956, *2*, 418-419; Cohen 1990), revivalism (H. S. Bender 1959, *4*, 308-310), the Social Gospel (C. J. Dyck 1990, *5*, 832-834) and many more.

The influence of the many Bible institutes (Regehr 1996, 234-235) was very mixed. H.S. Bender (1955 *1*, 331-332) has pointed out that while they increased missionary interest, they became divisive and harmful because they undermined Anabaptist values and promoted evangelicalism and fundamentalism.

For all Mennonite groups in America their heavy exposure to American evangelicalism has been the most problematical of all; for this reason evangelicalism will receive extensive attention both in the current history section and also in the next section containing readers responses.

Historian Frank Epp (1974, 252) has already pointed out that there have been some striking similarities in a number of developments among Mennonites, often thousands of miles apart and even under very different circumstances. For example, the early awakening in South Russia that produced the *Kleine Gemeinde* in 1814 (H. S. Bender 1957, *3*, 196-199) was paralleled by the appearance of Reformed Mennonites in America in 1812 (C. Smith & H. S. Bender 1959, *4*, 267-269). Likewise the organization of the Mennonite Brethren Church in South Russia in January 1860 (J. F. Harms 1924; J. H. Lohrenz 1957, 3, 595-602) had its counterpart in the organization of the General Conference Mennonite Church (E.G. Kaufman 1956, *2*, 465-471) in May of 1860.

CHAPTER 13

American Mennonites: Citizenship and Property

Coming to America

There were, as we have already said, numerous waves of Mennonite migration from Europe to America (Smith 1927). The various waves of the southern stream of Mennonites (H. S. Bender 1957, *3*, 611-616; 1959, *4*, 669-671; *4*, 776-782; Geiser 1931; G. Hein 1959, *4*, 110) are not the focus of this study. The very earliest northern-stream Mennonite groups who came to America seem to have been totally absorbed by other groups, also stated earlier.

Immigration from Russia

Some of the immigrants from Russia, however, have to a degree preserved their separate identity. This was also true in a lesser degree for many of the immigrants from Prussia, now Poland.

In the early 1870s the Russian czar began to renege on the eternal *privilegium* of total exemption from military service given to the Mennonites who had migrated to Russia nearly a century earlier. As soon as the Mennonite colonists became more aware of these new developments, many, especially those who could not accept some form of alternative service to active service in the military on which the Russian government was now insisting (Suderman 1943, 23-46), began to make plans to seek a new home in America (F. Epp 1974, 183; H. Loewen 1989, 127-146). The expressed reason for leaving was the loss of their nonresistant privilege, but we need to recognize that there were other economic factors as well (Flynn & Koop 1992; John B. Toews 1974, 8-14; 1986, 9-14). Several small groups left Russia immediately in 1872-74. After a committee of twelve authorized scouts had visited the new world and brought back a fairly positive report on the possibilities in America, the emigration became a veritable flood, not only from Russia but also from Poland, with some ten thousand immigrants settling in Canada and about eight thousand making a new home in the United States (Smith 1941, 638-39; Leibbrandt 1932, 205-226; 1933, 5-41; G. Lohrenz 1933, 5-41). By 1875 this flow of immigrants had begun to decrease sharply. All in all, more than one third of the fifty thousand Mennonites in Russia emigrated to the new world in this wave (F. Epp 1974, 185; G. Lohrenz 1933, 5-11; Klippenstein 1989, 13-42).

145

On the prairies and plains of North America these new immigrants tried to replicate the entire social and economic structure they had developed in South Russia as closely and as fully as possible. The Canadian scene lent itself to an almost complete replication of the Russian commonwealth system (Epp-Tiessen 1982, 40). That meant that Mennonites also became functional citizens immediately on their arrival in Canada (Ens 1994, 69-88). In the United States, however, such a complete replication of the Russian commonwealth patterns was not feasible. Nevertheless the immigrants functioned as citizens there almost from the day of their arrival (Spaulding 1984).

Since the military exemption situation in Russia remained precarious for quite a period, the migration to America continued in smaller groups sporadically, with a bigger wave coming during the years 1922 to 1927, after which the Russian communist government finally forbade all further emigration from the country. It is estimated that this second exodus involved another twenty thousand individuals (C. Krahn 1959, 4, 391). However, in November of 1929, when some 25,000 Mennonites came to Moscow seeking exit permission, actually only 1500 managed to get that exit permission. The rest were all sent to concentration camps in Siberia in cattle cars (G. Fast 1956, 32-110; 1957; Krahn 1959, 4, 520; 1959, 4, 848). Author Loewen (then seven years old) was in that small group that was able to leave Russia in 1929 (C. C. Peters & H. Willms 1960, 1-148).

In 1943, when the German army had to withdraw from the Ukraine during World War II, many Mennonites from that region accompanied the retreating German forces to Poland and Germany. Of these one-third, or about twelve thousand, were eventually able to emigrate to the Americas during 1945-1948 (C. Krahn 1957, 3, 685; 1959, 4, 391). Of these a substantial number settled in Paraguay, where they were able to perpetuate the Russian commonwealth more or less in its entirety (P. P. Klassen 1988, 348-365).

Two-kingdom citizenship

Russian Mennonites, as longtime citizens of the Mennonite commonwealth there, already took Luther's two-kingdom view for granted. They had lived that way for almost a century. In their daily life, the immigrants had functioned as full-fledged citizens from the day of their arrival in Russia.

When they arrived in the new world, these Mennonites again tried to settle in homogeneous clusters, just as they had lived in Russia (G. Wiebe 1900; B. Unruh 1930-1931, 28-41, 267). These concentrations permitted them to carry on many of their traditional religious and cultural practices, especially in rural areas of the United States, where they could also control the municipal governments and local school boards. In such situations they functioned as citizens immediately on arrival. The same is true of Canada, where their identification with the Quakers gave them automatic military exemption and their isolation permitted the replication of the Russian commonwealth structure (Ens 1994, 70).

Historian James Juhnke (1975, 7) has suggested that the American frontier, with its emphasis on local self-government, seemed so similar to the Russian commonwealth that many Mennonites immediately entered municipal politics and ran for school boards, road commissioners and justices of the peace (J. Redekop 1972b; 1983, 79-105). Thus the 1870s immigrants lost their political isolation locally in a mere ten years and at the state level in twenty years (Juhnke 1975,7ff).

Exemption from military service

The Mennonite immigrants from Russia (1870-1884) had already abandoned Menno Simons' only-the-sword-of-the-Spirit lifestyle long ago in Europe. They were left only with a deep concern to be totally exempt from any military service. At least that was why they said they were leaving Russia and emigrating to the recently-opened Midwestern states like Kansas, Nebraska and Minnesota. But as Juhnke (1975, 12) has pointed out, these Mennonites either were very naive or they completely failed to understand the American democratic system. Those who settled in Kansas mistakenly assumed that exemption from service in the national guard meant they would have total exemption from military service in the United States (Prentis 1889, 1909; D. Wiebe 1959, 6).

When the official Mennonite delegation from South Russia arrived in America in 1873, they went to Washington to negotiate immigration privileges. Their petition to President Ulysses S. Grant (Grant 1871, 301ff; 1873, 253ff; Richardson 1904-1910) on August 8, 1873 included a request for exemption from military service and control of their own schools. Grant was sympathetic but informed the delegation that such exemptions required an act of Congress. He assured them, however, that no war was foreseen, and no compulsory draft was in effect or contemplated. The Mennonite petition, in the form of a bill, was debated in Congress, but eventually was shelved and never brought up again (Correll 1935, 147; L. Harder 1949, 55-65; C. Hiebert 1974, 65; Hofer 1931, 216; Krahn 1949, 8-9).

Meanwhile an entirely separate and private effort to secure exemptions was underway. Cornelius Jansen, his son Peter, and J. B. Wood, a Quaker, visited President Grant on November 4, 1873 to present him with a petition (Jansen 1921). The two Russian Mennonites were shocked at the "ordinariness" of the president and the secretary of state. In Russia officials always wore uniforms and medals and had appropriately dressed armed guards. Audiences with them were highly formal affairs. Here all the officials were friendly and informal. The Jansens were disappointed that the president would not make a personal decision like the tsar had always done. Their desire was for a personal presidential concession that did not involve Congress. This illustrates Juhnke's contention that Mennonites did not understand the American system. The president received them well and gave them the same assurances he had given the earlier delegation, but ultimately nothing had changed. There was no special national military exemption privilege for Mennonites in the U.S. (Reimer & Gaeddert 1956, 87-90; Juhnke 1975, 12).

In Canada, where laws like the Militia Act of 1757 already exempted Quakers, Mennonites and Tunkers from bearing arms, this exemption was readily granted in an Order-in Council dated April 26, 1873 (F. Epp 1974, 51; C. Hiebert 1974, 27, 44). Many Mennonites settled on recently-vacated Indian lands in Manitoba—the so-called East and West Reserves (C. Redekop 1980, 71-90). Since they were permitted to operate their own schools in the German language, they saw no need to take the citizenship question seriously. Soon, however, their locally-born children would become Canadian citizens by birth (A. J. Dueck 1994; F. Epp 1974, 51; C. Hiebert 1974, 27, 44).

U.S. Mennonites in World War I

Given the initial confusion about their military status, it is hardly surprising that when the United States belatedly entered WWI, that neither the government nor the Mennonites were prepared to handle their conscientious objections to war. As a result many Mennonite men of draft age underwent severe testing. In the absence of an overall government policy, each regional military commander did what was right in his own eyes. Hundreds of Mennonites were placed in military detention. Many of them were sentenced to prison by military courts, with sentences ranging from one year to life. James Juhnke identified 504 Mennonite conscientious objectors and noted that about two-thirds of the draftees were sentenced to ten, fifteen and twenty-five-year prison terms. Only one was totally acquitted. Most of the condemned young men were pardoned as soon as the war ended (F. Epp 1974, 396; Juhnke 1989, 276).

At the height of this widespread sentencing of conscientious objectors (Schlissel 1968; Sibley & Jacob 1952), some relief appeared. Secretary of War, Newton D. Baker, influenced by the acute shortage of farm labor, permitted all conscientious objectors still held in detention camps to be sent out as farm laborers. Of conscientious objectors held in camp, 60 percent were sent to work on farms, 30 percent remained in detention camps and a handful were sent to do relief work in France (F. Epp 1974, 396; Hartzler 1922).

North American Mennonites in World War II

One would expect Mennonites in North America to have learned from World War I that they needed to be prepared for such contingencies. It seems, however, that they accepted the general line of wishful thinking that this had been the "war to end all wars."

Even though the United States proclaimed its neutrality in September 1939, it began to supply arms to Britain and prepared a peacetime draft bill. This prompted Mennonite Central Committee—which had maintained some contact with the US government even in peacetime—to send a delegation of Mennonites with a plan for action to President Franklin Roosevelt. By September 1940, when a military draft was authorized by Congress, it also passed the Burke-Wadsworth Bill, generally called the Selective Service Act. The result was Civilian Public Service (CPS), an alternative service program for conscientious objectors to war. From 1941 to 1947 some 11,996 conscientious objectors served in CPS. Of this total 4,665 were Mennonites. Many of these men developed leadership skills in the CPS camps and became postwar leaders in Mennonite churches and Mennonite Central Committee (U. Bender 1969; M. Gingerich 1949; 1957, 262-274; R. Kreider 1991, 4-11; Prieb 1990, 94-98).

During World War II, just twenty-some years after the Russian *Selbstschutz* debacle, one still found the Mennonites ambivalent about how to express their concern for peace. It seems the overwhelming identification of peace concerns with the refusal to bear arms in war had made their peace principles largely irrelevant during the interim. James Juhnke suggested Mennonites in America have even debated whether their peace position should in fact extend beyond the refusal to go to war and have several times consciously decided to limit it to just that (Juhnke 1989, 294).

As a result of this ambivalence, 54 percent of all North American Mennonite young men chose active military service during World War II instead of going into alternative service, which both U.S. and Canadian laws permitted. Canada not only provided Civilian Public Service in the forestry camps, it also opened a noncombatant medical corp under military auspices, similar to that of Russia in World War I. The Mennonite Brethren Church had only about 30 percent of its young men opt for active military service, somewhat better than the Mennonite average (J. A. Toews 1975, 350-360).

Why North American Mennonites are still so ambivalent about *Gewaltlosigkeit*

There has been a tremendous revival of interest in Anabaptist/Mennonite values, including peace principles, in Mennonite colleges and seminaries since Harold S. Bender launched the rediscovery of the "Anabaptist Vision" (Keim & Stoltzfus 1988). Why has this not helped Mennonites make peace a more prominent value in their daily and church life? At least three problems seem to paralyze some Mennonite groups when it comes to teaching and practicing peace in peace time. They are: the separation of *Gewaltlosigkeit* from the core of the gospel, the tendency to see military exemption as a privilege of "ethnic" Mennonites, and the fear of peace activism.

The separation of *Gewaltlosigkeit* from the core of the gospel

Clarence Bauman (1968, 38) has asserted that for early Anabaptists *Gewaltlosigkeit* was the premise that permitted these disciples of Jesus to witness boldly and that then also validated their Christian witness. But more recent Mennonites have not only separated peace from the message of conversion, but they have often treated it as unimportant for non-Mennonites, even when the latter were converts of Mennonite evangelism. A personal story illustrates this reality. We were on our way to Colombia as missionaries. We had packed our trunks, had said our good-byes, had received the blessing of our home church and had begun traveling toward the Hillsboro mission office for our final instructions. On an intermediate stop we were seen off by a long-time mission board member who gave us his final words of advice. Most of what he said met our expectations, but one thing jolted both of us severely. He said in German, "*Aber die Wehrlosigkeit, die lasst nur zu Hause, die hat dort keine Anwendung*" (But nonresistance, you had better leave at home, it has no application over there).

In 1950, Mennonite Central Committee convened a meeting in Winona Lake, Indiana, with representatives from all the Mennonite mission boards and proposed that Mennonites begin a joint peace witness as part of their overseas evangelism (Council of Mission Board

Secretaries: 1958, minutes). The Mennonite Brethren representatives, joined by some Mennonite Church delegates, immediately expressed opposition. Nonetheless, the recommendation was approved by the majority and the peace emissaries were appointed to serve alongside the "regular" missionaries of the four Mennonite mission boards then serving in Japan.

No sooner had the appointment taken place, the Mennonite Brethren began a campaign of opposition against these emissaries. In an effort to resolve the dispute, the peace missionaries returned from Japan and went directly to Hillsboro, Kansas, to meet with Mennonite Brethren mission representatives. The Mennonite Brethren correctly argued that peace should not be separated from the gospel witness and the total discipling process. They insisted that separate non-Mennonite Brethren peace missionaries in their Mennonite Brethren mission fields in Japan were creating a wrong dichotomy for young believers. Mennonite Central Committee then offered to discontinue its peace missionaries, provided that the mission boards would incorporate the peace witness into their discipling process.

But MCC soon realized that the mission boards were not, in fact, including the peace witness in their overseas work. For this reason MCC proposed a Joint Mission of Christian Testimony at the 1958 Council of Mission Board Secretaries (J. D. Graber 1950). Again, the Mennonite Brethren served notice that they would not participate. Furthermore, they argued that MCC was going beyond its mandate with the proposal. However, all the mission boards together agreed that the peace witness was an integral part of the gospel, and made a "statement of repentance," admitting that they had fallen far short in their witness to it. MCC in turn again offered to withdraw its peace missionaries from Japan if mission boards would now act upon their repentance. It was only then that the Mennonite Brethren delegates expressed their real concern: they feared that openly identifying peace issues with the message of evangelism would seriously reduce the number of converts (J. A. Loewen 1988, 4-5; also see J. D. Graber 1950; 1957, 152-166).

The tendency to see the military exemption as reserved for "ethnic" Mennonites

In 1963 author Loewen had a six-month Mennonite Central Committee assignment in Paraguay. He observed an intense ongoing debate about whether native Paraguayan and tribal Indian converts of Mennonite mission efforts were entitled to seek exemption from military service. The matter came to a head when the MCC Peace Section appointed a person to spearhead the teaching of peace principles to "non-ethnic" converts in the various mission efforts of North American and local Mennonite churches. The overall Mennonite feeling was that peace was not a thing to be taught to Paraguayans and Indians. Mennonite leaders said without hesitation that if Paraguayan converts would claim the right to refuse to bear arms, it would endanger the privilege of "ethnic Mennonites." MCC was forced to stop encouraging the teaching of peace to Paraguayans and indigenous Indians.

The fear of peace activism

Some facets of culture refuse to die easily. Even though most North American Mennonites today are in or very close to the mainstream of American culture, when it comes to protest for "conscience" sake they still like to think of themselves as "the quiet in the land" (Stayer 1990-1991, 24-37). They are troubled by those who demonstrate in front of military and nuclear installations. They are suspicious of those who withhold the military portion of their federal taxes (Hopkins 1985, 247-262). They are dubious about civil disobedience in the name of peace. They question the propriety of strident public condemnations of certain government actions, even though they may personally feel embarrassed about what the government is doing. Some even wonder why they feel that way. Maybe the real reason is that most Mennonites have never really learned to practice peace at home, at work, or even in church. Obviously most Mennonites are no longer aware that Menno Simons insisted on an only-the-sword-of-the-Spirit lifestyle in all of life, and certainly no less in times of peace.

Recently the Mennonite Brethren ambivalence about peacetime *Gewaltlosigkeit* (H. Loewen 1989, 127-146) came into focus again when MCC spearheaded the idea of establishing Mennonite peacemaking teams (D. K. Friesen 1986; also see: Churches like Christian peacemaker teams. . . 1987, *1*, 5-8; Christian peacemaker teams. . . 1988, 5), which would go to local or international trouble spots and serve as reconcilers (D. K. Friesen 1986; R. Kraybill 1980; Kraybill & Brubaker 1988). Once again the Mennonite Brethren Church opposed the joint effort and finally withdrew officially from all involvement in such peacemaking efforts ("Churches like Christian . . . " 1987, 1,8; "Peace Section Urged. . ." 1987, 1-2; Ruth-Heffelbower 1991; J. E. Toews 1986a). In spite of this type of opposition, a number of efforts at demonstrating peacetime peace efforts were launched under MCC auspices, e.g., reconciliation efforts (Bontrager 1987; R. Kraybill 1980; Kraybill & Brubaker 1988, 4-7; Mediating Inter-personal. . .n.d.; Zehr n.d.), help in times of disaster (K. Wiebe 1976), helping the underprivileged and the abused

(Jackson 1981), working against racism and sexism (Ruether 1972), mutual aid (C. J. Dyck 1970, 155-197; Fretz 1964, 154-156; 1970, 1-35; 1975, 5-7; P. J. Klassen 1970, 551-568), correcting environmental abuse (Kroeker 1989, 1-4; Kritzinger 1991, 4-19; McDonagh 1986, McHarg 1973, 171-186, Olivier 1991, 20-32; C. Redekop 1986, 387-403, Santmire 1985), in liberation theology (Ruether 1972; Yoder 1988, 338-350), etc.

CHAPTER 14

Social Class and Wealth

The Anabaptist ancestors of the northern stream of American Mennonites were heavily shaped by their European experience. They had all begun with the ideal of being citizens of only the Kingdom of God and ideally they strove for an internal society of equals in which even the clergy/laity distinction would be absent. Class distinction based on wealth or education or whatever, were definitely taboo on the basis of their reading of Scripture.

Economically, while on the whole rejecting the communal ownership of the Hutterites (Rideman 1950, 1970), they visualized a society of stewards of property that was shared among all its members, especially with the needy, both inside and outside of the believing community (Fretz 1957, 194-201). These ideals, however, had already been violated with increasing frequency in Holland (Brons 1891, 156; Mueller 1887, 53, 127), in Germany (A. Fast 1947, 6; B. C. Roosen 1887, 3; Sutter 1982, 117), and in Poland (W. Mannhardt 1863, 56). In South Russia, as our study has shown, a class-structured society became an express goal of those who exercised colony control (Görz 1993, 131; Reimer & Gaeddert 1956, 13). Currently in North America this distinction is reflected in a de facto church segregation, in that certain congregations are known for their wealthy members, while others have more "ordinary" members.

Early Mennonites were both urban and rural. The former were involved in business, shipping and trade, while the latter were largely peasant farmers and artisans. During their Prussian/Polish sojourn the urban Mennonites represented only a small minority in the cities of Danzig, Königsberg and Elbing. In Prussia/Poland, South Russia and in early America the majority have always been land-based. Farmers might develop sideline trades like blacksmithing, house building, furniture making or distilling, but their linkage to the soil remained fundamental. Thus in the early 1900s most Mennonites in North America were still land-based. This continued without much change in the United States until World War I and in Canada largely until World War II. Of the Canadian Mennonites, Ted Regehr says: ". . .in 1939 [they] were still simple, rural and agricultural people who sought to separate themselves as much as possible from outside influences and to build their own communities, churches, and families in the way that Jesus and the Scriptures taught" (Regehr 1996, 31; also see C. Redekop 1985b, 83-84). From then on their residence and work patterns began to change rapidly and fundamentally. They abandoned their colony-type isolation, they forsook their Anabaptist distinctives, and swiftly began to merge with the North American mainstream, especially the evangelical center (Redekop, Ainley and Siemens 1995; Regehr 1996, 126-127).

The loss of the "stewards only" ideal

Urbanization, education, professionalization and the rapid increase in prosperity soon revealed a deep conflict between the earlier Anabaptist "stewards only" philosophy and the Mennonites' current life-style (J. Redekop 1985, 54-59). The hard sayings of Jesus about wealth were now "theologically softened" by talking about "responsible" stewardship and church giving (Driedger 1990a; Regehr 1996, 193).

From the 87 percent rural farm population in 1941, they quickly moved to the cities until in 1991 the urban-rural statistics were completely reversed—the 87 percent were now urban (Regehr 1996, 126 and Fig. 6.1, 127).

In their rather comprehensive 1970 study of Mennonites, Kauffmann and Harder (1975) discovered that about 35 percent of American Mennonites already lived in urban centers with populations of 2,500 or more. By the end of the 1980s the shift to urban residence had reached at least 50 percent. Meanwhile, the number of farms declined from 25 percent in 1970 to 15 percent in 1980 (Kauffmann & Driedger 1991, 27-29). The specific application of the previous study to the Mennonite Brethren was made in a separate study (J. B. Toews, Konrad & Dueck 1985, 3-42; also see Vogt 1980, 137-148).

This shift in residence thrust Mennonites directly into the modern urban marketplace. Here they faced a host of new opportunities to stray from the narrow road of the Anabaptist "stewards only" ideal. Since 1945 Canadian Mennonites began their rapid professionalization (Regehr 1996, 166-168 quoting L. Driedger 1993, 304-322), social-class change and class differentiation (H. M. Martens 1977), and immersion in capitalism, (Redekop 1985a, 95-107).

Already during the commonwealth period (after 1880) in Russia when Mennonite colonies introduced internal property taxes to pay for their alternative service expenses, the very wealthy did not always provide accurate figures of their actual property worth. If this already happened internally, one can readily imagine that the temptation to cut corners would be even greater when Mennonites began to participate in the public market place and moved into different social classes in America (Urry 1989a, 116).

The rest of this chapter will focus on the Mennonite community in lower British Columbia in Canada (largely Mennonite Brethren with a much smaller contingent of General Conference Mennonites and only a smattering of Old Mennonites) in the post-World War II era and detail some economic and social developments after Mennonites in this specific region had largely given up subsistence farming during the World War II wartime boom and had become urban professional, trades and business people (L. Driedger 1993, 304-322).

The overall Mennonite community in North America has been diagramed in its diversity (Redekop, Ainley & Siemens 1995, 12-13), studied in its socio-economic aspects by Kauffman and Harder (1975; also see R. Loewen 1983; H. M. Martens 1977) and restudied some fifteen years later by Kauffman and Driedger (1991). These studies have already adequately described the shifts in residence, profession and economic and social values. The entrepreneurship of Mennonites has been adequately treated by Redekop, Ainley and Siemens (1995, 1-195; also see C. Kreider 1980, J. G. Toews 1974, 199-228). This study will not attempt to replicate any of the aforementioned efforts and will instead focus on some of the worldview and ethical standard changes that have taken place in this area in recent local Mennonite experience.

One also needs to underscore that both the changes documented in the previous studies and in this present effort represent a dramatic shift from the original Anabaptist stewardship (J. D. Graber 1957, 163) view of property and possessions to one of "possessive individual ownership" (J. A. Reimer 1988, 20; also see A. Dueck 1985, 50-53). This shift has been rather universal and rather comprehensive. There are no more Mennonite subsistence farmers left in the Fraser Valley. Mennonites now are engaged in professions, trades and entrepreneurship. The aim of Mennonites in the Fraser Valley now is to "get ahead" and to accumulate personal wealth, but not without a certain degree of unease (Redekop, Ainley & Siemens 1995, 27, 29). Mennonite millionaires are now commonplace in the region. In fact, during the sharp economic downturn in the early 1980s several churches had to organize special Sunday school classes for bankrupt millionaires, especially building developers. One church had a class of twenty-five and another a class of fifteen.

During this study, author Loewen interviewed in great detail about fifteen builders, real estate developers, real estate brokers and factory owners who had all been schoolmates of his when he grew up in the Fraser Valley half a century ago. This study of the local Mennonite scene makes one painfully aware of the dramatic shifts Mennonites have undergone during the recent past. It shows that their ethical accommodation to North American business practices has not only involved the noble and good, but also some of the less desirable traits.

The temptations of the marketplace

The major temptations that faced Mennonites entrepreneurs in the marketplace can be classified as: (1) legal, but not necessarily ethical, (2) probably less than legal, and (3) clearly illegal. Unhappily, modern Mennonites have, on occasion, succumbed in all three areas. The examples cited are all actual, regardless of the form of their literary presentation. To protect the anonymity of those who provided information on the basis of longstanding friendship, no names, dates or places have been mentioned.

Legal, but not necessarily ethical

The more laws a society has, the more loopholes individuals will discover as clever people seek to find their way around them. Among them are a number of practices that are basically legal, but not necessarily ethical.

Foreclosure

Lending money and then foreclosing when the debtor is unable to repay is not a North American invention, even in Mennonite experience. It was used already by Mennonites in Prussia in the Werder area to get control of several *coelmer* villages. Mennonites advanced money to Lutheran farmers in those villages and when the latter were unable to repay, they took over the farms one by one (Baerg 1977, 14-18).

This mechanism was also used in North America by some monied Mennonites. When it is used by a realtor, it can become an effective way to build wealth. For example, an apartment building owner has a big mortgage, which he pays off from his rental income. When the rental economy suddenly hits a slump, and his occupancy rate falls and rental income drops below his mortgage payments, he needs outside cash to meet the deficiency. Here a second mortgage can be a lifesaver. But, should the rental economy not improve quickly and he again falls behind on his payments, the second mortgage holder can foreclose, pay out the original mortgage and become the new owner. If the second mortgage holder is a realtor, very often the real estate commission itself is enough to buy out the previous owner's equity once the property has been remortgaged. On the other hand, foreclosure by banks and other lending agencies have also wiped out a lot of Mennonite real estate developers in the Fraser Valley of British Columbia. As already said earlier, during the market downturn in the latter 1970s and early 1980s several larger churches had Sunday classes made up of only bankrupt millionaires.

Bankruptcy

Declaring bankruptcy is a legal way to walk out of an impossible debt situation (Sutherland 1991). But it can also wipe out a person, because all assets are used to pay off the various creditors. Many elderly Mennonites have been seriously hurt financially when they invested with fellow Mennonites whom they trusted, but who then found themselves forced to declare bankruptcy.

A single bankruptcy does not necessarily imply impropriety or under-the-table deals. But when a person goes through several bankruptcies, then the repeated use of this legal mechanism becomes suspect.

When bankrupt persons emerge shortly after their collapse and quickly climb to previous equity levels, then suspicion grows that some money was secreted away beyond the reach of creditors. This, of course, is not legal. Bankruptcy laws demand full disclosure of all assets at the time of bankruptcy.

To their credit, a number of Mennonites who have gone under in bankruptcy have made serious efforts to repay all their former creditors once they were able to recover following a new beginning.

Taking advantage of naivete, ignorance and emotional distress

This can include a wide variety of circumstances. Victims often share part of the blame or responsibility; after all they are adults who should properly assess the situation. If they fail to do so, there is no legal recourse.

For example, a developer had been using a certain building contractor for several projects. A mutual trust had grown between them. The developer now produced a new set of plans and asked the contractor to build it for him on a per-square-foot basis. The contractor, without much investigation, agreed. In order to meet the mortgage application requirements, the developer asked the contractor to sign a "white contract." Usually this paper simply states that the contractor promises to build the building according to blueprint specifications. But this specific white contract also specified "the supplying of adequate plumbing and heating."

Even before he began building, the contractor realized he had underbid. Instead of just forfeiting his deposit he spoke to the developer about several new items he had not noticed earlier in the building plans and that would make profit next to impossible for him. The developer and the builder then made a gentleman's agreement, with the developer promising to make good any reasonable overruns. And he did! However when next winter's first cold spell arrived, the heating in the building proved to be grossly inadequate. The builder realized that on the basis of the white contract he was now legally responsible. Neither he nor the developer had arranged for a heating engineer to approve the plans. The contractor had assumed this had been done by the developer. The developer, meanwhile, had known that the heating was inadequate for emergencies, but hoped he could get by with it. The building contractor was financially ruined installing an adequate heating system. He had been blinded by naive trust. When he talked to the developer's lawyer about it, the latter merely shrugged and said, "You have just learned that not everything that's legal is necessarily ethical."

Another example might be when someone is under extreme emotional stress, such as after the death of a spouse. The survivor wants to be free of the business the couple had operated and accepts the first offer no matter how low. The Mennonite purchaser realizes a profit many times the amount paid but does nothing to share the windfall with the seller. Obviously the seller was very naive, but the Mennonite clearly took advantage of the seller's weakened emotional state. This may well have been legal, but it certainly was not ethical.

Taking advantage of trades and contractors

Mennonite developer X decided not to use any of his own money in building projects, and to depend solely on mortgage installment payouts to pay his suppliers, workers and sub-contracting trades. Every worker or supplier had to wait for the next mortgage payout to get paid. If the amount of mortgage money received did not cover all the debts, each one got only a percentage with the promise to pay the rest later. Should the developer in the end overrun the amount of the mortgage, he just left a percentage of his debts unpaid. Obviously word got around so that eventually this builder no longer found trusting workers or trade bidders on his new projects. But the approach worked long enough to launch this builder on his way to becoming a multimillionaire.

Not necessarily legal
Kickbacks

In kickbacks the person making the contract with a supplier or contractor gets some personal advantage for choosing a specific bidder. For example, a builder of several highrise apartment buildings might build his own residence or some "for-sale" houses at the same time he is building the highrises. All the bidders, from form-builders to suppliers of curtains, agree to outfit not only the apartment buildings but—at no extra cost—the builder's side project as well. The builder thus gets a free house or houses that he can turn into additional personal profit. In private business kickbacks seldom attract much attention, but when a public official engages in the practice, the consequences can be serious.

Bribes

Bribes, of course, are the other side of kickbacks. In fact, kickbacks could be considered bribes paid by the suppliers. Bribes can range from a free weekend at a resort to large sums of undocumented money paid to get a contract or facilitate some kind of special deal.

Definitely illegal

A developer who always sold portions of a given venture to other investors demanded that his building contractors supply him with inflated cost invoices, while he paid out only the actual costs. By using the inflated invoices for his investment partners this developer was able to accumulate enormous equities in properties at no cost to himself. His fellow investors always wound up paying for his share of the investment. The tax department finally caught up with him.

Another illegal practice, somewhat related, is double-bookkeeping—one set of books for the creditors and another for the tax office. A Mennonite merchant who was losing money in his implement business did this. He trusted that a sharp upturn in business would help him pay off his debts so he could go back to single bookkeeping. However, he went under before he could recover.

Cheating on income tax is another ploy not unknown to some heirs of Menno Simons. This temptation afflicts not only businesspeople but other self-employed people and even some wage earners. An older minister who became the confidante of many dying Fraser Valley Mennonites finally moved away from the community because he could no longer handle all the deathbed confessions of this nature.

While the abuses described do not represent all Mennonites, they indicate the degree to which some have strayed from Menno Simons' vision. While they may claim to hold a theology of peace, they have not applied its implications to the economics of the public marketplace. Redekop, Ainley and Siemens (1995, 178) have observed that North American Mennonite entrepreneurs display many of the same characteristics exhibited by the wealthy in South Russia. They soon feel uncomfortable in rural Mennonite churches and move to cosmopolitan areas (G. Epp 1989b, 239-260). They withdraw from the day-to-day scrutiny that the rural Mennonite communities still practice. Many of them eventually found their spiritual and intellectual stimulation outside of Mennonite churches and communities.

The Canon and the Congregation

Early Anabaptists joined Luther in their devotion to *Sola Scriptura* (Scripture alone) motto (P. Yoder 1988, 73), but as noted previously, they differed from him both in their view of the canon and the locus of Scripture interpretation (Poettcker 1964, 110-111; Kuiper 1967, 223-234; Wenger 1957, 167-179).

The early Anabaptists/Mennonites adhered to a focused canon with Jesus Christ as the center. Jesus' life and teaching were the prism through which all Scripture was to be interpreted (J. A. Toews 1975b, 17-20). The responsibility for the interpretation of Scripture, meanwhile, rested with the congregation rather than in the hands of preachers or theologians, as Luther insisted. The congregation was also the seat of governance. Its officers, called servants, merely carried out the wishes of the congregation under the direction of God's Spirit. The congregational assembly made its decisions in exegesis and in the choice of servants by means of group consensus. Once consensus was reached, it had the force of law. All members were duty bound to obey these decisions by translating the precepts gleaned into a daily life of discipleship. But just as in Europe, these original ideals were also weakened or undermined over time among the Mennonites in North America (Poettcker 1964, 112).

Losing the "focused" view of the canon

Early Mennonite immigrants to North America intentionally settled in homogeneous clusters. These concentrations, especially during the earlier pioneer years, provided a high degree of group isolation, especially for those groups who had not participated in any of the renewal currents, such as the Old Colony groups found in a few enclaves in Canada and in larger groupings in various parts of Latin America. This isolation permitted them to carry on their religious and cultural traditions without much external influence. It also, however, left them without outside mirrors that might have prompted them to examine themselves. This isolation, accentuated by only minimal internal education, over time had a tragic effect on the group's view of and use of the Bible and of their obedience to its teachings.

In this isolation the exegetical community became inoperative, the servants of the church became its authoritarian masters and its spiritual life began to wither. As a result, Mennonite piety often degenerated into an external façade in the form of conservative dress, traditional customs and the rejection of innovations like electricity, rubber tires and automobiles (Liechty 1980, 19-21). In fact, Melvin Gingerich (1970, 123; also see Kraybill 1987, 298-320) has suggested that Mennonite concentration on traditional mores, including dress, often absorbed so much of their time and energy that critical spiritual life issues, like live Bible study and genuine discipleship, drained away like water from a dried-out wooden bucket (Neff 1985, 3, 351; H. Quiring 1936, 98-102).

In the northern stream, stress on men's clothing had died out already in Russia in the more progressive Molotschna, especially among the Mennonite Brethren. But among the descendants of Chortitza colony it still persists even today in the dress of ministers in Mexico and some other Latin American colonies of originally northern-stream Mennonites.

For women the emphasis on not wearing men's clothing (Deut. 22:5)—for example, women wearing slacks persisted in Canada at least until the 1940s, and it still is a very live issue among the *Umsiedler* (the resettled ones) who are still moving from Russia to Germany. The head covering for married women has persisted in Russia through communist times, albeit under the guise of the peasant kerchief, which is traditional in Russia. In Canada it persisted even among married Mennonite Brethren women in the form of a black bow worn in church at least until the start of World War II. In Old Colony circles in Latin America, likewise, it is still very much alive today in the form of an elaborate black bonnet worn by women in church. Spiritual decay expressed in petty concerns of this kind is still strong in the Mexican and Bolivian colonies to which Canadian Old Colony Mennonites fled to escape the encroaching "world."

This attitude of extreme isolation did not remain universal in the northern stream. Both the General Conference Mennonite and the Mennonite Brethren churches in America started Bible schools and liberal arts colleges and fostered education. However, even in these groups live congregational Bible study began to lapse as paid pastors became the fashion.

Much of this internal decay came because live Bible study lapsed. Congregations felt that truth had already been established by their forebears and all that was still needed was to maintain the status quo. In many groups ministers had minimal training—and in the isolating groups, like the Old Colony people—none at all. They no longer developed new sermons, they simply read old sermons written by deceased former ministers.

Fortunately such tragic entropy did not become universal among North American Mennonites. New beginnings shook up the ship of tradition and original Anabaptist/Mennonite biblical values were "rediscovered." Dying embers of spiritual life burst forth in new flame, such as the revivals that have rekindled spiritual life in many *Kleine Gemeinde* (Bender 1957, *2*, 242-244), *Sommerfelder* (Bender 1959, *4*, 576-578), *Reinländer* (I. Dyck 1970; Zacharias 1976), *Bergthaler* (Schroeder 1986) and Old Colony Mennonites (Krahn 1959. *4*, 38-42). In Manitoba the revivals have produced the active Evangelical Mennonite Church (Henry Fast 1990, *5*, 278-280). Elsewhere other revived groups have been born. The revival fires have produced some very active and live believers, however they have generally become mainstream evangelicals rather than returning to a vision of Anabaptist discipleship. Most have accepted the fundamentalist evangelical view of the inerrant "flat" Bible rather than returning to the focused canon of their forebears.

Internal entropy was not the only reason for the loss of the focused canon. Outside influences produced similar effects. Among these were especially dispensationalism and fundamentalism. Their impact was significant though varied. One important area of impact was on the church's definition of the canon and its practice of exegesis.

Dispensationalism

The dispensational view of God's plan for the world originated with the teachings of John Nelson Darby (1800-1882), a Plymouth Brethren Bible teacher. It made its first appearance among Mennonites in Russia as a result of students returning from theological studies in Germany, especially from schools associated with the Blankenburg Conference. It took root in the teaching of a number of well-known Mennonite Brethren ministers. When Mennonites emigrated to North America from Russia, they brought this view of Scripture with them. Among them was minister Jacob W. Reimer, who spent many years teaching this view in American Mennonite churches. However, Mennonites in North America also came under its influence due to popular evangelical preachers who were dispensationalists, like C. I. Scofield, Lewis Sperry Chafer, Arno C. Gaebelein and Harry A. Ironside (D. Ewert 1990, 241; J. A. Toews 1975a, 327).

Dispensationalism sees God's work in terms of six (sometimes seven) successive dispensations of time, which in turn are bounded by eternity at both ends. The dispensations are: the creative age, the age of conscience, the age of the law, the age of the church, the kingdom age and the perfect age (Bullinger 1931; Larkin 1920). This teaching undercut the Mennonites' focused view of the canon, because it viewed certain sections of Scripture as relating only to certain specific ages, rendering them largely irrelevant for current believers.

Author Loewen recalls preaching a message on the Great Commission (Matt. 28:20) in one Canadian Mennonite Brethren church. Later the dispensational-minded minister commended the quality of his thoughts but categorically stated that the entire biblical basis of the message was in error. Matthew 28:20 was a kingdom age (millennium) Scripture and was addressed to Jews, not Gentiles. As far as this minister was concerned, this nullified the whole message.

While only a minority of Mennonite Brethren ministers held strong dispensational views, their influence seriously undermined a large part of the denomination's Anabaptist/Mennonite view of the canon and discouraged lay participation in public Bible studies. After all, only these "dispensational experts" knew which Scriptures applied to which eras. Because of their superior insights they could authoritatively dismiss any Scriptures that they felt applied to another dispensational age.

C. Norman Kraus (1958, 9) also pointed out how dispensationalism contradicted the Anabaptist/Mennonite view of the Sermon on the Mount. This Scripture was a critical part of the Anabaptist/Mennonite core canon, but the dispensational view transferred it from the era of the church to the dispensation of the millennium, and thus to Israel. The result was that the very foundation of Anabaptist/Mennonite discipleship was undermined (J. A. Toews 1975a, 78).

Fundamentalism

Another outside influence that eroded the focused canon view has been fundamentalism. Like Mennonites, fundamentalists also emphasized *Sola Scriptura*, though their premises were very different. Anabaptists emphasized studying Scripture collectively to determine its meaning and then applying the recognized truth in daily discipleship. Fundamentalists, however, were not so much concerned about discipleship as they were about whether Scripture was inerrant and God-breathed, if not literally dictated (Wenger 1957, 167-179). This view clashed with the Anabaptist/Mennonite view that the value of individual Scriptures was determined by how closely they coincided with Jesus' life and teaching (Poettcker 1964, 110-111; Schlabach 1980, 110-112).

Fundamentalists rejected any suggestion that the Old Testament was not completely equal in value to the New Testament. As Mennonite interest in fundamentalism increased, their view of the Christ-centered canon gradually eroded. Today the focused canon view is probably held by only a minuscule minority of Anabaptist-oriented Mennonite biblical scholars. Mennonite pastors on the whole feel more at home with the fundamentalist view of the Bible. Most Mennonite seminaries teach a focused-canon view, but many pastors still feel more at home with the flat canon. Many are unaware of their forebears' view of Scripture. Being "orthodox" in the fundamentalist sense meant that Mennonites became more concerned about correctly formulating their statement of faith than about incarnating it in daily life (Schlabach 1980, 110-111, 119).

Changes in Mennonite Brethren congregations

The professionalization of the ministry and of the study of the Bible

After World War I in the United States and World War II in Canada, the practice of multiple lay ministers waned as Mennonite churches opted for having one trained and paid pastor. This shift changed the nature of congregational Bible study. The trained minister now was an academically recognized authority on Scripture, not just another lay member of the congregation. Furthermore, he usually was imported from the outside rather than being home-grown. Bit by bit "unversed" lay members gave up attempting to interpret Scripture. This subtly changed the earlier participatory group study into an expository lecture by the Bible teacher. Eventually, lay Bible teachers also began to follow the pastoral lecture model. Bible study, formerly a free exchange of ideas between equals, now became a Bible lecture largely indistinguishable from an exegetical sermon. The result was the decline of the congregation as an exegetical community. Church members became consumers of exegesis rather than producers of it. They became spectators at exegetical performances rather than active players in it (D. Kraybill 1988, 171).

The recent development of cell groups in some Mennonite churches has helped counter this trend somewhat. If a teacher in such a group believes in an inductive approach, Bible study in these groups can approximate the original free exchange of ideas in exegesis of early Anabaptists/Mennonites. But many small group Bible teachers feel uncomfortable with this method of teaching; they feel more in control when they can deliver an expository lecture. This type of lecture-teaching further undercuts consensus decision-making. The chief task of the audience becomes that of listeners, not that of joint shapers of a congregational vision.

The democratic majority vote

In early Anabaptist/Mennonite congregations consensus was the preferred method to decide not only major church issues but all church concerns. And consensus, as author Loewen has observed in dozens of societies on several continents during his decades of overseas service, does not mean unanimity. It means that a matter has been discussed until all parties feel that their concerns have been adequately heard by all and that everyone is now agreed to let the general consensus prevail without further dissent. Majority voting, in contrast, does not ask: Does everyone feel that he or she has been heard adequately? It merely registers the percentage for or against, a proposition which has been presented. It, as it were, makes all dissent obvious; while consensus minimizes dissent.

When democratic voting emerged as the preferred mechanism to make decisions in society, even Anabaptists were affected. At first only the lesser "housekeeping" issues became matters of majority vote. As the preference for majority vote grew, voting became the decision-making mechanism of choice, even in the selection of pastors to be hired. Soon it became necessary to also give hired pastors a periodic vote of confidence. Unanimous votes gave way to mere majority votes. An increasing part of the congregation was no longer committed to what the majority had decided and so factions developed. But by far the most serious problem was the "us" and "them" division that arose between church members and paid professional leaders.

Church governance: the "will to power" in Mennonite churches

A recent and recurring power contention in Mennonite churches has centered on the issue of central (denominational) versus congregational control. This was already noted during Menno Simons' lifetime, when he and the other elders met to set church polity in Wismar without any congregational involvement (Clasen 1972, 251ff).

In South Russia this issue was manifest in the elders, who defined themselves as a governing body that could act independently of ministers and congregations. Thus a concern in the 1860 renewal movement in Russia was the return to congregational government. That the renewal movement was not alone in wanting a greater congregational voice can be seen in the fact that the parent church in Russia found it expedient to adopt the church-wide general conference format only a few years later (see Gerber 1983, 20-26).

In the Mennonite Brethren context the issues of power have been focused largely on two areas. At the denominational level the issue has been that of central conference control versus congregational autonomy. At the local church level the issue has involved the power of ministers versus member-controlled congregational assemblies.

There is no question that when the Mennonite Brethren Church began in 1860 it represented a reaction against the newly centralized power of the elders in the parent church. The renewal movement rejected this hierarchical development as unbiblical and un-Mennonite and insisted on a return to full congregational government. But the issue of power did not automatically fade away. In fact, the "will to power" has raised its head within the Mennonite Brethren Church itself, again and again, sometimes under very different guises, but often in almost identical forms.

Within the first months of Mennonite Brethren existence, the "will to power" manifested itself in the so-called "apostles" movement, in which several ministers unilaterally declared themselves divinely authorized to operate independently of the consensus of any congregation. However, since the new Mennonite Brethren fellowship was committed to congregational consensus-type government with ministers and lay people ranking as equals, it dealt with the movement swiftly and severely. In fact, as soon as the Mennonite Brethren Church had overcome its initial insecurity, it discontinued even the office of elder entirely.

The spirit of congregational control was nurtured wherever Mennonite Brethren churches were established (J. F. Harms 1924). The rapid development of daughter colonies in Russia and the establishment of many small new congregations in the new world demanded ever-increasing lay involvement in operating the church program at the local level. Previous concerns with authoritarianism gradually faded from memory. This permitted the "will to power" to reappear.

The paid ministry

Like the loss of the Dutch language in Prussia in the mid-eighteenth century (Duerksen 1967, 107-109), so the loss of the German language in America in the mid-twentieth century (J. Loewen 1986, 1-33) and the breakdown of closed communities helped move Mennonite churches toward ever-broader participation in national religious life in North America. One development brought about by this movement was the professional pastorate. Its effects underline the Mennonites' lack of an adequate theology of power.

Since the ministry in most Mennonite churches now is salaried, a special class of paid professional clergy has emerged. In the days of the non-salaried ministry, ministers farmed or worked at jobs like everyone else in the congregation. Furthermore, most churches had several such ministers. Under these conditions the ministers' major source of authority was their moral character, rather than the position they held or the degree of education they had achieved. Even though one of them was selected as leading minister, no individual minister wielded exclusive power or even the major power (J. Peters 1989, 167-182). The leading minister was merely the first among equals. Decisions were made by consensus, with everyone involved.

The earliest paid ministers in America often had little theological education and even less training in administration. As a result they often were not the best and certainly not the most experienced church administrators. Furthermore, when they did not come from the local congregation, they were not always considered full local church members, and were often marginalized in the day-to-day affairs of the church. They were not seen as the local church's natural leaders but rather as paid preachers whose home churches were located elsewhere. Many of them felt excluded from the power they thought was rightfully theirs on the basis of the position they held. When such ministers tried to exercise some authority, however, they quickly lost their vote of confidence and had to move on. The result was a period of widespread instability in the Mennonite pastorate.

Pastoral versus congregational control

Most pastors today are paid religious professionals who have both theological and administrative preparation. Most feel they are uniquely qualified not only to be preachers, but also to govern the church. Thus it seems that ministers are currently fighting back and are struggling to establish more control over local congregations. Some pastors are moving to establish boards of elders, and are downgrading the day-to-day control of traditional member-controlled church assemblies.

A typical process begins with a new pastor, especially a new senior pastor, asking the congregation to establish a small group of elders to help the minister keep his ministry relevant and assure that all the members get adequate "soul-care." The congregation, with the pastor's help, thus selects a nucleus of six to twelve people and establishes the requested board of elders. Then, however, the congregation is gradually eased out of decision-making, as that function shifts to the board of elders, of which the pastor is the chief executive officer. Before long the congregation discovers it has been moved into a mere advisory position.

A recent addition in some churches is a doctrinal purity pledge drawn up by the pastor and the board of elders that all future elders and elected officers of the church must sign. Anyone who questions the validity of such a pledge becomes doctrinally suspect.

Often a well-functioning board of elders also means there no longer will be nominees from the floor for various positions in the work of the church. The elders or a board-appointed nominating committee now prepares a slate of nominees and either asks the church to choose one of several candidates or, especially in smaller churches, merely asks for approval of the entire slate.

Many church members, who formerly enjoyed congregational government, are today quite frustrated. For unlike the earlier screening council (*Vorberat*), which brought issues to the entire assembly for debate and decision, the board of elders now makes the decisions for which it may or may not seek congregational ratification.

A new hierarchy in the ministry

An even more ominous power-phenomenon on the Mennonite Brethren horizon is that of an elder under the name of "conference minister." Author Loewen was a member of the Home Mission Board of the Southern District Conference of Mennonite Brethren Churches when it appointed its first conference minister in 1964. At that time there was deep concern that professional pastors had nowhere to turn with their own spiritual growth concerns. Many pastors who shared personal spiritual concerns with church members were getting into difficulty. Parishioners seemingly wanted to live under the illusion of having a perfect pastor. The best answer at that time seemed to be to appoint a "pastor to pastors" who could be a burden-bearer and spiritual counselor to active ministers.

Today, however, the office of conference minister in some areas seems to have taken a very different turn. Some see themselves as an elder or at least as a district superintendent with power superior to pastors of congregations. Some seem to see themselves guardians of church purity and a few even want to override congregational decisions with which they do not agree.

Unease on the Mennonite Brethren Church leadership scene today

Ron Geddert's editorial "Wanted: Handcuffed Pastors," which appeared in the *Mennonite Brethren Herald* (1 June 1990), highlighted the fact that many pastors no longer were secure enough in their positions to feel comfortable to take a firm position on issues. It generated many letters of reaction from both frustrated pastors and unhappy parishioners. The debate revealed that Mennonite Brethren churches today lack a biblical ethic of leadership. Pastors claim to be subject to a paralyzing insecurity because of the ever-present "no confidence" vote, while parishioners complain about the pastors' lust for power (Coggins 1989, 7; Derksen 1992, 3; A. J. Dueck 1990, 18-27).

When author Loewen surveyed his church colleagues about how to establish the parameters for an ethic of power, they suggested a catalogue of abuses of power was a first concern. It would highlight the need for such an ethic, as well as clarify some of the issues that such an ethic should address.

Despite the foregoing criticism of the current ministerial situation, it is important to note that in its 130-year history the Mennonite Brethren Church has had a long line of selfless ministers and church workers who have led, fed and nurtured the flocks under their care. Hundreds of genuine servants of God sought neither fame nor power during an entire life of serving the church. A few did engage in abusive practices. But often this happened because they lacked the necessary guidelines or were unaware of the implications of their actions. On the other hand, there always have also been those who sought position and power and it is these on whom this study now wants to focus attention.

Power abuses in Mennonite church leadership

To compile the suggested catalogue of leadership problems (French & Raven 1959, 150-167), Loewen consulted about a dozen church people, mostly Mennonite Brethren and General Conference Mennonite lay people, including some ex-Mennonites. He asked them to recount firsthand experiences with leadership abuse. The number and the similarity of these experiences was striking. The hurts and scars these abuses had left were often still visible and painful. The responses of these dozen respondents identified close to a hundred cases of pastoral or ministeral abuse. Since the examples were so many it became necessary to group them into categories. There is some overlap between them, and in several individual experiences more than one category of abuse was involved.

Authoritarianism

Abuses in this category seem to grow out of several tendencies: (1) the human "will to power" and the widespread urge to lord it over others, and (2) the subtle temptation for human leaders, especially in the church, to see themselves as God's personal representatives with a divine "power of attorney." In the exercise of authority such leaders become dictatorial, always ready to make arbitrary decisions which underlings or parishioners are not permitted to question. They also establish hierarchical distinctions in which those who govern carry status superior to those being governed.

The ultimate form of authoritarianism is illustrated in Dostoyevski's fictionalized account of the inquisition in which the grand inquisitor imprisons the returned Jesus Christ himself and in a midnight conversation with him in prison declares that the church hierarchy knows what is good for the church and that it will not let even the returned Jesus Christ himself interfere with the way it is building the church here on earth (Dostoyevski 1957, 227-244).

As such ruling hierarchies become entrenched, they often are blinded by their own point of view and they become increasingly intolerant of ambiguity or different points of view among their parishioners. Right and wrong are sharply defined and dissent in all forms is frowned upon. Here the Roman Catholic hierarchy comes to mind, but every branch of the Mennonite church has its own examples of authoritarian leaders who exercised arbitrary power. Some have expelled women for having feathers in their hats or for wearing makeup, earrings or silk stockings. Others have been excommunicated for marrying a Mennonite outside of their specific group, using a telephone, buying a car or even buying a car with too much chrome on it (B. S. Hostetler 1987, 295-302; Janzen & Giesbrecht 1978, 79; Juhnke 1989, 77).

Clericalism

For several centuries Mennonites in Europe and America chose their ministers from the ranks of their own members. Some had had the privilege of post-elementary schooling or even some Bible training, but the majority had learned to know their Bible in the *Bibelstunden* (Bible studies) carried on by the local church. In such Bible studies the entire congregation struggled together to understand what the Bible was saying and what its message meant for daily life.

Since Mennonites traditionally made no distinction between secular and sacred work, ministers and lay people worked at the same jobs, and in the Bible studies all of them contributed as they were able. Even though a few people were chosen to be ministers and were consecrated as such, their status was really no higher than that of other respected lay members in the church and community. Their authority grew out of the quality of the biblical instruction they provided for the church and in the example of their daily Christian living. Even the elders basically carried no more authority than other respected members of the congregation. Some elders, of course, like Warkentin and Wiens in South Russia, aspired to greater control (Krahn 1956b, 120-127).

One of the first real developments of clericalism, or a hierarchical split between the ministry and the laity in South Russia, came when the elders, frustrated by repeated outside intervention, organized a *Kirchenkonvent* in 1851, which authorized itself to act independently of the congregations. Until then, an elder had served only in the congregation of which he was a part and in which decisions were made largely by consensus. When an elder was invited into another congregation, it was only in an advisory capacity.

After World War I in the United States and World War II in Canada, with the loss of the German language, Mennonite churches changed from the multiple lay ministry to paid professional ministers. Elsewhere, we have pointed out some of the problems that developed. Thus today, with only fully-trained professional ministers in most Mennonite churches and with some larger churches having a number of such paid individuals on their staff, hierarchical differences are becoming increasingly evident. Many ministers are not content with merely preaching and nurturing church members; they feel qualified also to govern the church. When members resist such efforts, conflicting images about the role of the membership and of the pastor begin to manifest themselves. A letter to the editor of the *Mennonite Brethren Herald* illustrated this conflict well: "Today ministers are the 'we' and the congregation is the 'they,' and the 'we's' are complaining that the 'they's' do not let them govern the local church" (Hubert 1990, 8).

Clericalism has never been popular for long in Mennonite circles. When the elders in South Russia cut loose from the congregations, the revolt by the laity produced first the Mennonite Brethren Church and later also a general conference structure for even the parent church. This structure provided a new forum in which lay members could again participate fully in all decisions of the church at large.

Abuse of position

Positions of authority provide access both to the levers of power and to the resources of the group. The levers of power can be used to punish those who question or oppose authority and the resources of the group can readily be used to reward those underlings loyal to the leader.

Punishment can involve exclusion from certain positions, discipline, or even being forced out of the church. Abusive church leaders have often excommunicated opponents on flimsy or even manufactured charges. Some are willing to use misinformation, gossip, innuendo and blacklisting to silence opposing voices. Such campaigns can be very effective, especially when conducted under the guise of protecting the purity of the church or defending its doctrine.

Rewards, meanwhile, can be visible subordinate leadership roles, delegation to attend conferences and access to insider information. They can also involve perks such as trips to the Holy Land. Churches restructured with a board of elders of which the senior pastor is the actual or de facto head or chief executive officer have enormous potential for good. When a large church of several hundred members is divided into house-church groups in which all members feel free to speak, an elder member of such a group can help facilitate the bi-directional flow of information. Such churches can actually work together in decision-making by having all groups process the issues and arrive at consensus, which is then brought to the entire congregation for final action. By the same token, locally-felt needs can be communicated directly to the highest levels for immediate attention.

But if a church with a chief executive officer/board structure does not have successfully functioning house-church groups or if only a few people take part in such groups, then a board structure can quickly cut the congregation out of the decision-making process. On the pretext that the church is too large and takes too long to act, the board now makes the decisions. In fact, such a centralized structure in the hands of a power-hungry leader has the potential for dictatorial thought control.

Breach of trust

In recent years the media has been full of accounts of priests who abused their positions of trust, often in a sexual fashion. In Mennonite circles this type of abuse has also been present. Probably the most common breach or abuse of trust among Mennonites has been the violation of private confession. When Author Loewen visited a Mennonite colony in Latin America some years ago he was deluged by people seeking help with specific problems. They felt they could not confess to a local minister because the latter would make their private confession public.

Nor are North American Mennonites immune to violating the trust of private confession. During the height of the drug craze in the early 1970s, author Loewen's family was home on furlough from Africa and was able to help a teen-aged church member escape drugs and the accompanying life of sex and stealing that had financed the habit. Loewen knew this young person's conscience would eventually require a confession to the pastor and so he called on the pastor and discreetly inquired whether the pastor could listen to a confession of a healed drug addict church member without making it a matter of public discipline. Loewen felt the request was appropriate, since the offenses had happened outside the church's knowledge. Furthermore, because the person had left the life of drugs and illicit sex behind, it seemed a pastoral absolution should be sufficient in this case. The pastor agreed fully, but when the penitent actually came forward some months later, the pastor felt obliged to share the story with the board of elders. Some elders with a punitive bent insisted on at least a one-year probationary excommunication, even though the young person at this time had been free from both drugs and sexual misconduct for some time and had made restitution for all the remembered thefts. This church action not only violated Menno Simons' instruction that "if the sinner is repentant or has already repented, the ban is no longer appropriate," (Simons 1876, A:387) but it also drove that young person from the Mennonite church.

Loewen also remembers what he observed as a young man in his home church when genuinely pastoral leading ministers, having listened to private confessions, wanted to deal only with the broad outlines of a situation in public. However, many of the (largely inactive) ministers who made up the bulk of the church council would insist on publicly exposing lurid details, often permanently damaging the reputations of those who had voluntarily confessed.

When church members abuse power

The North American cultural system has penetrated deeply into every Mennonite church member's life (Cartwright 1959). In the culture at large the more financially successful tend to wield more power. This increased access to power is manifested not only in the business and political realms, but even in the church.

Pastors frequently complain of feeling pressure from wealthy parishioners to avoid certain subjects in their sermons or to support certain proposals or projects which the affluent want and often offer to pay for. The implications of this became very real to author Loewen recently when he complimented a newly-retired minister on the power and relevance of his latest sermons. The retired pastor leaned back contentedly and said: "It's wonderful! Now I can finally preach what God lays on my heart. I don't have to worry about my job. I don't have to listen to what powerful elders or millionaire church members want me to say!"

CHAPTER 16

Vulnerability to Outside Influences

Early Mennonite immigrants to North America usually managed to settle in homogeneous clusters. These concentrations permitted them to carry on many of their traditional religious and cultural practices, especially in situations where they also controlled the municipal governments and the local school boards. But after several decades the pressures of the new world melting pot began to have an impact. Bit by bit they lost their radical outlook and commitment and began to blend into the American religious scene (C. Redekop 1988, 190-192; Zuercher 1985, 5).

Historian Frank Epp has noted striking similarities in the ongoing religious experiences of Mennonites in Russia and those who came to North America, such as the renewal in the United States during the early nineteenth century and the emergence of the 1860s renewal in Russia. These similarities included their reactions to the kinds of external influences that impinged on them.

Fundamentalism

Fundamentalism in North America is usually credited as beginning with W. B. Riley of Northwestern Bible Institute in Minneapolis. The movement's name grew out of the 1909 publication of twelve booklets stressing the so-called "fundamentals of the faith." The movement stressed verbal inspiration and a literal interpretation of the Scriptures and often was prone to legalism.

Stewart Grant Cole (1931, 34) suggested that fundamentalism has a five-point doctrinal core: (1) the inerrancy of the Scriptures; (2) the deity of Christ; (3) his virgin birth; (4) the substitutionary atonement of Christ; (5) his physical resurrection and his bodily return to earth. To this list one must usually add millennarianism—the dispensationalist, premillennial return of Jesus Christ (Sandeen 1970).

Marsden (1990, 23) in addition, points out that true fundamentalism distinguishes itself from strait-laced evangelicalism by its militancy. George W. Dollar (1973, xv), a scholar of and participant in the fundamentalist world, corroborates with this definition: "Historic fundamentalism is the literal exposition of all affirmations and attributes of the Bible and the *militant* exposure of all non-Biblical affirmations and attitudes." This movement reached its peak shortly after the end of World War I.

Mennonites, with their traditional emphasis on the importance of Scripture, were soon drawn into a variety of fundamentalist associations. When the National Association of Evangelicals (NEA) was organized in 1942, the Mennonite Brethren Church, the Evangelical Mennonite Brethren (H. F. Epp 1956, 262-264; Esau 1990, 75-86) and the Evangelical Mennonite Church joined this fundamentalist-oriented organization. Other Mennonites might have joined but could not because they had already become members of the National Council of Churches in Christ, which the NEA considered theologically too liberal (J. A. Toews 1975a, 375-376; P. Toews 1983, 241-256).

How fundamentalism changed the Mennonite gospel

Probably the most systematic and most revealing study of fundamentalist influence on a Mennonite group is Theron Schlabach's 1980 study *Gospel Versus Gospel*. While concentrating on the Mennonite Church, the examples cited could be duplicated in most Mennonite church groups, including the Mennonite Brethren. Schlabach listed the following seductive influences: (1) the separation of body and soul; (2) an increased emphasis on authority and orthodoxy; (3) a shift in their view and treatment of Scripture.

Early Mennonites did not separate sharply between the here-and-now needs of a person and the eternal salvation of the soul. But when Mennonites under the influence of fundamentalism exchanged discipleship with "plan of salvation" language, the "spiritual needs" of humankind quickly gained pre-eminence over their need for medicine, food, clothes, shelter and justice (Schlabach 1980, 109). As a result the "lived gospel" was edged aside and direct verbal evangelism was elevated as the supreme value. Humanitarian aid was downgraded and ultimately became suspect as "social gospel." Schlabach (1988) credited evangelist Samuel Coffman with introducing the separation of personal salvation from discipleship and the incarnate gospel into Mennonite circles. Isaac Block (1985, 76-81) observed that today discipleship is often spiritualized and detached from personal behavior and linked to preaching a pure gospel.

Revivalism

Closely linked with fundamentalism was revivalism, whose impact on Mennonites has been a double-edged sword. On the positive side, Mennonites in Russia prior to 1860 and the Swiss Mennonite immigrants to North America, who had both developed into "a people without a missionary spirit" (J. J. Toews 1967, 135ff), were reawakened to missionary work by revivalism. This quickening occurred both in Russia and in America, and the resulting outreach has served to keep Mennonite churches vital. Mennonites did not, however, recapture a global vision of the church not tied to a single nation or ethnic group, as the early Anabaptists had (J. D. Graber 1957, 154; Juhnke 1989, 78; Löwen 1989, 35-37; Schlabach 1980, 10, 47; 1988, 166).

Ever since the re-introduction of *Reiseprediger*, the traveling preachers popularized in Russia after the 1860 revival, the Mennonite Brethren have been conducting revivals. Author Loewen underwent his first conversion experience when a missionary on furlough conducted a traveling tent revival campaign in Manitoba in the early 1930s. But the large scale tent revivals like those conducted by the Brunk Brothers after World War II were already patterned after the American revival movement (J. A. Hostetler 1954).

In these later revivals conversions no longer took place within the local congregational context where there was nurture and follow-up. The campaign now was community-wide, involving a variety of denominations, and conversion meant signing a pledge card in a large tent-gathering. Furthermore, many of the revival preachers now employed in Mennonite communities were outside fundamentalists, such as those who came to the annual revival week at Tabor College during the author Loewen's student days there.

As the American revival spirit took hold in Mennonite communities in the early 1940s, especially the young who spoke English—Author Loewen among them—were busily waving an interdenominational banner at Valley-wide revival campaigns. The Mennonite Brethren Church as a body joined the movement and launched West Coast Children's Mission, as its interdenominational front for all church outreach in British Columbia (Peter Penner 1959).

Evangelicalism

Mennonites, since their inception, believed in the need for new birth and personal renewal through the work of the Spirit of God. In that sense they have always been traditional evangelicals. The label "evangelicalism," as it is here used, however, does not refer to these positive aspects but rather to its individualistic piety and to some of the negative accouterments that today characterize segments of the North American evangelical mainstream.

Of all the outside influences, evangelicalism has been one of the most subtly dangerous for Mennonites. Ever since the nineteenth century, when it found easy entry into Mennonite churches through gospel hymns (Schlabach 1983, 224), it has made deep inroads into

Mennonite churches and communities. The reason why it poses a threat is because so many Mennonites felt there was an almost total overlap between Mennonite concerns and the central concerns of evangelicalism. There is some overlap, but it must be underscored that evangelicalism's basic values and fundamental Anabaptist/Mennonite values lie largely outside of each other's domains (Schlabach 1988, 91).

Evangelicalism is especially troubling also because it has a rather militant right wing, which has held strong attraction for some Mennonites. Juhnke (1975, 7ff) pointed out that the attraction of the patriotic militant fundamentalist right is not new to Mennonites. It has happened before. In the years 1931-1942 Gerald B. Winrod, the publisher of *The Defender Magazine*, had widespread Mennonite support in central Kansas. In fact, the Mennonite Brethren Publishing House printed his magazine for a number of years.

Evangelicalism and Anabaptism compared

Evangelicalism stresses orthodoxy over orthopraxy. Clark Pinnock (1988, 64) suggested that evangelicalism's current struggle for orthodoxy is absorbing all its energies at the expense of orthopraxy (cf. Kraus 1979b, 21). For committed Anabaptists the priority is reversed. That is why Matthew 24 was so central to the Anabaptist "canon within the canon." As a result, Mennonites stressed discipleship more than verbally confessed faith. This, as the C. N. Kraus (1979b, 9ff; 1979d, 169-182) edited book has effectively demonstrated, has a series of implications:

(1) Because evangelicalism lacks the Anabaptist/Mennonite emphasis on discipleship, it often finds itself promoting "cheap grace" (Kraus 1979b, 20). Peter C. Hiebert, first and long term chairman of Mennonite Central Committee, said it was not only in piety but by sharing with people in need that "we do the works of Him who sent us" (Juhnke 1989, 257).

(2) A further result is that evangelicalism vigorously promotes conversion, but often neglects ongoing spiritual growth and disciplined living. More recently this soul-winning emphasis has been renamed and upgraded as "church growth," but the emphasis remains on numerical increase rather than on spiritual growth (J. L. Burkholder 1979, 28-29; Michaelson 1979, 65).

(3) Evangelicalism joins "the modern American world" by emphasizing individualism (Kraus 1979b, 20; Michaelson 1979, 65). Both conversion and subsequent Christian living are treated as highly personal. The newly-converted are not inducted into a warm corporate

body where the individual will be nurtured and disciplined as Anabaptists/Mennonites have traditionally stressed (Kraus 1979d, 178; Michaelson 1979, 65).

(4) Evangelicalism falls short in community. In Pietism and evangelicalism the church is an assembly of the individually redeemed; in functional Anabaptism no one can become a member of the kingdom except in the context of brothers and sisters in the faith (Friedmann 1944, 117-122; 1957, 105ff).

(5) Evangelicalism lacks Anabaptist/Mennonite concern "to be separate from the world." As a result it has adopted capitalism and materialism almost completely and uncritically (Kraus 1979b, 20). It lacks a feel for simplicity and a concern for the poor and the outcast, which Anabaptists have traditionally manifested (Michaelson 1979, 72, 78-79; Sider 1989a).

(6) Evangelicalism, especially of the Christian Coalition cast, tends to be politically involved (Kraus 1979c, 39-61; Lapp 1979, 82-100), highly nationalistic, sometimes even militaristic. As a result it reduces God to a "tribal deity" (Koyama 1982, 106-112; 1984) who blesses evangelicals because they defend American democracy (Lapp 1979, 90-93). Menno Simons saw true believers as completely separated from any nation state.

(7) Evangelicalism, as the heir to fundamentalism, is more concerned about the defense of the inerrancy of Scriptures than in stressing the believers' obedience to its dictates, which is Anabaptism's primary concern (Schlabach 1983, 222-240; Wenger 1957, 167-179).

(8) Ron Sider (1979, 154) has already pointed out that as a result of the above shortcomings evangelicalism's gospel is a very partial one. It is concerned largely with the soul and the hereafter and fears involvement in seeking justice for the poor and the downtrodden, while it is treatment of the latter which seems to be the criterion for identifying true disciples of Jesus in Matthew 24.

If nonresistance was crucial in keeping Mennonites from being absorbed completely into the fundamentalist camp (Juhnke 1989, 259), it probably has been Mennonite Central Committee that has kept the Mennonites from becoming completely absorbed in the evangelical mainstream (R. J. Sawatsky 1973). Mennonite concern with relief and welfare—nurtured by MCC—has always made other evangelicals somewhat nervous, because to them it sounded like "social gospel." Even though individual Mennonite ministers have condemned MCC for its lack of "soul-winning" and have urged church members to boycott it, the older generation of Russian Mennonites who experienced MCC famine relief in the 1920s always remained its loyal supporters. Furthermore, the steady stream of young volunteers for MCC service provided an "anchor" of people who have directly experienced the value of Mennonite service ideals as reflected in Matthew 24.

Modernity

A recent outside influence on Mennonites in North America has been modernity. It has insidiously undermined Anabaptist/Mennonite values in all major groups, particularly in General Conference and Mennonite Brethren churches. Few Mennonites have as yet become aware of how fundamentally modernity has changed them.

Ted Koontz, a Mennonite ethicist, has demonstrated (1989, 415) how Mennonite churches are abandoning traditional Anabaptist/Mennonite values and wholeheartedly embracing modernity. In some cases unwary church leaders are actively hastening the process by undercutting what little is left of the traditional Mennonite vision. This is usually done under the banner of getting rid of "ethnic Mennonitism" and becoming truly evangelical churches.

To make the Mennonite drift into modernity more apparent, Koontz contrasts traditional worldviews with modernity's view. The following chart presents some of his comparative material in a highly abbreviated and adapted form:

The Traditional World	**The modern world**
Under control of the supernatural	Under control of science and technology
Leadership is charismatic and informal, guided by unwritten tradition	Leadership is bureaucratic, governed by highly codified written laws
People expect to live like their parents did	People have high aspirations for achievement in life
Most people are poor	Most people are wealthy
Change is feared and resisted	Change is expected and welcomed
The social unit is the extended family	The nuclear family or even the single-parent family is the norm
Residence is in small rural communities	Residence is urban or suburban
Religion is central to life	Religion is peripheral and of minor importance

Koontz (1989, 415) is probably correct when he says that while some Mennonites still bemoan "value" losses, most are moving "full

steam ahead" into modernity's mainstream. The following could be considered indicators of Mennonites embracing modernity:
- rapid upward social mobility
- even more rapid upward economic movement
- high levels of education, increasing professionalism
- growing individualism, focus on individual rights
- increasing recourse to courts to settle economic conflicts
- lessening of family ties, increased divorce
- refusal of group counsel, discernment and discipline
- growing lack of consensus about what life means
- church leadership styles copy the modern corporate example

Postmodernity

Recently political and ethical thinkers (Hauerwas 1981; 1983; MacIntyre 1981; Sandel 1983) have challenged modernity's outlook and values. Their thinking, often labeled "communitarianism," challenges the notion that the individual's access to rights, freedom and happiness are "the only center" of intrinsic value. Instead, they suggest that larger human endeavors (in church language, the building of the kingdom of God) is of equal, if not of greater value.

Communitarianism's challenge to modernity can be illustrated with the following comparative listing:

Modernity	**Postmodernity**
Liberalism is the dominant political and ethical philosophy	Calls for communitarianism
The individual is *the* central value	The individual, while valuable, is not the only center of value. The community also has rights
The individual's rights, freedom and happiness represent ultimate fulfillment	The individual is truly fulfilled when the community he or she identifies with is bettered
Good society protects the individual's rights and freedoms	Good society is virtuous. It balances the individual's rights over against the rights of others
The function of the state is to remove obstacles for individuals and to create conditions for their development	The function of the church is to help individuals develop their gifts for serving their community of faith and the world at large
Key words: individualism, rights, justice.	Key words: love, benevolence, compassion, self-sacrifice

There is no doubt that early Anabaptists/Mennonites had a communitarian outlook, very much like the one proposed by postmodern thinking. They believed in a personal decision to become a disciple of Jesus, but they then saw that individual as being "born again into a family of believers." In this communal context the believers pursued "the good" and "virtue" defined in consensus with the other members of the community. Again, the individual communities of believers or churches formed co-dependent larger bodies, which we today call denominations. The goal at both levels was to form character and to equip members to serve God and others. Thus postmodern communitarianism is really a call for Mennonites to return to their roots, reclothed in present-day cultural values (D. Kraybill 1988, 171; P. Peachy 1957, 340).

It is probably true that the Mennonite mainstream is still eagerly pursuing modernity, but many individual Mennonites are becoming increasingly uneasy about their upward mobility, their quest for wealth, status and power, and their corresponding loss of simplicity, compassion and community. Perhaps postmodernity's communitarianism can nudge us to become committed Anabaptists once more.

PART THREE

THE TWELVE ANABAPTIST VALUES AND READERS' RESPONSES TO THEM

This section seeks to interpret the history of the northern stream of Mennonites through the prism of the twelve Anabaptist values described earlier. The previous section has documented the slippage in regard to these values on the American Mennonite scene. This section now reviews these values and lets members of Mennonite congregations respond as to their relevance for them personally.

To achieve such dialogue, drafts of this study were circulated locally, across the Americas, and even in Europe. Scholars, church leaders, and interested lay people were all included in the dialogue. The responses were extremely varied. Some provided illustrative material. Some expressed reservations. Some disagreed forcefully. A number of these reactions, including several voices from previous centuries, have been included in this dialogue about Anabaptist values and their loss.

When Mennonites Adjusted Their Worldview to Become Two-Kingdom Citizens

This chapter treats the first two of the twelve value adjustments that took place during the history of Menno's descendants after the early persecution ended or at least greatly decreased after 1581 in southern Holland and after 1614 in northwestern Germany. Soon the very same Mennonites, who began as citizens only of God's kingdom of peace characterized by a lifestyle that renounced all force and coercion which Menno Simons called an "only-the-sword-of-the-Spirit" lifestyle now also became citizens of the earthly kingdom in which they resided and in which coercion was an integral part of daily social, legislative and economic life. Now these same Mennonites narrowed their understanding of peace to merely renouncing the swords of government and war.

The issue of a Christian's citizenship: single or dual?

Chapter One presented Menno Simons as unequivocal in his belief that the genuine child of God, who follows Jesus' teaching and example faithfully, can be a citizen of only one kingdom—God's kingdom of peace. This view clashed with that of the magisterial reformers who insisted that a believer had to function as a citizen of two kingdoms—the kingdom of God in the spiritual realm and the kingdom of the prince of the region in which the believer resided. The magisterial reformers quoted Paul (Rom. 13) to prove that Christians owed obedience to the state in addition to their commitment to God. They also quoted Jesus' words, "Render therefore to Caesar the things that are Caesar's and to God the things that are God's" (Matt. 22:21) and stressed that a Christian had two relatively equal loyalties: God and Caesar (Bauman 1964, 37-49).

Menno Simons disagreed with this interpretation. Believers, he said, do not give equal unlimited loyalty to both kingdoms. They obey Caesar only as long as Caesar's commands do not conflict with those of the Prince of Peace. As soon as there is any conflict between the commands of the respective princes, God's commands take precedence over Caesar's dictates.

Menno Simons and the early Anabaptists were clear in their understanding that the genuine child of God, because of the new birth, could be a citizen of only one kingdom, God's kingdom of peace. They took this position because of Jesus' unambiguous instructions that "no one can serve two masters" (Matt. 6:24). Their citizenship in the kingdom of peace demanded absolute loyalty to the prince of that kingdom.

Furthermore, they viewed their life on earth as no mere accident. The born-again needed to be perfected in their obedience to God and his Word. Their earthly sojourn was the necessary training arena for them to become like Christ in outlook and behavior. With Jesus they said, "My kingship is not of this world" (John 18:36). For this reason, they could not become citizens of earthly kingdoms; they were mere pilgrims and sojourners. Their prototype was Abraham, who, in obedience to God's call left Ur and Haran in Mesopotamia and sojourned in Canaan as an alien and stranger. Menno Simons and his early followers firmly believed they would always be a transient minority in this world. After all, Jesus had predicted that few people would find the narrow gate and even fewer would be willing to follow the narrow road all the way to its end (Matt. 7:14).

This status of sojourners or pilgrims also explained their limited obedience to the authorities of all earthly kingdoms. They did not truly belong. They obeyed the laws of the earthly kingdoms only where they did not conflict with the commands of their Lord in the kingdom of peace. This limited loyalty to earthly rulers was to be matched by an "only-the-sword-of-the-Spirit" lifestyle characterized by love, self-giving and sharing. Menno and his followers would not disengage from the world, nor relegate the ethics of the Sermon of the Mount to some future dispensation. They daily followed Jesus as redeemed nonconformists (J. Redekop 1987a).

Readers respond:

A Mennonite professor of Mennonite history speaks: I believe this study is overstating the case for Menno Simons' single-minded and total dedication to the one-kingdom-citizenship view and to his denial that a Christian could ever serve as a magistrate of the court or as an official of government. Consider Menno Simons' ambiguous statement in his early writing to Jan Laski where he affirms the Schleitheim Confession and states that the sword of magistracy is outside of the perfection of Christ. Then, however, he adds the proviso, "except the ordinary sword of the magistrate, when it must be used" (Menno Simons 1876, B:470).

Further, has not William Keeney correctly pointed out that Münster and Oude Cloister, where Menno Simons' brother was killed, moved him to condemn every use of the sword—be that the sword—war, of capital punishment, or even of ordinary magistracy? However, in later life, when he found refuge on the lands of the very tolerant nobleman, Bartholemäus von Ahlefeldt, he began to reconsider this position, thinking that if the ruler were of the von Ahlefeldt kind, Christians possibly could participate in government (Keeney 1968, 129).

Or are Peter Brock, William Keeney and van der Zijpp in error when they insist that Menno Simons wavered in his position and that there was an inherent ambivalence in his stance on the sword of government throughout? (Brock 1991b, 99; Keeney 1968, 131; van der Zijpp 1930, 15).

A modern Mennonite "realist," firmly integrated into European academics, says: *So you're going to make another attempt, á la H. S. Bender, to sell Menno Simons' vision! Don't you realize how futile that is? Sure, like H. S. Bender, you're going to cause a considerable—maybe even worthwhile—stir, but eventually nothing is going to come of it. I think it is high time for us to grab the bull by the horns and to admit we're citizens of this world's kingdoms without any "but" or "if." The sooner we come to terms with this fact, the sooner we can proceed to develop worship and lifestyle patterns for Christians who will have an impact on the world of the twenty-first century. We cannot all become rural and agricultural again. There are no places left in the world where we can build new Mennonite commonwealths. It's time some thinking Mennonites stopped trying to pick up the "spilled milk" of Menno Simons' vision. We need to create a new one all our own.*

Refusal to participate in the swords of government and war

When the Schleitheim Confession was drawn up in 1527 by Swiss Anabaptists, Menno Simons was still a Roman Catholic priest in Pingjum. When the Anabaptists later shared this confession with him, he not only endorsed it, he also became the spokesperson who translated the peace principles that the confession outlined into a comprehensive lifestyle for citizens of the kingdom of peace (Stayer 1972, 319, fn.40; Wenger 1945, 243-253).

There were sharp regional differences in the various places of Mennonite origin. These had a bearing on the discrepancy between Menno Simons' view and the views of the Swiss Anabaptists. The early Swiss Anabaptists lived under a cantonally-controlled governmental system. This brought them into intimate contact with the issues of government, and the government's necessary dependence on the sword to enforce its legal demands on its citizens. Thus they continually faced the question: "How far can a child of God, as a citizen of the kingdom of peace, participate in an effort which, by its very nature, belongs to the kingdom of this world?"

In Holland, by contrast, the Holy Roman Empire was far away. Furthermore, it was in a state of advanced decay. Nationalist independence movements were arising everywhere, often under the very banner of the Reformation. In southern Holland urban Mennonites were quite ready to cooperate with such independence movements. In northern Holland, however, Menno Simons was far removed from the authorities of both the holy Roman Empire and the budding independence movements. He and his followers were experiencing some persecution both from the remnants of the Catholic empire and from the mainstream of the Reformation spilling over from Germany. When Jan van Leyden of Münster and the dissidents of Oude Cloister, all of whom had joined the Reformation, resorted to arms to establish the kingdom of God on earth, Menno Simons unequivocally opposed such use of force for three reasons: (1) God's kingdom of peace can be established only by God himself; (2) people can become citizens of God's kingdom of peace only by free personal choice; (3) the kingdom of God by its very nature is peace; thus it has absolutely no room for the "sword of iron" (H. Isaak 1992b, 57-82).

Since the nature of the kingdom in which Christians are citizens is peace, Menno Simons saw little place for Christians to cooperate with governments who wielded the sword. This attitude was heightened by the fact that all the authorities Menno and his northern followers were exposed to were hostile to them. Participating with them was out of question. Furthermore, Scripture taught that governments always rely on force (the sword), which, according to Menno's understanding, had no place in the hands of citizens of the kingdom of peace.

When the persecution finally eased up, the Mennonites began the gradual shift to becoming citizens also of their earthly kingdoms. Yet they were still determined not to be just ordinary citizens. They maintained their own special status, reserving the right to refuse to swear the oath or to participate in government and war. The consequence of this was that Menno Simons' comprehensive "only-the-sword-of-the-Spirit" lifestyle was now effectively reduced to the doctrine of nonresistance (Ehrt 1932, 3).

Even this principle, limited as it was, brought Mennonites into continual difficulties with the authorities. On one hand, regional governments did not look with favor on citizens who unilaterally limited their obedience to the state. On the other hand, this shift to mere nonresistance opened a Pandora's box of possibilities for the use of force and coercion in all other areas of life. While outright persecution gradually diminished, their limited obedience to the state still subjected them to all types of harassment and difficulties, such as demands for monetary payment in exchange for military exemption, restrictions in land ownership, and limited entrance into professions.

In addition, there was the ill will of other citizens who felt the Mennonites were shirking their civic duties and thus loading a greater burden on non-Mennonites. Local citizens' antagonism can be understood, especially in those areas where military recruitment was acreage-based. The more land the Mennonites controlled and the fewer draftees they supplied, the greater was the recruitment burden imposed on their non-Mennonite neighbors (W. Mannhardt 1863, 52).

Another issue was the poll tax support for the recognized state churches. The greater the number of Mennonites in a given state church territory, the smaller was the support base for the government-recognized church. Authorities finally levied both Catholic and Lutheran poll taxes on the Mennonites, requiring them to support not only their own churches but also both state-recognized churches (Nottarp 1929, 26).

Perhaps these continued pressures allowed Mennonites to delude themselves that they were still keeping faith with Menno Simons. Several Mennonite leaders of the period felt that Menno had not spelled out the Christian position on nonresistance clearly enough. They complained that he had not developed a convincing systematic theology to defend the nonresistant position. They also correctly argued that just because Menno had said little about abstaining from the swords of government and war did not imply that he condoned such involvement by his disciples. As a general rule, though, it can be said that early Mennonites were convinced that "David's armor and sword" were not for the citizens of God's kingdom of peace. Those items were part of the "earthly Israel's" inventory (W. Mannhardt 1863, 22-30).

Readers respond:

A seventeenth-century Waterlander Mennonite objects: We believe that Menno Simons did not object to the use of the sword of government per se, he only insisted that no Christian should use the sword for revenge or aggression. For this reason we do not call ourselves "defenseless," as some of the baptism-minded do, we call ourselves "revengeless." This means that we will refuse to use the sword to avenge ourselves personally or when our nation is wronged. We will not commit aggression, or attack another person or nation. However, we feel that God permits, or even instructs us, to defend ourselves and our property when we are attacked personally or nationally.

A late twentieth-century Mennonite legislator opines: As a Christian I am grateful for the freedom of worship and the pursuit of livelihood and happiness which our country provides. I am grateful for the police and the armed forces who protect our communities and our country. Thus I feel that the least I can do is to serve in government to help provide legislation so that the good I believe in can flourish. I oppose wars of aggression, but when a cause is obviously just, like the recent war against Iraq under the United Nations banner, I think it is my Christian duty to support it and, if necessary, to participate in it.

A European Mennonite and scholar comments: When I first heard about this project of trying to make Menno Simons' vision relevant for the twenty-first century, I thought that the writers might not be aware that a number of modern scholars of Menno Simons' teachings are having second thoughts about the degree to which he was committed to nonresistance. Now, however, having read their analysis of the shifts Menno Simons' vision underwent in the northern Mennonite stream's history, I think they have clarified at least three major concerns for me.

First, by demonstrating that Menno Simons' vision involved a complete lifestyle of renouncing force they have shown convincingly why nonresistance did not get more systematic treatment in Menno Simons' writings—it was just a small part of a much larger whole.

Second, by showing that nonresistance came to the fore as "the big issue" only after Mennonites had compromised their original one-kingdom citizenship and now also began to function as citizens of the earthly kingdoms in which they lived, they made nonresistance the visible marker that distinguished them from other Christian citizens.

Finally, their analysis has identified why there has been so much unease among Mennonites about nonresistance. When Mennonites made a small part of the original vision into the whole, they were effectively betraying Menno Simons' larger vision of renouncing force in all areas of life. Obviously this betrayal could not take place without some guilt.

From Stewardship to Ownership and a Social-Class-Based Society

When Mennonites became earthly-kingdom citizens in addition to their citizenship in the heavenly kingdom of peace, a fundamental shift in their view of and relationship to property emerged. This shift seriously affected the cohesiveness and the egalitarian social order of their church and community.

Stewardship versus ownership of property

With the demise of feudalism in the late fifteenth and early sixteenth centuries, under which peasant farmers had functioned merely as serfs, the potential of peasant ownership of the land became a reality. Occupational statistics revealed that only about one-third of the former serfs actually became landowners. The others made their living in the many new trades and crafts that were developing in Europe at the time.

Owners of large tracts of idle and often undesirable land regarded Mennonites fleeing the persecution as an economic attraction. Ludolff Bentheim, a late seventeenth-century observer, advised such owners to put their land—however wild, swampy or barren—into the hands of Mennonite refugees. They would drain it, irrigate it, terrace it—whatever it took to make it productive. Indeed, they would establish a viable local economy on the land (Bentheim 1698, chapter 19).

Since these Mennonites made no attempt to achieve ownership of the land they were improving, nobles found they could make a good profit sheltering them from their persecutors. All the refugees wanted was to survive and be able to practice their faith. The added value they produced went to the landowners who gave them shelter.

An early Anabaptist/Mennonite property question concerned private versus communal ownership. The Hutterites, a group of Anabaptists that developed in Moravia, opted for communal ownership, feeling that private ownership brought with it too many temptations for the individual. Without private property, they felt, no one would become overly attached to material possessions and work would not be done for personal gain but for the benefit of the group. They based their thinking on the early church's sharing of material goods. However, even communal Hutterites became owners of land, albeit collective owners.

Menno Simons disagreed with the Hutterites. He noted that the church in Acts was forced to abandon the communal ownership model because it was based on the false premise that Jesus Christ was returning soon to set up the kingdom of God on earth and that further physical work was therefore unnecessary.

Menno joined Marpeck to criticize also the Hutterite approach because it used coercion to make property communal (Hutter 1938). This violated the Anabaptist/Mennonite voluntary stewardship ideals (P. J. Klassen 1963, 85; 1970, 551-568; W. Klassen 1968, 103). On the other hand, Menno Simons had no use for those who refused to work. The Anabaptist/Mennonite rule was: "Live a simple life, but always eat your own bread" (Brons 1891, 119).

Menno did agree with the communalists that Christians were not to set their hearts on the things of this world and that the products of their labors should not be used for personal benefit only. Benefits should be freely shared with others. Christ's followers should gratefully accept material blessings as a gift from God, but their attitude should always be that of stewards rather than owners. Since the persecution kept Mennonites on the move, Menno did not foresee that individual Mennonites would ever accumulate large amounts of material possessions. As pilgrims and sojourners they could not afford to be tied down by a lot of immovables. They asked only for physical safety, minimal clothes, food, shelter and enough surplus to help others in need. Beyond that they felt no urge for permanent ownership, no need to accumulate wealth, and no desire for increasing profit (O. Graber 1970, 218; Stayer 1991, 161; Verduin 1964, 232).

As soon as persecution decreased, however, Mennonites' increased liberty, coupled with their diligence, put land ownership, profit and wealth within reach. As a result their attitude to private property soon changed.

Even before they were accepted as full citizens Mennonites were permitted to operate in a restricted number of trades and businesses. They could also lease real estate. Even as resident aliens they were recognized as an economic asset.

Before long, they began to control whole segments of the economy: brewing, banking, shipping, whaling, textiles, lace work, and others. Although distant central governments might order their expulsion from a given region because of their dissident religion, local business leaders recognized them as an essential cog in the economy. Expulsion orders were frequently ignored. Gradually the Mennonites became full-fledged citizens and owners of property.

As their wealth increased, Mennonites found it necessary to protect their interests by working in local governments to assure a suitable economic climate for themselves. Eventually they became so wealthy and so acculturated to the surrounding milieu that the protection of their community and their property even by the sword seemed increasingly more reasonable.

Readers respond:

A modern Mennonite millionaire says: The authors correctly point out that Menno Simons' philosophy of property developed during the persecution. Since Menno Simons could not foresee a situation without persecution, he thus did not develop a theology of property adequate for our day. We today need large church facilities; we need top-notch educational institutions; and we need millions of dollars for missions, Mennonite Central Committee and other charities. Even wage-earners who tithe can never contribute the large sums of money needed to operate the church's program today.

I know "millionaire" is still a bad word in Mennonite circles, but during World War I in Russia it was the estate-owning "millionaires" who made Mennonite alternative service in the forests and in the medical corps possible. And today it is the "millionaires" who make our schools, colleges, seminaries and our vast outreach programs in missions and relief possible. Being a "millionaire" does not make the "owner" attitude inevitable, nor the stewardship outlook impossible. Let's not get carried away in our praise of poverty. There isn't much virtue in it.

A young "radical" couple says: The modern military state is an all-encompassing institution which through taxes and other social and economic systems makes everyone part and parcel of a very abusive machine. Since we take Menno Simons' lifestyle concerns seriously, the only workable way we see for ourselves today is not to own our home, not to hold full-time jobs, not to own anything worth being garnisheed. In this way we can avoid paying taxes to a military state. Furthermore, the free time we have permits us to help the less fortunate. Everyone who works full-time, owns property or a business, or has any investments automatically becomes a cog in the dehumanizing economic machine that makes the rich richer and bleeds the poor into ever greater poverty. This is true not only on a national scale. Through our giant multinational corporations, it's a worldwide problem.

A former homesteader on a Canadian prairie farm and earlier estate owner in Russia who lost everything at the hands of revolutionaries after World War I says: In church in Russia we used to sing "Von der Erde reiss mich los...," "Lord, tear me away from all my earthly attachments." I, too, sang that song heartily, because I didn't realize how many and how deep my attachments to wealth and possessions had become. When the anarchist bandits took what they could carry off and burned what they couldn't, I was grateful that at least all the members of our family were able to escape without physical harm. It wasn't easy for me to homestead in Canada and to have to borrow things from my neighbors, because I now couldn't afford to buy the things I needed for myself. While in Russia I always thought I was freely sharing my benefits, but once I experienced their painful loss, I realized that I had "fallen in love" with my possessions. I had come to see them as my own. I had become an owner in attitude. I know today that I should have shared more freely with all the Russian workers I employed. Maybe if we had shared more, we would have been able to prevent much of the violence and plundering our own workers inflicted on us during the unstable times following World War I.

Concern for maintaining a functional community of equals

The believing community Menno Simons envisioned was to be one of equals. The Radical Reformation flatly rejected as unbiblical both the feudal pattern of nobles and serfs and a medieval church governed by a hierarchy of professional clergy. Also rejected were the magisterial reformation churches with their clergy and laity distinction. Only one Lord and Master in the fellowship of believers was recognized—the Lord Jesus Christ—and all members of that fellowship as equals. When some members were chosen to fulfill leadership functions they were not called "leaders" but "servants." Even though there were several kinds of "servants" in the congregation, and one of them served as the coordinator of all the other servants and of the congregation, this "full servant" or "elder" was to be the first among equals, rather than having any higher governing status. Authority did not rest in the office of leadership, but rather in the congregation that called individual members to fill whatever positions the fellowship needed to function properly. Since the Epistle of James was part of their core canon, the Anabaptists felt that to distinguish between fellow-believers in the congregation on the basis of wealth or status was a serious sin. The Anabaptist ideal firmly insisted that there was no distinction between clergy and laity, no difference between secular and sacred work, no distinction between social classes and no deference due those who might currently be stewards of a larger quantity of material goods or of delegated authority.

This egalitarian ideal suffered severely with rising affluence. As church members became wealthy they began to separate into social classes based on wealth. Fissures in the "community of equals" developed as the Mennonites' increasing wealth enabled some of them to buy special government concessions. For example, Mennonites had become accustomed to making financial payments in lieu of military service. This produced class tensions in congregations because only the wealthy families could pay for their sons' military exemption without difficulty. Poor Mennonites who were unable to make such payments had to emigrate or succumb to government pressure and serve in the military.

Readers respond:

A former wealthy estate owner in Russia says: While it was easily possible for us to live in our home village in the colony, we quickly opted to build our family home on our estate. We still were members of the church in our former colony village, but we only attended there on special occasions. We often had church services in our own parlor with stimulating visitors from abroad. We found the jealousy and the inquisitiveness of the colony villagers too uncomfortable. Furthermore, they were so provincial. They had no appreciation for art, architecture or culture, things we really enjoyed. So we just made sizeable contributions to the village church's efforts. This usually kept the church happy and permitted us to function the way we liked, largely outside of their narrow and outdated mores.

A wealthy North American church member speaks about equality in the church: We live in a democratic society and we practice one-person-one-vote also in the church. That is equality. It is true that when I want some resolution passed in the church, I can marshal my church-member employees and their families to lobby on behalf of the proposed resolution. Since there are so many people indebted to me, I can also do some pretty effective arm-twisting so that I can usually swing a majority vote whenever I want something badly enough. I recognize I am using a lot of financial "clout" to achieve my end, but I see nothing wrong with that. I have worked hard and God has blessed my efforts. God also has given me insights through my business experience from which the church can benefit. So I feel perfectly happy with the fact that some of us are a little more equal than others.

When Mennonites Developed A Church State And Decided To Defend It With The Sword

In their effort to be physically separated from the world, Mennonites, wherever possible, chose to live in closed in-group communities. Little did they realize that this type of settlement pattern made it necessary to nurture their own "world" in their midst—a world whose existence they did not even recognize.

The issue of a Mennonite civil government: Establishing the "sword of government" in the bosom of a closed Mennonite community

Early Mennonites in urban centers like Amsterdam, Hamburg, Danzig and Königsberg, who were able to get official recognition as "worthy" citizens, invariably were successful entrepreneurs who established themselves as vital cogs in the local economy. When distant central governments periodically found it expedient to issue expulsion decrees against them, the semi-autonomous Hansa cities along the coast often ignored or challenged such orders because they considered the Mennonites essential to their economic health, if not survival. When cities did fall in line with such expulsion decrees their local economies usually took a severe beating (Neff 1957, 3, 114).

Such urban Mennonite populations usually were not large, but their members' success in business frequently earned them public positions and made it possible to buy favored treatment like exemption for their sons from military service (H. S. Bender 1956, 2, 496; 1957, 3, 689). Thus urban Mennonites from the very beginning established the pattern of making financial payment to purchase and preserve the privileges they coveted.

In rural areas the Mennonite situation was quite different. Groups of Mennonite families were invited to lease and develop larger tracts of land and establish local economies. When Mennonites were invited to lease lands from a Catholic archbishop, the Polish crown, or even privately controlled lands in the Polish *Werder* area, they would make long-term (twenty to forty-year) leases with inheritance clauses. The lessors wanted a guaranteed financial return without further administrative responsibility, so a contract might make the lessee group responsible to organize internally, collect the annual rent from the individual families and make the annual lump sum payment to the lessor. Such lease agreements might specify that the Mennonite lessees were responsible to appoint their own village mayor, councillors or dyking officers (Baerg 1977, 12, 23). On the basis of these lease agreements Mennonites living on such tracts of land were pushed to develop some degree of internal civil government. As a result, the Mennonite church community no longer was governed solely by a *Lehramt* (ministers and teachers) but also by a budding *Gebietsamt* (civil government). The overall Mennonite exemption from police, militia and military service also tended to push Mennonites toward some civil governmental functions, such as community policing. This kept the nation's police out of their closed communities (Baerg 1977, 12).

By the time the Mennonites were invited to colonize South Russia, the pattern of local Mennonite civil government had already become an established part of their tradition. The invitation to Russia also specified that the settlers should organize their own internal civil government, so colonies had a civil structure right from the start. All these local colony governments in Russia reported to a supervisory committee set up by the Russian crown. It was known as the Settlement Guardians Committee. During the Johann Cornies' era, Mennonite colony administrations were moved ever further into the Russian government orbit. Since Cornies' seeming high-handedness had offended both the *Lehramt* and the *Gebietsamt*, the two were eventually drawn into a conspiracy to field a common candidate for *Oberschulze* (paramount mayor) following Cornies' death. The result was an informal church-state merger that violated a basic premise of the Radical Reformation (Loewen & Prieb 1996, 32-37).

The drift away from the principles undergirding the Radical Reformation had by now progressed to the degree that Mennonites were exercising the sword of government as a "state within the state." Unconsciously they had developed an almost Constantinian merger of church and state, duplicating, as it were, the religious conditions that led to the Reformation (D. H. Epp 1984, 74-75; Klippenstein 1984, 23ff; H. Loewen 1991, 145-168).

Readers respond:

A former resident of Yarrow, British Columbia recalls: There was no provision in Canada for the Yarrow community to set up a civil government. Yarrow belonged to Chilliwack municipality as far as the Canadian government was concerned. But this did not stop the Yarrow community from having a de facto Schulze *and a constabulary. At first it was sort of ad hoc that Mennonite X and his cronies on behalf of the community beat up the rowdies who overstepped the community norms from time to time. Later, when Yarrow installed running water from a mountain spring, the water board headed by the earlier ad hoc authority became the de facto civil government. Even the provincial police tacitly recognized its existence, because they always worked in close liaison with the water board whenever police concerns in Yarrow developed. Even though it had no legal status, this de facto local government operated for several decades. Old customs die hard!*

A resident from a Mennonite community remembers: The Mennonite Brethren Church controlled the local city hall. When the church saw that the number of young people who attended midweek Bible study and prayer services was steadily declining, the church council passed a resolution asking its church members, who controlled city hall, to pass a city ordinance to close the pool hall and the bowling alley on Wednesday nights, so as to encourage (force?) young people to come to church. The few church council members who objected to this approach lost their seats on the church council in the next election.

The question of self-defense and national defense with the sword

Mennonite willingness to organize a self-defense army in South Russia did not begin with the breakdown of law and order following the collapse of the tsarist regime at the end of World War I. That collapse was merely the occasion for bringing into being this specific self-defense event.

The persecution of Anabaptists that erupted in the middle of the sixteenth century was occasioned by their dissident radical views, which offended both the medieval Catholic Church and the emerging Magisterial Reformation. The passion of the day was the destruction of heresy. This was most crassly exemplified in the Holy Office of the Inquisition, but it was an attitude shared by the reformers. The magisterial reformers, who like the Catholic Church made accommodations with the governments of their domains, carried on the inquisitors' use of the sword to root out heresy. Even the Anabaptists had some concerns about heresy, hence the use of the ban to exclude people with heretical views from their fellowship. The difference was that the Catholics and the magisterial reformers used the literal sword to defend the truth, while the Anabaptists ideally tried to do so with redemptive love, admonition and, where necessary, the ban. Thus all groups, including Mennonites, had self-defense mechanisms.

Wealthy Mennonites in the urban Waterlander area of Holland became the first to use money as a means of self-defense. When William I of Orange, regent of the territory under the Spanish crown, became a Calvinist and started an independence movement in 1568, the Mennonites brought him a substantial cash contribution to be used as he saw fit (Brock 1991b, 101-102; Brons 1891, 45). This act, wittingly or unwittingly, began a pattern of self-defense that Mennonites employed for the next three-and-a-half centuries.

One of the earliest Mennonite property defenses was the arming of Mennonite-owned merchant ships (M. Driedger 1993, 11, 68-69; W. Mannhardt 1863, 33-34). Both Dutch and German Mennonite churches passed ordinances forbidding church members' involvement with armed vessels. In Holland this prohibition was eventually reduced to the "little ban," in which a Mennonite aboard an armed ship was excluded from the communion table as long as he was on the ship. As soon as he came ashore the "little ban" was lifted (Dollinger 1937, 2, 241; W. Mannhardt 1863, 33-34).

The next step was the justification of actual armed self-defense. The first argument of this type appeared (in about 1580) when the Dutch Mennonites split into the "defenseless" group who renounced all involvement with weapons, and the "revengeless" group which merely rejected aggression, revenge and attack but permitted defense of self or nation.

In Royal, West and East Prussia Mennonites maintained their aversion to arms well into the eighteenth century, especially since they were generally able to purchase group exemption from the Polish crown. But this aversion faded when they began to develop their own civil government, which, when it was re-established and expanded in South Russia, eventually culminated in the formation of a Mennonite self-defense army (Ehrt 1932).

The more Mennonites felt "at home" as citizens and the more wealth and power they accumulated, the more willing they were to participate in local and eventually also national governments. Once they identified with regional or national governments, feelings of responsibility for participation in national defense became inevitable (H. Quiring 1958, 3, 135; Teufel & Hein 1967, 4, 140). The rise of nationalism was often sparked by individual enlistment in armed forces (K. Bartel 1981, 43; Brock 1981, 33; Erb 1939, 75-82; Francis 1955, 109; W. Mannhardt 1863, 50-51, 198-199). As more and more Mennonite church members enlisted, church leadership felt intimidated and in a number of cases modified its doctrine to match the lifestyle of its members.

Readers respond:

An American Mennonite district minister, speaking at a conference that was trying to reconfirm nonresistance as an integral part of its faith: More than 50 percent of the current male church members in my district have served in the military or intend to do so, if the draft is revived. It is wrong for us to condemn these people as "inferior or disobedient." They are as sincere and as genuinely Christian as you nonresistance advocates are. I plead with you, let's make both military service and the conscientious objector position optional. Let people decide for themselves whether to take the conscientious objector stance or to serve in the military.

A Mennonite historian who spoke thirty minutes before the above plea, **said:** As a historian I am troubled by the many times Mennonites have adjusted their doctrine to match current less-demanding lifestyles. I have a feeling we are at such a critical crossroad again in regard to the sword of war.

A Mennonite member of parliament testifies: I am proud to be able to represent my faith in government service. Our country was founded on an implicit faith in God. Today secularism, materialism and relativism have undercut many of the moral foundations of our country and nation. I feel it is my Christian obligation to maintain some of the values on which our country was founded. I know politics is based on the art of the possible and compromise is the operative rule, but I still feel it is wrong to retreat from involvement and then complain that our country is going to the dogs.

When Mennonites Shifted Their View of the Canon

The Anabaptists have always stood with the mainline reformers in upholding the concept of *Sola Scriptura*. In spite of this common slogan, however, fundamental differences separated them in their approach to the Scriptures. First was the difference in their concept of the canon itself. The magisterial reformers all accepted a "flat" canon, while the radical reformers insisted on a "focused" view of the canon (H. Fast 1970, 29-36; Hein 1936, 6-10; Hillerbrand 1958, 101; Klaassen 1966b, 83-96; 1966a, 149; P. Yoder 1988, 70).

In Luther's "flat" view the New and Old Testaments had equal redemptive value and within the two Testaments all truth had relatively equal importance. The Anabaptists disagreed. For them, the incarnate Jesus Christ was the ultimate and maximal communication from God to humankind. Thus Jesus Christ was the supreme value in Scripture. All Scripture that concorded with Jesus' life and teaching was at the heart of what God wants to communicate to human beings, while those Scriptures that did not accord with or which related to Jesus' words and example only marginally were of lesser importance. On the basis of this, some have spoken of the Anabaptists as recognizing "a canon within the canon." This core canon included the Synoptic Gospels, especially the Sermon on the Mount, Matthew 24 and 25, and the Epistle of James (H. Fast 1970, 28-36; W. Klaassen 1964, 113-116; 1966a, 148-156; J. A. Toews 1981, 75; P. Yoder 1988, 73-74).

William Keeney (1968, 37-38) observed that Menno Simons and Dirk Philips both insisted that the Old Testament should be interpreted Christocentrically and that both of them demonstrated this in their writings—New Testament passages were placed in the text and Old Testament references placed in the margin. This focused use of Scripture has also been documented in a wider study by Yoder and Hochstetler (1969).

The focused canon was a powerful exegetical principle. It defined not only the core value of Scripture—Jesus' life and teaching—but by giving equal rank to teaching and life it postulated that word and deed are inseparable dimensions of faith. Furthermore, Jesus' teaching and life functioned as a prism through which all scriptural truth was to be filtered for interpretation. Dale Schrag (1989, 12-18) has said that the Anabaptists actually moved from *Sola Scriptura* to *Solus Christus* in their view of Scripture.

The implications of the preceding view can be demonstrated in the Anabaptist treatment of Luther's famous insight: "The righteous shall live by his faith" (Hab. 2:4). For Luther this dictum stressed the primacy of the act of faith. It demonstrated to him that when persons accepted God as real and his Word as true, they became children of God. The Anabaptists did not question the importance of accepting and believing in God and his Word—they also regarded such faith as being of primary importance. But they also expressed additional concerns.

When Abraham "believed" God (Rom. 4:3), was his faith expressed only in his act of believing—accepting God's Word as true and as valid—as the German/English words (*glauben/belie e*) seem to imply? The Anabaptists denied this, claiming that it resided in the fact that Abraham acted upon his faith. He left his homeland and followed God's leading to a new and strange land. Mere head belief is never enough. One has to act on what one believes. The Anabaptist emphasized that "doing" was the only actual proof of "real faith" (cf. Burkholder 1959, 4, 1079). For them the Epistle of James provided the solid scriptural foundation for this conviction. Hans Denck (Täuferakten 1956) expressed the Anabaptist view succinctly when he said, "One cannot know Christ, unless one actually follows him in life" (P. Yoder 1988, 75).

Hermann Mannhardt (1919, 30) maintained that Menno Simons liked to paraphrase Luther's famous dictum, "The just shall live by faith," as "those whose lives show that they live what they believe shall be saved." Williams (1962, 819), on the other hand, said that Luther moved from *Sola Scriptura* to *Sola Fides* (by faith alone). As a result the Epistle of James seemed like an "epistle of straw" to him. Luther felt that James did not support or expand the Romans dictum of "by faith alone." He therefore saw the epistle as promoting human works.

When Anabaptist/Mennonites shifted from their focused view to a flat view of the canon

Unlike the reformers, the early Anabaptists used a focused rather than flat canon. Martin Luther, for example, held monogamy and marital fidelity as core values of the church bearing his name. However, once he had made his accommodation with the political princes and for all practical purposes made the church the official church of the state, he had to face the problem that rulers did not always follow the behavior expected of members of the church. For Luther this happened when his chief protector, Philip of Hesse, became involved with a second woman. Luther's answer to the dilemma was found in the Old Testament. Kings and princes, as the Old Testament record plainly showed, often had more than one wife. Thus as long as Philip received the church's blessing for both women, he was not violating the church's marriage rule since the Old Testament clearly exempted rulers from the one-wife restriction. Did not King David, the man after God's heart, have multiple wives? Thus Prince Philip of Hesse, the man after Luther's heart, could do likewise (Keeney 1968, 35)!

William Keeney (1968, 35) has pointed out that the "level" Bible view was at the heart of the Münster episode. Israel's Old Testament conquest of Canaan with the sword was the model and example for ushering in the kingdom of God at Münster. Likewise, Jan van Leiden's encouragement of polygamy at Münster was also drawn from Old Testament sources.

At this point other Anabaptists, who utilized a focused canon, protested vigorously (Gen. 2:24, Matt. 5:27, 31-33). They did not dispute the historical fact that Old Testament kings had multiple wives, but they considered such situations as disobedience to God's original design and to Jesus' own words. And even if Jesus had not reaffirmed God's original design, Anabaptist students of Scripture would have said Philip of Hesse's polygamy was wrong, because their core canon made no such provisions.

Why and when did the Mennonites abandon their Christocentric view? There is no single or simple answer. It happened at different points in time in different places and to differing degrees. Whenever the church ceased to function as an exegetical community and began to operate on tradition, such as reading old sermons instead of having the congregation engage in live exegetical study of the Scriptures, their Christocentric stance lapsed. In fact, when the church abandoned live Bible study and leaned exclusively on old sermons, the spiritual life of the church declined.

The shift continued whenever early Mennonites opted for educated ministers who had been trained in flat-Bible institutions. Since there were few or no Mennonite seminaries at that time, it was difficult for early trained ministers to develop or nourish a Christocentric interpretive framework of Scripture. A classic example of the flat view of the Bible in Mennonite practice was the Lichtenau meeting on whether or not to organize a *Selbstschutz*. Benjamin H. Unruh, the most educated Mennonite Brethren minister and leader at the time, tipped the scale when he quoted Old Testament military examples to support the notion of a self-defense army. He was operating on a flat canon view that he had learned in German pietistic schools.

A more recent Mennonite Brethren example of the tension between the flat and the focused view of the Bible occurred in connection with a discussion of capital punishment in the Scriptures. Elmer Martens, an Old Testament scholar, represented the flat view, asserting that capital punishment was biblical because the overall orientation of the Bible argued in its favor, though the examples he cited were exclusively Old Testament. John Redekop, a political scientist, argued against capital punishment. He recognized the heavy Old Testament support for capital punishment but reasoned that the Sermon of the Mount and Jesus' whole ministry argued for an entirely new ethic. Obviously Redekop was utilizing the focused canon view of the Anabaptists. Ironically, in the subsequent debate over this issue John Redekop and Frank C. Peters were berated for their Anabaptist view of the Bible and were called liberals. The critics of these two men were no longer aware of the Anabaptist focused canon (E. Martens 1987, 3-4; F. C. Peters 1987, 8-9; J. Redekop 1987, 4-6).

A third reason for the loss of the focused canon came from outside influences. Dispensationalism divided the message of the Bible into different epochs or dispensations. This influence had already begun in South Russia. Next, in North America there was the powerful influence of fundamentalism, which stressed the literal interpretation of Scripture and thus led to the practise of proof-texting—citing specific isolated sections of Scripture "to prove" that dogmatic statements were true. While dispensationalism is no longer influential for most Mennonites today, fundamentalism still exerts enormous pressure in North America.

Readers respond:

An octogenarian, on being asked whether he remembered any flat Bible uses from his many years of Mennonite church experience, told the following: When I was still young one of our senior, relatively educated preachers and long-term Bible school teachers was discovered to have secretly "enslaved" several girls under twenty. He always used what you here call the "flat Bible" in his approach while seducing them. He read the Bible—the Old Testament with these girls and showed them in Scripture how God had provided David with a nubile young woman to "keep him warm" in his old age (1 Kings 1:1-4). He then went on telling the young women that they (individually) were God's gift to him in his old age. One must surmise that he had forgotten to read the last part of verse four in that passage, for there it clearly states that David was no longer active sexually. This preacher/teacher was still very active!

A Mennonite Brethren, who married a Canadian Indian woman in his youth, speaks about his experience: When I was nineteen, I fell in love with the woman who has been my wife for over forty years now--a Canadian Indian. When the news of my forthcoming marriage became community gossip, I was visited by a delegation from the Vorberat *(the church council)* and warned that God's Word forbids his "chosen" people to marry pagans. They quoted many verses of Scripture from the Old Testament like Ezra 10:2-3 and Neh. 13:27-8 and warned me of very grave consequences, like Solomon who strayed from the Lord when his pagan wives turned his heart. When I countered that the girl I wanted to marry was a member of the Anglican church, the brethren just dismissed that with a wave of the hand. When I insisted on going through with the wedding, I was forbidden the use of the church where I was a member. After my wedding in the Anglican church, I was excommunicated. Today when I look back on the experience I say "thank God," because I don't want to belong to a church of bigots. Now talking with you, I realize that the people who visited me and who excommunicated me were doing so on the premise of a flat canon. They couldn't find any New Testament support for their position, so they resorted to the Old. Isn't it strange how we use Scripture to defend our prejudices.

A northern stream Mennonite who has found a new home in Paraguay but operates on a flat Bible view says: My English is not very good, but I think I understood enough of what you are saying in your book to express wholehearted disagreement with your opinions. I firmly believe that God rescued us from Russia in 1929 and gave us a new "homeland" here in the Chaco of Paraguay. We Mennonites are a part of God's "chosen people." Just like God gave his Old Testament people of Israel their own land and independence, we, his New Testament people here in the Chaco, have likewise received our own colony with its own government. I think Peter Klassen's book Reich Gottes und Reich dieser Welt *(Kingdom of God and Kingdom of this world)* puts it just right.

CHAPTER 21

When the Function of Mennonite Congregations Changed

For Luther and the other reformers interpreting Scripture was the responsibility of an official, educated and duly-installed clergy. Here the Anabaptists again disagreed sharply. They considered the exegesis of Scripture to be the responsibility of the entire congregation. Under the guidance of God's Spirit, the Supreme Interpreter, believers studied the Word and then formed a consensus both as to the meaning of the passage and its implications for life and behavior. Thus the Anabaptists saw the congregation as the actual locus of all authority under Christ and under the guidance and empowerment of God's Spirit. This view differed radically from the magisterial reformers. Zwingli, for example, would not trust the congregation to make even worship decisions. That was the responsibility of the clergy and the Zurich city council (Haas 1975, 50ff; 1980, 76; Rues 1743, 10).

In time the Anabaptists/Mennonites were "de-radicalized," making three shifts in the role of the congregation in church and community life: (1) the congregation discontinued its function as exegetical community, (2) the congregation shifted from consensus decision-making to "democratic" majority voting, and (3) the locus of authority moved from the congregation to its paid professional clergy or to the leadership of the conference or denomination.

Who is responsible for the exegesis of Scripture: the congregation or its professionally trained leaders?

Luther proclaimed that faith in correctly and "officially" interpreted Scripture is the cornerstone of salvation. Correct scriptural interpretation, according to Luther, was the responsibility of an educated and officially-appointed clergy. Here the Anabaptists objected strenuously: arguing that it was the task of the congregation of believers. They believed in having ministers and teachers in the congregation, but these were mere servants of the fellowship and not its masters. As one Anabaptist put it, "the servants of the Word read it; but the congregation as a whole interprets it" (H.-J. Goertz 1988a, 52). The ministers' voices carried weight only insofar as they expressed what the entire congregation recognized as the truth. The Anabaptists strongly believed in "the rule of Paul": a scriptural text is best understood in the context of a congregation led by God's Spirit (P. Yoder 1988, 74-75, also see Huebner 1990).

The other dimension of exegetical concern was the translation of truth into daily behavior and lifestyle. The Anabaptists asked how biblical truth affects people's behavior. This emphasis downplayed the role of creeds, which were a central concern for the mainline reformers. For the early Anabaptists creeds, confessions of faith, and doctrinal statements could never be considered ultimate. They could always be improved upon as the Spirit of God led the congregation to new insights during the communal study of Scripture (P. Yoder 1988, 78).

Menno Simons expected the community to translate the exegeted word into lifestyle and behavior. The communal quest to understand and obey God's Word served as the corrective to prevent individual error (W. Klassen 1968, 77-87). William Keeney (1968, 34-35) has underscored that Menno and his followers were more interested in translating scriptural truth into a lifestyle of obedience than in intellectual or theological debate. This fact had already been stated in Hans Denck's famous and frequently quoted dictum: "You cannot understand the Scriptures until you obey them."

Menno correctly anticipated that once the Word had been understood and translated into behavior, the congregation would be inclined to establish this as a fixed creed in the form of rules of behavior. This happened early on in Holland (1555-1570) and eventually led to the *Sonnist-Lammist* struggle in the seventeenth century. The *Lammists* promoted continuing live exegesis; the *Sonnists* demanded a clearly-defined creed and specific rules of behavior (Brons 1891, 151).

Menno feared that these creeds and rules would become "set in stone" and degenerate into the kind of dead legalism demonstrated by the Pharisees and denounced by Jesus as following the letter of the law but violating its spirit (Mark 7:1-13; H.-J. Goertz 1988a, 56; Hein 1939, 10-11; H. G. Mannhardt 1919, 9).

Repeatedly, however, the church has shifted the exegetical responsibility to its paid pastors (or did paid pastors expropriate the exegetical responsibility from the congregation?). There were several reasons for the intimate connection between paid pastors and this shift in exegetical responsibility.

First, when many early Mennonites wanted educated ministers, they had no seminaries of their own. Their home-grown ministers had always been "formed" in the bosom of an active exegetical community (Ens 1990, 60-89). Those pastors who wanted further training had to attended non-Mennonite institutions where they were trained to personally fulfill the exegetical function. It was only natural that they would attempt to take over the exegesis when they were called to serve a Mennonite church as its minister.

Moreover, as members of the congregation moved up the economic and social ladder, the "one mind" of the congregation became increasingly more difficult to achieve. For some it no longer was comfortable to exegete and apply Scripture by the entire congregation. The paid preacher-exegete became an easy compromise in such cases.

New class distinctions further undermined the exegetical community. The upper class no longer felt comfortable when less-educated and poorer members of the congregation expressed their opinions on the meaning and application of specific Scriptures to life. Professional exegetes, paid for by the wealthier members, helped avoid embarrassing confrontations. The Waterlanders in Holland were the first to institute a paid professional ministry in 1568 for this reason (Keeney 1968, 56).

Wherever paid pastors were institutionalized in Mennonite churches, exegetical specialists and itinerant Bible teachers (*Reiseprediger*) soon followed. The latter now toured the churches, giving expositional lectures to more-or-less passive consumer audiences. Eventually such visiting professional Bible expositors were invited not only from the Mennonite church family, but also from other streams of faith. Thus, Mennonite churches were exposed to a variety of interpretations, some of which clashed in principle with their original in-group exegesis or even undermined their original values.

Readers respond:

A parent, whose two children hold doctorates in New Testament studies, asks: Are you really suggesting that our children do not have the right to share with Mennonite churches what they have learned in their studies? When I compare the insights into the Scriptures that our children can provide with the warmed-over shallow platitudes that uneducated old Reverend P. always spouts, I say: "Thank God, we now have some educated ministers and Bible teachers who can tell us what the Bible really says."

A professor of Mennonite biblical theology and frequent Bible expositor at conferences, when asked by a student how he squared his lecture-exegesis approach with the Anabaptist/ Mennonite ideal of the congregation as exegetical community, ventures: I do not claim that the lecture approach is the only or even the best approach to Bible study in the local church. I feel that I am but one educated individual among many in the church today and I see no reason why the theologically trained, the professionally educated and highly literate lay people cannot all work together to re-establish the pattern of communal exegesis. Indeed, I would be in favor of it. To be frank, however, I find that many church people have a decided preference for being "entertained" by a stimulating exegetical lecture, rather than having to personally engage in dialogue with the text in the context of all the members of their church community. Some, I think, are afraid that they might personally be embarrassed, if all members of the church were allowed to express their views on the Scriptures and on their application to daily life. Others just don't want to put forth the necessary effort.

A retired minister, from the days of the multiple lay ministry, opines: I sometimes have the feeling that the reason we now have Bible lectures instead of congregational Bible studies is because too many church people are afraid to have Scripture applied to life in a completely open situation. The truth may cut "too close to the bone" for some of those people who make their livelihood in the grey areas of the marketplace. Such people find it safer to hire a professional person whom one pays to give a lecture, because such educated people "know how to be discreet." It could become awfully embarrassing, if everyone were allowed to express his or her opinion about how a given Scripture should be applied in life, especially when some people have no understanding of the difficulties a person faces in the workplace or the marketplace.

A rather quiet member of the church cautions: I agree with this study that by and large our MB Church has forsaken congregational Bible study and exegesis. However, I would like to caution that there still are some bright spots. Our Wednesday night Bible studies, even though they are attended by less than one-third of our church members, still have some groups that function as actual exegetical communities. I feel our church leadership needs to be encouraged to push for greater participation by all members and to look for group leaders who can stimulate group exegesis, rather than doing a monologue on their personal interpretation. Maybe the church needs a class for Bible study group leaders in which they are taught how to lead discussions rather than give lectures.

How best to make decisions within the believing community?

In the Roman Catholic Church and in most mainline Protestant churches the average believer has no role in shaping the church creed.

The result is that church members accept the official creed in varying degrees. Only the most timid will express no reservations. The average believer may have quite a number of reservations, some of them serious.

Menno Simons believed that the church should always hold its doctrinal positions open for review and revision. Furthermore, he held that the statement of faith of a given congregation of believers should be reached on the basis of that group's internal consensus. Menno's hope was to develop a church in which all members felt they had had a hand in shaping their statement of faith and in which all individual members were committed to living out that statement in its entirety. Such consensus applied both to the interpretation of Scripture and to its application.

The sixteenth-century Reformation was marked by a heightened concern about heresy. The Holy Office of the Inquisition was responsible for making heresy a matter of life and death. The early Anabaptists felt that as long as exegetical decisions were being made on the basis of group consensus under the guidance of God's Spirit, heresy need never be a primary concern. Whenever there was a doctrinal or lifestyle disagreement, the whole fellowship, aiming to be of one accord, would seek the mind of God together until it could conclude: "It pleased the Spirit of God and us" (Acts 15:25-28).

When the persecution ended, however, Mennonites began to de-radicalize and compromise their "only-the-sword-of-the-Spirit" lifestyle. The result was a renewed concern about purity of doctrine. It is an observable fact of church life that shortfall in obedience often is compensated for by heightened concern about purity of doctrine.

As lifestyle slippage increased and concern over purity of doctrine multiplied, fractures began to divide the Mennonite family. Groups hardened in certain positions, no longer willing to seek consensus with those who were of a slightly different mind. Difficulties arose over the application of the ban, the attitude toward the sword of war, and matters of external dress, language and lifestyle.

The more social differences a congregation harbored, the more difficult consensus became. Some groups soon sought to alleviate this discomfort by opting for professional preachers and a more creedal approach to faith. This in turn meant that the members of a given fellowship began to vary greatly in their degree of commitment to the church's statement of faith and behavioral precepts.

From time to time certain wise leaders were able to maintain or to re-establish the exegetical community of believers as a consensus-forming body. For example, the Balk community in Holland continued with its lay ministry and the exegetical community approach long after the major Mennonite groups around them had already opted for the paid professional ministry (Barthel 1913, *1*, 112-114; Brüsewitz 1956, 19-31).

At times the revival of consensus occurred when individuals were stimulated to begin studying the Scriptures together again and as a result experienced spiritual renewal, for example, the Mennonite Brethren renewal in South Russia, or the more recent renewal among Mennonites in southern Manitoba.

Consensus decision-making received a fatal blow from the popularization of the democratic majority vote. This is probably the most widely-used decision-making mechanism in Mennonite churches today. Unless a vote is unanimous, however, the majority vote approach always leaves some "losers." Most Mennonite churches today seem to be reconciled to operating with a sizeable minority of dissenting voices. A few congregations are trying to revive consensus-style decision-making, but they are a minuscule minority. Most Mennonite churches and leaders today are too time-conscious to even consider the consensus approach.

Many churches are, in fact, moving in a very different direction, namely to a more centralized authority structure. A typical pattern involves the modern corporate model in which the day-to-day decisions are made by a chief executive officer guided by a board, which in turn reports periodically to its stockholders (church members). In this approach only those issues the board deems worthy of general assembly consideration are brought forward for group discussion. As a result the congregation becomes largely a rubber-stamping body. Many Mennonite church members, who have grown up in a situation in which the assembled congregation made all major decisions, are today severely frustrated, because under the new board-of-elders structure they have become all but irrelevant to the decision-making process.

Readers respond:

A church member, frustrated by the new pastor-Chief Executive Officer and board-of-elder structure, fumes: In the past our church council always screened issues before they came up for church assembly discussion, but it was always possible to introduce an issue from the floor. Today, with the board of elders, we are no longer presented with the issues to be discussed and to be decided. We are faced with decisions that have already been made and we are asked to "rubber-stamp"—politely called "to ratify"—decisions that we had no part in making. I find it scandalous. It is completely unlike the Mennonite church I have known for sixty years. Somebody has hijacked my church!

A senior pastor of a church of 1,200 members, when asked about his attitude toward consensus decision-making, said: I think consensus decision-making in a large church like mine is utterly unrealistic. To attempt it is an absolute waste of time. In fact, I find that even the democratic majority vote often is a waste of time. But I guess it is a necessary concession to keep church members happy. I prefer the board of elders structure of which I am the chairperson (Chief Executive Officer) overseeing board members whom I have personally selected from among spiritual people who are on my wavelength. With such an arrangement, decision-making is quick and easy. Then it is also easy to operate a successful church. Most of the church members don't have the spiritual maturity to make the necessary judgments.

A young moderator of a church of 250-plus, which operates on consensus decision-making, says: Any church leader who says that consensus decision-making in a church our size is for the birds understands neither it nor the function of genuine Anabaptist leadership. Consensus decision-making demands a lot of leadership (servanthood?). The leader has to make sure he understands and digests both the very hesitant and the most passionate or farthest-out opinions. It is up to him to discover what the actual differences between all these points of view are. It is up to him to help the group establish the relative value rating among these differences of opinion. If he can make everyone feel that their voice is being heard and then helps the group as a whole to attach price tags to these differences, consensus usually is not far away. I believe in consensus! It makes a world of a difference in membership support and loyalty.

Where does authority in the church reside: in the congregation or its paid pastor?

Scholars of early Anabaptist/Mennonite history agree that the Radical Reformation placed the seat of authority in the congregation. In fact, Menno himself insisted that "the temple of God" was not the individual born-again believer nor the minister of the congregation, but the collective body of the congregation itself. This insistence grew stronger as Menno grew older (Bornhäuser 1970, 20, 23). The fellowship of believers collectively searched the Scriptures and under the guidance of God's Spirit they both formulated the doctrines of the church and specified their application in daily life. The congregation was the highest court of appeal in theology and lifestyle. If the issue in question was bigger than any local congregation, then all the congregations concerned considered the issue jointly and reached a consensus decision (W. Klassen 1968, 77-79).

Likewise it was the congregation that selected and called its leaders under the Spirit's guidance. To remind the persons selected of where the actual authority resided, these chosen leaders were called "servants of the church." Even though there was an implicit distinction of gifts and services among servants—simple servants (deacons), servants of the Word (ministers) and full servants (elders)—the church saw the difference between them as a matter of function and not authority (Loserth 1913, 438).

These "servants" quickly lost the attitude of servanthood and equality with all other members of the congregation, and began to see themselves as occupying positions of power. And since "full servants" or "elders" were vested with certain exclusive functions, like ordination of other servants, these were readily interpreted as giving them superior authority. We see this in the case of Leenaert Bouwens, Menno Simons' co-elder, who had to be sidelined for some time because he began to exercise arbitrary powers (Vos 1913, *1*, 251). In this case the church quickly reasserted its authority. But eventually the power of elders became institutionalized (Bender 1956b, 128-132). In Germany, where local congregations often had multiple elders, their authority was thereby downplayed, but elsewhere with single bishops the office was soon invested with increased powers.

A recurrent leadership problem in Anabaptist/Mennonite history had rested in the authority to apply the ban. The earliest view was that only the exegetical community could decide matters of truth and error. Thus only the believing community as a whole could apply the ban. Ministers alone could not do so. This became a problem in the Altona-Hamburg congregation when elders single-handedly imposed the ban, but the congregation paid no attention to such actions. It became a serious problem in South Russia when the elders organized themselves as a *Kirchenkonvent*.

As noted elsewhere, the problem of ministerial authority was greatly worsened when churches discontinued their original multiple lay ministry and shifted to paid professional ministers. This frequently happened when the church became more affluent and inequalities in the membership undermined the decision-making and exegetical functions of the fellowship.

A recent phenomenon in the shift of authority away from its locus in the congregation has involved the development of more centralized conference or denominational structures. In the case of the

Mennonite Brethren Church this struggle is reflected in the ongoing battle over the conference name: Is it the Conference of Mennonite Brethren Churches with ultimate authority resting in the individual congregations (thus making general conference resolutions only serious fraternal counsel), or is it the Conference of the Mennonite Brethren Church with ultimate authority resting in the leadership of the conference (thus making general conference resolutions binding on all congregations)?

Readers respond:

Frustrated church members of a congregation whose pastor is authoritarian, if not dictatorial, say: We are tired of being tongue-lashed from the pulpit as if we were naughty children. We resent being labeled "unspiritual." We feel that we have as deep a concern for this church as the pastor does. Since we have grown up here and he is only a recent arrival in our community, we feel that we understand the local situation as well, if not better, than he does. Furthermore, we think we have some positive input to make. What's happened to his "servant" attitude?

A frustrated pastor, in a letter to the editor of the church paper, says: I feel that God called me to the ministry and also to the ministry in this specific church. Furthermore this church extended a call to me to be its leader. But how can I lead, when the congregation won't follow? How am I to exercise my gifts and carry out the vision God has given me, when the congregation continually insists on writing its own agenda, and then demands that I follow it? Since when does the flock dictate how its shepherd should lead?

A district minister confides: What worries me most about our churches is how many ministers feel inhibited, if not bound, by powerful factions in their churches. Much of the tension that pastors express comes from having to weigh every word in terms of "will this offend" a powerful person or group within the church? Time and again pastors feel they have to compromise their integrity in order to avoid being pushed out prematurely by an offended group in the congregation.

An older Mennonite Brethren member, grown up under congregational control, who suddenly found himself sidelined by a board of elders of which the pastor is the Chief Executive Officer, laments: Church meetings have become a farce. We ordinary mem-

bers no longer make decisions as a congregation. The board of elders makes the decisions and occasionally it asks us to rubberstamp some of them. I feel like someone or some group has hijacked the church and reduced the congregation to second-class bystanders.

A congregation under an authoritarian minister complains: *We don't dispute that our minister has God's call to be a minister. However, we resent his authoritarian attitude. He sees himself alone as being spiritual and all the rest of us in the congregation as unspiritual. He will not permit consensus decisions. He considers such decisions to represent the "lowest common denominator." Oh, that our ministers could again operate in a "serving" rather than "governing" attitude!*

When Mennonites Achieved Physical Isolation as "God's Chosen People" in Their Own "Promised Land" and Then Lost Their Reason to be

As citizens of the kingdom of peace the early Mennonites regarded themselves as a perpetual minority. When their "separateness" brought persecution upon them, they quickly identified with "God's chosen people," the Old Testament children of Israel, who repeatedly had been hounded by their more powerful neighbors.

When Mennonites began to drain the Vistula Delta in 1547 and were able to lease large tracts of land for twenty to forty-year periods with inheritance and renewal provisions, they were suddenly able to extend their ideological and behavioral separation by means of relative physical isolation; they could, as per lease contract, establish their own homogeneous, largely self-governing villages. They could now actually be physically separate in their own villages. This physical isolation was further augmented when Mennonites were able to establish large self-governing colonies in South Russia. God's separated people had finally achieved their own Promised Land (H. Penner 1955, 69, 75).

The negative consequences of the "chosen people" complex

The feeling of being God's chosen people had far-reaching effects on Old Testament Israel. They saw themselves as the sole heirs to all of God's blessings, spiritual and material. They saw God as being on their side unconditionally. All other peoples were expendable in Israel's interest. In fact, they saw God as actively helping them drive out, exterminate, enslave or subjugate the "pagan" peoples surrounding them.

According to J. C. Toews (1954, August 4, 2-3), Mennonites in Russia always felt that Russian laws did not apply to them. Hence they felt fully justified to bribe officials to get their way. If a Mennonite had to deal with some local or regional Russian official, he always made sure his wagon or sleigh carried enough sausage and ham to achieve his ends. This above-the-law feeling of a group with a chosen people complex has been very apparent also among Mennonites in Canada who live along the U.S. border. Customs regulations, for example, were often described contemptuously as *domme Jesatze* (stupid laws), to be broken at will. Observers of the Mennonite colonies in Paraguay have noted similar attitudes there.

Among the benefits Mennonites as chosen people enjoyed, the exemption from military service—the highly abbreviated relic of their earlier lifestyle of peace and renunciation of force—was prized above all. It was seen as an exclusive in-group privilege and something that need not be shared. As a result Mennonites in Russia began to separate their peace witness from the rest of their gospel message. This separation has been an endemic Mennonite problem ever since (Bender 1935; 1950, 149-155).

Once the gospel of salvation had been detached from the lifestyle of peace, more features of the original only-the-sword-of-the-Spirit lifestyle were neglected. The gospel focus continued to narrow until it eventually became largely a concern with soul-winning—getting people to accept Christ as their Savior so they "would be ready for heaven." Conversion became the supreme focus of Christian evangelism and, as a result, discipleship, spiritual growth and stewardship attitudes toward property retreated as relatively unimportant concerns to be managed by individuals as they saw fit. The ultimate consequence in North America has been what Abraham Friesen (1988, 86) has called "the Mennonite drift toward rootless, rudderless evangelicalism" or as H.-J. Goertz (1988b, 3) put it, the "community of God" now often became the "city without God."

Readers respond:

*A **Honduran Mennonite pastor** says: Not one Mennonite missionary from North America came to us as a committed Anabaptist. Mennonite missionaries, except for some idiosyncrasies in dress, were utterly indistinguishable from all the other soul-winning evangelicals around us.*

*A **recent convert, now a member of a Mennonite church, reports**: I recently attended my first North American conference of our church. The sermons and other presentations at the sessions were superb. The mealtime fellowship was excellent. But whenever a delegate met me in the halls or outside between sessions and looked at my name tag—MacPherson—I discovered that I did not really belong to "God's chosen people." Invariably people blurted out: "Oh you're not a Mennonite!" Or asked, "Was your mother a Mennonite?" I realized that because my name was not Friesen, Reimer, Klassen, etc., I* *was seen as an outsider! Some apologized for their rudeness and their implicit ethnocentrism, saying, "We're so used to our in-group names that we forget that even people of Scottish or Irish ancestry can be converted and become Mennonites by conviction."*

The issue of Mennonite loss of identity and the resulting susceptibility to outside partisan influences

Whenever Mennonites, for whatever reasons, began to doubt their chosenness or uniqueness, their self-identity came under pressure. Today in North America the chosen people complex is all but extinct, but it has not been succeeded by a healthy sense of spiritual identity. As a result, Mennonite identity today is in severe crisis (G. Ediger 1986, 47). This crisis causes individuals and churches to drink from all sorts of theological fountains in search of a new identity (L. Driedger 1990b, 159-175; W. Klaassen 1990, 13-26; Zuercher 1985, 5). The current pervasive insecurity has made Mennonites exceedingly vulnerable to many outside influences (L. Driedger 1988, 9-208; Redekop & Steiner 1988, 1-202; R. Reimer 1985, 69-75; J. A. Toews 1972, 2-4, 25) and to being assimilated to the surrounding cultural milieu (L. Driedger 1990b, 159-175).

Contributing to this susceptibility is the loss of the exegetical community. This loss makes it increasingly difficult for Mennonite churches to reach collective decisions about the value of new ideas and new practices introduced from the outside. Many Mennonite churches, having lost their capacity for discernment and their appreciation of their original Anabaptist values, seemingly drift along helplessly, carried by a variety of popular currents.

Aggravating this situation is the paid-pastor/spectator-congregation trend, which characterizes so many Mennonite churches today. With pastors usually selected from outside of the local church, the congregation often has only scant knowledge of the new pastor's philosophy, theology and lifestyle. New pastors can easily introduce alien interpretations and practices without the congregation realizing how its theological orientation is being undermined.

Mennonite history is replete with examples of outside influence. One of the earliest examples involved the Remonstrants in Southern Holland. Remonstrants accepted Calvin's doctrine of predestination, but they were moderates and believed in religious liberty and tolerance for all (Brons 1891, 148; Zijpp 1959, 4, 296). As moderate Calvinists they objected to the extreme positions taken by some Reformed leaders. Their name actually derives from five "articles of remonstrance" objecting to the extreme position of the Reformed Church that they sent to government and church authorities. Collegiants, on the other hand, felt that no existing church could claim continuity with the New Testament church in Acts. They wanted no formal organization and no church buildings; but they emphasized adult believers' baptism and the priesthood of believers (Kolakowski 1990, 259-297, 385-416; Zijpp 1955, *1*, 640). The Remonstrants' influence was imported largely through Mennonite ministers who had trained in Remonstrant seminaries. John Smyth's baptistic Pietism seems to have created much smaller ripples there (Coggins, 1991, 101-107). In Hamburg-Altona it was the Dompelaars and the Quakers who caused severe disruptions in the Mennonite churches. Dompelaars, also called "Dunkers," emphasized adult baptism by immersion and footwashing before communion (Brons 1891, 140-141; Neff & Zijpp 1956, *2*, 81-82; B. C. Roosen 1886, 40). The Quakers were founded in England by George Fox in 1650 who called his followers "Friends of Truth." He stressed a return to simple Christianity in which believers followed their "inner light," the image of God implanted at creation (Gen. 1:26). Quakers worshiped without sacraments or clergy (H. S. Bender 1959, *4*, 561; H. Penner 1987, 173; B. C. Roosen 1886, 45). In Prussia, Lutheranism seems to have offered a way out for many Mennonites who chafed under the status restrictions they had to endure as Mennonites.

In the 1860 renewal in Russia, the overwhelming outside influence was Pietism which had both positive and negative effects. In North America fundamentalism has been one of the most powerful factors undermining Mennonite fidelity to an only-the-sword-of-the-Spirit lifestyle. Revivalism and evangelicalism have run a close second. Of late, individualism (Ainley 1990, 135-153), materialism and modernism have also become very powerful. Increasingly, North American Mennonites' loyalty to the values of Anabaptism diminishes as they have moved into popular evangelicalism and cultural religion (J. E. Toews 1985, 60-68).

Readers respond:

A current pastor of a Mennonite church trained in Christian and Missionary Alliance schools says: I find Mennonite peace principles and the so-called Anabaptist distinctives irrelevant relics of the past and impediments to our current soul-winning and church growth efforts.

A self-styled progressive Mennonite church member believes: I think it is high time Mennonites as a whole jettisoned their "burden of tradition" and stepped into the twentieth century. I think that the future of the church lies with soul-winning evangelicalism and we should get into that stream as quickly and as completely as possible.

An "evangelical" Mennonite says: *I resent the fact that the authors seem to imply that we have sold "our Anabaptist birthright" for a mess of "evangelical pottage." I am proud to identify with Billy Graham, Campus Crusade and interdenominational faith missions like Gospel Missionary Union, The Evangelical Alliance Mission, etc. Even Mennonite stalwarts like H. S. Bender and John Redekop spoke and speak about "evangelical Anabaptists." I want to belong to a soul-winning, growing, evangelical church. I see evangelicalism as something very positive.*

An ardent supporter of Mennonite Brethren evangelicalism objects: *I think this study does a grave injustice to evangelicalism by treating it so negatively. I acknowledge that it avoids setting up "straw men"—like treating evangelicals as traditional reactionaries of limited intelligence, as fundamentalist ignoramuses, as dishonest opportunists, or as religious fanatics who endanger civil liberties—but I still feel it does an injustice to mainstream evangelicalism. I agree with the study in several aspects. I, too, am embarrassed by evangelists like Billy Graham praying for the U.S. war effort. I wish evangelicalism were not so chummy with materialism and individualism. I, too, wish it would emphasize more orthopraxy, not only orthodoxy. On the other hand, it is the evangelicals who send the most missionaries, sponsor the major evangelistic campaigns worldwide and who provide some of the best radio and television religious programming in America and worldwide today.*

PART FOUR
THE HOPE

While there have been many embarrassing adjustments and compromises among the heirs of the Menno Simons' vision, there is hope, deep-seated hope, for the Mennonite church. There have been just as many examples of moving fidelity throughout the northern streams of history, as there have been embarrassing infidelities. Even though this study suggests that currently many Mennonites are drifting into evangelicalism, it recognizes that the "only-the-sword-of-the-Spirit" lifestyle can be recovered by all those who want to open more areas of their life to God. To encourage and facilitate such a recovery, this study concludes with two chapters of hope.

Despite the dizzying number of occasions when our family of faith has fallen short, there also have been countless occasions of profound, faithful discipleship. Some of them appear in the next chapter. The final chapter, then, involves a Bible-based appeal for turning more "rooms" of our lives over to Jesus, our Lord. This appeal is based on John Howard Yoder's discovery that the Radical Reformation is a model for recurrent or ongoing renewal (also see Abr. Friesen 1994). The house-with-many-rooms metaphor is then illustrated by a personal and family testimony. This is followed by a rationale for considering conversion, renewal and Christian growth as necessarily ongoing processes. This fourth part concludes with a final appeal for today's Anabaptist/Mennonite churches to change their direction radically—to return to their founding vision.

Stories of Fidelity

A vision remains only a vision until it is fleshed out in action or life. The redemptive plan of God became believable when "the Word became flesh and dwelt among us." Jesus, the incarnated Word, attracted followers because he not only "talked" about the narrow road of obedience (Heb. 5:8), he also "walked" it.

Fifteen centuries after Christ, Menno Simons studied the Word and rediscovered new birth and discipleship. He, too, decided to "talk and walk" the gospel! He described his understanding of discipleship as "living by the sword of the Spirit." Like Jesus Christ, Menno's example also inspired many people to lead lives of Christian discipleship.

Many believers who followed Jesus in the early church or during the Reformation were persecuted as enemies of the state and its associated church powers. In both eras the disciples of Jesus, though they expected his early return, refused to wait for a future dispensation to practice obedience. They were convinced that as citizens of the kingdom of God they could never join the kingdoms of this world, but were to penetrate them as salt and light. They saw themselves as pilgrims and strangers in transit through an alien world. They firmly believed that Jesus called them to walk the "narrow road" after him. They were to live a life of redemptive nonconformity to "take up the cross" of self-denial and self-sacrifice and follow Jesus (Wenger 1951). They recognized that the world would persecute them for this, but they were ready to lay down their lives for their faith.

The Golden Mean or the Golden Rule?

Some church leaders, evangelists and others may complain that the ideals of the Sermon on the Mount are extremist, impossible or unrealistic. They invite others to "be born again," but neglect calling these converts to follow Jesus in a life of obedience. As a result, many who claim to be believers continue to live by the "Golden Mean" of Greek philosophy—the middle road of cultural accommodation—rather than the "Golden Rule," the narrow road "of loving God and their neighbor as they love themselves."

Absolute fidelity is, of course, beyond human reach. But if Christ and the Spirit indwell the believer, fidelity—not perfection—is possible. One should not assume that fidelity will always lead to martyrdom, or that persecution is a prerequisite for fidelity. Fidelity can happen anywhere, anytime, and in the most unexpected places. Any person or group accepting Christ as Savior and following him obediently as Lord can become a model of fidelity.

The Martyrs' Mirror

The testimonies of some eight hundred Christian martyrs who serve as vivid examples of this possibility have been preserved in a 1,290-page book, commonly known as the *Martyrs' Mirror*, first published by Thielman van Braght in 1660. Van Braght, a Mennonite church elder in Dordrecht, compiled this book to call the church back to willingness to suffer for its faith. He saw the church of his day, softened by prosperity and affluence, as compromising its biblical faith for the sake of security.

Van Braght desired to pass on the faith by publishing stories of the martyrs' fidelity. He agreed with Tertullian, the early church father, who said, "The more you mow us down, the more we grow, the blood of the martyrs is the seed of the church." No book except the Bible has been more influential in nurturing the Mennonite faith than the *Martyrs' Mirror* (Oyer & Kreider, 1990, 7,9).

Van Braght begins his long line of martyrs with Jesus who died on the cross. Then comes John the Baptist, who was beheaded (A.D.32). He is followed by Stephen, the deacon (A.D.34), the first Christian martyr in the church, who forgave his enemies as they stoned him, praying: "Lord, do not hold this sin against them" (Acts 7:60). Nearly all of the disciples, apostles and early church leaders died as martyrs. Century by century stories of those who died for their faith are retold. Most of van Braght's Anabaptist martyr stories are drawn from the seven decades of persecution in the sixteenth century, when more than 2,500 Anabaptists died for their faith.

People of fidelity always have to pay a price for their faithfulness. Discipleship is costly. Every period of church history shows that sacrifice is unavoidable. Persecution by execution may be less common today, but tension between the two kingdoms continues. "Narrow road" living still has its costs.

The stories of fidelity that follow are taken from the *Martyrs' Mirror* and other sources (A. A. Toews 1949-1954, 2 vols.). Some are old and some are recent, but they are included here to inspire and encourage believers to accept Christ's call of discipleship. They illustrate fidelity to values that so often have suffered slippage or compromise. These testimonies offer a viable alternative to the empty and fruitless fast-lane lifestyle of many compromised Christians who live as comfortable citizens in the kingdoms of the world. Perhaps these examples will encourage some to decide to live as citizens of the kingdom of peace and as sojourners or pilgrims during their life on earth.

They died for their faith
"My son, hear the instructions of your mother"

Anneken Jans of Rotterdam was sentenced to die for her Christian convictions. She was drowned on January 24, 1539. At the site of execution she offered her infant son, Isaiah, together with a purse of money, to anyone who would promise to take care of the child. A baker with six children took the child.

In a letter written to her son, the mother counseled him to live as Jesus taught:

> My son, hear the instruction of your mother; open your ears to hear the words of my mouth. Behold, I go today the way of the prophets, apostles and martyrs, and drink of the cup of which they all have drunk. . . My child, do not regard the great number, nor walk in their ways . . . Where you hear of a poor, simple, cast-off little flock, which is despised and rejected by the world, join them; for where you hear of the cross, there is Christ; from there do not depart . . . Take the fear of the Lord to be your father, and wisdom shall be the mother of your understanding (adapted from Braght, 1938, 453-454; Oyer & Kreider, 1990, 38-39).

He wouldn't run away

Joris Wippe of Dordrecht was a highly respected cloth dyer. He was a kind man who gave food and material aid to the poor. When the authorities discovered that he was an Anabaptist, they hoped he would flee. They did not want to kill him. They did not even try to dissuade him from his faith because his faith and life were so authentic.

Because the law demanded it, Wippe was finally sentenced to death. But for seven weeks he lay in prison unpunished. No one was willing to execute him. Finally a soldier volunteered. He drowned Wippe in a barrel inside the prison to avoid a public outcry.

Before his death Wippe wrote letters full of joy, consolation and assurance to his wife and children (Braght 1938, 584-588; Oyer & Kreider 1990, 34-35).

To stop her from testifying they filled her mouth with gunpowder

Dutch Mennonites for centuries have sung hymns based on the story of Anneken Hendricks. She was active in circles of Bible-reading Christians and freely shared her faith in public. At her execution (c.1571) her mouth was filled with gunpowder to prevent her from witnessing (Braght 1938, 872-874; Oyer & Kreider 1990, 24-25).

No marble shaft marks the spot

Clayton Kratz became the first martyr among Mennonite Central Committee workers. He came to Russia to help save Mennonites and Russians from starvation during the famine following WWI. In the midst of his service he disappeared. Some say he was arrested and secretly killed. Others say that he fell ill on a trip and died as an unknown stranger in a Russian village. No one really knows how he met his end. Regardless of the manner of death, however, he died while serving others in need (G. Harder 1971).

> No marble shaft marks the spot where his body returned to earth. But his name is graven on the ears of thousands and thousands whom he came to help. Their children and children's children will repeat the story of the Mennonite youth who came from far away America to save their lives and gave his own. "Greater love hath no man than this, that a man lay down his life for his friends" (Prieb, 1990, 58).

They testified to the power of the Lamb

A modern Hans Denck

In *The Ephrata Story*, here greatly abbreviated, Ira S. Franck (1964) describes the power of the Lamb when Michael Whitman, a loyalist during the American Revolution and owner of a tavern in Ephrata, Pennsylvania, spat in Peter Miller's face without provocation. Miller, a nonresistant Christian, served as the leader of the Ephrata Cloister, where the *Martyrs' Mirror* was translated into German and printed for Mennonite homes in America.

Miller did not retaliate. A few days later he received word that Whitman had been arrested for treason by General Washington and sentenced to be hanged at Valley Forge. Miller put his work aside and trudged seventy miles to Valley Forge to see Washington. The conversation between the two went something like this:

Washington: Please state briefly and clearly the purpose of your coming here.

Miller: I have come here from Ephrata upon hearing that Michael Whitman has been sentenced to be hanged. I have come to plead that he be permitted to live. I pledge myself to act as his sponsor.

Washington: Are you aware of the gravity of the charge against this man? I suppose this man is your friend and that it is for this reason that you ask me to spare his life.

Miller: Sorry, sir, this man is not my friend. Indeed, he considers himself my bitterest enemy (shortened and adapted).

To confirm his statement, Miller recounted for the general the spitting insult. The general was so moved that he granted the plea and spared Whitman's life.

The sword of the Spirit overcomes

Missionary John C. Paton tells the story of how a converted South Pacific island chief and four other Christian men responded when they were greeted with a hail of spears as they entered a hostile village. Addressing the villagers the Christian chief said, "We come to you without weapons of war! We come to tell you about Jesus." The villagers were surprised that these Christians had come without weapons. They were even more surprised when they refused to throw back the spears hurled at them. They stopped fighting. Then the Christian chief spoke again: "Once we would have thrown your spears back at you and tried to kill you. Now God has changed our hearts. He now asks you, too, to lay down all weapons of war, and to hear what we can tell you about the love of God, our Father." The witness of this Christian chief and his four friends led the whole tribe to become Christians (Toews & Nickel 1986, 117).

A nun gives her life for her faith

Elizabeth, a nun and teacher, heard about martyrs who died for their faith. Deeply moved, she began to study the Scriptures and discovered the truth. She escaped the nunnery and joined an Anabaptist community. Eventually she was captured and in 1549 was examined before a judge. The *Martyrs' Mirror* describes her interrogation, from which the following dialogue is adapted. Elizabeth was asked to swear whether she was married or not. She answered, "I am not permitted to swear, our words are yes or no, I know no man." When asked to name the students she had influenced, she refused, saying, "I cannot tell you their names, because you will persecute them."

Inquisitor: "What do you think of our mass?"

Elizabeth: "My lords, I do not think much of your mass because it does not agree with God's Word."

Inquisitor: "What do you think of the sacraments?"

Elizabeth: "I find nowhere in the Scriptures that it is called a sacrament. We do celebrate the Lord's Supper."

Inquisitor: "What do you think of infant baptism, since you had yourself rebaptized?"

Elizabeth: "No my lords, I have no intention to be rebaptized. I was baptized once on the confession of my faith."

Inquisitor: "Do you not seek salvation through baptism?"

Elizabeth: "No my lord, salvation only comes if we love God above all else and our neighbor as ourselves."

Inquisitor: "Does the priest have power to forgive sins?"

Elizabeth: "No my lord, Christ is the only one who can forgive sins."

From here she was taken to the torture chamber. When torture did not move her, she was drowned (abbreviated and adapted from Brons 1891:108-113).

Catalysts for Christ

A catalyst helps feuding Christians become a Christian community

A Quechua Indian community in Ecuador was troubled by family feuds that dated back centuries. The missionaries among this group of

Quechua had worked there for twenty-five years. They had won many individuals and numerous families to accept Christ as their Savior, but due to the endemic feuds no church organization had been possible. Missionary/anthropologist I. M. Friedmann was called in to help find a solution.

Following a Bible study about Mary washing Jesus' feet with her tears and drying them with her hair (John 11:2), Friedmann was introduced as a visiting anthropologist. Not knowing what "anthropologist" meant to the people, Friedmann asked them, "Do you know what anthropologists do?" One person answered, "They dig up dead people's bones." Friedmann then went on to say he was a different kind of anthropologist. He studied culture, the way people lived. Furthermore he was a Christian.

He then went back to the Bible study just finished and told them about a personal experience that had really crushed him. He ended by asking: "Have any of you ever been deeply upset about some bad things you have done, just as Mary in this story was?"

After a short period of silence a man asked: "What should one do if one had thrown his brother-in-law in jail and now felt bad about it?"

Not knowing whether the question was real or hypothetical, Friedmann continued: "In my culture I know, but what should one do in your culture? Maybe our friends can help us."

Immediately people responded with, "He should apologize! He should be reconciled! He should ask his relative to forgive him! He should love his brother-in-law again!"

Friedmann then turned to the questioner and said: "I think our friends have spoken well!"

No sooner had he said this, the man walked across the room knelt down before another man and begged: "Brother-in-law, will you forgive me and love me again?" The two embraced. Then he moved over and said to the man's wife: "Sister, will you forgive me and love me again!" They, too, embraced with tears freely flowing.

Soon there was movement all over the room as people knelt before others to be reconciled. At this point Friedmann slipped out. His catalytic function was finished.

Within days these Christians asked the mission whether they could organize a church (adapted from I. M. Friedmann, 1990, 63-65).

They solved conflict like kingdom citizens

Two Mennonites go to court to solve a boundary dispute

Two Mennonites with adjoining properties had a boundary dispute. They took it to the church, but the church could not solve it and so asked them to go to the civil courts. On the appointed day, Mennonite one called on his neighbor and said, "Today's the day, let's go to court together!" The neighbor countered, "Brother, if I don't hill my potatoes today, I'm going to lose my crop. You know my side of the story, why don't you represent both of us." The first Mennonite went to court, told both sides of the dispute and the court decided in favor of Mennonite two. In the evening on his way back from court Mennonite one stopped by his neighbor to report. It was suppertime so he joined the family at the table and reported, "I told both your story and mine. The court decided in your favor, so let's thank God" (Erb 1939, 80).

Common or individual communion cup? They reached con sensus!

During the 1930s the Hillsboro (Kansas) Mennonite Brethren Church struggled over the issue of changing from the common cup to individual communion cups. After several congregational meetings, consensus began to emerge in favor of individual cups. But John F. Harms, the long-time Mennonite Brethren publisher, ardently defended the established tradition of the common cup. Jacob W. Vogt, the minister, made a suggestion. "Brothers and sisters, let's wait and continue to pray for further guidance from God."

In the intervening time a health crisis developed in the rural school districts of the area. The problem was traced to germs spreading via the common dipper used for drinking in schools. The county health department promptly eliminated the common dipper in public drinking places. Younger parents now confronted the older Harms with the new health regulations. Harms, convinced by his concern for public health, changed his mind. At a congregational vote in 1944 ninety percent voted for the change (O. Harms 1987, 178).

Salt and light pilgrims

He gave them bread

Jacob G. Ewert, a close friend of Peter C. Hiebert, had been an invalid for twenty-five years. Both his legs were cramped and his joints were immovable with arthritis. His left arm was crippled. His jaw was ossified. All his food had to be administered in liquid form through an opening made by removing his first molar tooth. His neck was immobile. He could only use his right arm when it was suspended in a sling, and on his right hand he could move only the thumb and one finger.

Ewert was a brilliant man. He was master of both English and German, and a scholar of Greek, Latin and Hebrew. He had a reading and writing knowledge of seven additional modern European languages, including Russian.

This man, who should have been the object of relief help, became an agent for a food remittance plan to aid the starving Mennonites in Russia. With his right arm hanging in the sling, he punched keys on a typewriter placed on his bed. His brother, David, also an invalid, had some control of his hands. He moved the typewriter carriage and fed in new sheets of paper when needed. Peter C. Hiebert described how the brothers worked (Prieb 1990, 67).

> For hours at a time and during the days of the food-draft rush, from early morning till often past midnight, these two men would work without ever a word of complaint or murmuring. While Jacob, the elder, would peck away on the keys to fill the line, David would sit motionless near at hand with a small string attached to the carriage of the machine. As soon as the line was complete, the shift was made with one pull of the string. Thus they proceeded from line to line until the letter was finished or the page was full. Then David, the quiet brother of whom the world knows very little, would feed another sheet of paper and set the machine ready for a repetition of the former operation.

On March 14, 1923, the day when the last applications for food drafts were accepted, Ewert was very busy all day. When the last of the applications had been completed, he transmitted the money and the last of the $89,000 worth of applications to the First National Bank with these notable words: "I have written the last food draft application. My work is done!" A few days later he died (Prieb 1990, 67-68).

An expelled Mennonite minister is asked to return

In 1636 Geeritt Roosen, a Mennonite minister in Hamburg, was expelled from the city for baptizing the family's maid. Roosen was such a personable individual and such a successful entrepreneur, however, that the local business community quickly requested his return. As a result of his humble lifestyle and his charity he is credited with achieving, almost "singlehandedly," tolerance for the "heretical" Mennonites.

Soon the Mennonites were no longer depreciated. A Lutheran pastor now complained that "everyone" was attending Roosen's church (B. C. Roosen 1854a, 10; 1886, 31; Shepansky 1980, 60).

He learned to have concern for the needy

Peter C. Hiebert, the first chairman of Mennonite Central Committee, was deeply influenced by his parents. Early in life the Hiebert children learned from their parents the meaning of discipleship and sharing. Their home served as a kind of way station for many immigrant families who needed temporary shelter until they could find permanent homes. Sometimes the guests stayed a week, a month or longer. One family remained through the entire winter because the father was lame with a badly infected foot.

One evening Peter's father could not sleep because he was concerned about a poor family that had recently arrived from Europe. He got up at night and awakened his wife. They agreed that the new family probably needed food. During the night, Hiebert mounted his horse and delivered a sack of flour, placing it on the porch of the poor family. Later they learned the needy family had been praying for food at the very time the flour was being delivered (Prieb 1990, 8; P. C. Hiebert 1962).

Protection from Los Angeles Rioters

A more contemporary example is the story told by Al Ewert, a Mennonite administrator with World Impact, an inner-city mission in Los Angeles. He tells about the unexpected protection from the rioters who were torching buildings all around them. In the midst of all the burning, the property of World Impact was spared. Later Ewert learned that some people who knew about World Impact's work with ghetto families, especially children, had protected the organization's property and staff (interview with Al Ewert, Jan. 1993).

Faithful Bible readers

They had to read the Bible on a boat

Early Anabaptists in southern Holland found it difficult to find secret places to worship and read Scriptures together. One day Peter Pieterz, a ferryman on the Amstel River in Amsterdam, had an idea. He suggested that the congregation meet on his ferryboat. From then on whenever they wanted to study the Scriptures together and pray, Peter would load up his ferryboat and the congregation would go to an isolated place on the river to worship. He was, however, eventually discovered. He was arrested and burned at the stake February 26, 1569 (Braght 1950, 738-738; Oyer & Kreider 1990, 48-49).

A Doxology

Through their faith these men and women—among many others—proved the truth of God's promises. Some returned to their families from certain death, while others were tortured and refused to be ransomed because they wanted to deserve a more honorable resurrection in the world to come. Some were exposed to the test of public mockery and flogging, and to the torture of being sawn in two; they were tempted by false promises of release and then were killed with the sword. Many became refugees with nothing but sheepskins or goatskins to cover them. They lost everything, and were still spurned and ill-treated by a world that was too self-centered to see their worth. They lived as vagrants in deserts, on mountains, or in caves or even holes in the ground.

All these rendered glowing testimony to their faith, but they did not immediately receive the fulfillment of the divine promise. God had something better planned for them, but it was not his plan that they should reach perfection without us (adapted from Heb. 11:23-29).

CHAPTER 24

The Hope for Ongoing Renewal

A Bible-based call for renewal (by Wesley J. Prieb)

People of hope are people of faith and courage. It will take hope, faith and courage to recover Menno Simons' vision of living only by the sword of the Spirit. Only Christ through the Spirit can empower the church to achieve this kind of fidelity, as stated in the verse that Menno took as his theme: "For no man can lay a foundation other than the one which is laid, which is Jesus Christ" (1 Cor. 3:11 NASB).

Jesus stands at the door of our lives: "Behold, I stand at the door and knock; if any one hears My voice and opens the door, I will come in to him, and will dine with him, and he with Me" (Rev. 3:20 NASB).

In the third chapter of Revelation this message of hope and renewal is directed to the church in Laodicea. The church there had become lukewarm—neither hot nor cold—through wealth and affluence. Prosperity and self-sufficiency had blinded the church, and its members were not aware of their spiritual poverty. They had to be jolted to see their real condition. Christ rebuked them: "You do not know that you are wretched and miserable and poor and blind and naked" (Rev. 3:17 NASB). "I know your deeds, that you are neither cold nor hot . . . I will spit you out of My mouth" (Rev. 3:15-16 NASB). Then he calls for repentance: "Those whom I love, I reprove and discipline; be zealous therefore and repent" (Rev. 3:19 NASB).

Repentance leads to cleansing and forgiveness. It also leads to a radical turning around—to renewal. Through repentance the compromised Laodiceans (or Mennonites) can have their gold converted—"refined by fire"—to become stewards of entrusted benefits. They can experience their sins forgiven, and their eyes can be opened to a renewed vision of an "only-the-sword-of-the-Spirit" life.

Jesus wants to take full possession of the house, but he never forces entry. The latch is always on the inside. Only the person on the inside can open the door. Jesus, by gently knocking, calls for a voluntary response, not forced obedience. If the door is opened, Jesus will enter, sit down and dine with the owner of the house. Jesus becomes an integral part of the family circle. He empowers the family to surrender life and property to kingdom concerns.

If the owner does invite Jesus to enter the house and dine, then Jesus promises that he, in turn, will be a good host and invite the renewed person to dwell in his Father's house: "He who overcomes, I will grant to him to sit down with Me on My throne, as I also overcame, and sat down with My Father on His throne" (Rev. 3:21 NASB).

This is John's vision of a renewed life revealed in a metaphor of a house. This is also Menno Simons' vision. If we open our house voluntarily, Jesus will enter and take possession of both the occupants and the contents of the house. Radical repentance will purify the house. Jesus will "turn it up-side down." He is the new owner of the occupants and their property. The occupants become citizens and assets of God's kingdom of peace, both now and in the future.

The house, however, is not one-roomed; it has many rooms and many doors, each with its own latch. Progressive renewal will happen as room after room is opened to Christ. Jesus will continue to knock on closed door after closed door. It could take years before all the rooms of a life are surrendered to the Lord. This is the progressive renewal individual Christians and the church as a whole need.

The Radical Reformation as a paradigm for new beginnings and ongoing renewal

In the course of this study we discovered that we were not the first to see the Radical Reformation as a model or paradigm for ongoing renewal; John Howard Yoder (1984, 4-5; see also Smith 1992) had already recognized this truth. He rejected the "single instantiation" idea of renewal and pointed out that the Waldensians and the Hussites had followed the same model a full century before Conrad Grebel, Michael Sattler or Menno Simons. Furthermore, a century later the Quakers in England had followed the same paradigm. In the current century the Churches of Christ in the United States and the Kimbanguists in Zaire have likewise made use of that model.

Yoder asserted that radical reform is not the "property" of any church or ethnic group. Mennonites do not have a unique claim on it. It is a model available to all peoples everywhere for all times. On the other hand, since Mennonites owe their origin to it, they ought to feel no hesitation about being open to it again and again.

Furthermore, according to Yoder, radical reform can never be a one-time event, because entropy afflicts radically-reformed individuals and radically-reformed groups, just like it afflicts everything else. Just as God does not have grandchildren, so the Radical Reformation cannot have grandchildren. Each successive generation must individually and collectively be reborn and reformed anew. Especially when there are major changes in the circumstances or in the cultural milieu, new radical decisions about spiritual renewal are imperative.

Many people in Mennonite circles today are becoming convinced that Mennonite churches in America are overdue for a radical renewal experience. Most churches have become so affluent, so acculturated to the individualistic capitalistic American scene, that the principles of simplicity, of being mere stewards of the material benefits they have gained, of discipleship, of the priesthood of all believers, of the pursuit of peace, are really alien to them. Perhaps a radical renewal is the only way that Mennonites at the end of the twentieth century can recover the vision and lifestyle that their forebears saw operating in Jesus' disciples when the early church was formed.

Conversion and ongoing renewal: a personal testimony (by Jacob A. Loewen)

As soon as I became accustomed to viewing the Radical Reformation as a model, I realized there was a precedent for this kind of ongoing renewal in my own Christian experience. I had been raised in a milieu that taught that conversion or new birth was a once-and-for-all experience that instantly transformed repentant sinners into children of God.

When I faced my own faith experience honestly, however, I found that my conversion experience had not been an instantaneous once-and-for-all event. It actually had been an ongoing process. Furthermore, the experiences of my wife and of our four children all followed a similar pattern (Loewen & Loewen 1969, 2-6).

I had been taught that a sinner, when converted, became a "totally new creature" in Christ. Old things passed away and everything became new. This is what I expected would happen to me when I went forward in response to an altar call in a Manitoba tent revival.

I was nine years old and desperate to become "a new creature." I lived on an isolated farm in Manitoba with three adults: my working parents and the widower farm-owner. The three adults worked in the fields from dawn to dark, spring to winter, while I either tagged along or amused myself alone. I was desperately lonesome. Whenever I got permission to visit some children on a neighboring farm for a few hours, I always overstayed the allotted time. I then came home with fanciful explanations of why it had been absolutely necessary for me to stay so long. My mother interpreted these explanations as sheer lies and proceeded to wean me from what she diagnosed as serious habitual lying. She used a piece of doubled-up canvas gas-pump hose, vigorously applied to my "seat of understanding."

The "weaning" process began with five lashes, plus five more for each additional infraction. By twenty lashes my bottom was sore for weeks, and I had no desire for further visiting. But eventually my behind always healed and my loneliness goaded me to try again. This brought twenty-five lashes.

This coincided with the summer's revival meetings. By this time I was desperate to overcome my "lying" problem. I wanted to become a "new creature" who would not tell lies any more and who would come home at the specified time. So I went forward during a tent revival meeting and was converted.

For a few weeks things went along just fine. But then I slipped back into the old behavior pattern. I overstayed my visiting time and came back with another elaborate explanation—all to no avail. Thirty lashes. Then thirty-five lashes! I was devastated. My conversion had not worked. I had not become a "new creature."

Between the ages of 10 and 15 I went to the altar repeatedly to be converted or to rededicate my life to Christ, only to find that within weeks or months old unwanted behavior patterns again reasserted themselves. The once-and-for-all conversion I had been taught to believe in just did not work in my life. In desperation I tried to atone for what I saw as a character defect: I volunteered to become a missionary.

Then came our own children. My wife and I were determined that our children should be older than we had been before they were converted. We hoped that then the conversion would "take" better than ours had. But to our dismay, living in a soul-winning mission field context our children all made their first decisions to accept Jesus as their Savior before they reached the age of six. It was while observing our children's conversions that my wife and I suddenly realized that conversion was, indeed, a process. Four- or five-year-olds just weren't aware of many facets of life when they made that first decision for Christ and so there was little chance that these unrecognized areas of life would all be included in the renewal experience.

Once we as parents were ready to take the idea of process conversion seriously, we developed the metaphor of the house with many rooms to encourage ongoing renewal. We told our children that when they had first invited Jesus to come into their lives, they had invited him into the front room. But the house of their lives contained many rooms, some of which they did not yet even know about. Some day they might discover that they had a lying-room, or a cheating-room, or an anger-room. When that happened, they would have to stop and consciously ask Jesus to come into that room too. The children sometimes had to undergo weeks of struggle with one of their newly-discovered "unconverted" rooms before they were willing to invite Jesus into it.

I, too, have continued discovering new "unconverted" rooms in my inner house. At about thirty-five I discovered my self-image room. There lived a totally unregenerated self-protecting self-image that exerted significant control over my life. It took a real crisis before I was able to turn that room over to Jesus. Now in my seventies I have become painfully aware of my aggressive-tongue room. I am currently trying to let Christ gain control of my sharp tongue (Menno, behold another true son of yours!). Progress is painfully slow and intermittent. Change this late in life is more difficult than ever.

Our family received reinforcement for the concept of process renewal from a very unexpected source. It came from a young church that emerged in the Choco where we had been sent as missionaries. When that church was first organized, a notorious local drunk also accepted Christ. He, too, was baptized and became a member of the church along with many others. Six weeks later, however, I saw the newly baptized convert lying in the gutter in the market town, roaring drunk. When I got back, I approached the pastor about how we might helpfully discipline the drunk for his backsliding, but the leader gently laid his arm on mine and said, "Jake, you have never been a slave of hard liquor. You do not know how hard it is to convert a drunkard's stomach. I was one and I know what I'm talking about. We are praying for this man and talking with him. We are assuring him that one of these days his conversion will reach his stomach. When that happens, his stomach will rebel against alcohol and he will vomit it right out. Until then, however, we must just be patient and continue to encourage him."

I had to admit that my home church teaching had not prepared me for such a longsuffering approach to conversion.

When I returned to the Choco church a year later, however, the now ex-drunk could give a moving testimony in the church assembly of how his conversion had finally reached his stomach. Three months ago he had slipped into drinking again and then, for the first time in his life, his stomach had rebelled. He had failed a few more times and tried to drink, but each time his stomach reacted even more violently. Now he was ready to vomit at the mere sight of a whisky bottle. Praise God! His conversion had finally reached his stomach and made it new.

When my wife and I first described our experience with process conversion in the *Mennonite Brethren Herald*, dozens of parents called or wrote telling us that they, too, had had that kind of an experience and had always believed there was something wrong with them when their renewal had not been instantaneous.

Why should conversion and radical church renewal be treated as processes?

There are several compelling reasons why for most people, conversion should be seen as a process rather than a once-and-for-all renewal experience. First, any change like conversion or church renewal is never complete when it first happens. Human beings and their situations in life are complex and many-faceted. Change never penetrates all facets of life totally or equally. Those parts of life that are in focus at the time will be changed most. Other facets not in focus may be changed only very little, maybe not at all. One always hopes that the change will spread and penetrate even those areas that were not in focus at the time, but all too often the reverse happens. If the untouched or little-changed area or segment of the group is large and very resistant, then there will be enormous internal pressures to revert to the earlier status quo. Only if change is treated as a process and steps are taken to insure ongoing renewal is there any hope that it can become lasting and deep.

Second, even if change were able to reach most facets of life or most individuals in a group, life's ongoing experiences always create new and previously unknown situations. New dimensions of personality, or previously unrecognized culture traits, suddenly come into focus. That was the experience of our children when they discovered they could cheat in school or steal a candy bar at the store. Unless the newly-discovered "room of life" or culture trait in a society is now consciously subjected to the change experience, the original change impact will be diminished. For our children, as we have already said, extending the change to an additional "room" often was a far more difficult step than the original decision to accept Jesus as Savior had been. They often battled for weeks before they could "open the room for Jesus." The experience of a church trying to develop an "only-the-sword-of-the-Spirit" lifestyle for the twenty-first century will be no different.

Our Anabaptist/Mennonite forebears, likewise, discovered that when persecution ended and they were able to own and accumulate property, the "sharing room" of their Christian experience had not really changed that much. They quickly abandoned sharing freely and began accumulating wealth individually. Today, in fact, one could venture that the "sharing room" of most North American Mennonites is not really "converted" at all. On the whole Mennonites today are as selfish and materialistic as the non-church people around them.

As a professor at one of our church colleges, I was severely jolted by the high percentage of Mennonite Brethren students who seriously doubted the validity of their original childhood conversion experiences.

When I checked with them individually, I discovered that the problem was all the "unchanged rooms" they had discovered in their lives since their original conversion. Alas, no one had helped them to include these newly discovered unconverted rooms in their renewal experience.

Third, even when change has been fairly universal and complete, human behavior, like everything else in nature, is subject to the second law of thermodynamics, often called the law of entropy. This law says: "Things in motion will slow down, unless new outside momentum is applied. Hot things in cold environments, or cold things in warm environments, will gradually assume the temperature of the environment." By the same token, new converts will find that in a few weeks or months their zeal for an "only-the-sword-of-the-Spirit" lifestyle is diminishing. The renewed church will discover that many of the old problems and temptations still exert enormous pull, and their enthusiasm for the new soon begins to wane.

The history of the early church teaches the same lesson. Few would question that the church of New Testament times was truly the church Christ wanted to establish. However, it took only four centuries until that very church, which had begun as completely separated from the world, was ready to join the world and become the religion of the state under Constantine. Once this compromise had been made, the church found itself on a rapid road of entropy. How much compromise have Mennonite churches today made to accommodate the world of their day? How many unconverted rooms are they currently aware of, but still have not included in their renewal experience? In what areas have they, like the Jews of Jesus' day, replaced the commandment of God with human rules? This raises a serious question: With how many unconverted rooms can a person or a church live, before that the link to Christ, the center, is completely choked off?

The house-with-many-rooms metaphor in the experience of college students

Christian college students, like many other Christians, frequently discover unconverted rooms in their lives. Their recovery and subsequent growth experiences shed additional light on how the house-with-many-rooms metaphor can help Christians, individually or as groups, achieving ongoing renewal.

One Sunday night a number of students at a small church college were caught breaking into a college office to steal examination papers. The sheriff took them to jail. When more students came to me to confess that they too had been involved, I called the sheriff and asked what should be done with these additional culprits. The sheriff said: "If you can talk to them and help them, I don't want them. If they turn arrogant or stubborn, however, call me and I'll 'soften' them up a bit."

I thus worked with several of these equally guilty culprits. I called them into my office individually, passed on the sheriff's message and asked if they were serious about solving the problem. They were! I then suggested that stealing exams was probably not the only unsolved problem in their lives. In order to establish an honest student/counselor relationship, I asked each student to provide me with a list of all the other problems or unconverted rooms in their lives of which they were aware. The lists varied from eight to thirteen. I then took each list and ceremoniously signed it in the presence of the student, telling the person that I now assumed responsibility for all the problems except the one on which the two of us would be working.

The individual student's first assignment was to choose the most painful, or the most burning problem on his or her list. That was the problem the two of us together would try to overcome. All the other problems were my burden now. The students might want to report to me whenever they did any one of the other items on the list again, but they were not to worry about them. Judgment on them was suspended temporarily.

We then began working on the first problem, the one chosen as most vital. In several cases it involved more thefts. So as the student got the necessary money together the two of us went to make good the offenses. When all debts were paid off, the student selected the next most urgent problem. Usually by the time the third or fourth problem had been solved or the bad habit had been broken, the student would suddenly burst into my office without an appointment and happily report, "I've licked the whole damn list." When I asked what had happened, they invariably reported: "After years of failure I had so little confidence in myself and in the power of Christianity, everything seemed so utterly hopeless. But now as I learned how to lick the problems one at a time, I suddenly found faith and self-confidence to trust that I could lick all of them with God's help."

Can the church today benefit from this model and deal with the unconverted rooms it discovers in its effort to recover an "only-the-sword-of-the-Spirit" lifestyle? Should it, too, begin by tackling one problem at a time?

A final appeal (by Wesley J. Prieb)

The risen Christ is pleading with a church and all its individual members: "Behold, I stand knocking at the door." Once Jesus enters the main room of the house and takes up residence with the host, repentance begins a lifelong room-by-room cleansing. Progressive renewal is often slow. Room after room must be opened until the entire household and its contents become kingdom assets. Jesus wants to take possession of every room. That is why the host must invite Jesus to be a permanent resident. Then he will keep knocking on unchanged rooms as long as we keep opening the doors. He wants to renew the whole house and everything that is in it.

A serious reminder: "If any one hears his voice" (Heb. 3:7, Ps. 95:7 NASB) but doesn't respond, that person's heart will be hardened. Jesus, sensing the rejection of the host, will then withdraw. Eventually the unrepentant host cannot even hear Jesus knocking anymore. Jesus gives us freedom of choice. Every person—and church must—choose either to host or to reject the divine caller.

CHAPTER 25

Personal Reflections on the *Only-the-sword-of-the-spirit* Ideal

(by Jacob A. Loewen)

How I Found My Roots In *Gewaltverzicht*

The issue comes to a head

In 1984 our only son, Bill, left the Mennonite Brethren Church because he felt it was diluting its statement of faith to the point where it was no longer able to take a clear stand on some crucial peace principles. When the two of us talked about what had happened, Bill chided me, saying, "Dad, you have provided me with foundations in so many areas of life! But why in the world did you never teach me Anabaptist/Mennonite peace principles?" This poignant indictment brought me face to face with the personal unease that I had experienced at different periods in my life over my own and my Mennonite Brethren Church's ambivalent loyalty to peace. Then and there I resolved to do something about it.

In 1988, in an open letter to Bill (J. A. Loewen 1988, 2-5), I gave a very preliminary answer to his troubling question. In response to that writing many parents telephoned, wrote or personally told us how they too felt painful guilt concerning their children in regard to this issue. But, like myself, their basic problem was ignorance. We did not know enough about the basic Anabaptist/Mennonite principles involved. None of us seemed to know how to make this fundamental Anabaptist teaching relevant in our day. For this reason I felt I owed it to myself and to others to do an in-depth study of the issues involved, so that I would be able to make up my own mind as to where I personally wanted to take my stand, and then begin working toward developing a coherent lifestyle which would reflect these convictions. I was also hoping to atone, at least in part, for my failure toward my own children by providing some of the insights I would gain for my grandchildren, to whom I dedicate my share of this effort.

How my pilgrimage began

When World War II erupted in 1939, I was just turning seventeen. Until then, to my knowledge, the Mennonite peace principles had received only scant attention in the preaching and teaching of the Mennonite Brethren churches in which I grew up. But as soon as war

253

was declared and the draft became imminent in Canada, the church dusted off its doctrine of nonresistance and began to catechize its young men. I, of course, accepted the church's position on war when my call-up came. I had been instructed to avoid arguments and theoretical discussions with the examining draft board members. I was only to affirm, again and again if necessary, "My conscience does not allow me to take up arms to kill other people."

How I became uneasy

I had occasion to use that quote only once before the examining draft board. The chairman followed my initial statement with the question, "What will you then do if Hitler rapes your mother or your sister?" Before I could answer, he fired off a rapid stream of similar questions, but he never stopped long enough for me to answer any of them. Then, as abruptly as it had begun, his stream of questions dried up. He stamped my papers and said, "Next please!" That's how I became a conscientious objector. The utter frivolousness of the experience stirred up a host of questions in my psyche. I felt I needed to do some serious study to find out whether my professed peace position was really a personal conviction or merely an oddity I followed because of tradition and social pressure.

To meet my alternative service obligation, I served in a large urban general hospital. Many Mennonite conscientious objectors served in forestry camps in British Columbia and some came home after the war severely disillusioned. Their camp service had given them little satisfaction. Many of their coworkers had been nothing more than war dodgers whose lives did not reflect even basic Christianity, not to mention peace principles (Enns 1981, 10-11; 1985). As a result the serious conscientious objectors felt their peace witness had been seriously compromised.

When I compared my lot with theirs, I felt fortunate. I had been able to express my Christian faith in helping sick people to a degree that I had never experienced before. As a service to my fellow human beings, my hospital work had been exciting and deeply meaningful. But again and again, when patients asked why I was doing alternative service as a conscientious objector it became clear that I was dead set against war but fuzzy about why. Worse, I did not know what I was really for. As my unease grew, I vowed to study the matter to discover what I was really "for" in my peace position.

But then the war ended. I went back to school and after graduation the Mennonite Brethren Board of Missions sent my wife and me to

Colombia as missionaries. The felt need to pursue the foundations of nonresistance was pushed out of my consciousness. After all, as a missionary I was working to reconcile the heathen to God and that seemed like a very positive kind of peacemaking.

How my unease grew

Shortly after our arrival in Colombia the persecution of Protestants in that country erupted. I was quickly drawn into the battle to keep our mission's churches, schools and dispensaries open. These mission projects had all been approved by the highest authorities of the land, but they were now being disrupted and closed by provincial or local officials who were under pressure by the local state-church authorities to "stand up for their Catholic faith" and drive the "Protestant heretics" out of their communities, if not, out of their country.

The struggle to keep our mission institutions open forced us to carry our fight all the way to the highest levels of the capital. These officials, while conceding that our operating documents were valid (many, in fact, bore their personal signatures), still refused to reverse the lower authorities' actions because they, in turn, had the papal nuncio breathing down their necks, reminding them that hell would be hot if they did not act like obedient sons of the church to defend the true faith.

To force the Colombian government to give us what we felt was elementary justice, we involved lawyers, embassies, the United States Congress, newspaper reporters and any other possible source of world opinion. Suddenly it dawned on me that I was engaged in a "war" in which, short of physical violence, I was using every vocal, legal and diplomatic weapon available to defend our right to operate as a peace church! After eighteen months of fighting, I became convinced that this approach of verbal, legal, and shame aggression did not agree with my peace position any more than did the use of the gun or the sword in time of war. But I still had not developed an adequate rationale to explain why I felt so uneasy.

This experience made me deeply aware that peace principles could never be merely a wartime issue, as my church had been teaching. Such a peace stance had to involve all of life if it was to have any validity! All our interpersonal interactions needed to be guided by it. When I thus became convinced that I could no longer fight, harass and embarrass the Colombian government and its officials in good conscience, I notified the mission board that I was bowing out of that fight for good. The mission saw me as a poor "soldier of the cross," but despite their displeasure with my decision, I was convinced that I could not use every verbal, legal and diplomatic weapon to defend peace and truth. But before I had sorted out the issues, however, a new agreement, negotiated between the state church and the government, made our work with the Waunana Indians illegal, and we were thus forced to leave Colombia and return to North America.

How my unease grew still more

I finished graduate school, and accepted a teaching position at Tabor College in Hillsboro, Kansas. This move coincided with the early stages of the racial protests, marches and sit-ins in the southern United States. To put my budding peace principles into practice I naively, but enthusiastically, joined the ranks of the marchers and protesters, together with some students from Tabor College. In my classes I tried to help students recognize racism in our churches and communities. However, as my southern involvement increased, I became increasingly more uncomfortable with my fellow protesters. Among them I found dozens of hormonally-charged young fellows who saw these large protest gatherings as good places to find sex. Others claimed to be anarchists. There was also a wide array of leftists, and many were there just "to raise hell." Here, too, I soon realized that the nonviolent label can be very elastic. It included every use of force and verbal aggression short of physical violence. So I found myself withdrawing again, just like in Colombia.

Then the United Bible Societies offered me an overseas service opportunity. I was to train nationals to translate the Bible into their own languages. Here I worked with all kinds of churches, missions and ethnic groups. I soon observed many conflicts in the mission programs overseas. There were tensions between mission agencies, tensions between nationals and expatriates, tensions between various ethnic groups, and inter-generational tensions within the indigenous churches themselves. To my unexpected delight I discovered a wide variety of peacemaking opportunities (I. Friedmann 1990).

On the whole the peacemaking experience during my Bible Society service was very satisfying. When I tried to make it relevant for others, however, I found that the reconciliation process I had experienced involved a degree of cultural competence and counseling knowledge that average church people might not have. Furthermore, my peacemaking effort showed no clear relationship to the Anabaptist peace concerns I espoused in theory.

When I retired in 1984 and finally had time to pursue some of my personal interests, the peace issue unexpectedly came to a head —my son left the Mennonite Brethren Church. Now I faced my son's haunting question: "But why in the world did you never teach me the premises underlying the Anabaptist/Mennonite peace position?" (J. A. Loewen 1988, 2-5). The answer, of course, was that I had never done the necessary homework to develop my own personal convictions. But I decided then and there to do it. The result of this multi-year effort is contained in this book.

This study not only has led me to personal conviction on the peace position, it has also helped me develop a series of guidelines to govern my behavior in situations where I feel I must protest for conscience sake.

Toward a personal standard for evaluating protest for conscience' sake

As recounted earlier, I frequently grew uncomfortable with the use of coercion to accomplish "God's purposes." I withdrew from a number of situations but wasn't really sure just why. I had no personal standard by which to measure appropriate and inappropriate behavior in the furtherance of peace. Although more clarity gradually began to emerge, it was not until I began this study that I sorted out the issues and defined my personal guidelines for conscientious protest.

What Gandhi taught me

When I looked for actual life examples to illustrate these emerging guidelines, I found, much to my chagrin, that Gandhi's life provided some excellent modern examples. To add to my chagrin, when I showed my preliminary findings to a fellow Mennonite Brethren minister, he warned me not to use them because Gandhi, after all, was not a Christian. After some serious soul-searching, I, nevertheless, have decided to use Gandhi's life and protests as an example of putting Christ's peace principles into practice. If this supposed "non-Christian" is the best example of what a Christlike life of renouncing force and depending only on the moral force of love and self-giving looks like, so be it! I bow my "Christian" head in shame before the moral power and example of "non-Christian" Gandhi's life (Waltner 1962, 55-58).

James W. Douglass (1968, 55-56) gives us a powerful insight when he reports that Gandhi felt he had to reject organized Christianity because he wanted to be true to Jesus Christ and his teaching. Gandhi once said, "Today I rebel against orthodox Christianity, as I am convinced that it has distorted the message of Jesus." The New Testament, however, was a gold mine for him. He wrote in his autobiography:

> The New Testament . . . especially the Sermon on the Mount . . . went straight to my heart. I compared it with the Gita. The verses "But I say unto you, that ye resist not evil: but whosoever shall smite thee on thy right cheek, you turn to him the other also. And if any man take away thy coat let him have thy cloak too," delighted me beyond measure and put me in mind of [the Gujarati poet] Shamal Bhatt's "For a bowl of water, give a goodly meal," etc. My young mind tried to unify the teaching of the Gita, *The Light of Asia* and the Sermon on the Mount. That renunciation was the highest form of religion appealed to me greatly (as quoted in Brock 1991b, 267).

The first example of protest from Gandhi's life comes from his involvement from 1907 to 1914 in the struggle against South Africa's infamous passbook laws. When Gandhi's fellow protestors wanted to blockade the passbook offices to make it impossible for them to function, Gandhi refused. He insisted that the protestor for conscience' sake may not harass or impede those who had legitimate reasons to enter those offices. It did not matter whether they were whites who were employed there, or whether they were blacks who felt they had no alternative but to register to get a passbook. Gandhi also insisted that the protestors had no right to block the area in front of the offices, because that would impede and inconvenience ordinary passers-by who were not involved in the protest.

Because of these considerations, Gandhi assembled his fellow-protestors in the park across the street from the passbook office where no one was impeded or inconvenienced by the protest. Gandhi believed that clear visibility in the park across the street was an adequate form of nonviolent protest.

Later when Gandhi organized the strike of the textile workers in Southern India in 1915-1918, the mill owners were led by a close friend and faithful supporter of Gandhi. Before the strike was called, Gandhi carefully ascertained what level of wage increase would be manageable for the mill owners. The workers wanted more, but Gandhi told them that exorbitant demands would make it impossible for the mill owners to operate with a margin of profit. What Gandhi proposed was an increase that would improve the quality of life for the mill workers but would not cripple the textile mills. If a strike demand met the essential needs of both parties, Gandhi said, it could be considered a just demand.

During the early part of the strike Gandhi frequently dined with his mill owner friend and discussed the ramifications of the strike with him. Gandhi insisted that the protestor or striker may not be arrogant or hostile, nor subservient and begging. Both parties should be able to settle their differences while maintaining their mutual dignity.

When the strike dragged on, however, and the striking mill workers began to suffer hunger, Gandhi had to learn two additional lessons. First, he as the moral leader of the strikers also had to suffer, even though there was plenty of food at his ashram. Out of this came Gandhi's first hunger strike. Second, some of the mill workers and their families found it impossible to survive while on strike. Some of these workers thus broke rank and went back to work at the mills for their old wages. Other strikers now wanted to punish these strikebreakers, but again Gandhi opposed, saying that no one had the right to exercise violence on another. Furthermore, no one but the individual himself had the right to decide how much suffering he or she could bear (Erickson 1969, 410-423).

By 1918-1920, when Gandhi was on a hunger strike for his country's independence, several more issues had been clarified in his thinking. First, civil disobedience is a valid response if laws are patently unjust, as in his peaceful march to the sea to make salt. Second, only the person whose conscience is being violated by an abuse or an injustice may be called on to suffer. The protestor may not demand nor inflict suffering or humiliation on others, whether they be perpetrators or merely uninvolved bystanders. Gandhi felt that accepting suffering without flinching empowers the sufferer. Louis Fischer has pointed out that "the British beat the Indians with batons and rifle butts. The Indians neither cringed nor retreated. That made England powerless and India invincible" (L. Fischer 1962, 275).

Gandhi applied

As I worked through Gandhi's experience of nonviolent protest, I began to understand the causes of my inner discomfort in Colombia as I fought to keep our mission work going. We were using every possible means of coercion, all kinds of verbal aggression, short of physical violence, to shame, harass, cajole, embarrass and create discomfort for as many government officials as possible. We used the press, both local and foreign. We involved embassies. We marshaled public opinion against Colombia in the U.S. Congress. For Christians of genuine

Anabaptist persuasion, violating another person's dignity should be just as unacceptable as it was for Gandhi.

In the same light I can now also evaluate why I felt I had to withdraw from the racial protests in the American South. We blocked traffic, occupied seats in restaurants, tried to disrupt business, tried to embarrass people, argued fiercely with racists and tried to use courts to force our morality on people of different persuasion. As a result of our verbal—sword of the tongue—aggression, we protestors had little or no moral power. There was too much coercion of every type. Sider aptly says that one must always show love and respect for the person one opposes (Sider 1979, 45).

Today, having examined the issues carefully and in detail, I can affirm that my personal standard for protest for conscience' sake involves the following:

(1) My peace position demands that I abstain from force and coercion at all times and in all areas of life.

(2) When I am faced with situations in which I feel I must protest, I may not insult or humiliate those whose behavior I oppose.

(3) I may not harass underlings who are carrying out, in the line of duty, actions I oppose, because they are not the ones who are in a position to make the changes I feel are necessary.

(4) I may not impede or inconvenience people who may be present, but who are not really involved in the situation.

(5) If there is any embarrassment or suffering involved, I may not inflict it. I as the protester should be the one suffering it.

(6) If a law is patently unjust, I may violate it publicly but peacefully.

(7) Only the person whose conscience is violated may be called on to suffer. No one may force or coerce another person to protest or to suffer.

(8) If the protest results in suffering, protesters must decide for themselves how much suffering they can bear. No one may ridicule fellow protesters for dropping out because the suffering is greater than they can bear.

These eight guidelines have helped me evaluate and assess actions such as picketing at abortion clinics, lying down in front of vehicles carrying nuclear arms, or causing damage to nuclear facilities. They represent my studied position on *Gewaltverzicht*, (abstaining from the use of force or coercion,) á la Menno Simons.

HOW I BECAME PROUD TO BE A MENNONITE

This testimony involves a degree of pain. It passes judgment on important developmental phases in my life, and on the Mennonite Brethren Church and some of its leaders, many of whom played very meaningful roles in my life and development.

My church background

When I look back on my own spiritual development, I see many things which the Mennonite Brethren Church did for me spiritually as I was growing up. For these I am deeply grateful. In Sunday school and in Bible studies my church taught me the content of God's Word. During the many Bible discussions I learned how to exegete the Word, understand its meaning and how to apply the insights gained to real life situations. Later in life, when I had occasion to associate with trained seminarians, I found that I, as a non-seminarian, could hold my own with them in interpreting Scripture. Furthermore, I knew where those Scripture passages were located in the Bible.

My church also taught me to pray. Even as a teenager, I found real strength and joy in the weekly prayer meetings. This was in spite of what I now recognize to have been the built-in pressure that the meeting would probably not close until all present had prayed aloud. The young men's "prayer band," of which I was a founding member, played a very formative role in developing my philosophy of life and service.

In the church Bible school I learned how to teach God's Word, and how to preach it (even though my Bible school teachers advised me that I had better become a missionary abroad rather than try to become a preacher back home). My church made me efficient in talking about God (teaching and preaching) and in talking to God (praying), but it wasn't until much later in life that I learned, from the Quakers, about listening to God in silence.

But here I must also indict my church for not introducing me to our heritage of Anabaptist values. I had to learn many of these values from Third World Christians who had learned them from MCC workers. I realize that my elders had allowed Pietist ideals to drown out much of their Anabaptist heritage. My greatest problem, however, came on my retirement. After almost forty years of service abroad, I came home to a church that was in the process of shedding even its Mennonite name—a name that I now was proud to bear (H. W. Friesen 1990, 9). But it was not that way always!

Ashamed of the Mennonite name

During the late 1930s the British Columbia Mennonite Brethren churches organized the West Coast Children's Mission as a nondenominational outreach arm under whose aegis I and many of those my age began working in evangelism.

Looking back today I have to admit that we all were somewhat ashamed of our status as impoverished immigrants. We ducked our Mennonite name and carried the nondenominational banner of the West Coast Children's Mission as high as we possibly could. We taught Daily Vacation Bible School and were able to lead both children and some of their parents to the Lord. We were not content with merely winning people for Christ; we kept on visiting the converts and carrying on services to nurture them in their spiritual growth. Soon these new believers wanted to be baptized and join a church. We approached our home churches. They, much to our embarrassment, baptized only the Friesens and the Froeses, some of whom spoke no German, and the Brauers and Kietzmanns, who spoke German, and told all the others to find a Baptist or Alliance church in which to be baptized.

After serving a term on the mission field, my wife and I returned to British Columbia on furlough. We were surprised to learn that the Daily Vacation Bible School activities that used to be carried on in the surrounding communities in the Lower Fraser Valley had now been transferred into the interior of the province. One of the leaders actually explained that it had been too embarrassing to win people to the Lord and then not be able to invite them into our German-speaking church services.

Mennonites do have something to offer

Meanwhile on the mission field, I learned about other aspects of being a Mennonite. I was surprised when other missions invited us Mennonites to come and teach them how our unpaid lay ministry worked. They had discovered that the paid-pastor model was a noose around the neck of young churches in mission fields and they were looking for an alternative. Suddenly I became aware of the fact that I had inherited something that others saw as highly desirable. When we returned home on our first furlough (1953), however, our enthusiasm was dampened severely because our home churches were all busily abandoning the lay ministry and were rushing to get paid pastors.

Mennonites are esteemed abroad

The next thing I learned abroad was that the name "Mennonite" was one of the most esteemed religious names in the so-called Third

World. It did not matter whether I visited South Africa, Thailand, Bangladesh or Israel. Everywhere I went people's faces beamed when they heard that I was a Mennonite. "We know you people! You sent food to us during the famine and you kept us from certain starvation. We still thank God for you Mennonites every day." Or, they said, "Oh yes, you are the peace-loving people who don't make war and rather help people in need. You have been an inspiration to us in our own struggle against oppression."

Probably the most moving experience in this vein happened in Spain. I was attending a Bible Society conference there when a Madrid evangelical church asked for a preacher from our conference. I was sent. The driver got lost and we arrived at the church late. The desperate minister quickly left the pulpit and came to the back of the church to receive me. He then asked me from which church I came. When I said, "Mennonite," a most unexpected thing happened. He cupped his hands and shouted to his wife who was playing the organ, while the congregation was singing a hymn, "*Querida, un Menonita!*" (Sweetheart, it's a Mennonite). At once the organ music stopped. The organist rushed the length of the church on stockinged feet, threw her arms around my neck and gave me a resounding kiss. I was visibly embarrassed. When she realized that, she explained. "During the civil war, my family and I were kept alive by food that came in bags with clasped hands on them and a logo which said, 'In the name of Christ, Mennonite Central Committee.' As a family we then and there vowed that if anyone survived the war and ever met a Mennonite, that person was to kiss that Mennonite on behalf of the whole family." I happened to be that first Mennonite!

Something happened in my heart that moment. I became very proud to be a Mennonite. It is for this reason that it has been so painful for me to come home to Canada for retirement and find that so many of the ministers who occupy our Mennonite Brethren church pulpits are ashamed of the Mennonite name and the heritage it represents. That is why I was devastated, when a leading minister recently told me, "The first thing I do with every church I pastor is to get rid of the Mennonite name on the sign in front of the church. I consider it an impediment to evangelism." I repeat what I have said before: I think the reason we still have people who duck the Mennonite name is that so many of our people do not know the value it carries in the world at large. Furthermore, they are ignorant of the priceless heritage which that name brings with it. It is my earnest prayer that this writing may, in a small way, remedy that.

Bibliography

Abel, W. *Agrarkrisen und Agrarkonjunktur*. Hamburg: Paul Parey, 1978.

Adrian, V. "Born of Anabaptism and Pietism." *Mennonite Brethren Herald* (March 26, 1965): 2-3.

Ainlay, Stephen C. "Communal Commitment and Individualism." In *Anabaptist-Mennonite Identities in Ferment, Occasional Papers #14*, edited by Leo Driedger & Leland Harder, 135-153. Elkhart, IN: Institute of Mennonite Studies, 1990.

Anderson, A. B. "The sociology of Mennonite identity: A critical review." In *Mennonite identity: Historical and Contemporary Perspectives* edited by C. W. Redekop & S. J. Steiner, 193-201. Lanham, MD: University Press of America, 1988.

"Aus den Kolonien: Wahlprojeckt." *Odessaer Zeitung*. (October 26, 1863): 974-975.

Baasch, E. *Die Handelskammer zu Hamburg*. (Vol.1). Hamburg: Lucas Graefe and Sillem, 1915.

Baasch, E. *Holländische Wirtschaftsgeschichte*. Jena: Geestar Fischer, 1927.

Baer, M. *Westpreussen unter Friedrich des Grossen*. Leipzig: S. Hirschel, 1909.

Baerg, Donald M. "Citizenship and land tenure." *Mennonites in Brandenburg-Prussia during the 17th and 18th Centuries*. Master's thesis, Johann Wolfgang Goethe Universität, Frankfurt-am-Main, 1977.

Bainton, R. H. *Here I stand: A Life of Martin Luther*. New York: Abingdon-Cokesbury Press, 1950.

Bainton, R. H. *The Reformation of the Sixteenth Century*. Boston: The Beacon Press, 1952.

Bainton, R. H. *The Age of the Reformation*. Princeton: D. Van Nostrand Company, Inc, 1956.

Bainton, R. H. *Christian Attitudes Toward War and Peace: A Historical Survey and Critical Re-evaluation*. New York: Abingdon Press, 1960.

Bainton, R. H. "Anabaptism and the Reformation: The Left Wing of the Reformation." In *The Anabaptists and Thomas Müntzer* edited by J.

M. Stayer, & W. O. Packull, 41-45. Dubuque: Kendall/Hunt Publishing Company, 1980.

Balzer, H. "Faith and Reason: The Principles of Mennonitism Reconsidered, in a Treatise of 1833." *Mennonite Quarterly Review, 22,* R. Friedmann, Trans. and Ed.(1948): 75-93.

"Baptisten oder nicht?" *Odessaer Zeitung* (April 7, 20, 1901,): 23.

Bartel, Karl. "Ostfriesische Mennoniten in den Kriegerischen Zeiten des 18./19. Jahrhunderts." *Mennonitische Geschichtsblätter, 38* (1981): 33-48.

Bartel, Siegfried. *Living with Conviction. A German Army Captain Turns to Cultivating Peace.* Winnipeg: CMBC Publications, 1994.

Barthel, H.C. "Balk." In *Mennonitisches Lexikon, 1*(1913): 112-114.

Bartsch, F. *Unser Auszug nach Mittelasien.* Steinbach, MB: Echo Verlag, 1948. (Originally published Halbstadt: Raduga, 1907)

Bartsch, F. & C. Krahn. "Ak-Mechet." In *The Mennonite Encyclopedia, 1*(1955): 29-30.

Bartsch, F. "Epp, Claasz, Jr." In *The Mennonnite Encyclopedia, 2* (1956): 234.

Baumann, C. "The Theology of 'The Two Kingdoms': A comparison of Luther and the Anabaptists." *Mennonite Quarterly Review, 38* (1964): 37-49.

Baumann, C. *Gewaltlosigkeit im Täufertum, eine Untersuchung zur theologischen Ethik des oberdeutschen Täufertums der Reformationszeit.* Leiden: E. J. Brill, 1968.

Baumann, C. "Gewaltlosigkeit als Kennzeichen der Gemeinde." In *Die Mennoniten* edited by Hans-Jürgen Goertz, 128-140. Stuttgart: Evangelisches Verlagswerk, 1971.

Bekker, J. P. *Origin of the Mennonite Brethren Church.* Previously unpublished manuscript by one of the eighteen founders. (D. E. Pauls & A. E. Janzen, Trans.). Hillsboro, KS: The Mennonite Brethren Historical Society of the Midwest, 1973.

Belk, F. R. *The Great Trek of the Russian Mennonites to Central Asia: 1880-1884.* Scottdale: Herald Press, 1976.

Bellah, R. N., Madsen, R., Sullivan, M., Swidler, A., & Tipton, S. M. *Habits of the Heart: Individualism and Commitment in American Life.* Berkeley: University of California Press, 1985.

Bellah, R. N., Madsen, R., Sullivan, W. M., Swidler, A., & Tipton, S. M. *Individualism and Commitment in American Life: Readings on the Themes of Habits of the Heart.* New York: Harper & Row, 1987.

Bender, H. S. *Our Peace Testimony to the World—Goals and Methods. Report of the Mennonite Conference on Peace.* Goshen, IN: Goshen College, 1935.

Bender, H. S. "Church and State in Mennonite History." *Mennonite Quarterly Review,* 13 (1939): 83-103.

Bender, H. S. "The Anabaptist Vision." *Mennonite Quarterly Review,* 18 (1944): 67-88.

Bender, H. S. "Mennonite Peace Action Throughout the World." *Mennonite Quarterly Review,* 24 (1950): 149-155.

Bender, H. S., et al, (Eds.). *The Mennonite Encyclopedia,* (Vols. 1-4). Scottdale: The Mennonite Publishing House, 1955-1959.

Bender, H. S. "Bible Institute." In *The Mennonite Encyclopedia, 1* (1955): 330-332.

Bender, H. S. "Evangelism." In *The Mennonite Encyclopedia, 2* (1956): 269-273.

Bender, H. S. "Excommunication, Procedure and Grounds." In *The Mennonite Encylopedia, 2* (1956): 277-279.

Bender, H. S. "Fundamentalism." In *The Mennonite Encyclopedia, 2* (1956): 418-419.

Bender, H. S. "Germany." In *The Mennonite Encyclopedia, 2* (1956): 483-501.

Bender, H. S. "The Pacifism of the Sixteenth-century Anabaptists." *Mennonite Quartely Review, 30* (1956a): 5-18.

Bender, H. S. "The Office of Bishop in Anabaptist-Mennonite History." *Mennonite Quarterly Review, 30* (1956b): 128-132.

Bender, H. S. "The Anabaptist Vision." In *The Recovery of the Anabaptist Vision: A Sixtieth Anniversary Tribute to Harold S. Bender* edited by G. F. Hershberger, 29-56. Scottdale: Herald Press, 1957.

Bender, H. S. "Kleine Gemeinde." In *The Mennonite Encyclopedia, 3* (1957): 196-199.

Bender, H. S. "Krimmer Mennonite Brethren." In *The Mennonite Encyclopedia, 3* (1957): 242-244.

Bender, H. S. "Mennonite Church." In *The Mennonite Encyclopedia, 3* (1957): 611-616.

Bender, H. S. "Military Service in Europe." In *The Mennonite Encyclopedia*, *3* (1957): 688-690.

Bender, H. S. "New York." In *The Mennonite Encyclopedia*, *3* (1957): 863.

Bender, H. S. "Revival." In *The Mennonite Encyclopedia*, *4* (1959): 308-310.

Bender, H. S. "Schwer(d)tler (i.e., bearers of swords)." In *The Mennonite Encylopedia*, *4* (1959): 488-489.

Bender, H. S. "Society of Friends." In *The Mennonite Encyclopedia*, *4* (1959): 561-565.

Bender, H. S. "Sommerfeld Mennonites." In *The Mennonite Encyclopedia*, *4* (1959): 576-578.

Bender, H.S. "Stäbler." In *The Mennonite Encyclopedia*, *4* (1959): 607.

Bender, H. S. "Sunday School." In *The Mennonite Encyclopedia*, *4* (1959): 657-660.

Bender, H. S. "Swiss Brethren." In *The Mennonite Encyclopedia*, *4* (1959): 669-671.

Bender, H. S. "Unschuld und Gegen-Bericht." In *The Mennonite Encyclopedia*, *4* (1959): 786.

Bender, H. S. "United States of America." In *The Mennonite Encyclopedia*, *4* (1959): 776-782.

Bender, H. S. "The Anabaptist Vision." In *The Anabaptists and Thomas Müntzer* edited by J. M. Stayer, & W. O. Packull, 13-22. Dubuque, Iowa: Kendall/Hunt Publishing Company, 1980a.

Bender, H. S. "The Zwickau Prophets, Thomas Müntzer, and the Anabaptists." In *The Anabaptists and Thomas Müntzer* edited by J. M. Stayer, & W. O. Packull, 145-157. Dubuque, IA: Kendall/Hunt Publishing Company, 1980b.

Bender, H. S., & Horsch, J. *Menno Simons' Life and Writings. A Quadricentennial Tribute 1536-1936*. Scottdale: Mennonite Publishing House, 1936.

Bender, R. T., & Sell, A. P. F. (Eds.). *Baptism, Peace and the State in the Reformed and Mennonite traditions*. Waterloo, ON: Wilfrid Laurier University Press, 1991.

Bender, U. *Soldiers of Compassion*. Scottdale: Herald Press, 1969.

Beningha, E. *Volledige Chronyk van Oostfrieslant*. Emden: H. Meybohm, 1723.

Bentheim, H. L. "Von den Wiedertäufern und Socinianern im Niederland." In *Holländischer Kirchen-fund Schulenstaat* edited by H. Ludwig Bentheim, Chapter 19. Franckfurt und Leipzig: Nicolaus Foerster, 1698.

Berg, van den M. A. *Niet het zwaard Maar het Woord. Luther en Müntzer in dee Boerenoorlog van 1525*. Kampen: Uitgeverij de Groot Goudriaan, 1990.

Bethke, H. *Eid, Gewissen, Treuepflicht*. Frankfurt-am-Main: Shemme Verlag, 1965.

Block, I. "Discipleship and Evangelism." *Direction*, *14*(2) (1985): 76-81.

Block, I. "Issues in Church Polity for North American Mennonite Brethren." *Direction*, *19* (2)(1990): 28-38.

Bloesch, D. G. *The Evangelical Renaissance*. Grand Rapids: Wm. B. Eerdmans Publishing Co, 1973.

Blum, J. "The Rise of Serfdom in Eastern Europe." *The American Historical Review*, *63* (1957): 807-836.

Bolten, J. A. "Von den Kirchen der Fremden Religions-vervandten in Altona." In *Historische Kirchennachrichten von der Stadt Altona und deren verschiedenen Religions-parteien von der Herrschaft Pinneberg und von der Grafschaft Ranzau*, 270-427. Altona: J. F. Hammerich, 1790a.

Bolton, J. A. *Historische Kirchennachrichten von der Stadt Altona*. 2 Vols. Altona: J. F. Hammerich, 1790b.

Bontrager, W. D. *In search of Justice: Litigation vs Reconciliation*. Minneapolis: W. D. Bontrager, 1987.

Bornhäuser, C. "Die Gemeinde als Versammlung der Gottesfürchtigen bei Menno Simons." *Mennonitische Blätter*, *25* (1970): 19-36.

Bornhäuser, C. *Leben und Lehre Menno Simons: Ein Kampf um das Fundament des Glaubens (etwa 1496-1561)*. Tübingen: Neukirchner Verlag, 1973.

Braght, T. J. van *The Bloody Theater or Martyrs Mirror of Defenseless Christians*. Scottdale: Mennonite Publishing House, 1938.

Braght, T. J. van *The Bloody Theatre or Martyrs Mirror of Defenseless Christians*. Elkhart, Indiana: Mennonite Publishing Company, 1950.

Braun, A. "Forsteidienst." In *Mennonitisches Lexikon*, *1* (1913): 663-664.

Braun, A. "Landlose." In *Mennonitisches Lexikon*, *2* (1937): 612-613.

Braun-Ibersheim, A. *"Die Kirchlichen Spaltungen in den Russland-Deutschen Mennoniten-Gemeinden." Schriften Reihe des Mennonitischen Geschichtsvereins in Beiträge zur Geschichte den Mennoniten.* Weierhof: Mennonitscher Geschichtsverein, 1938: 7-24.

Braun, H. J. "Mennoniten oder Baptisten?" *Friedensstimme* (May 1910): 3-5.

Brinner, L. *Die deutsche Grönlandfahrt.* Berlin: Karl Curtis, 1913.

Brock, P. *Pacifism in the United States: From the Colonial Era to First World War.* Princeton: Princeton University Press, 1968.

Brock, P. *The Roots of War Resistance: Pacifism from the Early Church to Tolstoy.* Nyack, NY: The Fellowship of Reconciliation, 1981.

Brock, P. *Freedom from Violence: Sectarian Non-resistance from the Middle Ages to the Great War.* Toronto: University of Toronto Press, 1991a.

Brock, P. *Freedom from War: Nonsectarian Pacifism 1814-1914.* Toronto: University of Toronto Press, 1991b.

Brons, A. *Ursprung, Entwicklung und Schicksale der altevangelischen Taufgesinnten oder Mennoniten: kurzen Zügen übersichtlich dargestellt.* Norden: Diedr. Soltau, 1891.

Brown, D. "The Problem of Subjectivism in Pietism: A Redefinition with special reference to the theology of Phiipp Jakob Spener and August Hermann Franke." A dissertation, Northwestern University, 1962.

Brown, J. N. *The Life and Times of Menno: the celebrated Dutch Reformer with an accurate portrait.* Philadelphia: King & Baird for American Baptist Publication Society, 1853.

Brown, J. N. *Das Leben und Zeitalter Menno's: des berühmten holländischen Reformators.* Philadelphia: King & Baird for American Baptist Publication Society, 1854.

Brown, J. N. *Het Leven en de Arbeid van Menno Simons, Nederlands beroemden Hervormer.* Haarlem: G. Velthuijsen, 18--.

Brüsewitz, C. F. "The Mennonites of Balk, Friesland." *Mennonite Quarterly Review,* 30 (1956): 19-31.

Brunk, George R. III. "Conversion." In *The Mennonite Encyclopedia 5* (1990): 205-206.

Brunk, G. R, (Ed.). *Menno Simons, A Reappraisal: Essays in Honor of Irvin B. Horst on the 450th Anniversary of the Fundamentboek.* Harrisonburg, VA: Eastern Mennonite College, 1992.

Buesch, J. G. *Versuch einer Geschichte der Hamburgischen Handlung.* Hamburg: Benjamin Gottlob Hoffmann, 1797.

Bullinger, E. W. *The Foundations of Dispensational Truth: The Lord Hath Spoken, Heb. i. 2.* London: Eyre & Spottiswoode (Publishers) Ltd, 1931.

Burkholder, J. L. "The Anabaptist Vision of Discipleship." In *The Recovery of the Anabaptist Vision: A Sixtieth Anniversary Tribute to Harold S. Bender* edited by G. F. Hershberger, 135-151. Scottdale: Herald Press, 1957.

Burkholder, J. L. "Ethics." In *The Mennonite Encyclopedia,* 4 (1959): 1079-1083.

Burkholder, J. L. "Popular evangelicalism: An Appraisal." In *Evangelicalism and Anabaptism* edited by C. N. Kraus, 23-38. Scottdale: Herald Press, 1979.

Burkholder, P. *The Confession of Faith of Christians Known by the Name of Mennonites. . .* Winchester, VA: Robinson and Hollis, 1837.

Campbell, J. *Creative Mythology.* London: Penguin Books, 1968.

Canadian Conference of Mennonite Brethren Churches 75th Convention, Waterloo, Ontario, July 4-7, 1986.

Carstensen, F. V. *American Foreign Markets: Studies of Singer and International Harvester in Imperial Russia.* Chapel Hill: University of North Carolina Press, 1984.

Cartwright, D. (Ed.). *Studies in Social Power.* Ann Arbor: Institute for Social Research, University of Michigan, 1959.

Casalis, G. (Ed.). *Christliche Friedenskonferenz 1968-1971.* Wuppertal: Jugenddienst Verlag, 1971.

Cassel, D. K. *Geschichte der Mennoniten.* Philadelphia: I. Kohler, 1890.

Cate, S. B. ten *Geschiedenis der Doopsgezinden in Holland, Zeeland, Utrecht en Gelderland.* (Vols. 1-2). Amsterdam: P. N. Van Kampen, 1847.

Cattepoel, D. "Das Religiöse Leben in der Krefelder Mennonitengemeinde des 17. und 18. Jahrhunderts." In *Beiträge zur Geschichte rheinescher Mennoniten: Festgabe zum 5. Deutschen Mennoniten-Tag vom 17. bis 19. Juni 1939 zu Krefeld: Nr. 2. Schriftenreihe des Mennonitischen Geschichtsvereins,* 5-28. Weierhof: Mennonitischer Geschichtsverein, 1939.

Cattepoel, D. "Niederlandische Malerei." In *Mennonitisches Lexikon,* 3 (1958): 241.

Chawla, N. *Mother Teresa*. London: Sinclair-Stevenson, 1992.

Childe, V. G. *Man Makes Himself*. New York: The New American Library, 1951.

"Christian Peacemaker Teams: What is happening to the idea?" *Mennonite Reporter* (September 12, 1988): 5.

"Churches like Christian Peacemaker Teams idea but will revise action formula." *Mennonite Reporter, 1* (January 19, 1987): 5-8.

Clasen, C. P. *Anabaptism: A Social History, 1525-1618, Switzerland Austria, Moravia, South and Central Germany*. Ithaca: Cornell University Press, 1972.

Coggins, J. R. "About kings and horses and powerful people." *Christian Week* (November 7, 1989): 7.

Coggins, J. R. *John Smyth's Congregation: English separatism, Mennonite influence, and the elect nation: No. 32. Studies in Anabaptist and Mennonite History*. Scottdale: Herald Press, 1991.

Cohen, N. J. (Ed.). *The Fundamentalist Phenomenon: A View From Within; A Response From Without*. Grand Rapids: William B. Eerdmans Publishing Company, 1990.

Cole, S. G. *The History of Fundamentalism*. New York: R. R. Smith, 1931.

Council of Mission Board Secretaries (1958, January 24, September 18). Minutes of the Council of Mission Board Secretaries. Formerly COMBS now CIM, Council on International Mission.

Cornelius, C. A. *Der Anteil Ostfrieslands an der Reformation bis zum Jahr 1535*. Münster: Commissions-verlag von F. Cazin, 1852.

Correll, Ernst. "Friedensbewegung." In *Mennonitisches Lexikon, 1* (1913): 706-713.

Correll, E. "President Grant and the Mennonite immigration from Russia." *Mennonite Quarterly Review, 9* (1935):144-152.

Correll, E. "The congressional debates on the Mennonite immigration from Russia, 1873-74." *Mennonite Quarterly Review, 20* (1946):178-221.

Cramer, S. "Mennoniten." In *Realencyclopedie für Protestantische Theologie und Kirche, 12* [1902-3])by Herzog-Haucks (1896-1913): 611.

Cramer, S. "Menno Simons." In *Realencyclopedie für Protestantische Theologie und Kirche,7* by D. Albert Hauck, Graz, Austria reprint, (1971): 586-594.

Crichton, W. D. *Zür Geschichte der Mennoniten*. Königsberg: Gottlieb Lebrecht Hartung, 1786.

Crous, E. "Der Beitrag der Mennoniten Zum Wiederaufbau Deutschlands im Zeitalter des Dreissigjährigen Krieges." *Mennonitische Geschichstblätter*, 3 (1938): 22-32.

Crous, E. "Anabaptism, Pietism, Rationalism, and German Mennonites." In *The Recovery of the Anabaptist Vision: A Sixtieth Anniversary Tribute to Harold S. Bender*, edited by G. F. Hershberger, 237-248. Scottdale: Herald Press, 1957.

Crous, E. "Nonresistance." In *The Mennonite Encyclopedia*, 3 (1957): 897-907.

D.E. "Höppner, Jacob." In *Mennonitisches Lexikon*, 2 (1937): 346.

Daly, H. E. *Economics, Ecology, Ethics: Essays Toward a Steady-state Economy*. San Francisco: W. H. Freeman and Company, 1980.

Denck, H. *Schriften*: Vol. 24, no. 2. *Quellen und Forschungen zur Reformationsgeschichte*. Gütersloh: C. Bertelsmann Verlag, 1956.

Denner, J. *Einfältige und Christliche Betrachtungen Über die Jährlichen und Heiligen Evangelia*..... Altona: Selbstverlag, 1730.

Deppermann, K., Packull, W. O. & Stayer. J. M. "From monogenesis to polygenesis: The historical discussion of Anabaptist origins." *Mennonite Quarterly Review*, 49 (1975): 83-121.

Derksen, W. "A church and conference part company." *Mennonite Reporter*, (January 13, 1992): 3.

Dick, B. J. "Something about the Selbstschutz of the Mennonites in South Russia (July, 1918-March 1919)." *Journal of Mennonite Studies*, 4 (1986): 135-142.

Dick, M. "The story of the Anabaptists." In *The Power of the Lamb* edited by J. E. Toews, & G. Nickel, 67-76. Winnipeg: Kindred Press, 1986.

Doerksen, V. G. "Edward Wüst and Jerusalem." *Mennonite Quarterly Review*, 56 (1982): 169-178.

Doerksen, V. G. "The Mennonite world is not flat and one does not fall off the edge." In *Why I am a Mennonite: Essays on Mennonite Identity* edited by H. Loewen, 42-49. Scottdale: Herald Press, 1988.

Dollar, G. W. *A History of Fundamentalism in America*. Greenville, SC: Bob Jones University Press, 1973.

Dollinger, R. *Geschichte der Mennoniten in Schleswig-Holstein, Hamburg und Lübeck. - Quellen und Forschung zur Geschichte Schleswig-Holsteins (Vol. 17)*. Neumünster: Karl Wachholtz, 1930.

Dollinger, R. "Hamburg." In *Mennonitisches Lexikon, 2* (1937): 239-244.

Dollinger, R., & Smissen, H. van der. "Hamburg-Altona." In *The Mennonite Encyclopedia, 2* (1956): 639-643.

Dostoyevski, F. *The Brothers Karamazov*. New York: New American Library, Inc., 1957.

Douglas, J. W. *The Non-violent Cross: A Theology of Revolution and Peace*. New York: The Macmillan Company, 1968.

Driedger, A. "Marienburger Werder." In *The Mennonite Encyclopedia, 3* (1957): 481-482.

Driedger, L. *Mennonite Identity in Conflict: Vol. 19. Studies in Religion and Society*. Lewiston, NY: The Edwin Mellen Press, 1988.

Driedger, L. *Mennonites in Winnipeg*. Winnipeg: Kindred Press, 1990.

Driedger, L. "Identity and Assimilation." In *Anabaptist-Mennonite Identities in Ferment, Occasional Papers #14* edited by Leo Driedger & Leland Harder, 159-175. Elkhart, Indiana: Institute of Mennonite Studies, 1990.

Driedger, L. "From Martyrs to Muppies: The Mennonite Urban Professional Revolution." *Mennonite Quarterly Review 67*(3) (1993): 304-322.

Driedger, M. D. "Conflict and Adaptation in an Exile Community. Flemish Mennonites in Altona and Hamburg 1649-1711." A thesis submitted to the Department of History, Queen's University, Kingston, Ontario, Canada, 1993.

Driver, J. "The Anabaptist vision and social justice." In *Christian Mission and Social Justice* edited by S. Escobar, & J. Driver, 86-110. Scottdale: Herald Press, 1978.

Dueck, A. "Economics, faith and practise." *Direction, 14*(2) (1985): 50-53.

Dueck, A. J. "Mennonite churches and religious developments in Russia 1850-1914." In *Mennonites in Russia, 1788-1988: Essays in honor of Gerhard Lohrenz* edited by J. Friesen, 149-181. Winnipeg: CMBC Publications, 1989.

Dueck, A. J. "Church Leadership: A Historical Perspective." *Direction, 9*(2) (1990): 18-27.

Dueck, A. J. *Canadian Mennonites and the Challenge of Nationalism.* Winnipeg, Manitoba: Manitoba Mennonite Historical Society, 1994.

Dühren, I. van. *Geschichte der Märtyrer oder Kurze historische Nachricht von den Verfolgungen der Mennoniten.* Winnipeg: Rundschau Publishing House, 1939.

Duerksen, H. *Das du nicht vergessest der Geschichten: Lebenserrinnerungen.* Filadefia: Druckerei ASCIM, 1990.

Duerksen, J. A. "Transition from Dutch to German in West Prussia." *Mennonite Life*, 22(3), (1967): 107-109.

Dyck, C. J. "Mutual aid in a changing economy." In *The Compassionate Community: A Collection of Lectures Presented at Conferences of the Association of Mennonite Aid Societies* edited by H. R. Hernley, 155-197). Scottdale, PA: Association of Mennonite Aid Societies, 1970.

Dyck, C. J. "1525 revisited? A comparison of Anabaptist & Mennonite Brethren Origins." In *Pilgrims and Strangers: Essays in Mennonite Brethren History* edited by P. Toews, 55-77. Fresno, CA: Center for Mennonite Brethen Studies, 1977.

Dyck, C. J. (Ed. with Kreider, R. S., & Lapp, J. A.). *From the Files of MCC: Vol. 1. The Mennonite Central Committee story.* Scottdale: Herald Press, 1980.

Dyck, C. J. (Ed. with Kreider, R. S., & Lapp, J. A.). *Responding to Worldwide Needs: Vol. 2. The Mennonite Central Committee story.* Scottdale: Herald Press, 1980.

Dyck, C. J. (Ed. with Kreider, R. S., & Lapp, J. A.). *Witness and Service in North America: Vol. 3. The Mennonite Central Committee story.* Scottdale Herald Press, 1980.

Dyck, C. J., & Martin, D. D. (Eds.). *The Mennonite Encyclopedia: A Comprehensive Reference Work on the Anabaptist-Mennonite Movement*, (Vol. 5). Scottdale: Herald Press, 1990.

Dyck, C. J. "Social Gospel." In *The Mennonite Encyclopedia,* 5 (1990): 832-834.

Dyck, C. J., Keeney, W. A., & Beachy, A. J. (Trans. and Eds.). *The Writings of Dirk Philips 1504-1586: Vol. 6. Classics of the Radical Reformation.* Scottdale: Herald Press, 1992.

Dyck, H. L. "Russian servitor and Mennonite hero: Light and shadow in images of Johann Cornies." *Journal of Mennonite Studies, 2,* (1984a): 9-28.

Dyck, H. L. (Trans. and Ed.). "Agronomist Gavel's biography of Johann Cornies." *Journal of Mennonite Studies, 2* (1984b): 29-41.

Dyck, H. L. "Landlessness in the Old Colony: The Judenplan Experiment 1850-1880." In *Mennonites in Russia, 1788-1988: Essays in honour of Gerhard Lohrenz* edited by J. Friesen, 183-201. Winnipeg: CMBC Publications, 1989.

Dyck, H. L. (Trans. and Ed.). *A Mennonite in Russia: The Diaries of Jacob D. Epp, 1851-1880.* Toronto: University of Toronto Press, 1991.

Dyck, I. M. *Auswanderung der Reinländer Mennonitengemeinde von Canada nach Mexiko.* Cuauhtemoc: Imprenta Colonial, 1970.

Dyck, J. "The struggle for self-understanding: Two conceptions of Gemeinde amongst Russian Mennonites, 1914-1923." Paper presented at the Symposium on the Bicentennial of Mennonites in Russia, Winnipeg, Manitoba, November 9-11, 1989.

Ediger, G. "A Ministering People." *Direction, 15(2),* (1986): 45-56.

Ediger, H. (Ed.). *Beschlüsse der von den geistlichen und andern Vertretern der Mennoniten-gemeinden Russlands abgehaltenen Konferenzen für die Jahre 1879 bis 1913.* Berdjansk: Druck und Verlag von Heinrich Ediger, 1914.

Ehrenberg, R. *Gewerbefreiheit und Zunftzwang in Ottensen und Altona 1543 bis 1640. Altona unter Schauenburgischen Herrschaft.* Altona: J. Harder, 1893.

Ehrt, A. "Das Mennonitentum in Russland." *Russische Blätter: Das Christentum in Russland.* Wernigerode am Harz: Hans Harder Verlag. Heft 2, (1929): 76-79.

Ehrt, A. *Das Mennonitentum in Russland von seiner Einwanderung bis zur Gegenwart.* Berlin (Langensalza): Verlag von Julius Beltz, 1932.

Enns, J. H. "Conscientious objectors during the 2nd World War." [Letter to the Editor]. *Mennonite Brethren Herald* (December 18, 1981): 10-11.

Enns, J. H. "My experiences in alternative service during World War II." An unpublished manuscript in Jacob A. Loewen collection, 1985.

Ens, A. "Theology of the Hermeneutical Community in Anabaptist-Mennonite Thought." In *The Church as Theological Community* edited by H. Huebner, 60-89. Winnipeg, MB: CMBC Publications, 1990.

Ens, A. "Becoming British Citizens in Pre-WW I Canada." In *Canadian Mennonites and the Challenge of Nationalism* edited by A.J. Dueck, 69-88. Winnipeg: Manitoba Historical Society, 1994.

Epp, A. R. "Calvin reveals an early Anabaptist position statement." *Mennonite Life*, *41*(1),(1986): 12-15.

Epp, D. "Tagebuch geführt von David Epp in Chortitz." A handwritten manuscript in the Mennonite Heritage Centre Archives, Winnipeg, (September 20, 1838).

Epp, D. H. *Johann Cornies. Züge aus seinem Leben und Wirken.* Rosthern, SK: Echo Verlag, 1946 (1st publ. 1909).

Epp, D. H. "Höppner, Jacob." In *The Mennonite Encyclopedia*, *2*,(1956): 811.

Epp, D. H. *Die Chortitzer Mennoniten: Versuch einer Darstellung des Entwicklungsganges derselben.* Steinbach, MB: Die Mennonitische Post, 1984 (First published in Odessa: Selbstverlag, 1889).

Epp, D. H. "The emergence of German industry in the South Russian Colonies." (John B. Toews, Trans. and Ed.). *Mennonite Quarterly Review*, *55*, (1985): 289-371.

Epp, D. H. *Johann Cornies.* (Peter Pauls, Trans.). Winnipeg, MB: CMBC Publications, 1995.

Epp, F. H. *Mennonite Exodus: The Rescue and Resettlement of the Russian Mennonites Since the Communist Revolution.* Altona, MB: D. W. Friesen & Sons Ltd, 1962.

Epp, F. H. *Mennonites in Canada, 1786-1920: The History of a Separate People.* Toronto: Macmillan of Canada, 1974.

Epp, F. H. *Mennonites in Canada, 1920-1940: A People's Struggle for Survival.* Toronto: Macmillan of Canada, 1982.

Epp, G. "Mennonite-Ukrainian relations (1789-1945)." *Journal of Mennonite Studies*, 7 (1989a): 131-144.

Epp, G. "Urban Mennonites in Russia." *Mennonites in Russia 1788-1988: essays in honor of Gerhard Lohrenz* (pp.239-260). Winnipeg, MB: CBMC Publications, 1989b.

Epp, H. *Notizen aus dem Leben und Wirken des verstorbenen Ältesten Abraham Unger, dem Gründer der "Einlager-Mennoniten-Brüdergemeinde".* Halbstadt: Selbsverlag, 1907.

Epp, H. *Verschiedenheiten zwischen den Vereinigten Mennoniten-Brüder-gemeinden und den Baptisten, so wie den alten Mennonitengemeinden.* Odessa: Selbstverlag, 1907.

Epp, H.F. "Evangelical Mennonite Brethren". In *The Mennonite Encyclopedia, 2* (1956): 262-264.

Epp-Tiessen, E. *Altona: The Story of a Prairie Town*. Altona, MB: D. W. Friesen & Sons Ltd, 1982.

Erb, P. "Nonresistance and litigation." *Mennonite Quarterly Review, 13* (1939): 75-82.

Erickson, E. H. *Gandhi's Truth: On the Origins of Militant Nonviolence*. New York: W. W. Norton & Company Inc, 1969.

Esau, K. "The Biblical call to unity: Implications for Mennonite Brethren." *Direction, 19*(2), (1990): 75-86.

Ewert, A. Personal interview by Wesley J. Prieb.(January, 1993).

Ewert, D. "Dispensationalism." In *The Mennonite Encyclopedia, 5* (1990): 240-241.

Ewert, W. "A defence of the ancient Mennonite principle of non-resistance by a leading Prussian elder in 1873." *Mennonite Quarterly Review, 11* (1937): 284-290.

Fast, A. *Menno Simons vor 400 Jahren und die Mennoniten von heute*. Emden: Otto Wentzel, 1936.

Fast, A. *Die Kulturleistungen der Mennoniten in Ostfriesland und Münsterland*. Emden: A. Fast, 1947.

Fast, G. *Im Schatten des Todes*. Winnipeg: Regehr Printing, 1956.

Fast, G. (Ed.). *In den Steppen Siberiens*. Rosthern: Selbstverlag, 1957.

Fast, H. *Der linke Flügel der Reformation: Glaubenszeugnisse der Täufer, Spiritualisten, Schwärmer und Antitrinitarier*. Bremen: Carl Schünemann Verlag, 1962.

Fast, H. "Die Eidsverweigerung bei den Mennoniten". *Mennonitische Blätter, 22* (1965): 18-31.

Fast, H. "Die Frage nach der Autorität der Bibel auf dem Frankenthalle Täufergespräch 1571." *Mennonitische Blätter, 27* (1970): 28-38.

Fast, H. "Gewaltverzicht als Bestandteil des Christlichen Friedenszeugnisses." In J. Strauss (Ed.), *Tutzinger Texte: 10: Glauben und Gewalt* (pp. 29-43). Munich: Claudius Verlag, 1971.

Fast, H. "The Anabaptists as trouble makers." *Mennonite Life, 31*(1), (1976): 10-13.

Fast, H. *Beiträge zu einer Friedenstheologie: Eine Stimme aus den historischen Friedenskirchen*. Maxdorf: Agape Verlag, 1982.

Fast, H. "Mennoniten." *Evangelisches Kirchenlexikon*, 3rd edition, *3* (1991): 358-61.

Fast, Henry. "Evangelical Mennonite Conference (Kleine Gemeinde)." *The Mennonite Encyclopedia*, 5 (1990): 278-280.

Fast, J. "Crossing swords: The Christian response toward war and peace" In *The Power of the Lamb* edited by J. E. Toews and G. Nickel (57-66). Winnipeg: Kindred Press, 1992.

Fellmann, W. (Ed.). *Beiträge Zur Geschichte der Mennoniten (Festausgabe für D. Christian Neff zum 70. Geburtstag.)* Weierhof: Mennonitischer Geschichtsverein. 1938: 25-44.

Fischer, H. G. "Lutheranism and the vindication of the Anabaptist way." *Mennonite Quarterly Review*, 28 (1954): 27-38.

Fischer, L. *The Life of Mahatma Gandhi*. London: Collier Books, 1962.

Flynn, D. J., & Koop, A. P. "Economic and cultural factors in the migration of Mennonites: A study of two Mennonite communities in Manitoba." An unpublished paper written at King's College, London, Ontario, (1992) a copy in the Jacob A. Loewen collection.

Francis, E. K. "The Russian Mennonites: From religious to ethnic group." *The American Journal of Sociology*, 54 (1948): 101-107.

Francis, E. K. "The Mennonite Commonwealth in Russia, 1789-1914: A sociological interpretation." *Mennonite Quarterly Review*, 25 (1951): 173-82.

Francis, E. K. *In Search of Utopia: The Mennonites in Manitoba*. Altona, MB: D. W. Friesen & Sons Ltd, 1955.

Francis, E. K. "Anabaptism and colonization." In *The recovery of the Anabaptist vision: A sixteeth anniversary tribute to Harold S. Bender* edited by G.F. Hershberger, 249-261. Scottdale: Herald Press, 1957.

Franck, I. S. *The Ephrata story*. Ephrata, PA: Hocking Printing Company, Inc, 1964.

"Die Freiwirte in den deutschen Kolonien Südrusslands." *Odessaer Zeitung* (April 26, 1863): 370.

French, J. R. & Raven, B. "The bases of social power." In *Studies in Social Power*, edited by D. Cartwright, 150-167. Ann Arbor: Institute of Social Research, 1959.

Fretz, J.W. "Colonization." In *The Mennonite Encyclopedia*, 1 (1955): 644-646.

Fretz, J. W. "Brotherhood and the economic ethic of the Anabaptists." In G. F. Hershberger, (Ed.). *The recovery of the Anabaptist vision*, 194-201. Scottdale: Herald Press, 1957.

Fretz, J.W. "Mexico." *The Mennonite Encyclopedia, 3* (1957): 663-664.

Fretz, J. W. "Mennonite Encyclopedia: venture in brotherhood." *Mennonite Life, 19* (1964): 154-156.

Fretz, J. W. "Meditations on Christian mutual aid." In *The Compassionate Community: A Collection of Lectures Presented at Conferences of the Association of Mennonite Aid Societies,* edited by H. R. Hernley, 1-35. Scottdale: Association of Mennonite Aid Societies, 1970.

Fretz, J. W. "Mennonite community: Traditional or intentional." *Mennonite Life, 30*(4), (1975): 5-7.

Fretz, J. W. *The Mennonite Encyclopedia, Experiment, 1953-1978: Twenty-five Years of Experience in Helping "little people" to get Established in Their Own Businesses in over Twenty Countries Around the World.* Waterloo: Conrad Press, 1978.

Freund, P. *Myths of Creation.* New York: Washington Square Press, Inc., 1965.

Friedmann, I. M. *Helping Resolve Conflict.* Scottdale: Herald Press, 1990.

Friedmann, R. "Anabaptism and pietism." *Mennonite Quarterly Review, 14,* 90-128, (1940): 149-169.

Friedmann, R. "Spiritual changes in European Mennonitism, 1650-1750: [An appendix to "Anabaptism and pietism"]." *Mennonite Quarterly Review, 15* (1941): 33-45.

Friedmann, R. "On Mennonite historiography and on individualism and brotherhood: A communication from Dr. Robert Friedmann." *Mennonite Quarterly Review, 18* (1944): 117-122.

Friedmann, R. *Mennonite piety through the centuries: Its Genius and its Literature.* Goshen, IN: The Mennonite Historical Society, 1949.

Friedmann, R. "The Doctrine of Two Worlds." In *The Recovery of the Anabaptist Vision: A Sixtieth Anniversary Tribute to Harold S. Bender,* edited by G. F. Hershberger, 105-118. Scottdale: Herald Press, 1957.

Friedmann, R. *Hutterite Studies.* Goshen, IN: Mennonite Historical Society, 1961.

Friedmann, R. *The Theology of Anabaptism: An Interpretation.* Scottdale, PA: Herald Press, 1973.

Friedmann, R. "The doctrine of two worlds." In *The Anabaptists and Thomas Müntzer,* edited by J. M. Stayer & W. O. Packull, 23-27. Dubuque, IA: Kendall/Hunt Publishing Company, 1980.

Friesen, A. "Menschen auf bestialische Weise hingeschlachtet." *Odessaer Zeitung* (April 7, 1913): 2-3.

Friesen, Abr. "The Marxist Interpretion of Anabaptism." In *Sixteenth Century Essays and Studies I,* edited by C. S. Meyer, 17-34. St. Louis, MO: Foundation Reformation Research, 1970.

Friesen, Abr. "Social revolution or religious reform? Some salient aspects of Anabaptist historiography." In *Umstrittenes Täufertum, 1525-1975: Neue Forschungen,* edited by H. J. Goertz, 223-243. Göttingen: Vandenhoeck & Ruprecht, 1975.

Friesen, Abr. "The radical reformation revisited." *Journal of Mennonite Studies,* 2 (1984): 124-176.

Friesen, Abr. "Why I am a Mennonite." In *Why I am a Mennonite: Essays on Mennonite identity,* edited by H. Loewen, 78-89. Scottdale: Herald Press, 1988.

Friesen, Abr. *Thomas Müntzer, A Destroyer of the Godless. The Makings of a Sixteenth-Century Revolutionary.* Berkeley: University of California Press, 1990.

Friesen, Abr. "Menno and Münster: The Man and the Movement." In *Menno Simons: a Reappraisal,* edited by G. R. Brunk, 131-162. Harrisonburg: Eastern Mennonite College, 1992.

Friesen, Abr. "Baptist Interpretations of Anabaptist History." In *Mennonites & Baptists: A Continuing Conversation,* edited by P. Toews, 39-72. Winnipeg, MB: Kindred Press, 1993.

Friesen, Abr. *History and Renewal in the Anabaptist/Mennonite Tradition.* Cornelius H. Wedel Historical series: 7. North Newton: Bethel College, 1994.

Friesen, D. K. *Christian Peacemaking and International Conflict: A Realist Pacifist Perspective.* Scottdale: Herald Press, 1986.

Friesen, H. W. "In B.C. the Mennonite Brethren get set to jettison their embarrassing name." *Mennonite Mirror, 20*(4), (1990): 9.

Friesen, J. (Ed.). *Mennonites in Russia, 1788-1988: Essays in Honour of Gerhard Lohrenz.* Winnipeg: CMBC Publications, 1989.

Friesen, J. "The relationship of Prussian Mennonites to German nationalism." In *Mennonite images: Historical, cultural, and literary essays dealing with Mennonite issues,* edited by H. Loewen, 61-72. Winnipeg: Hyperion Press Limited, 1980.

Friesen, L. "Mennonites and the new fissuring of Russian society, 1860s-1905." Paper presented at the Symposium on the Bicentennial of Mennonites in Russia, Winnipeg, Manitoba.(November, 1989).

Friesen, M. W. *Kanadische Mennoniten bezwingen eine Wildnis. 50 Jahre Kolonie Menno: 1927-1977*. Asuncion: Artes Gráficas für Kolonie Menno, 1977.

Friesen, P. M. *Die Alt-Evangelische Mennonitische Brüderschaft (1789-1910) im Rahmen der mennonitischen Gesamtgeschichte*. Halbstadt: Raduga, 1977.

Friesen, P. M. *The Mennonite Brotherhood in Russia (1789-1910)*. (Translated and edited by J. B. Toews, A. Friesen, P. J. Klassen, & H. Loewen.). Fresno, CA: Board of Christian Literature General Conference of Mennonite Brethren Churches, 1978, revised 1980.

Froese, W. "Weltflucht und Weltzuwendung." *Mennonitische Blätter*, 32 (1990-1991):104-124.

Gandhi, M. "The Story of my Experiment with Truth." In *The Collected Works of Mahatma Gandhi*. New Delhi: Publications Division, Ministry of Broadcasting, Government of India, 1970: 1-402.

Geddert, R. "Wanted: handcuffed pastors." *Mennonite Brethren Herald.* (June 1, 1990): 2-3.

"Die gegenseitigen Verhältnisse der Landbesitzenden und Landlosen Molotschner Mennoniten." *Odessaer Zeitung.* (January 10, 1864): 25-27.

Geiser, S. *Die Taufgesinnten-gemeinden: eine Kurzgefasste Darstellung der wichtigsten Ereignisse des Täufertums*. Karlsruhe: Heinrich Schneider, 1931.

Geiser, S. "Switzerland. In *The Mennonite Encyclopedia*, 4 (1959): 673-677.

Year Book of the 45th General Conference of the Mennonite Brethren Church of North America. (1951). Hillsboro, KS: Mennonite Brethren Publishing House.

Gerber, S. "Das Mennonitische Gemeindeverständnis." *Mennonitisches Jahrbuch*, 83 (1983): 20-26.

Gingerich, B. N. "Property and the Gospel: Two Reformation perspectives." *Mennonite Quarterly Review*, 59 (1985):248-267.

Gingerich, M. *Service for Peace: A History of Mennonite Civilian Public Service*. Akron, PA: The Mennonite Central Committee, 1949.

Gingerich, M. "Discipleship expressed in alternative service." In G. F. Hershberger, (Ed.). *The Anabaptist Vision*, 262-274. Scottdale: Herald Press, 1957.

Gingerich, M. *Mennonite Attire Through Four Centuries*. Breiningsville, PA: The Pennsylvania German Society, 1970.

Gingerich, O. "Relations between the Russian Mennonites and the Friends during the nineteenthth century." *Mennonite Quarterly Review, 25* (1951): 283-295.

Gish, A. *The New Left and Christian Radicalism.* Grand Rapids, MI: William B. Eerdmans Publishing Company, 1970.

Göbel, E. "Hohenzollern." In *The Mennonite Encyclopedia, 2* (1956): 788.

Goertz, A. "Über die Mennoniten Altpreussens." *Altpreussische Geschlechterkunde* (September 1, 1966): 225.

Goertz, H.-J. (Ed.). *Umstrittines Täufertum, 1525-1975: Neue Forschungen.* Göttingen: Vandenhoeck & Ruprecht, 1975, 2nd ed. 1977.

Goertz, H.-J. "Nationale Erhebung und religiöser Niedergang: Missglückte Aneignung des täuferischen Leitbildes im Dritten Reich. In *Umstrittenes Täufertum, 1525-1975* edited by H.-J. Goertz, (2nd edition): 259-289. Göttingen: Vandenhoek & Ruprecht, 1977.

Goertz, H.-J. "Der fremde Menno Simons." In *The Dutch Dissenters: A Critical Companion to Their History and Ideas,* edited by I. B. Horst, 160-176. Leiden: E. J. Brill, 1986.

Goertz, H.-J. *Die Täufer: Geschichte und Deutung.* München: C. H. Beck [1980], 1988a. (Evangelische Verlagsanstalt reprint 1988).

Goertz, H.-J, "The confessional Heritage in its New Mold: What is Mennonite Self-Understanding Today?" In *Mennonite Identity: Historical and Contemporary Perspectives,* edited by C. W. Redekop & S. J. Steiner, 1-12. Lanham, MD: University Press of Maryland, 1988b.

Goertz, H.-J. & Klaassen, W. (Eds.). *Profiles of Radical Reformers: Biographical Sketches from Thomas Müntzer to Paracelsus.* Scottdale: Herald Press, 1982.

Gorjon, F. *La Iglesia y el Estado:Hacia una Filosofía Cristiana de las relaciones etre la Iglesia y el Estado.* Buenos Aires: Trenque Lauguen, 1948.

Görz, H. *Die Molotschnaer Ansiedlung: Entstehung, Entwicklung und Untergang.* Steinbach, MB: Echo Verlag, 1951.

Görz, Heinrich. *The Molotschna Settlement.* (English version of 1951 publication of book.) Translated by Al Reimer and John B. Toews. Winnipeg, MB: CMBC Publications, 1993.

Goverts, Ernst. "Das adelige Gut Fresenburg und die Mennoniten." *Zeitschrift der Zentralstelle für niedersächsische Familiengeschichte, 7,* (1925): 41-56, 69-86, 97-103.

Graber, E. "Menno Simons and the Scripture." Unpublished manuscript, Goshen College, 1944.

Graber, J. D. "Non-resistance and mission." Peace Section Report, available in the MCC Library, 1950.

Graber, J. D. "Anabaptism expressed in missions and social service." In *The Recovery of the Anabaptist Vision: A Sixtieth Anniversary Tribute to Harold S. Bender,* edited by G. F. Hershberger, 152-166. Scottdale: Herald Press, 1957.

Graber, O. C. "Why Christians help one another." In *The Compassionate Community: A Collection of Lectures Presented at Conferences of the Association of Mennonite Aid Societies,* edited by H. R. Hernley, 199-225. Scottdale: Association of Mennonite Aid Societies, 1870.

Grant, U. S. "Third annual message of Ulysses S. Grant, December 4, 1871." In *A Compilation of Messages and Papers of Presidents* edited by J. D. Richardson, (Vol. 6:301ff). Washington, DC: Bureau of National Literature and Art, 1871.

Grant, U. S. "Fifth annual message of Ulysses S. Grant, December 1, 1873." In J. D. Richardson, (Ed.). *A Compilation of Messages and Papers of Presidents* (Vol. 7:253ff). Washington, DC: Bureau of National Literature and Art, 1873.

Groff, Weyburn W., "Gandhi, Mohandas Karamchand (Oct. 2, 1869-Jan.30, 1948)". In *The Mennonite Encyclopedia,* 5 (1990): 323-324.

Groope, Wilmer D. "Alcohol among the Columbian County, Ohio Mennonites." *Mennonite Historical Bulletin.* (January 21, 1960), p. 1ff.

Gross, L. "Recasting the Anabaptist vision: the longer view." *Mennonite Quarterly Review,* 60 (1986): 352-363.

Gutmann, M. P. *Toward the Modern Economy: Early Industry in Europe 1500-1800.* Philadelphia: Temple University Press, 1988.

Ein Gutsbesitzer. "Illustration zur Frage eines Jünglings in Nr92." *Odessaer Zeitung* (August 9-22, 1907): 2.

Haas, M. "Der Weg der Täufer in die Absonderung." In H. J. Goertz, (Ed.). *Umstrittenes Täufertum, 1525-1975: Neue Forschungen,* 50-78. Göttingen: Vandenhoeck & Ruprecht, 1975, 2nd Ed. 1977.

Haas, M. "The path of Anabaptists into separation: The interdependence of theology and social behavior." In J. M. Stayer & W. O. Packull,

(Eds.). *The Anabaptists and Thomas Müntzer,* 72-84. Dubuque, IA: Kendall/Hunt Publishing Company, 1980.

Hamm, P. M. *Continuity & Change Among Canadian Mennonite Brethren.* Waterloo: Wilfrid Laurier University Press, 1987.

Händiges-Elbing, E. "Beiträge zur Geschichte der Mennonitengemeinde Elbing-Ellerwald auf Grund handschriftlicher und anderer Quellen." In *Beitrage zur Geschichte der Mennoniten: Festgabe für Christian Neff zum 70. Geburtstag,* 25-47. Weierhof: Mennonitischer Geschichtsverein, 1938.

Harder, G. G. *When Apples are Ripe: The Story of Clayton Kratz.* Scottdale: Herald Press, 1971.

Harder, J. "Der Exodus in die Wüste." *Mennonitisches Jahrbuch,* 80 (1980): 69-73.

Harder, L. "The Russian Mennonites and American Democracy under Grant." In *From the Steppes to the Prairies (1874-1949)* edited by C. Krahn, 54-67. Newton, KS: Mennonite Publication Office, 1949.

Harder, L. *Steinbach and its Churches.* Elkhart, IN: Mennonite Biblical Seminary, Work of the Church Department, 1970.

Harder, L. *General Conference Mennonite Church Fact Book of Congregational Membership.* Newton, KS: General Conference Mennonite Church, 1971.

Harms, J. F. "Wer sind die Mitglieder der Mennonitischen Brüdergemeinde?" *Zionsbote* (May 21, 1896): 3-4.

Harms, J. F. *Geschichte der Mennoniten Brüdergemeinde.* Hillsboro, KS: Mennonite Brethren Publishing House, 1924.

Harms, O. *The Journey of a Church: A Walk Through One Hundred Years of Life and Times of the Hillsboro Mennonite Brethren Church.* Hillsboro, KS: Centre for Mennonite Brethren Studies, 1987.

Harnack, A. *Militia Christi: The Christian Religion and the Military in the First Three Centuries,* translated by D. Gracie. Philadelphia: Fortress Press, 1981.

Hartknoch, Christopherus. *Preussische Kirchen-Historie.* Danzig, Frankfurt & Leipzig: Samon Beckstein, 1686.

Hartwich, A. *Geographisch-historische Landesbeschreibung derer dreyen im Polnischen Preussen liegenden Werdern.* Danzig: Rosenberg, 1722.

Hartzler, J. D. *Mennonites in the World War, or Non-resistance Under Test.* Scottdale: Mennonite Publishing House, 1922.

Hast, Johann. *Geschichte der Wiedertäufer von ihrer Enstehung bis auf zur ihren Sturz zu Münster in Westphalen.* Münster: J. H. Dieters, 1836.

Hauerwas, S. A. *Community of Character: Toward a Constructive Christian Social Ethic.* Notre Dame: University of Notre Dame Press, 1981.

Hauerwas, S. *The Peaceable Kingdom: A Primer in Christian Ethics.* Notre Dame: University of Notre Dame Press, 1983.

Hauerwas, S. & Willimon, H. W. *Resident Aliens: Life in the Christian Colony.* Nashville: Abingdon Press, 1989.

Haury, V. "Den Wehrdienst geleistet und dann verweigert." *Mennonitisches Jahrbuch,* 88 (1988):53-55.

Haxthausen, A. von. *Studies on the Interior of Russia*, Edited by S. F. Starr, Translated by E. L. M. Schmidt. Chicago: University of Chicago Press, 1972.

Hege, C. *Kurze Geschichte der Mennoniten.* Frankfurt-am-Main: Kommissionsverlag von Hermann Minjon, 1909.

Hege, C. "Deutsches Reich." In *Mennonitisches Lexikon, 1* (1913): 422-429.

Hege, C. & Christian Neff. *Mennonitisches Lexicon,* (Vol. 1 [1913]; Vol. 2 [1937]) Frankfurt am Main und Weierhof: Hege & Neff). Completed by H.S. Bender & Ernst Crous, (Vol. 3 [1958]; Vol. 4 [1967]). Karlsruhe: Heinrich Schneider, 1913-1967.

Hege, C. "Ältestenrat." In *The Mennonite Encyclopedia, 1* (1955): 19.

Hege, C. "East India Company." In *The Mennonite Encyclopedia, 2* (1956): 122.

Hege, C. "Norden." In *Mennonitisches Lexikon, 3* (1958): 269-270.

Hege, C. "The East Indies Company." In *Mennonitisches Lexikon, 3* (1958): 321-322.

Hege, C. & Zijpp, N. van der, "Mandates." In *The Mennonite Encyclopedia, 3* (1957): 446-452.

Hein, G. "Friedensgesinnung und Wehrlosigkeit." *Mennonitisches Jahrbuch, 33* (1933): 104-113.

Hein, G. "Das Alte Testament im Urteil unsrer Väter und der Gegenwart." *Mennonitisches Jahrbuch,* (1935):137-142, (1936):6-13.

Hein, G. "Leupold Scharnschlager. Ein Mitarbeiter Pilgram Marbecks." *Mennonitische Blätter, 4* (1939): 6-12.

Hein, G. "Palatinate." In *The Mennonite Encyclopedia, 4* (1959): 106-112.

Hein, G. "Vermahner." In *Mennonitisches Lexikon, 4* (1959): 424.

Hernley, H. R. (Ed.). *The Compassionate Community: A Collection of Lectures Presented at Conferences of the Association of Mennonite Aid Societies*. Scottdale: Association of Mennonite Aid Societies, 1970.

Hershberger, G. F. "The Mennonite attitude and the modern peace movement as illustrated by the St. Louis Meeting of the World Alliance." *Mennonite Quarterly Review*, 2 (1928): 111-118.

Hershberger, G. F. "Peace and war in the Old Testament." *Mennonite Quarterly Review, 17* (1943a): 1-22.

Hershberger, G. F. "Peace and war in the New Testament." *Mennonite Quarterly Review, 17* (1943b): 59-72.

Hershberger, G. F. "Christian non-resistance: Its foundation and its outreach." *Mennonite Quarterly Review, 24,* (1950): 156-162.

Hershberger, G. F. "Conscientious Objector." In *The Mennonite Encyclopedia, 1* (1955): 692-699.

Hershberger, G. F. (Ed.). *The Recovery of the Anabaptist Vision: A Sixtieth-anniversary Tribute to Harold S. Bender*. Scottdale: Herald Press, 1957.

Hershberger, G. F. *The Way of the Cross in Human Relations*. Scottdale: Herald Press, 1958.

Hershberger, G. F. "Pacifism." In *The Mennonite Encyclopedia, 4* (1959): 104-105.

Hershberger, G. F. *War, Peace, and Nonresistance* (3rd ed.). Scottdale: Herald Press, 1969.

Hertzler, H.A. "Nachfolge Jesu." *Mennonitische Blätter, 28* (1971): 19-27.

Hiebert, C. (Ed.). *Brothers in Deed to Brothers in Need: A Scrapbook About Mennonite Immigrants from Russia 1870-1885*. Newton, KS: Faith and Life Press, 1974.

Hiebert, C. "The developments of Mennonite Brethren Churches in North America: some reflections, interpretations and viewpoints." In *Pilgrims and Strangers: Essays in Mennonite Brethren History*, edited by P. Toews, 111-132. Fresno, CA: Center for Mennonite Brethren Studies, 1977.

Hiebert, P. C. "Memoirs." Handwritten manuscript in the MB Historical Society archives, Hillsboro, KS, 1962.

Hiebert, P. G. "Conversion, culture and cognitive categories." *Gospel in Context*. (October, 1978): 24-29.

Hiebert, P. G. "Sets and structures: A study of church patterns." In D. J. Hesselgrave, (Ed.). *New horizons in world mission: Evangelicals and the Christian mission in the 1980's*, 217-227. Grand Rapids: Baker Book House, 1979.

Hiebert, P. G. "The category Christian in the mission task." *International Review of Missions*, 72 (1983): 421-427.

Hiebert, P. G. "World trends and their implications for Mennonite Brethren Missions." *Mission Focus*, 16 (1988): 75-82.

Hiebert, W. D. "Who are the Mennonite Brethren?" *Christian Leader* (September 13, 1966): 6-7.

Hildebrand, P. *Erste Auswanderung der Mennoniten aus dem Danziger Gebiet nach Südrussland*. Halbstadt: A. Neufeld, 1888.

Hillerbrand, H. J. "The Anabaptist view of the state." *Mennonite Quarterly Review*, 32 (1958): 83-110.

Hillerbrand, H. J. "Menno Simons: sixteenth-century reformer." *Church History*, 31 (1962a): 387-399.

Hillerbrand, H. J. *A Bibliography of Anabaptism 1520-1630*. Elkhart: Institute of Mennonite Studies, 1962b.

Hillerbrand, H. J. *Sixteenth-century Bibliography I: A Bibliography of Anabaptism, 1520-1630; A sequel, 1962-1974*. St. Louis: Center for Reformation Research, 1975.

Hillerdal, G. *Gehorsam gegen Gott und Menschen: Luthers Lehre von der Obrigkeit und die moderne evangelische Staatsethik*. Göttingen: Vandenhoeck & Ruprecht, 1955.

Hofer, J. M. (Trans. & Ed.). "The diary of Paul Tschetter, 1873: II." *Mennonite Quarterly Review*, 4 (1931): 198-220.

Hoffman, C. "Bericht über die Kirchen Süd-russlands." *Süddeutsche Warte*, 11 (1855): 50.

Hollinger, D. P. "Evangelicalism." In *The Mennonite Encyclopedia*, 5 (1990): 281-283.

Hopkins, W. D. "Resistance to taxes for military purposes." In *The Peacemaking Struggle: Militarism and Resistance*, edited by R. H. Stone & D. W. Wilbanks, 247-262. Lanham, MD: University Press of America, 1985.

Horsch, J. "Menno Simons Verhältnis zu der Münsterischen Sekte." *Deutsche-Amerikanische Zeitschrift für Theologie und Kirche, 22*, (March-April, 1911): 80-87.

Horsch, J. *Die Biblische Lehre von der Wehrlosigkeit*. Scottdale: Mennonitische Verlagsanstalt, 1920.

Horsch, J. "The modern pacifist movement considered in the light of the writings of the early church fathers." *Gospel Herald*, (October 28, 1926): 663-666.

Horsch, J. "A few questions regarding the 'Conference of Pacifist Churches.'" *Gospel Herald*, (October 20, 1927): 650-652.

Horsch, J. "Menno Simons true position on 'avoidance.'" *Mennonite Quarterly Review, 13*, (1939): 210-212.

Horsch, J. *Mennonites in Europe, Volume 1: Mennonite History*. Scottdale: Mennonite Publishing House, 1950.

Horsch, J. *The Principle of Non-resistance as Held by the Mennonite Church: A Historical Survey*. Scottdale: Mennonite Publishing House, 1951.

Horst, I. B. *A Bibliography of Menno Simons*. The Hague: Nieuwkoop S. B. De Graff, 1962.

Horst, I. B. "Menno Simons: The new man in community." In H.J. Goertz & W. Klaassen, (Eds.). *Profiles of Radical Reformers: Biographical Sketches from Thomas Müntzer to Paracelsus*, 203-213. Scottdale: Herald Press, 1982.

Horst, I. B. (Ed.). *The Dutch Dissenters: A Critical Companion to Their History and Ideas*. Leiden: E. J. Brill, 1986a.

Horst, I. B. "Menno Simons: The road to a voluntary church." In *The Dutch Dissenters: A Critical Companion to Their History and Ideas*, edited by I. B. Horst, 194-203. Leiden: E. J. Brill, 1986b.

Horst, I. B. "The meaning of Menno Simons today." In *Menno Simons: A Reappraisal*, edited by G. R. Brunk, 163-180. Harrisonburg: Eastern Mennonite College, 1992.

Hostetler, B. S. *American Mennonites and Protestant Movements*. Scottdale: Herald Press, 1987.

Hostetler, J. A. *The Sociology of Mennonite Evangelism*. Scottdale: Herald Press, 1954.

Hubert, D. "The church is Christ's church, not the pastor's" [Letter to the editor]. *Mennonite Brethren Herald* (August 10, 1990): 8.

Huebert, H. T. *Hierschau: An Example of Russian Mennonite Life*. Winnipeg: Springfield Publishers, 1986.

Huebner, H. (Ed.). *The Church as Theological Community*. Essays in honour of David Schroeder. Winnipeg, MB: CMBC Publications, 1990.

Hutter, J. "Anschlag und Fürwenden der blinden und verkehrten Welt, und allen Gottlosen gegen die Frommen." In *Glaubenzeugnisse oberdeutschen Taufgesinnten I, Quellen zür Geschichte der Täufer III*, edited by L. Müller. Leipzig: Hensius Nachfolger, 1938.

Hylkema, C. B. "Isaak Molenaar ann Willem de Clerq." *Doopsgezinde Bijdragen, 51* (1911): 63-92.

"Ein ins-Leben-tretender Jüngling. Eine Frage." *Odessaer Zeitung* (April 19-May 2, 1907): 3.

Isaac, F. *Die Molotschnaer Mennoniten: Ein Beitrag zur Geschichte derselben*. Halbstadt: H. J. Braun, 1908.

Isaak, H. "Das Weltverständnis Menno Simons." *Mennonitische Blätter, 31* (1974): 44-60.

Isaak, H. "The struggle for an evangelical town." In *The Dutch Dissenters: A Critical Companion to Their History and Ideas*, edited by I. B. Horst, 66-82. Leiden: E. J. Brill, 1986.

Isaak, H. "The heavenly has descended upon this earth. Spiritual, Apocalyptical or Eschatological Anticipation of the Kingdom of God á la Menno Simons." (Dissertation in preparation at University of Amsterdam, 1992a).

Isaak, H. "Menno's vision of the anticipation of the kingdom of God in his early writings." In *Menno Simons: A Reappraisal. Essays in Honor of Irvin B. Horst*, edited by G. R. Brunk, 57-82. Harrisonburg, VA: Eastern Mennonite College, 1992b.

Jackson, D. *Dial 911: Peaceful Christians and Urban Violence*. Scottdale: Herald Press, 1981.

Jansen, P. *Memoirs of Peter Jansen: The Record of a Busy Life*. Beatrice, NB: Peter Jansen, 1921.

Jansma, L. G. "The rise of the Anabaptist movement and societal changes in the Netherlands." In *The Dutch Dissenters: A Critical Companion to Their History and Ideas*, edited by I. B. Horst, 85-104. Leiden: E. J. Brill, 1986.

Janz, B. B. "Grundzüge und Charackter der Glaubensstellung unserer Väter." Paper presented to a study conference of the Board of Reference and Counsel of the General Conference of Mennonite Brethren

Churches, Winnipeg, Man., December 12-15, 1956. Center for Mennonite Brethren Studies, Fresno, CA.

Janzen, A. E. "Paraguay." In *The Mennonite Encyclopedia,* 4 (1959)"117-120.

Janzen, A. E. *Mennonite Brethren Distinctives.* Hillsboro, KS: Mennonite Brethren Publishing House, 1966.

Janzen, A. E. & Giesbrecht, H. (Eds.). *We Recommend...: Recommendations and Resolutions of the General Conference of the Mennonite Brethren Churches.* Fresno, CA: The Board of Christian Literature of the General Conference of Mennonite Brethren Churches, 1978.

Janzen, H. H. "Chiliasm." In *The Mennonite Encyclopedia, 1* (1955): 559-560.

Janzen, H. H. "Russian Missions." In *The Mennonite Encyclopedia, 4* (1959): 393.

Janzen, J.H. *Wanderndes Volk,* 3. Buch. Waterloo, ON: J. H. Janzen, 1981, (First pub. 1949).

Jenny, B. "Das Täuferbekenntnis 1527." *Schaffhauser Beiträge zur vaterländischen Geschichte,* Heft 28. Thüringen: Druck und Verlag Karl Augustin, 1951.

Juhnke, J. C. *A People of Two Kingdoms.* Newton, KS: Faith and Life Press, 1975.

Juhnke, J. C. "Gemeindechristentum and Bible doctrine: Two Mennonite visions of the early twentieth century." *Mennonite Quarterly Review,* 57 (1983): 206-221.

Juhnke, J. C. "Mennonite history and self-understanding: North American Mennonitism as a bipolar mosaic." In *Mennonite Identity: Historical and Contemporary Perspectives,* edited by C. W. Redekop & S. J. Steiner, 83-99. Lanham, MD: University Press of America, 1988.

Juhnke, J. C. *Vision, Doctrine, War: Mennonite Identity and Organization in America 1890-1930: Vol. 3. The Mennonite Experience in America.* Scottdale, PA: Herald Press, 1989.

Just, L. R. "Influences of Johann Cornies upon the major social institutions of the Mennonites in south Russia." Unpublished thesis, University of Kansas, 1948.

Kahlstorf, E. "Rechtsgeschichte der Marienburger Werder." Dissertation Universität Würzburg, 1935.

Kasdorf, H. *Flammen unauslöschlich. Mission der Mennoniten unter Zaren und Sowjets 1789-1989.* Druckhaus Gummersbach: Logos, 1991.

Kauenhoven, K. "Mennonitensöhne auf dem Gymnasium in Elbing 1600-1784." *Mennonitische Blätter,* 18 (1961): 16-19.

Kaufman, E. G. (E.K.G. sic.) "General Conference Mennonite Church." In *The Mennonite Encyclopedia,* 2 (1956): 465-471.

Kauffman, J. H., & Driedger, L. *The Mennonite Mosaic: Identity and Modernization.* Scottdale: Herald Press, 1991.

Kauffman, J. H., & Harder, L. *Anabaptists Four Centuries Later: A Profile of Five Mennonite and Brethren in Christ Denominations.* Scottdale: Herald Press, 1975.

Keeney, W. E. "The new birth: Menno Simons and Dirk Philips speak." *Mennonite Life,* 16 (1961): 29-32.

Keeney, W. E. "Basic Beliefs of the Dutch Anabaptists." In *No Other Foundation,* edited by Klaassen, W., et al, 13-26. North Newton: Bethel College, 1962.

Keeney, W. E. *The Development of Dutch Anabaptist Thought and Practice from 1539-1564.* Nieuwkoop: B. De Graf, 1968.

Keeney, W. E. "The quiet revolution: Menno Simons." *Mennonite Life,* 25 (1970): 15-20.

Keeney, W. E. "Anabaptism confronts Menno Simons." *Mennonite Life,* 30 (1975): 15-18.

Keim, A. N. and Stoltzfus, G. H. *The Politics of Conscience. The Historic Peace Churches and America at War 1917-1955.* Scottdale: Herald Press, 1988.

"Keine Menschen nur Kleinhäusler." *Odessaer Zeitung,* (April 2, 1865): 151.

Keller, L. *Geschichte der Täufer und ihres Reiches zu Münster.* Osnabruck: Ackerstaff & Kuballe, 1980 (Original work published 1880).

Keyser, E. "Die Mennoniten im Weichsellande." *Mennonitische Blätter,* 6 (1940): 1-5.

Klaassen, W. "Speaking in simplicity: Balthasar Hubmaier." *Mennonite Quarterly Review,* 40 (1955):139-147.

Klaassen, W. "The biblical basis of nonresistance." *Mennonite Life,* 17, (1962a): 51-52.

Klaassen, W. "The Life and times of Menno Simons." In *No Other Foundation,* edited by Klaassen, W., et al, 1-12. North Newton: Bethel College, 1962b.

Klaassen, W. "The Anabaptist view of the Scriptures II." *Mennonite Life, 19* (1964): 113-116.

Klaassen, W. "The Bern Debate of 1538: Christ, the center of Scripture." *Mennonite Quarterly Review, 40* (1966a):148-156.

Klaassen, W. "Anabaptist Hermeneutics: The letter and the Spirit." *Mennonite Quarterly Review, 40* (1966b): 83-96.

Klaassen, W. *Anabaptism: Neither Catholic nor Protestant.* Waterloo, ON: Conrad/Grebel Press, 1973.

Klaassen, W. "The Anabaptist understanding of the separation of the church." *Church History, 46,* (1977): 421-436.

Klaassen, W. (Ed.). *Anabaptism in Outline: Selected Primary Sources: Vol. 3. Classics of the Radical Reformation.* Scottdale: Herald Press, 1981.

Klaassen, W. (English Ed.) *Profiles of Radical Reformers.* H.-J. Goertz, General Editor. Scottdale: Herald Press, 1982.

Klaassen, W. "Eschatalogical themes in early Dutch Anabaptism." In *The Dutch Dissenters: A Critical Companion to Their History and Ideas,* edited by I. B. Horst, 15-31. Leiden, E. J. Brill, 1986.

Klaassen, W. "The Quest for Anabaptist Identity." In *Anabaptist-Mennonite Identities in Ferment, Occasional Papers #14,* edited by Leo Driedger: Leland Harder, 13-26. Elkhart, IN: Institute of Mennonite Studies, 1990.

Klaassen, W. (Ed.). *Anabaptism Revisited.* Essays on Anabaptist/Mennonite Studies in honor of C. J. Dyck. Scottdale: Herald Press, 1992.

Klaassen, W., Keeney, W., Mast, R., Neufeld, V., & Krahn, C. *No Other Foundation. Commemorative Essays on Menno Simons.* North Newton: Bethel College, 1962.

Klassen, A. J. "The roots and development of Mennonite Brethren Theology to 1914." An M. A. thesis at Union School of Theology, Vancouver, Canada, 1965.

Klassen, E. S. *Trailblazer for the Brethren: The Story of Johann Claassen, A Leader in the Early Mennonite Brethren church.* Fresno, CA: The Board of Christian Literature of the General Conference of Mennonite Brethren Churches, 1978.

Klassen, G., & Neufeld, A. "Die Beziehungen der frühen Mennoniten Brüder und der Baptisten in der Mission." Unpublished paper, Mennonite Brethren Biblical Seminary, 1985.

Klassen, K. "Über den entsetzlichen Raubmord." *Odessaer Zeitung* (April 11-24, 1913): 2.

Klassen, P. J. "Mutual aid among the Anabaptists: Doctrine and practice." *Mennonite Quarterly Review*, 37 (1963): 79-95.

Klassen, P. J. *The Economics of Anabaptism: 1525-1560*. The Hague: Mouton & Co., 1964.

Klassen, P. J. "Mutual aid among the Anabaptists: Doctrine and practice." In *The Compassionate community: A collection of lectures presented at Conferences of the Association of Mennonite Aid Societies*, edited by H. R. Hernley, 551-568. Scottdale: Association of Mennonite Aid Societies, 1970.

Klassen, P. J. *Europe in the Reformation*. Englewood Cliffs, NJ.: Prentice-Hall, Inc., 1979.

Klassen, P. J. "Baptists and Mennonites in Poland and Prussia." In *Mennonites & Baptists: A Continuing Conversation*, edited by Paul Toews, 73-80. Winnipeg, MB: Kindred Press, 1993.

Klassen, P. P. *Die Mennoniten in Paraguay: Band 1. Reich Gottes und Reich dieser Welt*. Weierhof: Mennonitischer Geschichtsverein, 1988.

Klassen, P. P. *Die Deutsch-Völkische Zeit in der Kolonie Fernheim Chaco, Paraguay 1933-1945: Ein Beiträge zur Geschichte der auslandsdeutschen Mennoniten während des Dritten Reiches*. Bolanden-Weierhof: Mennonitischer Geschichtsverein, 1990.

Klassen, P. P. *Die Mennoniten in Paraguay: Band 2. Begegnung mit Indianern und Paraguayern*. Weierhof: Mennonitischer Geschichtsverein, 1991.

Klassen, W. "Anabaptist hermeneutics: The letter and the spirit." *Mennonite Quarterly Review*, 40, (1966): 83-96.

Klassen, W. *Covenant and Community: The life, writings and Hermeneutics of Pilgram Marpeck*. Grand Rapids: William B. Eerdmans Publishing Company, 1968.

Klaus, A. *Unsere Kolonien. Studien und Materialien zur Geschichte und Statistik der ausländischen Kolonisation in Russland* (J. Töws, Trans.). Odessa: L. Nitzsche, 1887.

Klimenko, M. "Anfänge des Baptismus in Südrussland (Ukraine) nach offiziellen Dokumenten." Unpublished dissertation, Friedrich-Alexander Universität, 1957.

Klippenstein, L. "Mennonite pacifism and state service in Russia, a case study in church-state relations: 1789-1936." Doctoral dissertation, University of Minnesota, 1984.

Klippenstein, L. "The Mennonite migration to Russia 1786-1806." In *Mennonites in Russia 1788-1988: Essays in Honour of Gerhard Lorenz*, edited by J. Friesen, 13-42. Winnipeg: CMBC Publications, 1989.

Köhler, W. "Martin Luther (1483-1546)." In *The Mennonite Encyclopedia, 3*, (1957): 416-421.

Kolakowski, L. "Dutch Seventeenth-Century Anticonfessional Ideas and Rational Religion: The Mennonite, Collegiant and Spinozan Connections." Translation and introduction by J. Satterwhite. *Mennonite Quarterly Review, 64*, 259-297, *64*, (1990): 385-416.

Koolman, J. T. D. "Amsterdam." In *The Mennonite Encyclopedia, 1*, (1955): 101-106.

Koontz, T. "Mennonites and Postmodernity." *Mennonite Quarterly Review, 63* (1989): 401-427.

Koyama, K. "Tribal Gods or Universal God." *Missionalia, 10*(3), (1982): 106-112.

Koyama, K. *Mount Fuji and Mount Sinai: A Pilgrimage in Theology*. London: SCM Press, 1984.

Krahn, C. "Some social attitudes of Mennonites in Russia." *Mennonite Quarterly Review, 9* (1935): 165-177.

Krahn, C. *Menno Simons (1496-1561). Ein Beitrag zur Geschichte und Theologie der Taufgesinnten*. Karlsruhe: Heinrich Schneider, 1936.

Krahn, C. (Ed.). *From the Steppes to the Prairies (1874-1949)*. Newton, KS: Mennonite Publication Office, 1949.

Krahn, C. "Agriculture among the Mennonites of Russia." *Mennonite Life, 10* (1955): 14-20.

Krahn, C. "Apostolische Brüdergemeinde." In *The Mennonite Encyclopedia, 1* (1955): 141-142.

Krahn, C. "Chortitza Mennonite Church." In *The Mennonite Encyclopedia, 1* (1955): 568.

Krahn, C. "Chortitza (Khortitsa) Mennonite Settlement." In *The Mennonite Encyclopedia, 1* (1955): 569-573.

Krahn, C. "The office of elder in Anabaptist-Mennonite history." *Mennonite Quarterly Review, 30* (1956): 120-127.

Krahn, C. "East Friesland." In *The Mennonite Encyclopedia, 2*, (1956): 119-122.

Krahn, C. "Fresenburg." In *The Mennonite Encyclopedia, 2* (1956): 394-395.

Krahn, C. "Manitoba." In *The Mennonite Encyclopedia, 3* (1957): 457-466.

Krahn, C. "Menno Simons." In *The Mennonite Encyclopedia, 3* (1957): 577-583.

Krahn, C. "Migrations of Mennonites." In *The Mennonite Encyclopedia, 3* (1957); 684-686.

Krahn, C. "Münster Anabaptists." In *The Mennonite Encyclopedia, 3* (1957): 777-782.

Krahn, C. "Old Colony Mennonites." In *The Mennonite Encyclopedia, 4* (1959): 38-42.

Krahn, C. "Orenburg Mennonite Settlement." In *The Mennonite Encyclopedia, 4,* (1959): 75-79.

Krahn, C. "Russia." In *The Mennonite Encyclopedia, 4* (1959): 381-392.

Krahn, C. "Schleswig-Holstein." In *The Mennonite Encyclopedia 4* (1959): 461-462.

Krahn, C. "Siberia." In *The Mennonite Encyclopedia, 4* (1959): 517-521.

Krahn, C. "Smissen, van der." In *The Mennonite Encyclopedia, 4* (1959): 549.

Krahn, C. "Stundism." In *The Mennonite Encyclopedia, 4* (1959): 649-650.

Krahn, C. "Temple (German, *Tempel*) Church." In *The Mennonite Encyclopedia 4* (1959): 693-694.

Krahn, C. "Vologda." In *The Mennonite Encyclopedia, 4* (1959): 848.

Krahn, C. "Bureau of Guardianship of the Foreign Colonists." In *The Mennonite Encyclopedia, 4,* (1959): 1068-1069).

Krahn, C. "Menno Simons and the Mennonite World Brotherhood." In *No Other Foundation,* edited by Klaassen, W., et al. 55-63. North Newton: Bethel College, 1962.

Krahn, C. *Dutch Anabaptism: Origin, Spread, Life and Thought, (1450-1600).* The Hague: Martinus Nijhoff, 1968.

Krahn, C. "Abraham Thiessen: A Mennonite revolutionary." *Mennonite Life, 24* (1969): 73-77.

Krahn, C. "A Mennonite 'Zionist' movement." *Mennonite Life, 25,* (1970): 171:173.

Krahn, C. "A pietiest revival comes to south Russia." *Mennonite Life, 33* (1978): 4-11.

Krahn, C. *Menno Simons (1496-1561): Ein Beitrag zur Geschichte und Theologie der Taufgesinnten*. Newton, KS: Faith and Life Press, 1982.

Kraus, C. N. *Dispensationalism in America: Its Rise and Development*. Richmond, VA: John Knox Press, 1958.

Kraus, C. N. "American Mennonites and the Bible, 1750-1950." *Mennonite Quarterly Review*, 41 (1967): 309-329.

Kraus, C. N. (Ed.). *Evangelicalism and Anabaptism*. Scottdale: Herald Press, 1979a.

Kraus, C. N. "Introduction: What is evangelicalism?" In *Evangelicalism and Anabaptism*, edited by C. N. Kraus, 9-22. Scottdale: Herald Press, 1979b.

Kraus, C. N. "Evangelicalism: The great coalition." In *Evangelicalism and Anabaptism*, edited by C. N. Kraus, 39-61. Scottdale: Herald Press, 1979c.

Kraus, C. N. "Anabaptism and Evangelicalism." In *Evangelicalism and Anabaptism*, edited by C. N. Kraus, 167-182. Scottdale: Herald Press, 1979d.

Kraus, C. N. "Shifting Mennonite Theological Orientations." In *Anabaptist-Mennonite Identities in Ferment, Occasional Papers #14*, edited by Leo Driedger : Leland Harder, 32-49. Elkhart, IN: Institute of Mennonite Studies, 1990.

Kraybill, D. B. *The Upside-down Kingdom*. Scottdale: Herald Press, 1978.

Kraybill, D. B. "Mennonite women's veiling: The rise and fall of a sacred symbol." *Mennonite Quarterly Review*, 61 (1987): 298-320.

Kraybill, D. B. "Modernity and Identity: The Transformation of Mennonite Ethnicity." In *Mennonite Identity: Historical and Contemporary Perspectives*, edited by C. W. Redekop & S. J. Steiner, 153-172. Lanham, MD: University Press of Maryland, 1988.

Kraybill, R. *Repairing the Breach: Ministering in Community Conflict*. Scottdale: Herald Press, 1980.

Kraybill, R. & Brubaker, D. "A resource for dealing with conflict: the Mennonite Conciliation Service." *Mennonite Life*, 43(1), (1988): 4-7.

Kreider, C. *The Christian Entrepreneur*. Scottdale: Herald Press, 1980.

Kreider, R. "The Anabaptist conception of the church in the Russian Mennonite environment: 1789-1870." *Mennonite Quarterly Review*, 25, (1951): 17-33.

Kreider, R. "Vocations of Swiss and south German Anabaptists." *Mennonite Life*, *8* (1953): 38-42.

Kreider, R. "The Teachers Abroad Program." *Mennonite Life, 17* (1962): 76-81.

Kreider, R. "The 'Good Boys of CPS.'" *Mennonite Life, 46*(3), (1991): 4-11.

Kritzinger, J. J. "The Ecological Crisis." *Missionalia, 19*(1), (1991): 4-19.

Kroeker, W. "What some Christians are doing about recycling." *Christian Week* (November 7, 1989): 1-4.

Die Kubaner Ansiedlung. Steinbach, MB: Echo Verlag, 1953.

Kühler, W. J. *Geschiedenis der Nederlandsche Doopsgezinden in de Zestiende Eeuw*. Haarlem: H. D. Tjeenk Willink & Zoon N.V., 1932.

Kühler, W. J. "Anabaptism in the Netherlands." In *The Anabaptists and Thomas Müntzer*, edited by J. M. Stayer & W. O. Packull, 92-103. Dubuque, IA: Kendall/Hunt Publishing Company, 1980.

Kuhn, W. "Die Mennonitische Altkolonie Chortitza in der Ukraine." *Deutsche Monatshefte: Zeitschrift für Geschichte und Gegenwart des Ost-deutschtums, 9* (1942): 1-44.

Kuiper, F. "The Pre-eminence of the Bible in Mennonite History." *Mennonite Quarterly Review*, *3* (1967): 223-234.

Lapp, J. A. "The Evangelical factor in American politics." In *Evangelicalism and Anabaptism*, edited by C. N. Kraus, 82-100. Scottdale: Herald Press, 1979.

Larkin, C. *Dispensational Truth: Or God's Plan and Purpose in the Ages*. Philadelphia: Clarence Larkin, 1920.

Lau, F. (Ed.). *Das Buch Weinsberg: Kölner Denkwürdigkeiten aus dem 16. Jahrhundert*. Bearbeitet von Konstantin Höhlbaum. (Vol. 3). Leipzig: A. Dürr, 1896-1897.

Leibbrandt, G. "The emigration of the German Mennonites from Russia to the United States and Canada in 1873-1880: I." *Mennonite Quarterly Review, 6* (1932): 205-226.

Leibbrandt, G. "The emigration of the German Mennonites from Russia to the United States and Canada, 1873-1880: II." *Mennonite Quarterly Review, 7*, (1933): 5-41.

Lichdi, D. G. *Mennoniten im Dritten Reich: Dokumentation und Deutung*. Weierhof/Pfalz: Mennonitischer Geschichtsvereins, 1977.

Lichti, O. "Friedensgessinnung und Wehrlosigkeit: Antwort und Gegenwort auf gleichnamigen Vortrags von S. Hein." *Mennonitisches Jahrbuch*, (1924): 76-87.

Liechty, J. C. "Humility: The foundation of the Mennonite outlook in the 1860s." *Mennonite Quarterly Review, 54*, (1980): 5-31.

Lindsell, H. *The Battle for the Bible*. Grand Rapids: Zondervan Publishing House, 1976.

Littell, F. H. "The Anabaptist Concept of the Church." In *The Recovery of the Anabaptist Vision: A Sixtieth Anniversary Tribute to Harold S. Bender*, edited by G. F. Hershberger, 119-134. Scottdale: Herald Press, 1957.

Litten, F., & Nottarp, H. *Ergänzungsgutachten über die Berechtigung der Heranziehung der in den Marienburger Werdernansässigen Mennoniten und Katholiken zu Leistungen für die Unterhaltung der dortigen Kirchensysteme*. Königsberg: Selbstverlag, 1931.

Loewen, H. (Ed.). *Mennonite Images: Historical, Cultural, and Literary Essays Dealing with Mennonite Issues*. Winnipeg: Hyperion Press Limited, 1980.

Loewen, H. "Echoes of drumbeats: The movement of exuberance among the Mennonite Brethren." *Journal of Mennonite Studies, 3* (1985): 118-127.

Loewen, H. (Ed.). *Why I am a Mennonite: Essays on Mennonite Identity*. Scottdale: Herald Press, 1988.

Loewen, H. "A house divided: Russian Mennonite nonresistance and emigration in the 1870's." In *Mennonites in Russia 1788-1988: Essays in Honor of Gerhard Lorenz*, edited by J. Friesen, 127-146. Winnipeg, MB: CBMC Publications, 1989.

Loewen, H., & Reimer, A. (Eds.). *Visions and Realities: Essays, Poems, and Fiction dealing with Mennonite issues*. Winnipeg: Hyperion Press, 1985.

Loewen, H. H., & Urry, J. "Protecting Mammon: Some dilemmas of Mennonite non-resistance in late imperial Russia and the origins of the Selbstschutz." *Journal of Mennonite Studies, 9* (1991): 34-53.

Loewen, H. J. *One Lord, one church, one hope, and one God: Mennonite Confessions of Faith in North America*. Elkhart, IN: Institute of Mennonite Studies, 1985.

Loewen, H. J. "Church and state in the Anabaptist-Mennonite Tradition: Christ Versus Caesar?" In *Baptism, Peace and the State in*

Reformed and Mennonite Traditions, edited by R. T. Bender & A. P. F. Sell, 145-168. Waterloo, ON: Wilfrid Laurier University Press, 1991.

Loewen, H. J. "Peace in the Mennonite tradition: Toward a theological understanding of a regulative concept." In *Baptism, Peace and the State in Reformed and Mennonite Traditions,* edited by R. T. Bender & A. P. F. Sell, 87-122. Waterloo, ON: Wilfrid Laurier University Press, 1991.

Loewen, J. A. "The German Language, Culture and Faith." A study paper read at the conference on the *Dynamics of Faith and Culture in Mennonite Brethren History* organized by the Centre for MB Studies held in Winnipeg, MB., Nov. 14-15, 1986.

Loewen, J. A. "Dear Bill." *Mennonite Brethren Herald,*(October 28, 1988): 2-5.

Loewen, J. A. "Russian Mennonites, property and the sword." In *Anabaptist/Mennonite Faith and Economics,* edited by C. W. Redekop, V. A. Krahn & S. J. Steiner, 41-65. Lanham, MD: University Press of America, 1990.

Loewen, J. A. & Loewen, A. "Can child conversion last? (Socialization and child conversion: a personal record)." *Mennonite Brethren Herald,*(October 17, 1969): 2-6.

Loewen, J. A. & W. J. Prieb. "The Abuse of Power Among Mennonites in South Russia 1789-1919."*Journal of Mennonite Studies, 14,* (1996): 17-44.

Loewen, R. *Blumenort: A Mennonite Community in Transition, 1874-1982.* Steinbach, MB: Blumenort Mennonite Historical Society, 1983.

Lohrenz, G. "The emigratiom of German Mennonites from Russia to the United States and Canada, 1873-1880." *Mennonite Quarterly Review, 17* (1933): 5-41.

Lohrenz, J. H. *The Mennonite Brethren Church.* Hillsboro, KS: The Board of Foreign Missions of The Conference of the Mennonite Brethren Church of North America, 1950.

Lohrenz, J. H. "Mennonite Brethren Church." In *The Mennonite Encyclopedia, 3* (1957): 595-602.

Loserth, J. "Diener am Wort." In *Mennonitisches Lexikon, 1* (1913): 438-440.

Loserth, J. "Reichsgesetze gegen die 'Wiedertäufer.'" *Mennonitische Blätter, 2* (1936): 27-29.

Löwen, H. *In Vergessenheit geratene Beziehungen: Frühe Begegnungen der Mennoniten-Brüdergemeinde mit dem Baptismus in Russland-*

-ein Überblick: Vol. 1. Beiträge zur osteuropäischen Kirchengeschichte. Bielefeld: Logos, 1989.

Ludwig, K.-H. *Zur Besiedlung des Weichseldeltas durch die Mennoniten. Die Siedlungen der Mennoniten im Territorium der Stadt Elbing und in der Ökonomie Marienburg bis zur Übernahme der Gebiete durch Preussen 1772.* Marburbg (Lahn): Wissenshaftliche. Beiträge zur Geschichte und Landeskunde Ost-Mitteleuropas: Johann Gottfried Herder-Institut, No. 57, Schriftleitung: Ernst Bahr, 1961.

Luther, K. "A Critical Review of Mennonite Philosophy." In *Mennonite Identity: Historical and Contemporary Perspectives,* edited by C. W. Redekop & S. J. Steiner, 39-62. Lanham, MD: University Press of America, 1988.

Luther, M. *Luther's Werke, kritische Gesammtausgabe.* Weimar: Herman Böhlau, 1883-1932.

Luther, M. "Lectures on Genesis chapters 1-5: Vol. 1." In *Luther's Works,* edited by J. Pelikan, St. Louis: Concordia Publishing House, 1955.

Luther, M. "Temporal authority: To what extent it should be obeyed" (J. J. Schindel, Trans.). In *The Christian in Society: II,* edited by W. I. Brandt, 81-129. Vol. 45, *Luther's works.* Philadelphia: Muehlenberg Press, 1962.

McDonagh, S. *To Care for the Earth: A Call to a new theology.* Santa Fe: Bar and Company, 1986.

McFarlane, S. "Buddhism." In *World Encyclopedia of Peace, 1*, 97-103. Oxford: Pergamum Press, 1986.

McHarg, I.L. "The Place of Nature in the City of Man." In *Western Man and Environmental Ethics: Attitudes Toward Nature and Technology,* edited by I. G. Barbour, 171-186. Reading, MA.: Addison-Wesley, 1973.

MacIntyre, A. *After Virtue: A Study in moral theology.* Notre Dame: University of Notre Dame Press, 1981.

MacMaster, R. K. *Land, piety, peoplehood: The Establishment of Mennonite Communities in America, 1683-1790: Vol. 1. The Mennonite Experience in America.* Scottdale: Herald Press, 1985.

MacMaster, R. K. (with Horst, S. M., & Ulle, R. F.). *Conscience in Crisis: Mennonites and other peace churches in America, 1739-1789, Interpretation and Documents: Vol. 20. Studies in Anabaptist and Mennonite History.* Scottdale: Herald Press, 1979.

Maercher, H. "Geschichte des Schwetzer Kreises." *Zeitschrift des Westpreusischen Geschichtsrereins, 2,* (1/3), (1888): 369.

Malowist, M. "Poland, Russia and western trade in the 15th and 16th centuries." *Past and Present, 13* (1958): 26-41.

Mannhardt, H. G. *Predigten und Reden aus fünfundzwanzig-jähriger Amtszeit.* Danzig: John & Rosenberg, 1913.

Mannhardt, H. G. *Die Danziger Mennonitengemeinde: Ihre Entstehung und ihre Geschichte von 1569-1919.* Danzig: Danziger Mennonitengemeinde, 1919.

Mannhardt, W. *Die Wehrfreiheit der Altpreussischen Mennoniten: Eine geschichtliche Erörterung.* Marienburg: Altpreussischen Mennonitengemeinden, 1863.

Marbeck, P. *Quellen und Forschungen zur Geschichte der Oberdeutschen Taufgesinnten im 16. Jahrhundert: Pilgram Marbeck's Antwort auf Kasper Schwenckfelds Beurteilung des Buches der Bundesbezeugung von 1542.* (J. Loserth, Ed.). Wien und Leipzig: Carl Fromme, 1929.

Marsden, G. M. *Religion and American Culture.* San Diego: Harcourt Brace Jovanovich, Publishers, 1990.

Martens, E. A. "Sorting out a position on capital punishment." *Mennonite Brethren Herald*, (April 17, 1987): 2-3.

Martens, E. A. "God's goal is shalom." In *The Power of the Lamb*, edited by J. E. Toews & G. Nickel, 25-34. Winnipeg: Kindred Press, 1992.

Martens, H. M. "The relationship of religious to socio-economic divisions among the Mennonites of Dutch-Prussian-Russian descent in Canada." Unpublished doctoral dissertation, University of Toronto, 1977.

Martin, T. "The Terekers' dilemma: A prelude to the Selbstschutz." *Mennonite Historian*, (December, 1991): 1-2.

Mast, R. L. "Menno Simons and the Scriptures." In *No Other Foundation*, edited by Klaassen, W., et al, 35-41. North Newton: Bethel College, 1962.

Mellink, A. F. *Documenta Anabaptistica Nederlandica: Eerste deel, Friesland en Groningen (1530-1550).* Leiden: E. J. Brill, 1975.

Mellink, A. F. *Amsterdam en de wederdopers in de zestiende eeuw.* Nijmegen: Socialistiese Uitgeverij, 1978.

Mellink, A. F. *Documenta Anabaptistica Nederlandica: Tweede deel, Amsterdam (1536-1578).* Leiden, E. J. Brill, 1980.

Mellink, A. F. "Anabaptism at Amsterdam after Münster." In *The Dutch Dissenters: A critical companion to their history and Ideas*, edited by I. B. Horst, 127-142. Leiden: E. J. Brill, 1986.

Mediating Inter-personal Disputes: A Practical Model. Akron, PA: Mennonite Central Committee, n.d.

Menchu, R. (E. Burgos-Debray, Ed., A. Wright, Trans.). *I, Rigoberta Menchu. An Indian Woman in Guatemala.* London: Verso, 1983.

Die Mennoniten-Gemeinden in Russland. Heilbronn Am Neckar: Kommissions-Verlag der Mennonitischen Flüchtlingsfürsorge, 1921.

Michaelson, W. "What nurtures us: The Streams of Church Tradition feeding a Radical Gospel." *Sojourners.* 7, (May, 1978): 16-19.

Michaelson, W. "Evangelicalism and radical discipleship." In *Evangelicalism and Anabaptism,* edited by C. N. Kraus, 63-82. Scottdale: Herald Press, 1979.

Miller, W. R. *Martin Luther King, Jr. His life, martyrdom and Meaning for the World.* New York: Weybright and Talley, 1968.

Mosemann, J. H. "The modern peace movement." *Gospel Herald*, (January 28, 1926): 898.

Mueller, J. P. *Die Mennoniten in Ostfriesland vom 16. bis zum 18. Jahrhundert.* Emalen & Borkum: W. Haynel, 1887.

Muente, H. "Das Altonaer Handlungshaus van der Smissen." Unpublished doctoral dissertation, University of Hamburg, 1932a.

Muente, H. *Das Altonaer Handlungshaus van der Smissen 1682-1824. Ein Beitrag zur Wirtschaftsgeschichte der Stadt Altona (Altonaische Zeitschrift für Geschichte und Heitmatkunde*, Vol. 2). Altona: Verlag Herm. Lorenzen, 1932b.

Muralt, L. von, & Schmid, W., (Eds.). *Zürich: Vol. 1. Quellen zur Geschichte der Täufer in der Schweiz.* Zürich: S. Hirzel Verlag, 1952.

N. F. "Ein bestialischer Raubmord." *Odessaer Zeitung*, (May 16-29, 1912): 2.

Neff, C. "Abgaben." In *Mennonitisches Lexikon, 1* (1913): 11.

Neff, C. "Allianz Gemeinden." In *Mennonitisches Lexikon, 1* (1913): 35.

Neff, C. "Bann." In *Mennonitisches Lexikon, 1* (1913): 115-119.

Neff, C. "Johann Bartsch." In *Mennonitisches Lexikon, 1* (1913): 128-129.

Neff, C. "Eggerick Beninga." In *Mennonitisches Lexikon, 1* (1913): 163.

Neff, C. "Bestrafung der Täufer." In *Mennonitisches Lexikon, 1* (1913): 201-209.

Neff, C. "Johannes Calvin." In *Mennonitisches Lexikon, 1* (1913): 314-317.

Neff, C. "Chiliasmus." In *Mennonitisches Lexikon*, *1* (1913): 342-347.

Neff, C. "Klaassen, Johannes." In *Mennonitisches Lexikon*, *1* (1913). 356-357.

Neff, C. "Cramer, Dr. Samuel." In *Mennonitisches Lexikon*, *1* (1913): 377-381.

Neff, C. "Emden." In *Mennonitisches Lexikon*, *1* (1913): 565-573.

Neff, C. "Enno I." In *Mennonitisches Lexikon*, *1* (1913): 592.

Neff, C. "Die Wehrlosigkeit der Mennoniten und der Weltkrieg." *Mennonitisches Jahrbuch*, (1924): 76-87.

Neff, C. (Ed.). *Gedenkschrift zum 400 Jährigen Jubiläum der Mennoniten oder Taufgesinnten, 1525-1925*. Ludwigshafen: Konferenz der Süddeutschen Mennoniten, 1925.

Neff, C. "Friedrichstadt." In *Mennonitisches Lexikon*, *2* (1937): 4-5.

Neff, C. "Friesische Mennoniten." In *Mennonitisches Lexikon*, *2* (1937): 8-9.

Neff, C. "Hoffmann, Christoph." In *Mennonitisches Lexikon*, *2* (1937): 325-326.

Neff, C. "The Mennonites of Germany including Danzig and Poland." *Mennonite Quarterly Review*, *11* (1937): 34-43.

Neff, C. "Anna von Oldenburg." In *The Mennonite Encyclopedia*, *1* (1955): 124.

Neff, C. "Ban." In *The Mennonite Encyclopedia*, *1* (1955): 219-223.

Neff, C. "Bartsch, Johann." In *The Mennonite Encyclopedia*, *1* (1955): 240.

Neff, C. "Beckerath, Hermann von." In *The Mennonite Encyclopedia*, *1* (1955): 259.

Neff, C. "Beningha, Eggerick (1490-1562)." In *The Mennonite Encyclopedia*, *1*, (1955): 274.

Neff, C. "Friedrichstadt." In *The Mennonite Encyclopedia*, *2* (1956): 401.

Neff, C. "John III, Sobieski." In *The Mennonite Encyclopedia*, *3* (1957): 114.

Neff, C. "Letters of Protection (*Schutzbriefe*)." In *The Mennonite Encyclopedia 3* (1957): 328.

Neff, C. "Molenaar, Isaak I." In *The Mennonite Encyclopedia*, *3* (1957): 724-725.

Neff, C. "Mannheim." In *Mennonitisches Lexikon*, *3* (1958): 21.

Neff, C. "Osthofen." In *Mennonitisches Lexikon, 3* (1958): 32.

Neff, C. "Menno Simons." In *Mennonitisches Lexikon, 3* (1958): 86-90.

Neff, C. "Mennoniten." In *Mennonitisches Lexikon, 3* (1958): 102.

Neff, C. "Perückenstreit." In *Mennonitisches Lexikon, 3* (1958): 351.

Neff, C. "Reiswitz (Reisswitz), George Leopold, Baron of." In *The Mennonite Encyclopedia, 4* (1959): 282-283.

Neff, C., Hege, C., & Epp, D. E. "Poor, care of." In *The Mennonite Encyclopedia, 4* (1959): 202.

Neff, C. & Zijpp, N. van der. "Dompelaars." In *The Mennonite Encyclopedia, 2,* (1956): 81-82.

Neff, C. & Zijpp, N. van der. "Flemish Mennonites (Dutch, *Vlamingen or Vlaamschen*)." In *The Mennonite Encyclopedia, 2* (1956): 337-340.

Neff, C. & Zijpp, N. van der. "Frisian Mennonites." In *The Mennonite Encyclopedia 2* (1956): 413-414.

Neff, C. & Zijpp, N. van der. "Oldeklooster (or Bloemkamp)." In *The Mennonite Encyclopedia, 4* (1959): 52-53.

Neff, C., & Zijpp, N. van der. "William I of Orange." In *The Mennonite Encyclopedia, 4* (1959): 956-957.

Neufeld, C. P. *The fate of Mennonites in Soviet Ukraine and the Crimea during the Soviet collectivization and the famine (1928-1933)*, (Vols. 1-2). Edmonton, AB: Colin Peter Neufeld, 1989.

Neufeld, D. *Mennonitentum in der Ukraine*. Emden: Grosse Osterstrasse, 37: Selbstverlag, 1922.

Neufeld, V. "Menno Simons and the Twentieth Century." In *No Other Foundation*, edited by Klaassen, W., et al. 43-54. North Newton: Bethel College, 1962.

Niebuhr, J. J. "Jakob G. Niebuhr Fabriken." *Mennonite Life, 9* (1955): 15-30.

Niepoth, Wilhelm. "Beckerath, von." In *The Mennonite Encyclopedia, 1,* (1955): 259.

Noll, M. A. *The Scandal of the Evangelical Mind*. Grand Rapids, MI: Wm. B. Eerdmans Publishing Company, 1994.

Nottarp, H. *Die Mennoniten in den Marienburger Werdern: Eine Kirchenrechtliche Untersuchung*. Halle: Max Niemeyer Verlag, 1929.

Olivier, D. F. "Ecology and mission: Notes on the history of the JPIC process and its relevance to theology." *Missionalia*, *19*(1),(1991): 20-32.

Oesau, W. *Schleswig-Holsteins Grönlandfahrt auf Walfischfang und Robbenschlag von 17. bis 19. Jahrhundert*. Glückstadt: J.J. Augustin, 1937.

Oesau, W. *Hamburgs Grönlandfahrt auf Walfischfang und Robbenschlag*. Gluckstadt und Hamburg: J. J. Augustin, 1955.

Oyer, J. S., & Kreider, R. S. *Mirror of the Martyrs: Stories of courage, inspiringly retold, of 16th Century Anabaptists who gave their lives for their faith*. Intercourse, PA: Good Books, 1990.

Pannabecker, S. "Mennonite foreign missions." In *The Mennonite Encyclopedia*, *3* (1957): 712-717.

"Peace Section urged to call for strong commitment from Mennonite youth." *Mennonite Reporter*, (January 5, 1987): 1-2.

Peachey, P. "The modern recovery of the Anabaptist vision." In *The Recovery of the Anabaptist Vision: A sixtieth anniversary tribute to Harold S. Bender*, edited by G. F. Hershberger, 327-340. Scottdale: Herald Press, 1957.

Peachey, T., & Peachey, L. G. *Seeking peace: True Stories of Mennonites around the world, struggling to live their belief in Peace. Full of courage and spirit!*. Intercourse, PA: Good Books, 1991.

Peck, M. S. *The Road Less Traveled*. New York: Simon and Schuster, 1978.

Peck, M. S. *The Different Drum: Community Making and Peace*. New York: Simon and Schuster, 1987.

Penner, H. "Ansiedlungen mennonitscher Niederländer in der Weichselmündung von der Mitte des 16. Jahrhunderts bis zum Beginn der Preussischen Zeit." Dissertation Universität Danzig, 1940.

Penner, H. "The Anabaptists and Mennonites of East Prussia." *Mennonite Quarterly Review*, *22* (1948): 212-225.

Penner, H. *Weltweite Bruderschaft: Ein Mennonitsches Geschichtsbuch*. Karlsruhe: Verlag Heinrich Schneider, 1955.

Penner, H. "Ostpreußen." In *Mennonitisches Lexikon*, *3* (1958): 322-325.

Penner, H. "West Prussia." In *The Mennonite Encyclopedia*, *4* (1959): 920-926.

Penner, H. *Ansiedlung Mennonitischer Niederländer in der Weichselmündungsgebiet von der Mitte des 16. Jahrhunderts bis zum Beginn der preussischen Zeit: Nr. 3. Schriftenreihe des Mennonitischen Geschichtsvereins.* Weierhof-Platz: Mennonitischen Geschichtsverein, 1963.

Penner, H. *Die ost- und westpreussischen Mennoniten in ihrem religiösen und sozialem Leben in ihren kulturellen und wirtschaftlichen Leistungen: Band II.* Kirchenheimbolanden: Horst Penner, 1987.

Penner, P. "Baptist in all but name: Molotschna Mennonite Brethren in India." *Mennonite Life,* 46(1), (1991): 17-23.

Penner, P. "The Russian Mennonite Brethren and the American Baptist Tandem in India (1890-1940)." In *Mennonites and Baptists.* A continuing conversation, edited by Paul Toews, 133-146. Winnipeg: Kindred Press, 1993.

Penner, P. *Reaching the Otherwise Unreached: An Historical Account of the West Coast Children's Mission of B.C.* Clearbrook: West Coast Children's Mission, 1959.

Peters, C. C. (Sponsor) & Willms H. (Compiler). *Vor den Toren Moskaus.* Yarrow, BC: Kommittee der Flüchtlinge, 1958.

Peters, F. C. "The ban in the writings of Menno Simons." *Mennonite Quarterly Review, 29* (1955): 16-33.

Peters, F. C. "The early Mennonite Brethren Church: Baptist or Anabaptist?" *Mennonite Life, 14* (1959): 176-178.

Peters, F. C. "Quo Vadis? Mennonite Brethren Church." *Christian Leader,* (September 9, 1969): 2-3.

Peters, F. C. "Decision making: Personal and corporate." In *The compassionate community: A Collection of lectures presented at Conferences of the Association of Mennonite Aid Societies,* edited by H. R. Hernley, 491-549. Scottdale: Association of Mennonite Aid Societies, 1970.

Peters, F. C. "Capital punishment: A Christian perspective." *Mennonite Brethren Herald,* (April 17, 1987): 8-9.

Peters, G. W. *Foundations of Mennonite Brethren Missions.* Winnipeg: Kindred Press, 1984.

Peters, J. "Changing leadership patterns: Conference of Mennonites in Canada." *Journal Of Mennonite Studies,* 7 (1989): 167-182.

Pinnock, C. H. "A critical response to A. James Reimer's Mennonite theological self-understanding." In *Mennonite Identity: Historical and Contemporary Perspectives,* edited by C. W. Redekop & S. J. Steiner, 63-67. Lanham, MD: University Press of America, 1988.

Piper, P. *Altona unter Schauenburgische Herrschaft: Die Reformierten und die Mennoniten Altonas.* Altona: J. Harder Verlag, 1893.

Piper, P. "Geeritt Roosen und seine Geschichte der Kriegsereignisse seiner Zeit." *Germania, 1*(6), (1899): 365-370.

Plett, C. F. *The Story of the Krimmer Mennonite Brethren Church.* Winnipeg: Kindred Press, 1985.

Plett, D. F. *The Golden years: The Mennonite Kleine Gemeinde in Russia (1812-1849).* Steinbach, MB: D. F. P. Publications, 1985.

Plett, D. F. *Storm and Triumph: The Mennonite Kleine Gemeinde (1850-1875).* Steinbach, MB: D. F. P. Publcations, 1986.

Plett, D. F. *Pioneers and Pilgrims: The Mennonite Kleine Gemeinde (1874-1882).* Steinbach, MB: D. F. P. Publications, 1990.

Poettcker, H. "The Anabaptist view of the scriptures: I." *Mennonite Life, 19,* (1964): 110-111.

Poettcker, H. "Menno Simons' encounter with the Bible." *Mennonite Quarterly Review, 40,* (1966): 112-126.

Poettcker, H., & Regehr, R. A. (Eds.). *Call to Faithfulness: Essays in Canadian Mennonite Studies.* Winnipeg: Canadian Mennonite Bible College, 1972.

Postma, J. S. *Das Niederlandische Erbe der Preussisch—Russländischen Mennoniten in Europa, Asien und Amerika.* Leeuwarden: Drukkerij A. Jongbloed c.v., 1959.

Prabhu, R. K. *What Jesus Means to Me.* India: Narajuiran Publishing House, 1959.

Prentis, N. L. *Kansas Miscellaneous.* Topeka, KS: Kansas Publishing House, 1889.

Prentis, N. L. *A History of Kansas.* Topeka, KS: Caroline Prentis, 1909.

Prieb, W. J. "The power of the lamb: Following the flag of a new kingdom." In *The Power of the Lamb,* edited by J. E. Toews & G. Nickel, 117-127. Winnipeg, MB: Kindred Press, 1986.

Prieb, W. J. *Peter C. Hiebert: "He Gave Them Bread".* Hillsboro, KS: Center for Mennonite Brethren Studies, 1990.

Prinz, J. *Die Kolonien der Brüdergemeinde: Ein Beitrag zur Geschichte der deuschen Kolonien Südrusslands.* Moscow: G. Lisner & A. Geshel, 1898.

Quiring, Heinz. *Herrschaft und Gemeinde nach mitteldeutschen Quellen des 12. bis 18. Jahrhunderts*. Göttingen: Vandenhoek & Ruprecht, 1952.

Quiring, H. "Der Danziger Perückenstreit." *Christlicher Gemeinde Kalender,* 45 (1936): 98-102.

Quiring, H. "Inquisition." In *Mennonitsches Lexikon,* 2 (1937): 422-423.

Quiring, H. "Königsberg." In *Mennonitisches Lexikon,* 2 (1937): 538.

Quiring, H. "Inquisition." In *The Mennonite Encyclopedia,* 3 (1957): 41-42.

Quiring, H. "Militärdienst." In *Mennonitisches Lexikon,* 3 (1958): 135-136.

Quiring, H., & Zijpp, N. van der. "Königsberg." In *The Mennonite Encyclopedia,* 3 (1957): 221-222.

Quiring, J. *Die Mundart von Chortitza in Süd-Russland*. München: Druckerei Studentenhaus München, Universitat, 1928.

Quiring, W. *Deutsche erschliessen Chaco*. Karlsruhe: Heinrich Schneider, 1936.

Quiring, W. *Russlanddeutsche suchen eine neue Heimat: Einwanderung in den Paraguayschen Chaco*. Karlsruhe: Heinrich Schneider, 1938.

Quiring, W. "Johann Cornies, der Russland-deutsche Bahnbrecher und Reformer." In *Grosse Deutsche in Ausland: Eine volksdeutsche Geschichte in Lebensbildern,* edited by H. J. Beyer & O. Lohr, (160-168). Stuttgart: Union Deutscher Verlagsgesellschaften, 1939.

Quiring, W. "Johann Cornies--A great pioneer. A centenary tribute (1848-1948)." *Mennonite Life,* 3(3), (1948): 30-34.

Quiring, W. *Im Schweisse Deines Angesichts*. Steinbach, MB: Derksen Printers Limited, 1953.

Quiring, W. & Helen Bartel. *Mennonites in Canada: A Pictorial Review*. Altona, MB: D. W. Friesen & Sons Ltd, 1961.

Ramseyer, R. L. (Ed.). *Mission and the peace witness: The Gospel and Christian Discipleship: Vol. 7. Institute of Mennonite Missionary Studies*. Scottdale: Herald Press, 1979.

Randt, E. "Die Mennoniten in Ostpreussen und Lituaen bis zum Jahre 1772." Unpublished doctoral dissertation, University of Königsberg, 1912.

Ratzlaff, E. L. *Im Weichselbogen: Mennonitensiedlungen in Zentralpolen*. Winnipeg: Christian Press, 1971.

Rauert, M. & A. Kuempers-Greve. *Van der Smissen. Eine mennonitische Familie vor dem Hintergrund der Geschichte Altonas und Schleswig-Holsteins.* Hamburg: Nord Magazin, 1992.

Redekop, C. W. *Strangers become neighbors: Indigenous Relations in the Paraguayan Chaco.* Scottdale: Herald Press, 1980.

Redekop, C. W. "Mennonite displacement of indigenous groups: An historical and sociological analysis." *Canadian Ethnic Studies, 14* (1982): 71-90.

Redekop, C. W. "The Mennonites' Romance with the Land." In *Visions and Realities: Essays, Poems, and fiction dealing with Mennonite Issues,* edited by H. Loewen & A. Reimer, 83-94. Winnipeg: Hyperion Press, 1985a.

Redekop, C. W. "The Mennonite transformation: From Gelassenheit to capitalism." In *Visions and Realities: Essays, Poems, and fiction dealing with Mennonite issues,* edited by H. Loewen & A. Reimer, 95-107. Winnipeg: Hyperion Press, 1985b.

Redekop, C. W. "Toward a Mennonite theology and ethic of creation." *Mennonite Quarterly Review, 60* (1986): 387-403.

Redekop, C. W. "The sociology of Mennonite identity: A second opinion." In *Mennonite Identity: Historical and contemporary perspectives,* edited by C. W. Redekop & S. J. Steiner, 173-192. Lanham, MD: University Press of Maryland, 1988.

Redekop, C. W. *Mennonite Society.* Baltimore: The Johns Hopkins University Press, 1989.

Redekop, C. W., Ainlay, S. C., & Siemens, R. *Mennonite Entrepreneurs.* Baltimore: The Johns Hopkins University Press, 1995.

Redekop, C. W., Krahn, V. A., & Steiner, S. J. (Eds.). *Anabaptist/Mennonite Faith and Economics.* Lanham, MD: University of America Press, 1994.

Redekop, C. W., & Steiner, S. J. (Eds.). *Mennonite Identity: Historical and contemporary perspectives.* Lanham, MD: University Press of America, 1988.

Redekop, J. H. (Ed.). *Labor Problems in Christian Perspective.* Grand Rapids: William B. Eerdmans Publishing Company, 1972a.

Redekop, J. H. *Making political decisions: A Christian Perspective: No. 23. Focal Pamphlet Series.* Scottdale: Herald Press, 1972b.

Redekop, J. H. "Mennonites and politics in Canada and the United States." *Journal Of Mennonite Studies, 1* (1983): 79-105.

Redekop, J. H. "The influence of rising levels of education." *Direction*, 14 (1985): 54-59.

Redekop, J. H. *A People Apart: Ethnicity and the Mennonite Brethren*. Winnipeg: Kindred Press, 1987a.

Redekop, J. H. . "The case against capital punishment." *Mennonite Brethren Herald*, (April 17, 1987b): 4-6.

Redekop, J. H. "Mennonite politicians." *Mennonite Brethren Herald* (December 23, 1988): 8.

Redekop, J. H. "Politics." In *The Mennonite Encyclopedia*, 5 (1990): 711-714.

Regehr, E. of Plowshares, an MCC supported group monitoring world arm sales, recently helped UN shape a resolution on registering world arms sales as a way of discouraging the proliferation of arms in all parts of the world. In M. L. Reimer, Plowshares . . . *Mennonite Observer* (September 2, 1991): 1-2.

Regehr, T. D. *Mennonites in Canada, 1939-1970: A People Transformed*. Mennonites in Canada, Vol. 3. Toronto: University of Toronto Press, 1996.

Reimer, A. A. "Wie es kam." *Der Rundschau Kalender*, 4, 1930, 36-47.

Reimer, A. J. "Mennonite Theological Self-Understanding, the Crisis of Modern Anthropocentricity, and the Challenge of the Third Millennium." In *Mennonite Identity: Historical and contemporary perspectives*, edited by C. W. Redekop & S. J. Steiner, 13-38. Lanham, MD: University Press of America, 1988.

Reimer, A. "Klaas Reimer: Rebel conservative, radical traditionalist." *Journal Of Mennonite Studies*, 3 (1985a), 108-117.

Reimer, A. *My Harp is Turned to Mourning: A novel*. Winnipeg: Hyperion Press, 1985b.

Reimer, A. "The Mennonite Gutsbesitzertum in Russia." Paper presented at the Symposium on the Bicentennial of Mennonites in Russia in Winnipeg, Manitoba (November 9-11, 1989).

Reimer, G. E., & Gaeddert, G. R. *Exiled by the Czar: Cornelius Jansen and the Great Mennonite Migration, 1874: No. 3. Mennonite Historical Series*. Newton, KS: Mennonite Publishing Office, 1956.

Reimer, M. L. "Plowshares director helps shape UN action on arms trade." *Mennonite Observer*, (September 2, 1991): 1-2.

Reimer, R. "Faith and practice in congregational life." *Direction*, 14 (1985): 69-75.

Rembert, K. & Crous, "Crefeld or (Krefeld)." In *The Mennonite Encyclopedia*, *1*, (1955): 733-738.

Reiswitz, G. L., & Wadzeck, F. *Beiträge Zur Kenntnis der Mennoniten-Gemeinden in Europa und America, statistichen, historischen und religiösen Inhalts*. Berlin: Reiswitz & Wadzeck, 1821.

Reiswitz, G. L., & Wadzeck, F. *Glaubensbekenntnis der Mennoniten und Nachricht von ihren Colonien nebst Lebensbeschreibung Menno Simons*. Berlin: August Rucker, 1824.

Reiswitz, G. L., & Wadzeck, F. *Beitrage zur Kenntnis der taufegesinnten Gemeinden oder Mennoniten, statistischen, historischen und religiösen, auch juristischen Inhalts (Vol. 2)*. Breslau: Carl Friedrich Fritsch, 1829.

Rempel, D. G. "The Mennonite colonies in Russia: A study of their settlement and economic development from 1789 to 1914." Unpublished doctoral dissertation, Stanford University, 1933.

Rempel, D. G. "The Mennonite commonwealth in Russia: A sketch of its founding and endurance, 1789-1919." *Mennonite Quarterly Review*, *47*, (1973): 259-308.

Rempel, D. G. "The Mennonite commonwealth in Russia: A sketch of its founding and endurance, 1789-1919." *Mennonite Quarterly Review*, *48*, (1974): 5-54.

Rempel, H. *Waffen der Wehrlosen: Ersatzdienst der Mennoniten in der UdSSR*. Winnipeg: CMBC Publications, 1980.

Richardson, J. D. *A Compilation of Messages and Papers of Presidents (Vols. 1-10)*. Washington, DC: Bureau of National Literature and Art, 1904-1910.

Rideman, P. *Account of our Religion, Doctrine and Faith, given by Peter Rideman of the Brothers whom men call Hutterians*. Bungay, UK: The Plough Publishing House, 1950.

Rideman, P. *Confession of Faith: Account of our Religion, Doctrine and Faith given by Peter Rideman of the Brothers whom men call Hutterites*. Rifton, NY: Plough Publishing House, 1970.

Risler, W. "Mennonites of Krefeld." *Mennonite Life*, *6*(2), (1951): 26-28.

Ritschl, A. *Geschichte des Pietismus*. (Vols. 1-3). Bonn: Adolf Marcus, 1880-1886.

Röbler, W. "Luther, Martin." In *Mennonitisches Lexikon*, *2*, (1937): 703-708.

Roloff, J. "Gewalt und Gewaltlosigkeit nach der Verkündigung Jesu." In J. Strauss, (Ed.). *Tutzinger Texte: 10: Glauben und Gewalt*, Munich: Claudius Verlag, (1971): 9-25

Roosen, B. C. "Kurze Zusammenfassung der Geschichte der Hamburg-Altonaer Mennoniten-Gemeinde, von ihrer Enstehung bis zum Altonaer Brandes." *Zeitschrift des Vereins für hamburgische Geschichte*, 3, (1851): 78-108.

Roosen, B. C. *Gerhard Roosen*. Hamburg: Rauhen Haus, 1854a.

Roosen, B. C. "Kurze Geschichte der Hamburg-Altona Mennoniten Gemeinde." *Mennonitische Blätter*, 1(March):9-14; (May):21-26; (July):33-38, 1854b.

Roosen, B. C. *Geschichte der Mennoniten Gemeinde zu Hamburg und Altona*. (Vols. 1-2). Hamburg: H. D. Persiehl, 1886-1887.

Roosen, B. C. *Geschichte unseres Hauses*. Hamgurg: Emma Roosen, 1905.

Roosen, G. *Nutzbahrer und Gründlicher Unterricht Von dem jetzo gewöhnlichen Brauch und Art Der Unrahtsahmen Kachel-Öfen*. Hamburg: Conrad Neuman, 1695.

Roosen, G. *Unschuld und Gegen-Bericht der Evangelischen Taufgesinneten Christen*. Hamburg: G. Roosen and Ratzeburg mit Sigismund Hoffmann, 1712.

Rues, M. S. F. *Aufrichtige Nachrichten von den gegenwärtigen Zustand der Mennoniten, oder Taufgesinnten*. Jena: J. R. Croeker's Widow, 1743.

Ruether, R. R. *Liberation Theology: Human hope confronts Christian History and American Power*. New York: Paulist Press, 1972.

Ruether, R. R. *New Woman, New Earth: Sexist Ideologies and Human Liberation*. New York: The Seabury Press, 1975.

Rupp, E. E. "Evangelical Church." In *The Mennonite Encyclopedia*, 2 (1956): 264-266.

Ruth-Heffelbower, D. *The Anabaptists are Back: Making Peace in a Dangerous World*. Scottdale: Herald Press, 1991.

Sandeen, E. R. *The Roots of Fundamentalism: British and American Millienarianism 1800-1930*. Chicago: University of Chicago Press, 1970.

Sandel, M. *Liberalism and the Limits of Justice*. Cambridge: Cambridge University Press, 1983.

Santmire, H. P. *The Travail of Nature: The Ambiguous Ecological Promise of Christian Theology*. Philadelphia: Fortress Press, 1985.

Sawatsky, H. L. "Mexico." In *The Mennonite Encyclopedia*, 5 (1990): 580-582.

Sawatsky, R. J. "The Influence of Fundamentalism on Mennonite Nonresistance 1908-1944." An M.A. thesis at the University of Minnesota, 1973.

Sawatsky, R. J. *Authority and Identity: The Dynamics of the General Conference Mennonite Church*. North Newton, KS.: Bethel College, 1987.

Sawatsky, R. J. "Beyond the Social History of the Mennonites: A Response to James C. Juhnke." In *Mennonite Identity: Historical and Contemporary Perspectives*, edited by C. W. Redekop & S. J. Steiner, Lanham, MD: University Press of Maryland, (1988): 101-108.

Sawatsky, R. J. "The One and the Many: The Recovery of Mennonite Pluralism." In *Anabaptism Revisited*, edited by W. Klaassen, Scottdale: Herald Press, (1992): 141-154.

Sawatsky, W. *Soviet Evangelicals Since World War II*. Scottdale: Herald Press, 1981.

Sawatsky, W. "Mennonite Commonwealth in Orthodox Lands." *AMBS Bulletin*, 52(1), (1988): 6-10.

Sawatsky, W. "Russian Mennonites and Baptists (1930-1990)." In *Mennonites & Baptists: A Continuing Conversation*, edited by Paul Toews, 113-132. Winnipeg, MB: Kindred Press, (1993)

Sawatzky, H. *Templer Mennonitscher Herkunft*. Winnipeg: Echo-Verlag, 1955.

Sawatzky, H. *Mennonite Templers*. Winnipeg, MB: CMBC Publications, 1990.

Schaeder, H. H. *Der Mensch in Orient und Okzident: Grundzüge einer eurasiatischen Geschichte*. München: R. Piper & Co., 1960.

Schafer, D., et al. *Christian Peacemaker Teams: A study document*. Akron, PA: Council of Moderators and Secretaries, MCC Peace Section, 1986.

Schellenberg, G. "Mein Weg zum Friedenszeugnis". *Mennonitisches Jahrbuch*, 88, (1988): 50-52.

Schepansky, E. W. "Mennoniten in Hamburg und Altona zur Zeit des Merkantilismus". *Mennonitische Geschichtsblätter*, 38, new series 32, (1980): 54-73.

Schlabach, T. F. *Gospel versus gospel: Mission and the Mennonite Church, 1863-1944: Studies in Anabaptist and Mennonite History, No. 21*, Scottdale: Herald Press, 1980.

Schlabach, T. F. "Mennonitism and Pietism in America, 1740-1880: Some thoughts on the Friedmann thesis." *Mennonite Quarterly Review*, 57, (1983): 222-240.

Schlabach, T. F. *Peace, Faith, Nation: Mennonites and Amish in Nineteenth Century America: The Mennonite Experience in America, Vol. 2*. Scottdale: Herald Press, 1988.

Schlissel, L. (Ed.). *Conscience in America: A documentary history of conscientious objectors in America, 1757-1967*. New York: E. P. Dutton & Co., Inc., 1968.

Schmidt, H. J. (Ed.). *Conversion: Doorway to Discipleship*. Hillsboro, KS: Mennonite Brethren Publishing House, 1980.

Schmidt, H. J. "The Mennonite Brethren Peace Witness." In *The Power of the Lamb*, edited by J. E. Toews and G. Nickel, 87-96. Winnipeg: Kindred Press, 1986

Schmiedehaus, W. *Ein Feste Burg ist unser Gott*. Chihuahua, Mexico: The Author, 1948.

Schmiedehaus, W. *Die Altkolonier Mennoniten in Mexiko*. Winnipeg: CMBC Publications. Revision of 1948 edition. (Germany edition, Bad Kreuznach: Pandion Verlag, 1984), 1982.

Schön, M. *Das Mennonitenthum in Westpreussen: Ein kirchen und kulturgeschichtlicher Beitrag zur Belehrung über das Wesen des Mennonitenthums*. Berlin: Friedrick Luckhardt, 1886.

Schowalter, O. "Altonaer Kaufleute des 18. Jahrunderts auf Reisen". *Christlicher Gemeinde-Kalender*, 46, (1937): 103-116.

Schowalter, O. "Kulturleistungen der Hamburger Mennoniten: Schiffahrt-Industrie-Welthandel". *Mennonitische Geschichtsblätter*, 3, (1938): 33-48.

Schowalter, O. "Quer durch Altona and Hamburg auf den Spuren mennonitischer Geschichte". *Christlicher Gemeinde-Kalender*, 48, (1939): 59-70.

Schrag, D. R. "Anabaptists and the Bible: From *Sola Scriptura* to *Solus Christus*." *Mennonite Life*, 44(3), (1989): 12-18.

Schrag, P. "The fellowship concerned about apostasy among Mennonites." *Mennonite Brethren Herald*, (January 10, 1992): 31.

Schreiber, W. I. *The fate of the Prussian Mennonites*. Göttingen: The Göttingen Research Committee, 1955.

Schroeder, W. *The Bergthal Colony*. Revised edition. Winnipeg, MB: CMBC Publications, 1986.

Schumacher, B. *Niederländische Ansiedlungen in Herzogtum Preussen zur Zeit Herzog Albrechts (1525-1565)*. Leipzig: Duncker & Humbolt, 1903.

Schumacher, B. *Aus der Geschichte Ost-Preussens*. Leer: Gerhard Rautenberg, 1957.

Schumacher, B. *Geschichte Ost- und Westpreussens*. Würzberg: Holzner Verlag, 1958.

Schumacher, E. F. "Buddhist economics." In *Economics, ecology, ethics: Essays Toward a steady-state economy*, edited by H. E. Daly, San Francisco: W. H. Freeman and Company, (1980): 138-145.

Scott, R. C. *Quakers in Russia*. London: Michael Joseph Ltd., 1964.

Seebass, G. "Luther's Stellung zur Verfolgung der Täufer und ihre Bedeutung für den Deutschen Protestantismus." *Mennonitische Blätter*, 40, (1982): 7-24.

Séguy, J. *Les Assemblées Anabaptistes--Mennonites de France*. Paris: Mouton, 1977.

Séguy, J. "Geschichte der Mennoniten in Frankreich." *Mennonitische Blätter*, 40, (1982): 84-96.

Shenk, W. S. "Missionary encounter with culture." *International Bulletin of Missionary Research*, 15, (1991): 104-109.

Shepansky, E. W. "Mennoniten in Hamburg zur Zeit des Merkantilismus." *Mennonitische Blätter*, 37, (1980): 54-73.

Shridharani, K. *War Without Violence: A Study of Gandhi's Method and its Accomplishments*. New York: Garland Publishing, Inc., 1972.

Sibley, M., & Jacob, P. *Conscription of Conscience: The American State and the Conscientious Objectors*. Ithaca, NY: Cornell University Press, 1952.

Sider, R. J. *Rich Christians in an Age of Hunger*. Downers Grove, IL: InterVarsity Press, 1977.

Sider, R. J. *Christ and Violence*. Scottdale: Herald Press, 1979.

Sider, R. J. *Nonviolence: The Invincible Weapon?* Dallas: Word Publishing, 1989a.

Sider, R. L. "Toward a Biblical Perspective on equality: Steps on the way toward Christian political engagement." *Interpretation 43*, (1989b): 156-169.

Simons, M. *Opera Omnia Theologica of alle de Godtgeleerde Wercken van Menno Symons*. Amsterdam: Joannes van Veen, 1681.

Simons, M. *Die Vollständigen Werke Menno Simons*. Elkhart, IN: Mennonitische Verlags-Handlung, 1876.

Simons, M. *The Complete Writings of Menno Simons, c.1496-1561*. (L. Verduin, Trans.). Scottdale: Herald Press, 1956.

Smissen, C. H. A. van der. *Festspiel zum 50 jäh Amtsjubiläum des Herrn Pastor B. C. Roosen aufgeführt am 13. Oktober 1895*. Altona: H. Dircks, 1895a.

Smissen, C. H. A. van der. *Kurzgefasste Geschichte und Glaubenslehre der Altevangelischen Taufgesinnten oder Mennoniten*. Summerfield, Iowa: Selbstverlag des Verfassers, 1895b.

Smissen, C. H. A. van der, Hege, C., & Krahn, C. "Ahlefeldt." In *The Mennonite Encyclopedia, 1* (1955): 27,

Smissen, H. van der. "Alba." In *Mennonitisches Lexikon, 1* (1913): 17,

Smissen, H. van der. "Altona." In *Mennonitisches Lexikon, 1*, (1913): 46-47.

Smissen, H. van der. "Brons, Anna (nee Cremer ten Doornkaat)." In *Mennonitisches Lexikon, 1*, (1913): 271-273.

Smissen, H. van der. "Brons, Anna (nee Cremer ten Doornkaat)." In *The Mennonite Encyclopedia, 1*, (1955): 436-437.

Smith, C. H. *The Coming of the Russian Mennonites*. Berne, IN: Mennonite Book Concern, 1927.

Smith, C. H. *Smith's Story of the Mennonites*. Newton: Faith and Life Press. 5th edition 1981, 1941.

Smith, C. H. "Pennsylvania." In *The Mennonite Encyclopedia, 4*, (1959): 136-141.

Smith, C. H. *Menno Simons: Apostle of the non-resistant life*. Berne, IN: Mennonite Book Concern, n. d.

Smith C. H. & Bender, H. S. "Reformed Mennonite Church." In *The Mennonite Encyclopedia, 4*, (1959): 267-270.

Smith, C. *Going to the Root: Nine proposals for Radical Church Renewal*. Scottdale: Herald Press, 1992.

Smith, W. H. "Paraguay." In *The Mennonite Encyclopedia, 4*, (1959): 117-119.

Smucker, D. E. "A Mennonite critique of the Pacifist Movement." *Mennonite Quarterly Review, 20*, (1946): 81-88.

Spaulding, J. L. "The changing economic base of the Mennonite community with special reference to certain central Kansas counties." Unpublished manuscript, Mennonite Historical Library, North Newton, KS., 1984.

Sprunger, M. S. "Rich Mennonites, poor Mennonites: Economics and theology in the Amsterdam Waterlander congregation during the Golden Age" (Doctoral dissertation, University of Illinois at Urbana-Champaign). Dissertation Abstracts International, 54(5), 1993, 1919A.

Sprunger, M. S. "Dutch Mennonites and the Golden Age Economy: The problem of social disparity in the Church." In C. W. Redekop, *Anabaptist/Mennonite Faith and Economics*, edited by V. A. Krahn, & S. J. Steiner, Lanham, 19-14. MD: University Press of America, 1994.

Stauffer, E. "Die Mennonitengemeinde in Hamburg-Altona." *Hamburgische Kirchenzeitung,* 4, 15-18, 39-42, (1928): 63-65.

Stayer, J. M. *Anabaptists and the Sword.* Lawrence, KS: Coronado Press, 1972.

Stayer, J. M. "The easy demise of a normative vision of Anabaptism." In *Mennonite Identity: Historical and contemporary perspectives*, edited by C. W. Redekop & S. J. Steiner, 109-116. Lanham, MD: University Press of America, 1988

Stayer, J. M. "Noch einmal besichtigt: 'Anabaptists and the Sword': Von der Radikalität zum Quietismus." *Mennonitische Geschichtsblätter,* 47/48, (1990/1991): 24-37.

Stayer, J. M. *The German Peasants' War and Anabaptist Community of Goods.* Montreal & Kingston: McGill-Queen's University Press, 1991.

Stayer, J. M., & Packull, W. O. (Eds.). *The Anabaptists and Thomas Müntzer.* Dubuque, IA: Kendall/Hunt Publishing Company, 1980.

Steinmetz, M. "Thomas Müntzer in the research of the present." In *The Anabaptists and Thomas Müntzer*, edited by J. M. Stayer & W. O. Packull,133-143. Dubuque, IA: Kendall/Hunt Publishing Company, 1980.

Stoltzfus, G. M. "Toward new horizons in Mennonite Mutual aid." In *The compassionate community: A Collection of Lectures Presented at Conferences of the Association of Mennonite Mutual Aid Societies*, edited by H. R. Hernley, 37-50. Scottdale: Association of Mennonite Aid Societies, 1970.

Stone, R. H. & Wilbanks, D. W. (Eds.). *The Peacemaking Struggle: Militarism and Resistance.* Essays prepared for the advisory Council on Church and Society. Lanham, MD: University of America Press, 1985.

Strauss, J. (Ed.). *Tutzinger Texte: 10: Glauben und Gewalt.* München: Claudius Verlag, 1971.

Stricker, G. (with Sawatsky, W.). "Mennonites in Russia and the Soviet Union: An Aspect of the church history of the Germans in Russia." Religion in Communist Lands, *12*(3), (1984): 293-314.

Studer, G. C. "Toward a theology of servanthood." In *The compassionate community: A Collection of Lectures Presented at Conferences of the Association of Mennonite Mutual Aid Societies*, edited by H. R. Hernley, 227-295. Scottdale: Association of Mennonite Aid Societies, 1970

Sudermann, J. "The Origin of Mennonite State Service in Russia, 1870-1880." *Mennonite Quarterly Review,* 17, (1943): 23-46.

Sutherland, J. R. *Going Broke: Bankruptcy, business ethics and the Bible.* Scottdale: Herald Press, 1991.

Sutter, S. C. "Friedrichstadt: An early German example of Mennonite magistrates." *Mennonite Quarterly Review,* 53, (1979): 299-305.

Sutter, S. C. "Die Anfänge der Mennonitengemeinde in Friedrichstadt 1621-1656." *Mennonitische Blätter,* 37, (1980): 42-53.

Sutter, S. C. "Friedrichstadt an der Eider: An early experience in religious toleration, 1621-1727." Unpublished doctoral dissertation, University of Chicago, 1982.

Swartzentruber, A. O. "The piety and theology of the Anabaptist martyrs in van Braght's *Martyrs' Mirror,* I." *Mennonite Quarterly Review,* 28, (1954): 5-26.

Swope, W. D. "Alcohol among the Columbiana County, Ohio, Mennonites." *Mennonite Historical Bulletin,* 21(1), (1960): 2.

Täuferakten (TA) *VI-2 Hans Denck Schriften, 2: Religiöse Schriften.* W. Fellmann, (Ed.). Gütersloh: (Quellen und Forschungen für Reformationsgeschichte XXVI), 1956.

Täuferakten Zürich (TA Zürich) *Quellen zur Geschichte der Täufer in der Schweiz,* Zürich: L. von Muralt & W. Schmid, 1952.

Teufel, E. & Hein G. "Schwertler." In *Mennonitisches Lexikon,* 4, (1967): 140.

Thiessen, A. *Die Agrarwirren bei den Mennoniten in Russland.* Berlin: H. Wigankow, 1887.

Todd, J. M. *Martin Luther: A biographical study*. London: Burns & Oates, 1964.

Toews, A. A. *Mennonitische Märtyrer: Der Jüngsten Vergangenheit und der Gegenwart*, (Vols. 1-2). North Clearbrook, BC: A. A. Toews, 1949-1954.

Toews, C. P., Friesen, H., & Dyck, A. *The Kuban Settlement*, Vol. 9. Echo historical series. Winnipeg: CMBC Publications, 1989.

Toews, J. A. *The Way of Peace (true nonresistance through Christ)*. Hillsboro, KS: Mennonite Brethren Church Christian Service Program, n. d.

Toews, J. A. *True Nonresistance Through Christ*. Winnipeg: MB Church of North America, 1955.

Toews, J. A. "Die Ersten Mennoniten Brüder und Menno Simons: Hinweg von Menno, oder zurück zu Menno." *The Voice*, 6(6), (1957): 1-3.

Toews, J. A. "In Search of Identity." *Mennonite Brethren Herald*, (March 10, 1972): 2-4, 25.

Toews, J. A. *A History of the Mennonite Brethren Church: Pilgrims and Pioneers*. Fresno, CA: General Conference of Mennonite Brethren Church Board of Christian Literature, 1975a.

Toews, J. A. "Eine Gemeinde radikaler Bibelleser." *Mennonitisches Jahrbuch*, 75, (1975b): 17-20.

Toews, J. A. "Mennonite Brethren: Past, present, and future." In *Pilgrims and Strangers: Essays in Mennonite Brethren History: No. 1. Perspectives on Mennonite Life and Thought*, edited by Paul Toews, Fresno, 170-181. CA: Center for Mennonite Brehtren Studies, 1977

Toews, J. A. *People of the Way: Selected Essays and Addresses*. Winnipeg: Historical Commitee, Board of Higher Education, Canadian Conference of Mennonite Brethren Churches, 1981.

Toews, J. B. "Mennonite Brethren Identity and Theological Diversity." In *Pilgrims and strangers: essays in Mennonite Brethren History*, edited by Paul Toews, Fresno, 133-157. CA: Center for Mennonite Brethren Studies, 1977

Toews, J. B. "Geleitwort." In H. Löwen. *In Vergessenheit geratene Beziehungen: Frühe Begegnungen der Mennoniten-Brüdergemeinde mit dem Baptismus in Russland--ein Überblick: Vol. 1. Beitrage zur osteuropäischen Kirchengeshichte*, Bielefeld: Logos, (1989): 7-8.

Toews, J. B., Konrad, A. G., & Dueck, A. "Mennonite Brethren Church Membership Profile, 1972-1982." *Direction*, 14(2), (1985): 3-42.

Toews, J.C. "Das Mennonitsche Gutsbesitzertum in Russland." *Der Bote*, June 30:3-4, July 7:3-4, July 14:5, July 21:3, Aug 4:1-3, Aug 11:4-5, Sept 1:3, Sept 8:4, Sept 15:4, Sept 19:4, (June 30-September 19, 1954).

Toews, J. E. "The meaning of Anabaptism for the Mennonite Brethren Church." In *Pilgrims and Strangers: Essays in Mennonite Brethren History: No. 1. Perspectives on Mennonite Life and Thought*, Fresno, edited by P. Toews, 161-169. CA: Center for Mennonite Brethren Studies, 1977.

Toews, J. E. "Theological Reflections." *Direction, 14*(2), (1985): 60-68.

Toews, J. E. "Kingdom-peace theology for modern Mennonites." Paper presented at the Mennonite Christian Peace Team Consultation, Chicago, IL., (December 16-18, 1986a).

Toews, J. E. "Peace Makers from the Start." In *The Power of the Lamb*, edited by J. E. Toews and G. Nickel, 45-56. Winnipeg: Kindred Press, 1986b.

Toews, J. E., & Nickel, G. (Eds.). *The Power of the Lamb*. Winnipeg: Kindred Press, 1986.

Toews, J. G. "Mennonite entrepreneurs." In *Manitoba Mennonite Memories: A century past but not forgotten*, edited by J. G. Toews & L. Klippenstein, 199-228. Altona, MB: Manitoba Mennonite Centennial Committee, 1974.

Toews, J. G., & Klippenstein, L. (Eds.). *Manitoba Mennonite Memories*. Altona, MB: Manitoba Mennonite Centennial Committee, 1974.

Toews, J. J. "Cultural background of the Mennonite Brethren Church." Unpublished thesis, University of Toronto, 1951.

Toews, J. J. "Benzien, Karl." In *The Mennonite Encyclopedia, 1* (1955): 275.

Toews, J. J. "Oncken, Johann Gerhard." In *The Mennonite Encyclopedia, 4* (1959): 60.

Toews, J. J. "Wieler, Johann." In *The Mennonite Encyclopedia, 4* (1959): 948.

Toews, J. J. "The missionary spirit of the Mennonite Brethren Church in Russia." In *The Church in mission: a sixtieth anniversary tribute to J. B. Toews,* edited by A. J. Klassen, 134-154. Fresno, CA: Board of Christian Literature, Mennonite Brethren Church, 1967.

Toews, John B. *Lost Fatherland: The Story of the Mennonite emigration from Soviet Russia, 1921-1927: No. 12. Studies in Anabaptist and Mennonite History*. Scottdale: Herald Press, 1967.

Toews, John B. "The Origins and Activities of the Mennonite *Selbstschutz* in the Ukraine (1918-1919)." *Mennonite Quarterly Review, 46* (1972): 5-40.

Toews, John B. "Nonresistance Reexamined: Why did Mennonites leave Russia in 1874." *Mennonite Life, 29* (1&2), (1974): 8-14.

Toews, John B. "The Russian origins of the Mennonite Brethren: Some observations." In *Pilgrims and Strangers: Essays in Mennonite Brethren History: No. 1. Perspectives on Mennonite Life and Thought*, edited by P. Toews, 78-107. Fresno, CA: Center for Mennonite Brethren Studies, 1977.

Toews, John B. *Czars, Soviets & Mennonites*. Newton, KS: Faith and Life Press, 1982.

Toews, John B. (Ed. & Trans.). "The Early Mennonite Brethren: Some outside views." *Mennonite Quarterly Review, 58* (1984): 83-124.

Toews, John B. (Ed. & Trans.). "Nonresistance and Migration in the 1870s: Two Personal Views." *Mennonite Life, 41*(2), (1986):9-14.

Toews, John B. *Perilous Journey: The Mennonite Brethren in Russia, 1860-1910: No. 4. Perspectives in Mennonite Life and Thought*. Winnipeg: Kindred Press, 1988.

Toews, John B. " Baptists and Mennonite Brethren in Russia (1790-1930)." In *Mennonites & Baptists: A Continuing Conversation*, edited by Paul Toews, 81-96. Winnipeg, MB: Kindred Press, 1993.

Toews, P. (Ed.). *Pilgrims and Strangers: Essays in Mennonite Brethren History: No. 1. Perspectives on Mennonite Life and Thought*. Fresno, CA: Center for Mennonite Brethren Studies, 1977.

Toews, P. "Fundamentalist conflict in Mennonite colleges: A response to cultural transitions?" *Mennonite Quarterly Review, 57* (1983): 241-256.

Toews, P. "The long weekend or the short week: Mennonite peace theology, 1935-1944." *Mennonite Quarterly Review, 60* (1986):38-57.

Toews, P. (Ed.). *Mennonites & Baptists: A Continuing Conversation*. Winnipeg, MB: Kindred Press, 1993.

Toews, Peter. *Eine Seltsame Begebenheit angehend der durch Peter von Riesen....* Hochstadt, MB.: Peter Toews, 1911.

Toorenenbergen, J. J. van, (Ed.). *Het oudste Niederlandsche verboden boek, 1523. Oecomencia Christiana Summa der godliker Scrifturen*. Leiden: E. J. Brill, 1882.

Trocmé, André. *Jesus and the Nonviolent Revolution*. Scottdale, PA: Herald Press, 1973.

Tulles, F. B. *Meeting House and Counting House: The Quaker Merchants of Colonial Philadelphia, 1682-1763*. New York: W. W. Norton & Company, 1963.

Umble, J. H. "Women and Choice: An Examination of the Martyrs' Mirror." Unpublished thesis, Southern Methodist University, Dallas, 1987.

Unger, W. "Focusing the Evangelical Vision." *Direction, 20*(1), (1991): 3-17.

Unruh, A. H. *Die Geschichte der Mennoniten-Brüdergemeinde, 1860-1954*. Hillsboro, KS: The General Conference of the Mennonite Brethren Church of North America, 1954.

Unruh, B. H. "Die Revolution 1525 und das Täufertum." In *Gedenkschrift zum 400 Jährigen Jubiläum: Der Mennoniten oder Taufgesinnten, 1525-1925*, edited by C. Neff, 19-47. Ludwigshafen: Konferenz der Süddeutschen Mennoniten, 1925.

Unruh, B. H. "The background and causes of the flight of the Mennonites from Russia in 1929." *Mennonite Quarterly Review*, (1930)4, 267-281; (1931) 5, 28-41.

Unruh, B. H. *Die niederländisch-niederdeutschen Hintergründe der Mennonitischen Ostwanderungen in 16., 18. Und 19. Jahrhundert*. Karlsruhe: Selbstverlag (gedruckt Heinrich Schneider), 1955.

Urry, J. "The closed and the open: Social and religious change amongst the Mennonites in Russia (1789-1889)." An unpublished doctoral dissertation, Oxford University, 1978.

Urry, J. "John Melville and the Mennonites: A British evangelist in South Russia, 1837-ca.1875." *Mennonite Quarterly Review, 54* (1980): 305-322.

Urry, J. "Through the eye of a needle: Wealth and the Mennonite experience in Imperial Russia." *Journal Of Mennonite Studies, 3* (1985): 7-35.

Urry, J. "The social background to the emergence of the Mennonite Brethren in nineteenth century Russia." *Journal Of Mennonite Studies, 6* (1988): 8-35.

Urry, J. "Mennonite economic development in the Russian mirror." In *Mennonites in Russia, 1788-1988: Essays in Honour of Gerhard Lohrenz*, edited by J. Friesen, 99-126. Winnipeg: CMBC Publications, 1989a.

Urry, J. *None But Saints: The Transformation of Mennonite Life in Russia 1789-1889*. Winnipeg: Hyperion Press Limited, 1989b.

Urry, J. "Prolegomena to the study of Mennonite society in Russia, 1880-1914." Paper presented at the Symposium on the Bicentennial of Mennonites in Russia: The experiences of Mennonites in Russia/Ukraine/USSR, 1789-1989, Winnipeg, MB, November 9-11, 1989c.

Urry, J. "The Russian state, the Mennonite world and the migration from Russia to North America in the 1870s." *Mennonite Life*, 46(1), (1991): 11-16.

Urry, J., & Klippenstein, L. "Mennonites and the Crimean War, 1854-1856." *Journal Of Mennonite Studies*, 7 (1989): 9-32.

Verduin, L. *The Reformers and their Stepchildren*. Grand Rapids: Wm. B. Eerdmanns Publishing Company, 1964.

Verheyden, A. L. E. *Anabaptism in Flanders, 1530-1650: A Century of Struggle: Vol. 9. Studies in Anabaptist and Mennonite History*. Scottdale: Herald Press, 1961.

Vogt, R. "The impact of economic and social class on Mennonite theology." In *Mennonite Images: Historical, Cultural, and Literary Essays Dealing with Mennonite Issues,* edited by H. Loewen, 137-148. Winnipeg, MB: Hyperion Press, 1980.

Vos, K. "De Keuze tot Doopsgezind Bisschop." In *Archief voor Kerkengeschiednis,* 195ff. Gravenhage: Martinus Nijhoff, 1921.

Vos, K. "Leenaert Bouwens." In *Mennonitisches Lexikon, 1*, (1913): 250-251.

Vos, K. *Menno Simons, 1496-1561*. Leiden: E. J. Brill, 1914.

Vos, K. "Leenaert Bouwens." In *The Mennonite Encyclopedia, 3* (1957): 305.

Vos, K. "Sicke Freerks." In *The Mennonite Encyclopedia, 4* (1959): 523.

Vries, Jan de. *The Dutch Rural Economy in the Golden Age, 1500-1700*. Newhaven and London: Yale University Press, 1974.

Walls, A. F. "Conversion and Christian Continuity." *Mission Focus*, 18(2), (1990): 17-21.

Waltner, O. "Mahatma Gandhi and World Peace." *Mennonite Life, 17* (1962): 55-58.

Ward, B. *Rich Nations and Poor Nations*. Toronto: CBC Publications, 1961.

"Was sind die Mitglieder der Mennoniten Brüdergemeinde? Juristisch? Wirklich?" *Odessaer Zeitung,* (July 16-28, 1896): 23.

Washington, J. M. (Ed). *A Testament of Hope: The Essential Writings of Martin Luther King, Jr*. San Francisco: Harper & Row, Publishers, 1986.

Weaver, J. D. "Mennonite theological self-understanding: A response to A. James Reimer." In *Mennonite Identity: Historical and contemporary perspectives*, edited by C. W. Redekop & S. J. Steiner, 39-61. Lanham, MD: University Press of America, 1988.

Wedel, C. H. *Abriss der Geschichte der Mennoniten* (Vols. 1-4). Newton, KS: Bethel College, 1900-1904.

Wenger, J. C. "The Schleitheim Confession of Faith." *Mennonite Quarterly Review, 19* (1945): 243-253.

Wenger, J. C. *Separated Unto God: A Plea for Christian Simplicity of Life and for a scriptural nonconformity to the World*. Scottdale: Mennonite Publishing House, 1951.

Wenger, J. C. "Avoidance." In *The Mennonite Encyclopedia, 1* (1955): 200-202.

Wenger, J.C. "Chiliasm." In *The Mennonite Encyclopedia, 1* (1955): 557-559.

Wenger, J. C. "The biblicism of the Anabaptists." In *The Recovery of the Anabaptist Vision*, edited by G. F. Hershberger, 167-179. Scottdale: Herald Press, 1957.

Wenger, J. C. *The Mennonite Church in America: Sometimes Called Old Mennonite: Vol. 2. Mennonite History*. Scottdale: Herald Press, 1966.

WEP Linus Pauling, (Hon. Ed-in-Ch.), Irven Laszlo & Jong Youl Yoo, (Ex. Eds.). *World Encyclopedia of Peace*. 4 Vols. Oxford: Pergamon Press, 1986.

Whaley, J. *Religious Toleration and social change in Hamburg 1529-1819*. Cambridge: Cambridge University Press, 1985.

White, L. "The historical roots of our ecological crisis." *Science, 155* (1967):1203-1207.

Wichmann, E. H. *Geschichte Altonas*. Altona: J. Harder, 1896.

Wiebe, D. V. *They Seek a Country: A Survey of Mennonite migrations with special reference to Kansas and Gnadenau*. Hillsboro, KS: The Mennonite Brethren Publishing House, 1959.

Wiebe, D. "A Philosophy for Mennonite Self-Understanding: Normative Self-Definition or Self-Deceptive Image Management?" In *Mennonite Identity: Historical and contemporary perspectives*, edited by

Redekop & Steiner, 137-146. Lanham, MD: University Press of Maryland, 1988.

Wiebe, G. *Ursachen und Geschichte der Auswanderung der Mennoniten aus Russland nach Amerika.* Chortitz, MB: Diedrich Wiebe,1900.(Reprinted 1962 Cuauhtémoc: Imprenta1 Rempel; 1987 Winnipeg: CMBC Publications).

Wiebe, G. *Causes and History of the Emigration of the Mennonites from Russia to America.* (H. Janzen, Trans.). Winnipeg: Manitoba Mennonite Historical Society, 1981.

Wiebe, G. "Urkundenbuch der Mennoniten-Gemeinde Heubuden." Unpublished manuscript in Mennonite Archives, Winnpeg, n. d.

Wiebe, H. *Das Siedlungswerk niederländischer Mennoniten im Weichseltal zwischen Forden und Weissenberg bis zum Ausgang des 18. Jahrhunderts: Vol. 3. Wissenschaftliche Beiträge zur Geschichte und Landeskunde Ost-Mitteleuropas.* Marburg: Johann Gottfried Herder-Institut, 1952.

Wiebe, K. F. *Day of Disaster.* Scottdale: Herald Press, 1976.

Wiebe, P. "Kurze Übersicht der im Molotschner Mennonitenbezirke zum 1. Januar 1849 im Bestand." *Unterhaltungsblatt für Deutsche Ansiedler im südlichen Russland,* (May 4, 1849): 3ff.

Wiebe, R. *Peace Shall Destroy Many.* Toronto: McClelland and Stewart Limited, 1962.

Wiebe, R. "Petronius and his Pew Pals." *Mennonite Brethren Herald, 1,* (March 30, 11; April 6, 12, 1962).

Wiens, D. "New Wineskins for Old Wine." *The Christian Leader,* (supplement), (October 12, 1965): 1-28.

Wiens, D. "Incarnation and ideal: The story of truth becoming heresy." In *Pilgrims and Strangers: Essays in Mennonite Brethren History: No. 1. Perspectives on Mennonite Thought and Life,* edited by P. Toews, 28-51. Fresno, CA: Center for Mennonite Brethren Studies, 1977.

Wiens, D. "Cultural change." *Direction, 14(2),* (1985): 43-49.

Wiens, D. "A philosophy of Mennonite self-understanding." In *Mennonite Identity: Historical and contemporary perspectives,* edited by C. W. Redekop & S. J. Steiner, 117-135. Lanham, MD: University Press of America, 1988.

Wiens, D. "Mennonite: Neither Liberal nor Evangelical." *Direction, 20(1),* (1991): 38-63.

Wiens, G. "Russo-German Bilingualism: A Case Study." *Modern Language Journal, 36* (1952):392ff.

Wiens, G. "Mother Tongue Frustration." *Mennonite Life, 9* (1954): 32-33.

Wiens, H. "Aus den Tagen des grossen Cornies." *Mennonitische Warte, 9-10,* (1935): 347-350, 367-371.

Wiens, H. J. *"... Dass die Heiden Miterben Seien:" Die Geschichte der Indianermission im paraguayischen Chaco.* Filadelfia: Konferenz der Mennoniten Brüdergemeinden in Paraguay, 1989.

Williams, G. H. *The Radical Reformation.* Philadelphia: The Westminster Press, 1962.

Wink, Walter. *Engaging the Powers. Discernment and Resistance in a World of Domination.* Minneapolis: Fortress Press, 1992.

Wingren, G. *Man and the Incarnation: A Study in the Biblical Theology of Irenaeus.* (MacKenzie, R., Trans). Philadelphia: Muhlenberg Press, 1959.

Wölk, H., & Wölk, G. *Die Mennoniten Brüdergemeinde in Russland 1925-1980: No. 4. Perspectives on Mennonite Life and Thought.* Fresno, CA: Center for Mennonite Brethren Studies, 1981.

Y. Eine Antwort auf die Frage eines Jünglings. *Odessaer Zeitung,*(May 23-June 5, 1907): 2.

Yarrow, C. H. M. *Quaker Experiences in international conciliation.* New Haven: Yale University Press, 1978.

Yoder, E. T., & Hochstetler, M. D. *Biblical References in Anabaptist Writings.* Aylmer, ON: Pathway Publishers, 1969.

Yoder, J. H. "The Hermeneutics of the Anabaptists." *Mennonite Quarterly Review, 41* (1967): 291-308.

Yoder, J. H. *Täufertum und Reformation im Gespräch: Dogmengeschichtliche Untersuchung der frühen Gespräche zwischen Schweizerischen Täufern und Reformatoren.* Zürich: EVZ-Verlag, 1968.

Yoder, J.H. *The Politics of Jesus.* Grand Rapids: Eerdmans, 1972.

Yoder, J. H. "Anabaptism and history: 'Restitution' and the possibility of renewal." In *Umstrittenes Täufertum, 1525-1975: Neue Forschungen,* edited by H.-J. Goertz, 244-258. Göttingen: Vandenhoeck & Ruprecht, 1975.

Yoder, J. H. "Mennonite political conservatism: Paradox or contradiction." In *Mennonite Images: Historical, Cultural, and literary es-*

says dealing with Mennonite issues, edited by H. Loewen, 7-16. Winnipeg: Hyperion Press, 1980.

Yoder, J. H. *The Priestly Kingdom: Social Ethics as Gospel*. Notre Dame: University of Notre Dame Press, 1984.

Yoder, J. H. "The Anabaptist shape of liberation." In *Why I am a Mennonite: Essays on Mennonite Identity*, edited by H. Loewen, 338-350. Scottdale: Herald Press, 1988.

Yoder, P. "The role of the Bible in Mennonite self-understanding." In C. W. Redekop & S. J. Steiner, (Eds.). *Mennonite Identity: Historical and contemporary perspectives*, 69-82. Lanham, MD: University Press of America, 1988.

Zacharias, P. D. *Reinland: An Experience in Community*. Reinland, MB: Reinland Centennial Committee, 1976.

Zehr, Howard, *Mediating the Victim-Offender Conflict*. Akron, PA: MCC, n.d.

Zuercher, Melanie Z. "On Being and Staying a Mennonite." *Festival Quarterly 12*(1), (1985): 5.

Zijpp, N. van der. *De vroegere Doopsgezinden en de Krijgsdienst*. Wolvega: N. V. Drukkerij en Boekhandel v.h. G. Taconis, 1930.

Zijpp, N. van der. "Lamisten." In *Mennonitisches Lexikon*, 2, (1937):606.

Zijpp, N. van der. *Geschiedenis der Doopsgezinden in Nederland*. Arnheim: Van Loghum Slaterus, 1952.

Zijpp, N. van der. "Collegiants." In *The Mennonite Encyclopedia, 1* (1955): 639-640.

Zijpp, N. van der. "Netherlands." In *The Mennonite Encyclopedia, 3* (1957): 824-843.

Zijpp, N. van der. "The Early Dutch Anabaptists." In *The Recovery of the Anabaptist vision: A Sixtieth Anniversary Tribute to Harold S. Bender*, edited by G. F. Hershberger, 69-82. Scottdale: Herald Press, 1957.

Zijpp, N. van der. "Philips, Dirk." *Mennonitisches Lexikon, 3* (1958): 368-369.

Zijpp, N. van der. "Patriots and Mennonites in the Netherlands." In *The Mennonite Encyclopedia, 4* (1959): 124-125.

Zijpp, N. van der. "Remonstrants." In *The Mennonite Encyclopedia, 4* (1959): 296-297.

Zijpp, N. van der. "Wismar Resolutions." In *The Mennonite Encyclopedia, 4* (1959): 966.

INDEX: Names and Selected Subjects

A

Abraham 8, 20, 140, 190, 208
abuse,
- abuse of power 103-4, 111, 172-3
- abuse by church members 111, 176
- abuse of the environment 124
- sexual abuse 100-1
- taking advantage of 159-60
- unfair labor practices 160

admonition 58
- admonition between believers rare 131
- mutual admonition 31, 82, 100

Agricultural Society 95, 106
- Agricultural Union 103, 110

Ahlefeldt, Bartolomaus von 34, 45, 58-9, 191

Ak Mechet 116

Aken, Gillis van 34, 58

Alba, Duke von/of 40, 55

Alexandrovsk 95

Allianz Gemeinde 117

Altdorf 75

alternative service 131
- in America 254
- in Holland 41
- in Prussia 65
- in Russia 97-8, 139
- first example 41
- alternative service men returning 139
- two alternative service possibilities 97

Ältestenkonvent 101

Altona 53, 59, 61-4

Amsterdam 37-8, 42, 50, 60, 68, 70

Anabaptist/Anabaptists 19, 31, 37-40, 44-5, 50, 53-5, 58-60, 65-72, 75, 113-4, 150, 155, 163, 166, 168, 217, 224, 226, 232
- Anabaptist concerns iii, 41
- revolutionary overtones of the Anabaptists 68
- Anabaptist values iii
- 12 core values x-xii, 13-8
- compromise of values 65-6, 165, 184, 225

Anabaptist vision v
- return to 66, 120, 131, 150
- renewal of 131-2
- shortcomings of 29-34
- Bender's Anabaptist vision v, 150
- Anabaptist vision: monogenetic or polygenetic? v-vi

Anabaptist/Mennonite I, iv-v, 9, 12, 37, 68, 101, 120-2, 129, 131, 150, 163, 166, 168, 182-3, 186, 195-6, 215, 220,

Anwohner 88-9, 92

apostles - see: exhuberant

Apostolische Brüdergemeinde 116

Arianism 79

armed ship/s 42, 49, 63, 204
- shipowner/s mounting cannons 62

329

Armenreihe 89
Aufwiegler 31
Ausgetretenen 118
Authoritarianism 169, 173
authority
- authority in the church 82, 170-1, 173-4,
- centralized authority structure 43-4, 69, 170-3
- locus of all authority 16

B

Baltic 67-8
ban
- banned, banning/s 101, 119, 132, 173, 211
- ban and shunning 31-2, 93, 101, 123
- banned by congregation 33, 203, 220
- banned by minister/s 34, 125, 220
- big ban 42
- little ban 42, 49, 204
- punitive ban 29, 32-3, 56, 176
banished/banishment 103, 106, 111
bankruptcy 129-30, 159
baptism 8, 30, 44, 133, 193, 262
- infant 3, 5, 31
- adult 43, 100, 120, 131, 226, 236
Baptist/Baptists 113-4, 118-22, 126, 137, 139-40
Bartsch, Johann 85, 99
Bauman, Clarence 150
Beckerath, Herman von 65
Bekker, Benjamin 125
believing community 14-6, 155, 198, 220

Bender, Harold S. v, 5, 143, 150, 191, 227
Beningha, Eggerink 53
Benzien, Karl 119, 127
Bergthaler 165
Bible institutes 143
- Bible school movement 143
Bible Society 114, 256, 263
Bible study/studies 78, 114, 120, 123, 164, 167, 203, 209, 216, 237
bishops/elders 4, 74-5, 83, 93, 101-2, 127, 132, 220
Blankenburg 113, 121-2, 127-8, 140, 165
Block, Isaac 180
board of elders - see: elders,
Bommel, an anabaptist 75
bounded set analogy xii-xiv
Bouwens, Leenart 32-3, 56, 58, 220
breach of trust 175
bribe/s 161, 223
Brons, Anna 57, 75
Brons, Isaac 57, 75
Brotbrecher 116
Buddha 20
bugger, drill bugger 95
Bundeskonferenz 122, 127
Busschaert, Hans 58

C

call
- of God 122, 125
- of the congregation 122
Calvin, John 3, 30, 225
- Calvinist 204, 225
Campbell, Joseph 19, 21
Canaan 190, 209
- heavenly Canaan 93

330

INDEX

canon 163, 165-6, 198, 207, 209
- canon within the canon 182
- flat canon x, 15, 165, 167, 207-11
- focused canon x, 128, 163, 165-7, 207-10
- Christ-centered canon 166, 209

capital punishment 191, 210
capitalism 156, 245
catalyst 236-7
Catherine the Great 81, 85
Catholic/Catholics 71, 74, 78, 83, 103, 137
- Catholic Church 5, 77, 84
- Catholic counter-reformers 5
- Catholic hierarchy 173

cell groups 167
centered set analogy xii-xiv
Charity 65, 83, 100, 239
- Algerian slaves 65
- offerings 65

cheating on income tax 161
child abuse - see: abuse,
chiliasm 38, 116
Chortitza 142, 164
"chosen people" 211, 223-5
Christian Coalition ii, 183
church governance 17, 132
- congregational governance 17, 58, 168-9
- governing elder 73, 82, 169
- conference control 68, 169
- seat of church authority - see: authority,

church
- discipline 6, 8, 43, 56, 124, 132
- dues 77, 83
- government 87, 91
- church/state collusion 15, 87, 98, 202
- collusion between church and colony authorities 93

church growth 63, 130, 182, 226
citizen/citizens 14, 189, 191-6, 204, 223, 231-2, 238, 244
- in Canada 146
- in Germany 60
- in Holland 40, 42
- in Prussia 70, 82
- in Russia 86-7, 97
- in the United States 146-7
- of a spiritual kingdom 9-10, 13-4, 70, 87
- of heaven v, 9, 128
- of the earthly kingdoms x, 190, 192, 194, 232
- from the day of their arrival in Russia 146
- two-kingdom 5, 146, 189, 191
- citizenship-one kingdom 155, 189-90, 194

Civilian Public Service 143, 149-50,
Claassen, Johann 115, 124-5
Clergy 14, 62, 138, 155, 198, 213, 226
clothing/dress,
- distinction/distinctive dress 163-4
- men's 164
- women's 164, 173
- head covering 164

coelmer - see: Hollanderies
coercion - see: force
Collegiants 225-6
collusion/s - see: church/state collusion
Cologne 58
Colombia 150, 255-6, 259
colony/ies 41, 101-3, 105-11, 117, 119, 129, 131, 156
- in South Russia 85-6, 89-93, 95-7, 101, 113, 223

331

- colony land 81, 96
commonwealth 85, 87, 97, 132, 146-7, 156, 191, 199
community 14-6, 43, 50, 58, 87, 89, 91, 96-7, 100-4, 109, 114-5, 120-1, 123, 128-9, 131-2, 155-7, 161, 163, 167, 173, 181, 183, 185-6, 195, 197-203, 209, 211, 213-8, 220-1, 224-5, 235-6, 239
compromise/s - see: anabaptist
concentration camp/s 146
conference control - see: church governance
conference minister 171
confession/s 100, 161, 191, 236
   - church doctrinal statement 43, 89, 140, 214
   - private 175-6
congregation/congregational
   - Bible study/studies 131, 164, 167, 173, 216
   - control 58, 62, 64, 111, 167, 174-5, 218-22, 238
   - government 82, 101-2, 107
   - rulers 14, 59, 125, 130, 169-71, 198
   - exegesis 16, 43, 62, 163, 209, 213-5
conscientious objections, conscientious objector/s 49, 66, 81, 103, 148-9, 205, 254
consensus - see: decision making
conspicous consumption 124
Constantine 21, 249
   - Constantinian compromise 4, 249
conversion 113, 120, 129, 131, 150, 181-2, 224
   - once and for all 129, 245-8
   - instantaneous 245
   - process 245-8
   - group 181

- "gateway to discipleship" 128
- converted 246
- dated 128-30
Cornies, Johann (Jr.) 110
Cornies, Johann 89, 95, 103-12, 115, 202
Cossacks - see: tribespeople
Council of Mission Board Secretaries 150-1
councillor/s 71, 105, 202
court 17, 57, 72, 74, 148, 185, 190, 219, 238, 260
creed/s 113, 214, 216-7
Crimean War 92, 104, 110, 119
Crusades 67
Culm 76, 78, 80
Czar 91, 145

D

Danzig 67-71, 73, 75, 78, 83, 85, 104, 155, 201
   - forecities 70
   - D. Werder - see: Vistula,
Darby, John Nelson 128, 165
deaconess/es 83
deacon/s 42, 82-3, 118, 220, 232
decision-making 175
   - consensus x, 167, 170, 213, 218-20
   - majority voting 168, 213, 218-9
   - one mind, one accord 17, 217
defenseless - see: nonresistance
Denck, Hans 208, 214, 234
Denner, Jacob 59
Dessiatine 91, 95, 105, 109
"development engine" 105
Dick, B.J. 140
Dirks, Heinrich 126
Dirks, Lijksen 54

discipleship iv, 29, 43, 51, 82,
    128, 130, 132, 163-6, 180,
    182, 224, 231-2, 240, 245
discipline 90, 93, 102, 121, 130,
    175, 182, 247
  - harsh 103
  - little church discipline 124
  - redemptive 32, 132
  - use church discipline 6, 8, 43,
    56, 102, 111, 132
dispensational 128, 143, 165-6,
    179, 210
doctrine/s
  - statement of 17, 49, 214, 217
Dompelaars 43, 226
Doopsgezinde 37, 39-44, 49-50
double-bookkeeping - see: ethical
draining - see: Vistula
Dubrovna 85, 100
Duma 87, 94
Dutch East Indies Company 41
Dyck, early Mennonite in Prussia
    73
dyeing - see: textile
dykes - also see: Vistula
  - dyking authorities 69, 202

E

education 43, 110, 155-6, 163-4,
    170, 185, 197
egalitarian - see: equality
Eiderstadt 59
Einlage 114, 117-9, 125
Einwohner 89
Elbing 67-8, 71-2, 155
elder/s, bishops 44, 58, 72, 82-3,
    101, 125, 132, 169, 171, 174,
    198
  - board of elders 171, 175, 218
  - complex 132

  - in Holland 33
  - eldership 132
  - multiple 220
Elizabeth, nun 235-6
Emden 37, 53, 56-7
emigrate, emigration 65, 78, 81,
    92, 202
  - to America 62, 135, 145-6, 165
  - to Mexico 142
  - to Paraguay 142
Enns, Elder Jakob 102
entrepreneurs 39, 46, 60-2, 108,
    162, 201, 239
  - entrepreneurship 41, 157-8
entrophy xi
Enuma Elish 19-20
Epistle of James 16, 198, 207-8
  - "epistle of straw" 208
Epp, Elder Claas 116
equality 132, 199, 220
  - first among equals 170, 198
estate/s 136-7
  - owner/s 136, 138, 197, 199
ethical violations
  - in business 124
  - double bookeeping 161
  - cheating on taxes 161
  - inflated invoices 161
  - kickbacks 161
  - taking advantage of 159-60
evangelical/s 62, 130, 181, 183-4,
    227, 263
  - diversity ii
  - Evangelical Left ii
  - evangelicalism 129, 143, 179,
    181-3, 224, 226-7
  - Evangelical Mainstream iii,
    156, 165
  - fundamentalist ii, 165
  - Evangelicalism and Anabaptism
    compared iii-iv, 182-4,
evangelism/evangelize ii-iii, 7,
    126, 150-1, 180-2, 224, 262-3

333

- Fundamentalist ii
- no missionary spirit 82
- biblical iv
- popular iv
- "cheap grace" iv, 182
- evangelists iv, 120, 227, 231

eviction/expulsion 58, 71
- orders 71, 79

Ewert, Al 240

Ewert, Jacob G. 238

excommunicated - see: ban

exegesis 165, 207, 214, 216, 220, 261
- by clergy 214-5
- in congregation of believers x, 43, 62, 163, 213, 217
- of Scripture 16, 128, 209
- exegetes, professional/specialists x, 215
- community/ies 16, 99, 114, 120, 123, 128, 131, 163, 167, 215-6, 225
- lecture-exegesis 167, 216

exemption/s 148, 202
- from military 41, 49, 121, 131, 147, 151, 201, 204
- from service in the national guard 147
- end of military exemption 135-6, 146

exile/exiled 99, 102

expository lecture - see: lecture - exegesis

exuberant movement 124-5
- Christian liberty 124
- die Starken 124
- die Hüpfer 124
- apostles 125
- die Fröhlichen 124
- "free grace" 117, 124
- shouts of praise 124
- spiritual despotism 125

F

faith as a rope and anchor - see: metaphors

famine relief 89, 183

Fast, Elder Bernard 114-5

Fast, Heinold A. Fast 26-7

fellowship 12
- of equals 14, 17, 89, 169, 198

Fernheim Colony 143

fidelity 6, 9, 18, 31, 37, 41, 50, 76, 81, 97, 128, 208, 226, 231-2, 243

fire brigades 69
- fire fighting 85
- fire insurance 69, 83

Flamish 42, 83, 85, 100

flogged/flogging 90, 111, 103, 241

Florissen, an anabaptist 75

force
- abstain from coercion 260
- abstain from 6, 7, 10, 25, 27, 99, 127, 260
- abstain from sword 6, 7, 10, 13, 25
- of arms 38
- renouncing force 4, 13, 15, 19-22, 27, 194, 224, 257
- name for the "renunciation of force" 26

foreclosure/foreclosing 38, 158

Franz, Heinrich 115

Fresenburg 53

Friedmann, Robert 42, 129

Friedrichstadt 53, 59, 63

Friends of Jerusalem 115-6

Friesen, Jacob 140

Friesen, Abraham and Maria 126

Friesen, Peter M. i, 32, 115, 117, 133

Frisians 32, 45, 59, 100

Froese, Jacob 126
fundamentalism/fundamentalist 143, 165-7, 179-83, 210, 226-7
Funk, Stephen 77

G

Gandhi, Mohandas K. 22, 27, 257-60
Gebietsamt
 - budding 85
 - in Russia xiv, 85-7, 92-3, 111, 202
Gelassenheit 43
Gellius Faber 8
General Conference Mennonite Church 142, 144
German,
 - language 113, 121, 139, 148, 169, 174
 - nationalism 64, 79, 139
Germany
 - North ix, 37, 50, 53, 189
Gewaltlosigkeit 26, 141, 150, 152
Gewaltverzicht 26-7, 29, 35, 140, 253, 260
Gnadenfeld 78, 114-7, 131, 140
Görz, Elder Franz 113
gospel
 - perverting the gospel 4-7, 14-5, 17, 22, 47, 121, 129, 150-1, 180-1, 183, 207, 224, 227, 231
government
 - participants in government 4-5, 9-10, 12, 15, 27, 41-3, 46, 48-9, 55, 57-8, 61, 65, 69, 71-3, 76, 78-81, 85-8, 90, 92, 94, 97, 105-6, 109-10, 125, 132, 145-9, 152, 168-9, 171, 201-5, 211, 225
Grant, Ulysses S. 147
Great Werder - see: Vistula

Grebel, Conrad 6, 244
Groningen 48, 50-1
Guardians Committee 85-6, 105-6, 110, 202
Gunpowder 60, 234

H

Halbstadt church 110-1
Hamburg 49, 53, 60, 62, 126, 201, 239
 - Baptists 118
 - Hamburg-Altona 9, 60-1, 65, 220, 226
Hansa 58, 60, 201
 - Hanseatic cities 39, 60, 67
 - Hanseatic League 61
Harms, John F. 238
Hausknecht, David 115
Haxberg, royal councillor 76
Hendricks, Anneken 234
heresy/heretical 6, 8, 37, 62, 79, 124, 203, 217, 239
Herrnhuter Brethren 78
Hiebert, Peter C. 182, 238-40
High German 59
high school records 72
Hillsboro 150-1, 238, 256
Hofacker, Ludwig 118
Hofen, Heinrich von 73
Hoffman, Melchior v, 37-8, 53-4, 68, 121
Hoffmann, Christoph 115
Hohenzollern 67, 80
Holland - see: Netherlands
Hollanderies
 - *coelmer* 69, 158
 - *emphyteusis* 68-9
Holy Roman Empire 40, 44, 46, 192

335

hope 38, 128, 141, 160, 217, 233, 243, 246, 248, 250
- eschatological 38
Höppner, Jacob 85, 99
- sentenced 99
Horsch, John 27, 58
house metaphor - see: metaphor of house
house-church groups 167
Hübert, Abram J. and Katharina 126
hunger strike 259
Hussites 244
Hutterites 155, 195-6

I

identity
- loss of x, 225
immigrants/immigration 85, 92, 97, 147, 163, 179-80, 240, 262
- early 142-3, 145
- later 146
incarnation 23, 167
India 126, 258-9
individualism 43, 129-32, 182, 185, 226-7
industry - see: Mennonite
inerrancy/inerrant
- of Scriptures 183
Inquisition/inquisition/inquisitional 38-9, 44-5, 67, 173
- Office of the 37, 203, 217
intolerance 8, 124
Isaac, Franz 111
Isaak, Helmut 47
Isolation 143, 147, 155, 163-4, 223

J

Jans, Anneken 54, 233
Jansen, Cornelius 148
Janz, Benjamin B. 140
Janzen, Jacob 104
Janzen, Cornelius 103
Jewish xi, 21
Johannes a Lasco 31
Jories, David 58
Jung-Stilling, Johann Heinrich 113
Juschanlee 105
just war 4

K

Kalleken Strings 54
Kampen, Jost van 71, 81
Kappes 117, 124
Keeney, William 190-1, 207, 209, 214
Keulen, Hans van 71
kickbacks - see: ethical
Kimbanguists 244
King, Martin Luther 22
kingdom
- earthly 189-90, 192, 194
- of peace - see: peace
- of heaven 10, 24
Kirchenkonvent 107, 111, 174, 220
Klassen, Peter 47, 211
Kleine Gemeinde 83, 103-4, 113, 143-4, 165
Kleinhäusler 89
Königsberg 65, 67, 72-4, 155, 201
Kontenius, Senator 105
Kratz, Clayton 234
Krefeld 50
Kreider, Robert 103

Krimmer Mennonite Brethren Church 143
Kroeker, Isaak 73
Kronsweide 117
Kujavien, Bishop of 74, 76-7

L

laborer/s 149
- Mennonite 88-90, 94, 96
- non-Mennonite 89-90, 94
laity 14, 138, 155, 174, 198
- lay ministers 62, 167, 174
Lammists 43-4, 214
land 9, 46-8, 68, 70, 74-7, 79-80, 85, 91-5
- landholders/landholding 47, 85, 87-91, 93, 108-9, 111
- landless 78, 85, 88-93, 96, 108-9, 111
- landless laborers 96
- rural and agricultural people 155
- rental - see: emphyteusis
- purchase - see: coelmer
- unused 91
land acquisition 68, 80
- purchase restricted 80
- purchase land outside of colonies 95
Lange, Johannes 116
leader/leadership 3, 14, 32, 38, 43, 82-3, 85-6, 97, 105, 109, 115-6, 122, 139, 170, 172, 184, 213
- servant/leader 14 -5, 17, 82, 163, 198, 220-1
- servanthood 220
leatherworking - see: trades
Leeuwarden 3, 37, 44
Lebramt x, 85-6, 99-101, 108, 111, 202

Lenzmann, Elder August 115
Lepp, Aron 118
Levies 83, 107
Leyden, Jan van 38, 192, 209
Liberty 39, 55, 117, 124, 196, 225
Liebig, August 119
lifestyle 3, 4, 10-11, 13-8, 22, 24, 27, 34, 43, 50-1, 66, 103, 129, 131
- of obedience 214
- of peace 224
loan/s 55-6
Loewen, Helmut-Harry 138
Loewen, Jacob A. i, 146, 151, 166, 168, 171-2, 175-6, 245, 253-263
Loewen, Johann 117
Loewen, Bill i, 253
love 20, 22, 25, 185, 190, 203, 231, 234-7, 257, 260
- love your enemies 23
Loysen 75
Lübeck 53, 58-9
Luther, Martin iii, ix, 3-6, 31, 146, 163, 207-9, 213
- Lutheran reformers 7

M

Madrid 263
magistracy/magistrates 29, 34, 57, 63, 71, 87, 103, 111, 190-1
Makhno, Nestor 137
Martens, Wilhelm 93
Martyrs
- anabaptist 38
- female 54
- numbers of 39, 55
Martyrs' Mirror 54-5, 232, 234-5
Materialism iv, 183, 205, 226-7
Matthies, Isaak 93

Matthys, Jan 38
Matties, Gordon 15
mayor/s 42, 57, 59, 69, 79
 - *obershulze* 86, 107, 109, 202
 - *shulze* 86
Melitopol 94, 136
melting pot 142, 179
Melville, John 114
Memel 67, 79
 - Delta 78-9
Menchu, Rigoberta 22
Mennists 45, 55, 68, 142
Menno Simons 26-7, 29-31, 130, 138, 152, 168, 176, 193, 208, 214, 231
 - as a priest at Pingjum vii, 3, 37, 191
 - ambivalence 29, 31-4
 - conversion 3, 37
 - life vii, 53, 58-9
 - monument 59
 - shifts 34
 - views iv, 6-10, 12, 19, 22-6, 128, 132, 183, 189-90, 192, 196, 207, 217
 - vision viii-ix, 13-8, 37-9, 111, 120, 198, 244
 - writings i, vi, 83, 104, 191, 207
 - concerns 4
 - visits Danzig 70
 - price on head 44
 - death - died in 1561 58
"Mennonite affliction" 31
Mennonite Brethren/MB 93, 111, 115, 117, 119-22, 127-8, 139-40, 144, 150-2, 166-7, 169, 171, 209
 - MB Church xiv, 110, 115, 118, 123-7, 130-2, 152, 172, 221, 253, 261
 - MB Document of Secession 115, 132

 - MB Herald 172, 174, 247
 - MB trademark- conversion 113, 129
Mennonite tsar 105
Mennonite/s 27, 32, 110-1, 113-4, 116, 119, 123-4, 126-8, 131-2, 135, 139, 142-4, 145-53, 156, 163, 165, 168, 179, 186, 203, 218
 - Mennonite Central Committee 143, 149-52, 182-3, 240
 - commonwealth 85, 146, 191
 - destinctive message - blurring on the American scene 157
 - estates 93, 136
 - manufacturers, industry 87
 - name 263
 - officeholders 57
 - peace principles 139, 253, 226
 - privileges - see: priveleges
 - state - see: commonwealth
 - women 164
 - ethnic privileges 152
 - coarse 42
 - fine 42
Mennonitisches Lexikon 39
metalworking - see: trades
metaphor of house vii, 244, 246
 - whole vii, 251
 - housecleaning vii, 251
 - many rooms 244, 246
 - invite Jesus in more rooms 251
 - unconverted room 246, 249, 251
metaphor of narrow road iv, vii, 26, 156, 190, 231
 - living 130, 232
Military 57, 64, 79, 92, 150, 193
 - active service 58, 66, 74, 76, 80, 119, 127
 - militarism iv, 121, 140
 - academy at Culm 80

- exemption 49, 51, 59, 61, 65, 71, 73, 76, 78, 80-1, 131, 145-8, 151, 201, 224
- substitutes 41, 76, 193, 199, 201

Miller, Peter 71, 234
millionaire/s 157-8, 160, 176, 197
minister/s 15, 42, 73, 82, 85, 107-8, 110, 161, 164, 166, 169-74, 176, 183, 213, 219-20, 226, 239, 263
- educated 43-4, 72, 167, 170, 209, 213-4

ministry 50, 82, 110, 121, 171, 174
- unpaid lay ministers 62, 167, 174, 217, 220, 262
- salaried ministers 62, 67, 164, 169-70, 174, 214-5, 218-9, 225

missionary/ies 57, 150-1, 180-1, 246, 255
- to India 126
- to Russians 114

mobility restriction/s - see: restrictions
modernity 184-6
Molenaar, Isaak 50
Molotschna 85, 95, 100, 106, 113, 118-9, 125, 136, 140, 142-3, 164
Moravian 113
- Brethren 114-5

Mother Teresa 22
Münster v-vi, 5, 34, 38, 60, 192, 209
Müntzer, Thomas 6

N

National Socialism 66
nationalism 20, 64, 79, 139, 204
- national defense iv, 203-4
- national loyalty 64

Netherlands 9, 45, 50
- northern Holland x, 37, 44-5, 47-8,192
- southern Holland 37-40, 42-4, 189, 192

new birth 22, 78, 116, 123, 126, 129, 181, 189, 231, 245
- born again 26, 123
- conversion/converted see: conversion

new villages 91
Nickel, Benjamin 118
Noe, Francis 61
Nogai/s - see: tribespeople
Nonconformity 231
nonresistance i, xi, 19, 26, 49-50, 58, 64-5, 80, 83, 138, 140, 150, 183, 192-3, 254-5
- nonresistant privilege 145

nonviolent protest 258
Norden 53, 55
North America 26-7, 49, 80, 117, 142, 146, 149-50, 152, 155-8, 162-5, 169, 175-6, 179-81, 184, 199, 210, 224-6, 248, 256

O

oath 71, 192
- for citizenship 42, 60
- of allegiance 59
- substitute 55

obedience 27, 100, 109, 152, 163, 182-3, 189-90, 209, 214, 217, 231, 243, 259
Oberschulze - see: *schulze*,
Odessaer Zeitung 109, 138-9
Officeholders 57
official religion,
- no single official religion 40

Old Order iii
Oldenburg
- Count Enno of 45, 53
- Anna von/ of 45, 53
Oncken, Johann G. 118
one-person-one-vote - see: voting
only-the-Sword-of-the-Spirit ix, 4, 13, 15, 18, 21-2, 50, 118, 243, 253
- only-the-sword-of-the-Spirit lifestyle ix-xi, xiv, 13, 34, 51, 147, 152, 189-90, 192, 217, 224, 226, 243, 248-50,
only-ordained-by-letter 99
order-in-council 65
orthodoxy 180, 182, 227
orthopraxy 182, 227
outside influence/s 113, 119, 124, 127, 144, 155, 166, 181, 184, 243, 255
owner/s, ownership
- communal ownership 155, 195
- ownership of property 15, 195

P

pacifist 34, 119
- Dutch 21
- Prussian 81
paid minister/ministry/pastor/s - see: ministry
Paton, John C. 235
Peace 7, 9-10, 12-3, 16, 26-7, 29, 34, 65-6, 77, 81, 94, 131-2, 138, 149, 161, 245, 256, 263
- Kingdom of iv, vii-viii, 13-5, 25, 38, 189-93, 195, 223, 233, 244
- Prince of viii, 189
- activism 152
- activism feared 150, 152
- emissaries 151
- position 5, 44, 127, 149, 254-5, 257, 260
- principles i, iii, 139, 149-50, 152, 191, 253-7
- separated from the message of conversion 150
- witness 151, 224, 254
- children of viii-ix
- peacemaker/s ii, xi, 4, 26, 152, 255-6
- peacemaker teams 152
peasant/s 5, 46, 138, 155, 195
- Revolution - see: Revolution
Penner, Bernard 125
Penner, Adolph 126
persecution/persecutes 8-9, 37, 39-41, 44-5, 47-8, 53-4, 57-8, 65, 68, 86, 121, 132, 192-3, 195-6, 203, 223, 231-2, 255
- end of 189, 217, 248
pestilence 72-3
Philadelphia Church of the Revelation 116, 135
Philip of Hesse 53, 208-9
Phillips, Dirk 32-3, 58, 207
Pieterz, Peter 240
Pietism/Pietists 42, 113-4, 120-1, 123, 129-31, 139, 226
- Blankenburg 113
- Moravian 113
- Würtemburg 113
Pilgrims 13, 15, 87, 190, 196, 231, 233, 238
poll tax 193
poor 24, 39, 49-50, 55-6, 65, 79, 83, 89, 91, 96, 183-4, 199, 215
- homes for the 74
Postmodernity 185-6
- "communitarianism" 185-6
pottery-making 46, 48
power 4, 20-2, 25-7, 67, 70, 82, 99, 101-2, 137, 172-3, 186,

    204, 257, 260
- ethic of 172
- political 5, 24, 28
- positions of 168-9, 220
- abuse/abuses of 5, 24, 103, 125, 172, 175-6
- economic 24, 65
- religious 24
- divine 24
- earthly 23
- renouncing 132

prayer 32, 59, 64, 81, 113, 203, 261, 263

preacher/pastor 16, 31, 58-9, 62, 65, 77, 82, 124, 126, 163, 165, 170, 181, 210, 215, 217, 261, 263
- paid (salaried) - see: professional
- educated - see: professional

Prieb, Wesley J. ii, 243-51

priesthood of all believers 226, 245

prism analogy xii, 163, 207

privilege/s 9-10, 14, 41, 48, 51, 53, 55, 57, 60-1, 65, 73, 77-9, 82-3, 85, 87-8, 91, 97-8, 100, 106, 114, 116, 118, 145, 147-8, 150, 152, 173, 224
- *privilegium* 97, 105, 126, 131, 145

Professional/s 56, 124
- clergyman 14, 62, 198
- exegetes x, 215
- preachers 130, 168-70, 174
- professionalism 130, 156, 167

proselytize - also see: evangelize
- no proselytizing 57, 60

protest for conscience' sake 257

Prussia 58, 64, 85, 95, 113, 145, 226
- Brandenburg 67, 73
- East 67, 73
- Polish 67
- West 67

punishment 12, 136, 210
- physical 91
- flogging 241

pure church 23, 31, 124, 131-2, 217

Q

Quakers 119, 147-8, 226, 244, 261

quarrels 34, 43, 62-3
- Ohrloff barley 111
- Halbstadt Church 110

quietism
- "quiet in the land" 38, 152

R

rabbits' defense 39

racial
- prejudice 124
- protests 256, 260

radical
- obedience 100
- reform 198, 244-5
- renewal 244-5

Reformation 39-40, 47, 84, 131, 192, 217, 231
- reform, reformers 5, 51, 83, 244
- Magisterial 5, 54, 189, 198, 203
- counter 6
- radical xi, 14, 17, 100, 198, 202, 219, 244-5
- Mainline Reformers 5-10, 207, 214

Reformed Mennonites in America 144

Reformed 13-4, 39-40, 42, 44, 54, 56, 58, 144, 225, 244

341

- Church 13-4
Reimer, Klaas 103
Reimer, Jacob W. 140, 165
Reiseprediger 126, 181, 215
Reiswitz, G. 48
rejection of innovations 163
rejection of force - see: force
Remonstrant/Remonstrants 43, 225-6
renewal/s 100, 113, 117, 120, 126, 132, 163, 179, 181, 218, 243, 248-9
- new beginnings 244
- movement/s 32, 113, 115-7, 123, 127, 131, 168-9
- renewed life 244, 250
- ongoing 244-6
- revival, revivalism 50, 120, 123, 125, 129-30, 142-3, 150, 165, 181, 218, 245-6
- dramatic testimonies of repentance 66
residence 60, 64, 69, 71, 155-7, 161, 184
- reside legally 73
- resident alien/s 70, 76
- short-term 47, 73
restricted/restriction/s 80-1, 94, 100, 193, 209, 226
- Mennonites restricted to certain trades 70, 196
- travel 92
return to Menno Simons 50, 83, 131
return of Jesus Christ 121
revenge 193
- revengeless 204
Revolution
- revolutionary/ies 10, 55, 60, 68-9, 93, 97, 109
- peasant 6, 68
- Russian 94, 128, 135-6

- Anabaptist accused 31, 68, 70
Rienex, Hoyte 58
Riesen, Peter von 83
Riga 63, 67, 69
right to exist 48
Roosen, Coordt 60
Roosen, Gerrit 62
Roosen, B.C. 39, 59
Russia 32, 65, 85-98, 105-6, 108-11, 135-8, 140, 142-50, 155-6, 158, 162, 164-5, 168-9, 173-4, 179-81, 183, 197-9, 202-4, 210-1, 218, 220, 223-4, 226, 234, 239
- Russian laborers - see: laborers
- southern 85, 94, 105, 113, 136, 155,
- Russo-Turkish war 85, 88, 92

S

sacred 14, 173, 198
Sattler, Michael 244
Satyagraha 27
Schaeder, Hans Heinrich 20-1
Schauenberg
- Counts of 61
- Count Ernest of 61
Schirmgeld - see: *schutzgeld*
schism (secede) 31, 110, 116
- document of secession 115, 132
- MB secession 140
- at Gnadenfeld 115
Schlabach, Theron 132, 180
Schleitheimer Confession 12, 103, 132, 180, 190-1
Schleswig-Holstein 34, 53, 58-9
Schmidt, Nicholas and Johann 115
Schottland 75
Schroeder, Jakob 73

Schulze - see: mayor
Schutzgeld (Schirmgeld) 41, 71, 76
Schwäermer 31
Schwertler v
Scofield, Cyrus Ingerson 128, 165
Scripture 19-20, 22, 26, 44-5, 54, 77, 81, 84, 118, 120, 123, 128, 131, 155, 163, 165-7, 179-80, 183, 192, 207, 209-11, 213-9, 235-6, 240, 261
sea wall - see: draining
secular 21-2, 58, 88
- secular/sacred work 198
- secularizing education 110
Seidlitz 75
Selbstschutz 136, 139-41, 209
- hired tribespeople 135
- hired Cossacks 136
- justification for the 140
- law/order breakdown 138
- secret 136
- antecedents to 135-6
- self-defense 140, 203
- self-defense army 135
Selective Service Act 149
self-given/self-giving/self sacrifice 21, 190, 257
self-government 147
- self-governing - colonies 86, 223
- self-governing - villages 69, 79
- local 79, 147
separation of church and state 15
serf/s, serfdom 14, 46, 89, 92, 94, 96, 138, 195, 198
Sermon on the Mount vii, 16, 23, 26, 101, 128, 140, 166, 207, 231, 258
servants 88, 94, 96
- household 90
- maids 88-9
share, shared, sharing 59, 60, 65, 90, 121, 139, 155, 159-60, 171, 176, 182, 190, 195, 203, 215, 224, 234, 253,
- freely 196, 248
Smissen, van der,
- family 59
- Heinrich 64
Snijder, Sicke Freerks 3, 37
Social Gospel 143, 180, 183
social classes- see: stratified society
Socinian/s 43
Sojourners ii, 190, 196, 233
Sola Scriptura 163, 166, 207-8
Sola Fides 208
Solus Christus 207
Sommerfelder 165
Sonnists 43, 214
soul winning 130, 139, 182-3, 224, 226-7, 246
South Africa 258, 262
specialize
- specialized farmers 47
Spronck, Pieters 73
Stäbler v
state church dues 77
steward/s, stewardship 9, 14-5, 155, 157, 195-8, 224, 243, 245
- only 156
stratified society 89
- class distinctions 95, 155
- social classes 14, 156, 198
- tiered 98, 108
Streams of Mennonites
- northern ix, 145, 164, 194, 229
- southern 145
stroke i, 58
Stundist movement 114
Sunday school movement 144
Sweden attacks 63

343

Swiss 13, 68, 180, 191
sword 4-5, 7, 11, 17, 25-6, 38, 42, 44, 86, 97, 119, 180, 192, 203, 209, 235, 241, 243, 255
- of the Spirit v, vii, ix, xi, 13-5, 22, 33, 37-8, 103, 231, 235
- for evangelism 7
- of government 189, 193, 201, 221-2
- of iron x, 192
- of war x, 5-6, 86, 97, 135, 189, 205, 217
- power 6, 8, 10, 12, 14, 20-1, 24, 87, 90, 104
- in church discipline 102
- in defense of truth 6
- to protect benefits 6, 8-9, 88, 138, 197
- swordless lifestyle 10, 19
- sword-power abuses 5, 111
- sharp tongue - see: tongue
- earthly 24
- renounce ./ non-use of 10

T

tax, taxes, taxation 55-6, 60, 63, 65, 68, 73, 76, 80, 82, 85, 87, 92-3, 96-7, 152, 156, 161, 193, 197
Temple Church 16, 115
temptation 120, 156, 158, 161, 182, 195, 249
Teutonic Knights 67, 69, 75
textile 79, 196, 258
   - weaving 46, 48, 56
   - factory/mill/industry 56, 73-4
   - dyeing 46
Thiessen, Abraham 93
Tielt, Herman van 58
Tilsit cheese 78
tobacco 103, 118

Toews, John A. 117
tongue/s 260
- sword of the tongue 29-31, 33, 247, 260
trades 56, 70, 73, 86, 107, 157, 160, 195-6
- pottery making 46, 48
- weaving - see: textile
- woodworking 46
- blacksmithing 155
- cloth dyeing - see: textile
Trappe, Baron von 85
tribespeople 88, 135
- Cossacks 88, 138
- Nogais 92
Trypmaker, Jan Volkerts 37
Tunkers 148
Two kingdom citizenship 5, 189
- in Holland 189, 192
- in Germany 50, 189
- in Prussia 81
- in Russia 146
- in North America 146

U

Unger, Cornelius 118
Unger, Abraham 118
Union of Utrecht 40
Unruh, Benjamin H. 140-1, 146, 209
untergeordnet 107
urban 42-3, 46, 56, 124, 155, 157, 192, 201, 204
- centers 53, 156
- residence 156, 184
- urbanization 131, 156
Urry, James 92, 132, 138

V

Vermahner 82
Vistula 65, 67-8, 78-9
- draining the Delta 75, 223
- Danzig Werder 74-6, 80
- Grosse Werder 74
- Marienburger Werder 74
- Kleine Werder 74
- drainage canals 76
- sea wall 76
- dykes 75
- wind mills 75, 95

Vogt, Jacob W. 156, 238
Volkskirche 99-100
Vorberat 171, 211
Voth, Tobias 113, 115
vote/voting 62, 88-9, 91, 108, 168
- ineligible to 91, 108
- no confidence 170, 172
- power 92, 111
- two votes for landholder 93, 109
- majority 168, 213, 218
- one person-one vote 199

Vreedzamen 38

W

Waldensians 54, 244
war/s 4, 10-2, 15, 27, 39, 41, 63, 65, 100, 132, 139-40, 147, 149, 189, 191-3, 227, 235, 253-4
- of aggression 194, 255
- of self-defense- see: *Selbstschutz*

Warkentin, Elder 104, 173
Waterlanders 33, 42, 193, 215
wealth 40, 42-4, 48, 85, 87, 94, 96-7, 115, 132, 136, 146-7, 155-8, 162, 173, 176, 184, 196, 191, 196, 198-9, 204, 215, 243, 248

Wedel, Elder Peter 114
Wehrlosigkeit 26, 150
West Coast Children's Mission 181, 262
whalers/whaling 9, 56, 62, 192
whole person iii
Wiebe, Adam 71
Wiebe, Philip 110
Wieler, Johann 126
Wieler, Gerhard 125
Wiens, Elder H. 106-7
Wiens, Delbert 129
will to power 19, 21-2, 27, 168-9, 172
Willems, Dirk 12-3,
William of Orange 39-41, 50, 60
- William I of Orange 204
- price on his head 40
Wink, Walter 20-1
Winkelprediger 31
Winrod, Gerald B. 182
Wippe, Joris 233
Wismar 57-9, 168
- Resolutions 58
Wladislaus, King 78
women 38, 54, 64, 74, 124, 164, 173, 209, 241
- status of 88-9
Word of God 11-2, 128
- study the 44
- to study personally 45
work 4-5, 7, 10, 14, 31, 42-3, 45-8, 53, 56, 58-9, 62-4, 75-6, 81, 83, 88-90, 93-4, 96-7, 103, 106, 108, 110-1, 113, 119, 122-3, 126, 130, 132, 149, 151-2, 155, 160, 165, 169, 171-3, 175, 181-2, 195-9, 203, 208-9, 216, 234, 236, 239-40, 245-6, 249-50, 253-9, 261-2

World War I 66, 98, 136, 138, 148-50, 155, 167, 174, 179, 197-8, 203
world 4, 10, 13-4, 19, 24, 87, 165, 183-4, 190, 196, 241
- domination systems 20-2
- separation from 9, 26, 39, 50, 201
worship privileges - see: privileges
Würtemberg 113
Wüst, Eduard 117
Wüstenfeld 53, 58-9

Y

Yarrow, British Columbia 202-3
Yoder, John H. 4, 21, 244

Z

Zijpp, N. van der 49, 191
Zwingli, Urich iii, 3-6, 31, 213
Zurich 5, 213